Talmud /AND/ Philosophy

NEW JEWISH PHILOSOPHY AND THOUGHT
ZACHARY J. BRAITERMAN

INDIANA UNIVERSITY PRESS

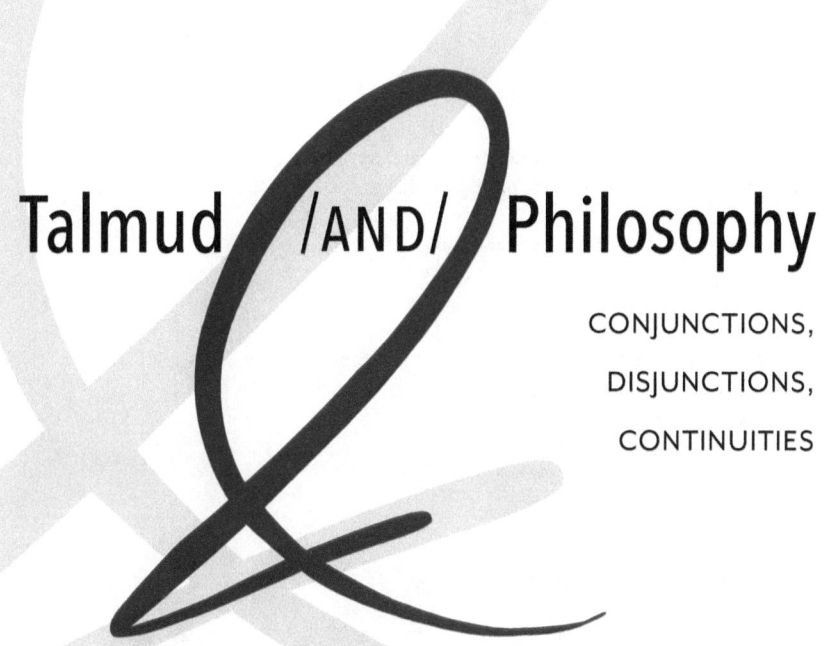

Talmud /AND/ Philosophy

CONJUNCTIONS,
DISJUNCTIONS,
CONTINUITIES

Edited by
Sergey Dolgopolski and
James Adam Redfield

This book is a publication of

Indiana University Press
Office of Scholarly Publishing
Herman B Wells Library 350
1320 East 10th Street
Bloomington, Indiana 47405 USA

iupress.org

© 2024 by Indiana University Press

All rights reserved

No part of this book may be reproduced or utilized in any form or by any means, electronic or mechanical, including photocopying and recording, or by any information storage and retrieval system, without permission in writing from the publisher.

Manufactured in the United States of America

First Printing 2024

Cataloging information is available from the Library of Congress.
978-0-253-07066-1 (hdbk)
978-0-253-07067-8 (pbk)
978-0-253-07068-5 (web PDF)

For Bruce Rosenstock,
in memoriam

CONTENTS

Foreword   ix

Acknowledgments   xi

Introduction / *Sergey Dolgopolski and James Adam Redfield*   1

1. To Refute God Himself: Talmud as Meta-Philosophy / *Agata Bielik-Robson*   21

2. Talmudic and Jewish Logo-Politics / *Elad Lapidot*   51

3. But I Say: The Political (Dis)appearance of the Past in Rabbinic Citation / *Sergey Dolgopolski*   85

4. Pragmatic Points of View: Kant and the Rabbis, Together Again / *James Adam Redfield*   112

5. Systematicity and Normative Closure in Lithuanian Talmudism / *Yonatan Y. Brafman*   155

6. The Talmudic Concept *hamar gamal* (Donkey Driver–Camel Driver): A Legal and Literary-Somatic Analysis of Talmudic Imagery / *Lynn Kaye*   177

7. The Language of Plants and Human-World Entanglement in Midrash and Walter Benjamin's Philosophy of Language / *Alexander Weisberg*   204

8. Between Philosophy and Rhetoric: The Mishnah Yoma as a Case Study / *Sophia Avants*   232

Postscript: Ein talmudisches Etwas über die philosophische Literatur: A Talmudic Observation on Philosophy / *Karma Ben-Johanan*   253

Bibliography   263

Index   281

FOREWORD

This volume charts an emerging form of inquiry, Talmud /and/ philosophy: an inquiry into the intersections, partitions, mutual illuminations and problematizations of these two traditions, disciplines, and bodies of thought. Rather than either apply philosophical ideas to the Talmud or make the Talmud relevant to philosophical problems, the goal of this inquiry is to rethink the copula *and* to show that *and* does not have to be a relationship between well-bounded or pregiven domains. The starting point for our inquiry—the contrary notion that Talmud must be clearly separated from Philosophy, both equally reified, to be related—has a long history. As Gérard Granel might say, philosophers and Talmudists inherit robust "traditions of tradition" (Gérard Granel, *Traditionis Traditio* [Paris: Gallimard, 1972]): preconceptions of themselves that presuppose what philosophy *and* Talmud should mean.

The traditions of these traditions did not arise equally over time, nor did they arise without violence. The question of what philosophy is has always been one of the central questions of philosophy. Paradoxically, this means that philosophies of Talmud often denied the latter the right to ask the same question about itself. Such asymmetry is apparent throughout even the most sympathetic and erudite efforts to systematize Talmud philosophically or "raise" it to the level of philosophy: from Maimonides's rationalization of its complex rhetoric by transforming it into a code of law; to Canpanton's appropriation of Aristotle to analyze and transmit the hidden logic of its dialectic; to Luzzatto's vision of the Talmud as the supreme example of enlightened reason; to Levinas's metaphorization of its language as the template for an ethics that philosophy had not yet realized; to Hermann Cohen's abstraction of its theology as the principled basis for a "religion of reason"; until the present, when this hegemony of the philosophical has consciously and unconsciously influenced even "traditional" interpreters of the Talmud—those who do read the text as a source of Jewish wisdom and a theoretical expression of Judaism, if not as a practical guide to daily life.

Still more remarkably, not until recently have "secular" readers of the Talmud who are less consciously beholden to theology or philosophy— scholars of philology, history, and culture—taken Talmud seriously as an independent tradition and mode of intellectual practice. On the contrary, in their hands, too, Talmud has been predominantly reified and pigeonholed as a "historical" object on the margins of Western thought. Often, *the* Talmud—a book rather than a mode of practice, whether the better-known Babylonian or more obscure Palestinian Talmud—has been taken as documenting the experience of Jews in late antiquity or representing the essence of Judaism as opposed to Christianity. Only recently have scholars in secular institutions begun to ask seriously what *Talmud* might have meant as a form of life and mode of thought, fully coeval with those of philosophy, since Talmud's birth in rhetorical schools of Roman Palestine. What might Talmud's "tradition of [its own] tradition" become if its reader focused on its original and singular discipline of thought rather than seeing *the* Talmud through a glass darkly as incoherent philosophy or unreliable historiography? This recent question, also the question of our volume, contributes to convergence not only between Talmudic and philosophical thought but also potentially between Talmudic readers in secular and religious settings—both of whom are centrally concerned, if for their own reasons, with the matter of what Talmud, like philosophy, is.

Rather than accept an axiomatic partition between Talmud and philosophy (even if it is mediated by "influences" or erased by gestures of "translation" and "conversion"), our volume opens a new door to Talmud /and/ philosophy by placing this very question of *and* at its center. Rather than posit and overcome the partition, we aim to interrogate and transform its structure. The essays responding to this challenge collectively demonstrate that asking the question of relation, not only between Talmud /and/ philosophy but also of each tradition to itself, can offer a critical contribution to relocating Jewish thought in, alongside, or against Western tradition.

ACKNOWLEDGMENTS

The editors would like to thank Chaya Halberstam, Moulie Vidas, and Zvi Septimus, who participated in a workshop on the topic at the University at Buffalo, SUNY, on April 14–15, 2015, as well as Jonathan Boyarin. Many conversations with them, both during and after those years, have proven deeply informative for the shape of this volume. We are thankful to Alex Weisberg for serving as assistant editor in earlier stages of the book's development. This is also an opportunity to recognize personally all of the contributors and our many conversations with them from which this book has emerged. We are deeply thankful to Zachary Braiterman, the series editor, for his initial interest in the project and his ongoing care as the project advanced through further stages, as well as Assistant Acquisitions Editor Anna Francis at Indiana University Press for her dedication to the project and Tim DeBold of Atramenti Editing for his expert hand in helping to prepare the volume for publication. We also thank Anthony Catanese for preparing the Index.

For their support in the publication process, we gratefully acknowledge the Gordon and Gretchen Gross Professorship in Jewish Thought of SUNY–Buffalo and the Saint Louis University Research Institute.

Talmud /AND/ Philosophy

Introduction

SERGEY DOLGOPOLSKI AND JAMES ADAM REDFIELD

This book is about Talmud *and* philosophy, not "Talmud" or "philosophy." Its critical contribution is to uncover and interrogate the work of this innocuous copula /and/ in order to determine whether it serves as a conjunction, disjunction, continuity, or other form of relationship between the terms. Before beginning a discussion on this /and/, we offer an articulation of our title's other orienting terms: *philosophy* and *Talmud*. Our presentation subsequently falls into two parts. The first is an "Attunement to the Theme of Talmud /and/ Philosophy" written by Sergey Dolgopolski that was sent to the contributors at the outset of our work together. Following this Attunement, we provide an introduction and chapter-by-chapter discussion of authors' responses to our common theme.

What is "philosophy" as expressed in our title? Rather than a body of texts (by writers who are identified as "philosophers" on one hand, or, on the other, *the* Talmud, two late ancient Jewish corpora by that title), we define the relationship of Philosophy and Talmud as one of traditions. More precisely, to quote Gérard Granel, we define Philosophy as well as Talmud as a "tradition of tradition": an inherited perception of what the tradition is. Practitioners accept this perception as given, even though they relate to one another's practices *of* the tradition in various ways, for example, as exemplars or antagonists, thereby constituting differences within a continuity. By inviting the two traditions of tradition into conversation, the volume opens up a mutual renegotiation of their boundaries.

Philosophy, as such a "tradition of tradition," is defined by many of its practitioners as unfolding from the pre-Socratics to Plato and Aristotle in ancient Greece; moving forward to the Platonisms and Aristotelianisms of late antiquity and Christian, Muslim, and Jewish Middle Ages; to the humanism and romanticism of the Renaissance and Enlightenment; and, finally, to the modern and postmodern eras—the focus of this volume's practitioners of philosophy when this tradition of tradition radically questioned its own scope and limits—emblematically in Feuerbach and Marx in the nineteenth century, and Heidegger and Levinas in the twentieth.

Talmud refers to a "tradition of tradition" that originates in but is not confined to late antiquity, nor is it limited to the medieval era when its literary product (*the* Talmuds of Jerusalem and Babylonia, which we designate consistently by the definite article) gradually gained hegemony as a normative text in Jewish life. This tradition of tradition—Talmud, as opposed to *the* Talmud—unfolds from rabbinic schools of rhetoric in late ancient Palestine and Babylonia to the medieval rabbinic interpretation and appropriation of the archives of these schools through practices of collection, transmission, editing, commentary, systematization, and jurisprudence; to the early modern period, when the Talmud remained a symbol for postbiblical Judaism even as Christian and humanist thinkers deepened their engagement with Talmud as a mode of thought; to the modern and postmodern eras, when Talmud was reabsorbed into the dominant currents of Western society, religion, and politics, even as it retained its symbolic role as an expression of what is most distinctive in Jewish thought. In short, as this volume shows, to be a practitioner of both philosophy and Talmud is to constantly renegotiate the boundaries of one's tradition and redefine one's tradition for itself.

ATTUNEMENT TO THE THEME OF TALMUD /AND/ PHILOSOPHY

The main intrigue in the theme of "Talmud and Philosophy" concerns this little word *and*, and we'll address that intrigue shortly. But there is another, more general intrigue at work here. The Talmud is what differentiates the

Jewish tradition of reading the Bible from other traditions—from Islamic and Christian traditions. The Christians have the church fathers; the Islamic traditions have sunna and hadith, the oral traditions of interpretations of their Scripture, Koran; and rabbinic communities or, in modern terms, Jewish communities, have Talmud. Talmud is the general name for two large corpora. One is called the Palestinian Talmud, or Jerusalem Talmud. Ironically, it was never written in Jerusalem because the city was not available to rabbis at the time of its composition ending approximately in the fourth century CE. This "Jerusalem" or "Palestinian" Talmud was then taken to Babylonia or further developed into the Babylonian Talmud, although the question of relationships between the Palestinian Talmud and the Babylonian Talmud is a difficult one. At any rate, there is a Talmud that is referred to as the Babylonian Talmud, and a version of it, a reification of it—and the term *reification* is very important in this account—is a set of typographically produced volumes of the Babylonian Talmud with its text filled with medieval commentaries, the object of very diligent study in rabbinic communities for almost a thousand years beginning from the Middle Ages. Currently, people outside of Jewish circles also have access to it. As a result, the readership of the Talmud is historically the largest it has ever been because of the availability of versions in English, modern Hebrew, German, and other renditions or translations.

And yet, we are only now beginning to *understand* what it is that has been studied for all those years in traditional settings and more recently in academic settings. We have taken the object of that study for granted and asked only about *how* to study it. We have also been asking questions concerning only the historical development and how to interpret the text. But the question of what this text is in the first place, what Talmud signifies, and what it represents is only now coming to the attention of researchers.

Let me therefore begin with a very preliminary history—we are not even sure we ought to say *history* but perhaps an approximation by way of a *story*—of the receptions or conceptions of what this text is, even if people never asked this question concerning what this text is but took what it is for granted. That said, they took it for granted in a variety of ways, and we will now map out this variety.

It all has to do with the relationship between philosophy and its traditional others. If we think and try to reconstruct the Talmudic text (i.e., if we try to reconstruct what the communities producing the Talmud looked like in late antiquity in Babylonia and Palestine), then the first approximation of this picture would be something along the following lines:

Rabbinic leaders in Babylonia, where they had relative administrative autonomy, needed training schools, which at that time were schools of rhetoric. Not only rabbinic leaders but also judges, community leaders, officers, officials, and so on were trained here. Rhetoric was understood not in the sense of the art of speaking nicely but rather as a school of thinking, a school of argumentation, a school of seeking justice, and a school of general education. The way rabbis trained at these institutions was exceptional. There are classical elements of rhetorical training, which, according to Ciceronian tradition, amount to the following:

1. *delivery*: how you present your speech
2. *invention*: the new point that you make in the speech
3. *memory*: techniques that an expert in rhetoric would need to deliver the speech because, at the time, there were no PowerPoint presentations or even paper records. The true expert was supposed to speak without any notes. In classical rhetorical schools, memory was thus a technique used to prepare for that type of oral delivery: memory for things and words, creating a palace of memory by associating what needs to be said and in which order with certain places. The elements of *invention*, *memory*, and *delivery* are followed by the remaining two elements:
4. *refutation*: an argument refuting the argument of another party, an important part of rhetorical training.
5. *example*.

These five elements were separated from each other as five different techniques. But in rabbinic academies, they were not separate. These schools of rhetoric did something that to the best of my knowledge had never been done before: they used refutation—the art of proving to the other speaker and the audience that this opposing point of view is wrong—as an instrument for remembering, a vehicle of memory. They also used refutation as an instrument for invention and to build character, to deliver or create a personality that therefore (in principle) became interpersonal rather than either an individual or collective (e.g., a chorus.) For one to say something, one had to be already refuting someone else;

otherwise, there was no point in talking. If what one had to say was obvious or called for no objections, then one was better off keeping silent. And everyone understood that. One should only open one's mouth if there was a point that was worth refuting.

There is an example of this in biblical Hebrew, which is not related to the texts discussed here, but it still provides a useful illustration. In biblical Hebrew, there is no word for *yes*, only for *no*. The biblical כן means *so* rather than *yes* because if your response is *yes*, you just do it; you comply with what you were told to do, and there is no need to actually say anything. *No*, by contrast, is a very important word. It conveys that you are not going to comply.

Refutation came to serve all the elements that the other rhetorical schools considered to be separate. The result was not a book but a skill and also a curriculum—an "archive," either oral or recorded, as modern scholars would call it. These are archives of the curricular activities of the rabbis in the academies of Sura, Nehardea, Pumbedita, and other places in Babylonia. The archives circulated in different forms, the earliest of which is responsa, which were the answers by *geonim*, or leaders of communities, sent as epistles to remote locations. Thus, the first embodiment of the Talmud was not a book or ink on paper but these rabbinic academies and a skill they taught: the skill of memorizing and using refutation to probe the memory for its validity.

The first and most characteristic figure in such a rhetorical school or academy, insofar as can be reconstructed from the arguments in the Talmud, is a *tanna*, who is simply a memorizer. The tanna mechanically remembers what is called the Mishnah, the instruction for rabbinic courts, which was composed in around 220 CE (Mishnah), followed in around 250 CE by the Tosefta (a collection of formulations parallel to those in the Mishnah and thus excluded from it). The tanna was also charged with remembering and reciting other apocryphal texts of the authorities who are mentioned in the Mishnah and Tosefta. These were not general instructions for teaching the law; rather, they were directions for how to rule or, more precisely, how to decide. The matter concerned decision rather than the application of a rule to a case. It was about cases and situations where *no* kind of rule could readily apply. That approach entailed the following: if there were rules (or rules could be produced), then there was nothing to decide. One could just apply the rules. But the issues discussed in the Mishnah (at least according to the way the Mishnah is approached in the Talmudic text, what in the printed editions of the Talmud is called Gemara, the "study" or "completion" of the Mishnah) were things that could not be sorted out by common sense or logic, or even by applying rules to a case. When there was an *uncertainty* as to which way to go (I gladly borrow this term from Chaya Halberstam, a term to which I owe a lot), that was when the Mishnah or rabbinic instruction was necessary. When there was certainty, there was no need for either. This text of the Gemara was scrutinized in rabbinic academies of later periods in Babylonia to ensure that the nature of these uncertainties would be remembered. If one wanted to understand anything in the Mishnah, one had to understand which uncertainties this Mishnah refuted or removed.

This attitude toward uncertainty led to a completely different protocol of a relationship to, or way of thinking about, the world than what we are used to. Speaking in very broad terms, philosophy stands in sharp contrast to this attitude. Philosophers, broadly speaking, have a variety of conceptions of truth. One of the simpler, more widely known, and most strongly criticized of such conceptions is called "correspondence theory." When a statement is made about something that corresponds to something in reality, it is true; if it does not correspond to something in reality, it is false. Without denying this idea of truth or this truth protocol, rabbinic academies developed a counterpart to it, a completely different idea of truth: claims are only true if they refute something, that is, if there is an uncertainty and there is something to be refuted given that uncertainty. Otherwise, claims have no point. There is no reason to tell someone that a ring is gold simply because it is—what is the point of saying so? But if there is an uncertainty about it (e.g., in a jewelry store in the fifteenth century), the salesperson could say to the customer, a groom-to-be, "Well, this is gold," thereby refuting or dispelling certain doubts that the groom-to-be might be having about buying this ring for his bride. Refutation becomes the criterion for truth. I can assert that a claim is true if I can determine what the claim is refuting. Things can be understood in their truth only if we understand what they come to refute.

How this conception of truth as refutation relates to other schools of rhetoric or philosophy—the key answer to this question, which has no final answer—is latent in the key word of the title. This key word is not *Talmud*. It is not *philosophy*. It is /and/.

In considering the ends of that word /and/, several scenarios become possible, one of which is philosophical. As already mentioned, Talmud was produced in the context of rhetorical schools. As was also briefly mentioned, rhetoric has an unstable position in the scope of traditional philosophy. According to Platonism, one of the leading traditions of philosophical thinking, rhetoric has no place in philosophy. It is the outcast, the outsider; it is the place of sophistry where people use arguments to make points about their private interests. Rhetoric is the way of trickery; it is the arch-other of what philosophy is. There is no truth to rhetoric whatsoever. The other, competing tradition is Aristotelian, which says that rhetoric does not belong to the core or center of philosophy, to its *canon*, but it does belong to philosophical knowledge, to its *organon*. So, then, we have two approaches: one that completely excludes rhetoric, and the other that lets rhetoric into the margins of philosophy—as a scandalous necessity—but not in the center.

Going back to the beginning of this introduction, where we explored a preliminary definition of the terms *Talmud* and *Philosophy* as parallel "traditions of tradition," let us reconsider the historically dominant paradigms for how this relationship *between* Talmud /and/ Philosophy has been understood. We might begin in the Middle Ages because that was the period in which people started talking about an object, a reification, which ultimately became "the" Talmud in the form of printed volumes. The first well-known person to start thinking about the Talmud as a reified object—in particular, as an object of philosophical negation—was Moses Maimonides. In the introduction to his *Mishneh Torah*, he expressed the idea of stripping the late ancient archives of rabbinic academies of their rhetorical form of refutations and counterrefutations because he thought this rhetorical form was extraneous to the "law," which Maimonides posits the Talmud contains and on which, in his view, the Talmud is centered. Very schematically, Maimonides's response is: Let's extract the law from the extraneous form of refutations and counterrefutations it had in late antiquity and present everything systematically—nicely, cleanly, "philosophically"—so that one mind (rather than two, let alone more minds) would be enough to establish what the law is. In rabbinic academies, no thinking is possible without at least four, but generally many more minds—one I disagree with, one about whom I disagree with another, and yet another one with whom the previous one disagrees. So there are at least four minds and sometimes many more. Against that complex multitude, Maimonides proposes to have one mind, one thinker, and one person. He aims to strip the Talmud of its rhetorical form and present everything systematically. That is what *Mishneh Torah* does.

In addition to losing the "extraneous" rhetorical form of the Talmud, there was another price the Talmudic tradition paid for the would-be-systematization: the partition of the Talmud into "legal" and "narrative" forms, or into halakhah and aggadah, respectively. Maimonides wrote another book, *The Guide for the Perplexed*, in which he addressed what remains of the Talmud when the law is systematically extracted from it. What remains is the second, poetic component in the Talmud: the individual sayings, interpretations, and deeds of certain rabbis. In the *Guide*, he addressed narratives that personal rabbis produced, or narratives attributed to personal rabbis in the Talmud, under the general rubric of aggadah—in the sense of poetic productions, a "figure of speech," *melitsah*—as opposed to what for him is the law, or halakhah. So he introduced the separation that we still suffer from today: the separation between the aggadah, or narrative—the part of the Talmud that is, as it were, added and "poetic," wherein, Maimonides would say, every rabbi acts and teaches in accordance with his own inspiration—and halakhah, the legal part, where everything is universal, and truly the law. This separation between aggadah and halakha continued to be a significant concern to both traditional and academic scholars of the Talmud. Yet we have to understand its source: a philosophical interest in distilling the law from the rhetoric.

Of course, the rhetoric cannot be completely stripped from the law—or, rather, the law cannot be extracted from the rhetoric. But to appreciate Maimonides's impulse to do such a thing, we should recall the political context of the history of receptions of the Talmud that he inherited. Central to this context was the Karaite political crisis. The Karaites were communities that separated themselves from rabbinic communities on grounds prepared by Islamic culture, where the art of grammar flourished (nurtured, as it was in many ways, by Jewish interpreters). The art of grammar reinforced a Stoic idea that one could have access to the meaning of a text if one understood the grammatical structures of the text. For example, the Karaites thought they could take the pronouncement at the beginning of the book of Genesis ("On the seventh day God rested") to mean vaguely "some time on the Sabbath" so that the Sabbath could start at noon, which is, after all, still "on the seventh day." Rabbinic communities were starting the Sabbath on Friday night, a very practical difference that had political implications. Rabbinic authorities needed to counter the argument of the Karaites who told the rabbis that they were just inventors and that others could legitimately read the actual chapters of the Bible grammatically and come up with practical interpretations, which the Karaites claimed were more straightforward as well as more correct than what the rabbis were coming up with. The rabbis' response to this argument was the *Iggeret [Epistle] of Rav Sherira Gaon* and an earlier book called *Seder [Order] of Tannaim and Amoraim*. These books outlined the continuity of authority through generations of rabbis in the Talmud to show that it was in keeping with, and the heir of, Moses's teaching. A common practice of the time was to create fantastical genealogies and topologies of certain things, and this was done with rabbinic tradition. (Its fantastical nature is best exemplified by the fact that, at the same time, a fantastical map of Roman administration had been created. People did not like horizontal connections; they wanted something vertical, so they produced a map of a Roman administration that never existed.)

These two books, the *Epistle* and the *Order*, fueled and reflected a growing hunger for genealogy within the rabbinic world. This yielded a genealogy of *Tannaim* and *Amoraim* (the latter meaning "speakers" who issue dicta or commentary on traditions of Tannaim, or "reciters" of the Mishnah), which showed that rabbis do have a tradition beginning from Moses and proceeding through each generation of scholars named in the Talmud. In this genealogy, names were given and relationships were established, so by the Middle Ages, there was a continuous authority of tradition. Therefore, the Sabbath must start on Friday night, not Saturday noon. That was the first step in transforming the Talmud into a reified object: first as a genealogy, then as an object of rejection or philosophical "reform" by Maimonides. A little later, by at least the thirteenth century, a single book was produced, which tried to include the entirety of the

Talmud. At the time, the idea was to collect everything in one volume and give the book as a bar mitzvah gift. There is a version of this book in the Bavarian State Library in Munich. It is not really everything, but it is an attempt at everything; the manuscript contains almost all of the Talmud. The scribe took half a year to produce the volume of the whole Talmud in very quick handwriting, probably realizing that it would not be read easily; it was a bar mitzvah gift for a boy who might continue the tradition of learning. The book itself was not the core; the core was memory. People were still memorizing things, and these writings were simply aids to memory. Yet the book did emerge: the codex of the Talmud.

Since then, the struggle over the relationship between Talmud and philosophy and over the /and/ continued. Maimonides said, or was understood to have said, that we do not need the Talmud, to which there were several important responses. The first was that the poetic/aggadic element of the Talmud remains important in mystical terms and has its own rationality, albeit not a philosophical one. Kabbalah was, in a sense, the result of that response to Maimonides. The other response was so-called Talmudic rationalism, which came from the schools of Aristotelian rhetoric, whereby rhetoric and the art of interpretation are very precise. According to this view, the Talmud is therefore rational and precise, not in the logical sense of precision but in the rhetorical and hermeneutical sense. The fifteenth-century book *Darkhei Hatalmud* by Rabbi Isaac Canpanton, which I was privileged to write about in the footsteps of Daniel Boyarin and Hayim Dimitrovski, was an important source in which this attitude to the rationality of the Talmud as *Talmud* (an intellectual discipline, a tradition of thinking, not a reified object of thought) took shape. Not entirely unlike Maimonides, Canpanton and others of his school were openly Aristotelian, so it is not quite appropriate to speak of "Talmud and Philosophy." Their philosophy was Aristotelian or post-Aristotelian, and there were schools of rhetoric and philosophy—or, in the case of Kabbalah and respective Kabbalistic interpretations of the materials in the Talmud, there were Neoplatonic schools.

In that context, glossing the phrase "Talmud *and* Philosophy" as a simple and direct conjunction is inappropriate even though, institutionally, it was that and it still is today. For Canpanton—or, more broadly, for

Talmudic rationalists—the Talmud was rational, but in a rhetorical sense, not a philosophical one. As a rhetorical object, *the* Talmud was the book privileged for rational *contemplation* (*iyyun*, to use Canpanton's term) or an ideal physical object as a printed book. Regardless, the readers of this book were Aristotelians. Within this Talmudic Aristotelianism, *Talmud* and *Philosophy* could not be two separate but conjoined entities. Institutionally, of course, there was a moment of partition; Talmud was practiced in Rabbinic institutions, such as Houses of Study where the Talmud was studied, whereas philosophy developed in scholastic academies and later in universities. Yet intellectually, Talmud and philosophy remained under the specter of Aristotelian traditions, leaving no room for *and* as a conjunction (unless the word is glossed as an internal *and*, between philosophy and rhetoric, *within* philosophy—a gloss that is also problematic).

This is why, by way of contrast, the moment of institutional separation between Talmud and philosophy goes back to the point from which I began: philosophical *rejection* or marginalization of rhetoric, which both sides—the philosophers and the Talmudists—have blindly and tacitly accepted. The result is two separate traditions, Talmud and (i.e., *or*) Philosophy—two schools or institutions of study that do not readily communicate. The time came to institutionalize what intellectually remains a continuum. That is why these traditions need to be studied as a continuum, including fissures that such a continuum might or even must entail.

This is not to say that there is no divide between Talmud and philosophy or that Talmud can or should be subsumed into philosophy. Rather, I offer the possibility that the Talmud represents an intellectual discipline of its own, with this moment of refutation as a vehicle of memory at its center—a discipline that offers ways of thinking about being and interpersonality. (I would not say intersubjectivity because both *subjectivity* and *intersubjectivity* are too philosophical.) Interpersonality here refers to ways of thinking in which one is not immersed in one's solitary thinking. Thinking is a collective enterprise, calling for thinking together without ever thinking as one, in the end.

I conclude this attunement with a quote from Franz Rosenzweig, who was also sensitive to the dangers of the little word *and*. He writes in the *Star of Redemption*:

The And is not the secret companion of the particular word, but of the sequence of words. It is the keystone that completes the vault of the cellar, above which is erected the edifice of logos, of reason in language.

[Das Und ist nicht der geheime Begleiter des einzelnen Worts, sondern des Wortzusammenhangs. Es ist der Schlußstein des Kellergewölbes, über welchem das Gebäude des Logos, der Sprachvernunft, errichtet ist.]

This edifice of logos, of "reason in language" is precisely what has been developed and criticized by philosophical tradition in its self-understanding: whether in conjunction with, or in disjunction from, Talmud. Philosophy, the "edifice of logos" (again, including critique thereof), is now the dominant intellectual paradigm in our society and our thinking about everything from informational technology to Talmud. I hope we will encompass possible continuities as well, starting by suspending the edifice of the /and/ in its disjunctive and, in particular, conjunctive and controlling powers, and that we will start looking into the walls and the ground, into the opening and, perhaps, the darkness behind it that lifting the veil of the /and/ can create.

* * *

It is no secret that introductions are written after the body of the book is already there. The same open secret holds for the balance of our introduction, where we reflect on essays written in response to the Attunement. The essays were written by scholars of both rabbinic texts and philosophical works, moving beyond partitions that the history of the word /and/ has imposed on our thought by way of trainings and institutions. The collaborative nature of our project anticipates that the book's readers are or will be similarly open to thinking beyond their various disciplines and backgrounds.

Moving beyond the /and/ has assumed different shapes and brought forth new questions. One focus of these questions is the stable axis of a relationship between philosophy and rhetoric, onto which the relationship between Talmud and philosophy has also been predominately projected; if not entirely incorrectly, then far too reductively.

Three major configurations fall along that axis: excluding rhetoric as a mimetic art from philosophy, in Platonisms; allowing rhetoric as a marginal discipline into the *organon* but not the *canon* of philosophy, in

Aristotelianisms; or placing rhetoric at the center, where it underlies any philosophical argument, in the modern philosophy of language. Talmud, in turn, has been aligned with these three major views of the relationship between philosophy and rhetoric. Talmud has been excluded from philosophy (Maimonides); included into philosophy in Talmudic rationalism (Canpanton); and privileged as the most advanced version of philosophical thinking, whether the best version of Enlightened reason (Luzzatto) or a "religion of reason from the sources of Judaism" (Cohen) on par with other philosophical religions of reason. An alternative fourth view has Talmud figuring as "ethics" in the sense of first philosophy, one at which other philosophies were envisioned as having yet to arrive (according to one interpretation of Levinas). Despite these oppositions among the three traditional philosophical positions (not to mention the fourth), locating the Talmud and its tradition, vis-à-vis philosophy, was invariably defined by a stable axis of relationship that philosophy had also posited between itself and its traditional other: rhetoric. In short, in the relationship of Talmud /and/ philosophy, the word /and/ has historically been glossed in four ways: as a disjunction (excluding Talmud *from* philosophy), as a conjunction (including Talmud *into* philosophy), as an origin (making Talmud the center, or *telos*, of philosophy), and as a horizon (figuring Talmud as the beginning of a philosophy yet to come). Regardless, because of its profound and often unconscious association with the traditional positioning of philosophy in relation to rhetoric, Talmud itself—as its own "tradition of tradition" and discipline of thought—has been obscured from view.

Authors responded to the attunement by resisting this reductive projection of Talmud onto the axis of relationships between philosophy and rhetoric, landing in various positions as they probed its stability and shook its very conceptual pillars. The essays study and chart strategies for moving beyond and above the axis, beyond and above the ends that the /and/ of philosophy /and/ Talmud has traditionally established, as if they were taken for granted. As a result, this book maps alternative possibilities for defusing the role of /and/ or lifting it up to view, without, however, sealing the gap between Talmud /and/ philosophy.

These modes of lifting up /and/ vary from essay to essay. Each author looks into the abyss behind the gap from a new angle. Each refuses to convert this abyss into a perspectival landscape, to reduce it to the vanishing point of a privileged perspective. With that critical impulse, the contributions are complementary and can be configured as orthogonal lines of flight from the traditional axis of relationships among Talmud, philosophy, and rhetoric. They reveal original ways of working with, rather than closing, the gap *between* Talmud /and/ philosophy that was traditionally configured as disjunction, conjunction, origin, or horizon.

The gap can open possibilities for a meta-view: one that Agata Bielik-Robson explores by probing a Talmudic discussion as a meta-space, irreducible to a single linear axis of relationship, where philosophy newly problematizes its own sense of tradition. Beyond a term that has been elided by reduction to rhetoric, she uses *Talmud* to assess and take philosophy's measure from the outside. Instead of simply inverting the traditional axis of relationship by making the Talmud dominant over philosophy, she interrupts the powers of the copula /and/, reframing its architectonics by reflecting on the Talmudic tradition of thought as a vantage point for reflecting on the tradition of philosophical thinking. She asks how philosophy would look if such a philosophy were born from the spirit of the Talmud and refused to cut the umbilical cord of its bond to the Talmud. This is not a Levinasian project of positing the Talmud as *already* a philosophy, one to which another philosophy will arrive. It is a much more open project of reflecting on and practically conceiving a new philosophy from the spirit of the Talmud. Others (e.g., de Man) have made a similar turn toward rhetoric of metaphor and metonymy by insisting that philosophy (e.g., Locke or Kant) had never parted from such rhetoric. Yet Bielik-Robson goes even further to suspend any sense of hierarchy or static architecture, any need for a stable genetic relationship around the /and/ to pose, instead, a truly open and fundamental question: How can philosophy rethink its dominance of rhetoric if a philosopher asks a Talmudic question about philosophy itself?

For Elad Lapidot, the gap rescales Talmud as a discipline of thought in rabbinic tradition. Lapidot interprets the "tradition of tradition" of Talmud on a still broader scale: as a task, a perspective, and the possibility of another beginning for human engagement with the world. For Lapidot, this rescaled vision of the tradition (lowercase "talmud") translates a discipline of rabbinic thought toward a horizon of human thought per se, in and beyond the scope of Heidegger's "other thinking," as a departure from Greek-Aristotelian-Christian-Jewish-Muslim traditions where Western philosophy has seen its past and future. Lapidot reconfigures the question of /and/ by articulating the ongoing task of moving from "*the* Talmud," as an archive of late ancient texts posited and interpreted since the Middle Ages, to this book's "Talmud," as an intellectual discipline of disagreement and memory, to his "talmud," as the always-open task of arriving at an intrinsically evolving "tradition of tradition." As his ongoing task, one that deals with the problem of the political or literary as a way for humans to engage the world and community, rethinking "talmud" means a perpetual questioning of the operations of the /and/ between Talmud and philosophy. Instead of settling on his rescaled "talmud" as "philosophy's other," let alone "philosophy's better," Lapidot invites us to rethink this "tradition of tradition" as an open call to *constantly* rethink and challenge the operations of the /and/.

The gap between Talmud /and/ philosophy exposes an abyss of forgetting within human memory, as Sergey Dolgopolski argues on the powers of citing the past in the Palestinian Talmud. The chapter focuses on forgetting and memory (in this order) and the role that citing from the body of work collected in the Palestinian Talmud can play in how we understand forgetting and remembering the past in both late ancient and modern contexts. The result is to set up a comparative framework for the Palestinian tradition of Talmud and the tradition of philosophy surrounding the question of forgetting and memory. To do so, Dolgopolski places a fragment from the Palestinian Talmud back into that *longue durée* of the history of forgetting as the default human condition. This history is a reversal. Memory and truth, the derivatives of forgetting, become the default while forgetting recedes to their would-be inverse. In the context of this reversal, partitions between the traditions of Talmud and philosophy emerge in a new perspective; one facet of which this essay sets out to explore.

Dolgopolski focuses on the rabbinic schools of rhetoric in Roman Palestine and their place in that *longue durée*. The rabbis cite and thereby remember the for-them-not-yet-fully-established procedural laws and obligations (*ius*, halakah) of Israel toward God; they do this so as not to forget their laws governing their obligations to God, thereby making the case for God not to forget God's promises-to-have-become-"obligations" to them. Thus the crucial question of the chapter is how to appreciate the role of citing the past (and in particular of the law of the past) as the rabbis and philosophers engage with, and struggle against, the powers of forgetting. Dolgopolski's exposition of that *longue durée* offers a new problematization of how the Palestinian Talmud is positioned vis-à-vis forgetting, an abyss that philosophy also faces repeatedly.

Lifting up the /and/ without sealing the resulting gap leads James Adam Redfield, a scholar of rabbinic anthropologies, to reimagine this gap's possible relationship to Kant's philosophical anthropology. Rabbinic thought transpires in his argument as a version of anthropology that is commensurable in scope, but irreducible to, Kant's philosophical-anthropological answer to the question "Who is human?" in the framework of Kant's defense of Enlightenment as a religion of reason. Rather than focusing on one gap, Redfield studies two in his novel "analogical" critique: the gap between anthropology and morality in a precritical Kant (as distinct from his three *Critiques*) and the gap between anthropology and morality in rabbinic literature. Redfield's essay shows how the tension between the precritical and critical Kant can illuminate the scope of relationships between anthropology and morality in rabbinic texts. His argument operates in the space between Kant's philosophy and rabbinic literature and is only sustainable as long as that difference does not collapse: rabbis are not to be reduced to an avatar of Kant or vice versa. In this, Redfield departs from the prevalent reception of both the rabbis (along the lines of the modern *halakhah*) and Kant—by those who read his anthropology in light of his *Critiques* alone and, therefore, tend not to accord his anthropology any significant purchase on his overall system. Just as Kant's "precritical" account of morality in his anthropology bears on his overall thought precisely *because* he takes a very different approach to morality in his later, critical works, so, too, Redfield argues, can we situate a selective (and by no means paradigmatic) rabbinic moral anthropology (*derekh erets*) within rabbinic thought precisely *through* the conceptual tensions and discontinuities between anthropology and morality. That juxtaposition does not conflate this rabbinic moral anthropology with Kant's precritical one; rather, it opens up a space between rabbinic thought on moral norms and human nature on one hand and a philosophical tradition of thinking through the same relationships on the other. Redfield's juxtaposition performs a critical interrogation of the /and/ in both traditions of tradition.

Yonatan Brafman places the modern discussion of rabbinic procedural law (halakhah) directly into the gap: a gap now reconceived as a no-one's-land, where we can no longer differentiate between pragmatic analysis of the law as such and halakhic analysis of the law. This gap arises because both the pragmatic and the halakhic analysis take up the law as the challenge for thought, one that is fully met neither by rabbinic codifications of divine law nor by the philosophy of a human-made (positive) law. For Brafman, this challenge initiates a self-reflective discussion on the nature of law and is thus congruent, in its modes of thought and analysis, with self-reflective discussions of law in analytic traditions of philosophy. While distinctly different in vocabulary, and variously imbued with the apparatus of Christian legal thinking, the analytical discussions of both rabbinic law and modern law meet in this gap between philosophy and Talmud. Together, they depart or break, as Brafman argues, from the reification of *the* Talmud, in the form of authoritative codes of law that unfolded from the Middle Ages to modernity.

A scholar of rabbinic thought, Lynn Kaye shows how images lurk behind the gap that neither form a copula with concepts nor support any sense of separation between concept and image. If such a separation has defined philosophy's self-differentiation from rhetoric, Kaye's rereading of rabbinic texts opens a different vista on rhetoric. By reconceiving dynamics between *thought* and *image* in rabbinic discourse, at right angles to Kant's understanding of their relationship, Kaye manages to articulate yet another irreducible gap behind the /and/ without sealing it shut. Kaye asks the reader to inhabit the space of thinking of a rabbinic discussion, where, unlike in philosophy, the question is not how to relate concepts to images or vice versa but rather what it means to develop a rigorous mode of thought *in* images from the start—and before the sheer distinction between concepts and images is assumed. Such thinking in images includes images in the sense of the personae of those who do such thinking in interaction with one another. Appropriately, Kaye's exposition includes images that she creates to develop her argument.

As an interpreter of the late ancient rabbis, Alexander Weisberg frames the gap as one between late ancient and modern thought on "language," "reality," and human-world ontologies. In reclaiming the rabbinic tradition in late antiquity as escaping the axis of relationships between these terms, Weisberg places that tradition in a heuristic schema marked, on its other end, by Benjamin's view of reality and language. Thus his reading of rabbinic texts interrogates the modernist philosophy of language. The asynchronicity of his analysis invites a fresh mode of encounter among traditions and across epistemes, negotiating their intellectual conjunctions and disjunctions rather than resolving or reassessing their historical relationships. The chapter discusses a plant-animal connection as one way to think about the relationships between philosophy and Talmud. Weisberg applies Walter Benjamin's philosophy of language to illustrate that relationship in an innovative way.

A scholar of rabbinic and classical thought, Sophia Avants threatens to reconfigure the hitherto dominant view of the relationship between the traditions of philosophy and rhetoric by reclaiming the Mishnah as the work of building a community around a third space: a constructive form of the gap. Avants reframes relationships between philosophy and rhetoric to allow the rhetoric of the Mishnah to interrupt philosophy's control of its partition from the *ars rhetorica*. Avants uses her act of interruption, that is, her violation of the rigid disjunction between philosophy and rhetoric, as a way to resituate the Mishnah—precisely in that third space between philosophy and philosophical figures for rhetoric and its tradition. Avants takes up the question of the Platonic and Aristotelian treatment of mimesis and the rhetorical syllogism, in contradistinction from rabbinic practices of the rhetorical syllogism or enthymeme, as one way to build a community. In this Mishnaic third space, rhetorical arguments clash, creating a space for discussion—rather than aiming at a community that is driven to agreement through public persuasion. Avants reframes the late ancient composition of the Mishnah as creating a space and community of this "in-between": reducible to neither philosophy's nor rhetoric's standard accounts of their own traditions. In contrast with Emmanuel Levinas's readings and translations of Talmudic discussions into the language of Greek philosophy, as an ethics of responsibility and forgiveness in a logocentric community, Avants pursues a different route. She explores the relationships between rhetoric as part of a philosophical canon and rhetoric as a formative principle in the Mishnah. Her analysis reveals a new sense of community in the Mishnah; predicated, as it is, on a reinterpretation of the enthymeme as a "rhetorical syllogism" of a life in indeterminacy, departing from a dominant philosophical view of the enthymeme as a "reduced logical syllogism." The contrast between the two syllogistics, a philosophy's *ideal* of logic in life versus the Mishnah's *reality* of rhetoric in life, translates into two distinct senses of community. One community is based on the default of logical certainty; the other is grounded on the programmatic uncertainty of a rhetorical syllogism.

Karma Ben-Johanan, a critical historian of relationships between Christianity and rabbinic literature, describes a genealogy of the emergence of the Talmud on the horizon of the Christian intellectual world. Sensitive to the theology of Christian supersessionism, which encountered the Talmud as "unexpected" evidence of the intellectual life of supposedly spiritless and even mindless Jews, Ben-Johanan pointedly signals the current danger of reverse supersessionism, a flip of the historical axis whereby a rediscovered talmud (see Lapidot, above) or Talmud (in our sense, above) strives for dominance with philosophy or a theological space dominated by Christianity. To avoid this danger, Ben-Johanan asks how lifting up the /and/, reopening the gap of Talmud /and/ philosophy today, could instead yield a "stubbornly unsupersessionist" version of supersessionism: this time, one of t/Talmud over philosophy, without simply reversing the old philosophy-rhetoric hierarchy. This leads her to critique the challenge of avoiding a power hierarchy between Talmud and philosophy and to her historical review of the obstacles to any unsupersessionist dialogue between the two, however "stubbornly" she, and we, would like.

Collectively, this volume invites a sustained rethinking of the tradition of the two traditions, that of Talmud *and* that of philosophy. The chapters commit to neither a common third category nor a common beginning from which to trace the emergence of the two traditions. Together, the contributions lay bare the very instability and complexity of the otherwise all-too-quiet and all-too-powerful effects of the /and/ on the tradition, in or against the sway of which a philosopher or a Talmudist always thinks.

How might this book be read? To whom is it addressed? Broadly, the book contributes to rethinking where the various areas of Jewish studies stand in relation to the humanities at large. As philosophy grounds the theoretical apparatus for many disciplines, developing the bridge between philosophy and the study of the Talmud can allow other disciplines to grasp their own connections with counterparts in Jewish studies. In that sense, the book invites new readerships across the humanities and beyond the partitions. More broadly still, the book addresses readerships interested in comparative perspectives on rabbinic tradition, philosophy, history, literature, and other areas beyond the humanities within the liberal arts university, as well as other readers who think and read across the traditions.

As each chapter responds to the initial Attunement to the theme, each in its own way, after reading this introduction and before reading the afterword, the chapters can be read in any order according to the interests of the reader.

1

TO REFUTE GOD HIMSELF
Talmud as Meta-Philosophy

AGATA BIELIK-ROBSON

> *Tell all the truth but tell it slant—*
> *Success in Circuit lies*
> *Too bright for our infirm Delight*
> *The Truth's superb surprise*
> *As Lightning to the Children eased*
> *With explanation kind*
> *The Truth must dazzle gradually*
> *Or every man be blind—*
>
> EMILY DICKINSON, Fragment no. 1263

> *The first real man among the philosophers was also the first to see God face to face—even if only to refute Him.*
>
> FRANZ ROSENZWEIG ON NIETZSCHE (*Star of Redemption*, 25)

There are many ways in which the positioning of Talmud *and* Philosophy can be understood: as conjunction (perhaps leading to some elusive synthesis), as neutral juxtaposition, or as opposition (*and* as *versus*). But I propose something else: a certain reading of Talmud as a *meta-philosophical* document, which first creates a necessary condition for *any* reason, be it a philosophical Logos or a rhetorical scriptural reasoning. By referring to the famous *lo bashamayim* fragment from Bava Metziʻa 59b—possibly the best-known Talmudic story, frequently quoted by Scholem, Levinas, Taubes, Biale, Boyarin, and many others, and the most exquisite example of the Talmudic tradition of refutation—I want to demonstrate that it delivers a set of transcendental conditions of any rational discussion, before any specific definition of the *ratio*, including the Western philosophical one.[1] I call this transcendental meta-philosophical position a *decentered theism*. In opposition to the theocentric "theological absolutism," which turns the divine infinite vantage point into the "measure of all things," the rabbinic decentering creates a distance from the overwhelming divine verdicts, which allows the finite minds to develop their own reasoning. The refutative no against the miraculous interventions from above, which automatically trump any argument from below, is here a necessary defense mechanism without which no "finite thinking" could ever emerge.[2]

RADICAL FINITUDE

The aggadic fragment from Bava Metziʿa 59b has always been one of the most discussed stories, but it is certainly due to Gershom Scholem's essay "Revelation and Tradition as Religious Categories in Judaism" that it became truly famous; more than that, it became almost a synecdoche of the whole Talmud, epitomizing the main tenets of the Jewish wisdom of commentary:

> Nothing demonstrates this authority, the authority of commentary over author, more triumphantly than the story of the oven of Akhnai which is told in the Talmud. Rabbi Eliezer ben Hyrkanos and the sages disputed about whether or not this oven, which had a particular type of construction, was subject to impurity in the sense of the Torah. Finally, against the opinion of Rabbi Eliezer, a majority declared it subject to impurification. On this matter the Talmudic account, which represents one of the most famous passages in Jewish literature, then continues:

> On that day Rabbi Eliezer brought forward all the arguments in the world, but they were not accepted. He said to them: "If the Halakhah [the proper decision] agrees with me, let this carob tree prove it." Thereupon the carob tree was uprooted a hundred cubits from its place; some say, four hundred cubits. They replied: "No proof may be brought from a carob tree." Then he said: "If the Halakhah agrees with me, let this stream of water prove it." Thereupon the stream of water flowed backwards. They replied: "No proof may be brought from a stream of water." Then he said: "If the Halakhah agrees with me let the walls of the schoolhouse prove it." Thereupon the

walls of the schoolhouse began to totter. But Rabbi Joshua rebuked them and said: "When scholars are engaged in halakhic dispute, what concern is it of yours?" Thus the walls "did not topple, in honor of Rabbi Joshua, but neither did they return to their upright position, in honor of Rabbi Eliezer; still today they stand inclined." Then he said: "If the Halakhah agrees with me, let it be proved from Heaven." Thereupon a heavenly voice was heard saying: "Why do you dispute with Rabbi Eliezer? The Halakhah always agrees with him." But Rabbi Joshua arose and said (Deut. 30:12): "It is not in heaven." What did he mean by that? Rabbi Jeremiah replied: "The Torah has already been given at Mount Sinai [and is thus no longer in Heaven]. We pay no heed to any heavenly voice, because already at Mount Sinai You wrote in the Torah (Exod. 23:2): 'One must incline after the majority.'" Rabbi Nathan met the prophet Elijah and asked him: "What did the Holy One, blessed be He, do in that hour?" He replied: "God smiled and said: My children have defeated Me, My children have defeated Me."[3]

According to Scholem, the moral of the story is the unequivocal praise of *mediation* as a necessary *medium* through which the divine word becomes apprehensible:

> In Judaism, tradition becomes the reflective impulse that intervenes between the absoluteness of the divine word—revelation—and its receiver. Tradition thus raises a question about the possibility of immediacy in man's relationship to the divine, even though it has been incorporated in revelation. To put it another way: Can the divine word confront us without mediation? And, can it be fulfilled without mediation? Or, given the assumption of the Jewish tradition which we have formulated, does the divine word rather not require just such mediation by tradition in order to be apprehensible and therefore fulfillable? For rabbinic Judaism, the answer is in the affirmative.[4]

This mediation, however, also changes the status of the "divine word": it is no longer a *spoken* word but a *written* one. The rabbinic insistence on the scriptural character of revelation—"already at Mount Sinai You wrote in the Torah"—contains both a defensive and an agonistic element that wards off the absoluteness of God's message in order to let imperfect human beings enter the game. Without this self-defense, which protects the receiver as an autonomous pole in the asymmetrical relationship between the finite human and the infinite God, the former would simply collapse under the enormous impact of the latter. To insist, therefore, on the scriptural *mediation/medium* of the revelation is to allow—in Harold Bloom's words—a certain *ratio* to be established between otherwise incommensurable dimensions.⁵ This self-defense must take the form of the attack capable of stripping the Infinite of its overwhelming and traumatizing glory (which constitutes the main theme of the book of Job, in which the terrifying divine manifestation thunders "from the whirlwind" to crush the precarious human). Yet this defensive mechanism is not set against God but rather for God's sake. If God is to reveal himself as God and enter into a relation of the covenant, he has to allow for the "defeat" of his absoluteness: the Christian narrative of *kenosis* begins here, in the very logic of the divine-human relationship.⁶

The moral of the story, therefore, is to vigorously refute God's attempt to enter the argument in a way that completely disregards the rules of the game. These rules were established precisely to ward off the repetition of the *trauma* of revelation but also to allow *revelation* as such, relieved of its blinding effect. The defeat is thus quite literal: God started the game, but he has been surpassed by his children.⁷ But this also means something deeply un-Greek: that the First, *arche*, does not possess the highest authority of the veridictive vantage point; that coming late or second, further removed from the origin, does not disqualify or disadvantage the "children" in the rational process of truth-seeking. The further removed from the absolutist perspective that always privileges the arche as "the mystical foundation of authority," the better; the less overwhelmed by God's presence or the proximity of origin, the more quickly the Talmudic rationality will develop its own finite thinking in the element of *différance*/disagreement, which can only benefit from the divine nonpresence.⁸

The divine defeat has a double sense here. It is a necessary condition of God entering and maintaining the covenantal relationship with finite human beings, but it also confirms the written nature of the revelatory gift. Exodus 23:2, quoted by Rabbi Joshua, declares (and this is not a mistake) that God specifically *tells* people not to side with the majority or follow the crowd on moral judgments "to do evil" (*lera'ot*) and "to pervert [justice]" (*lehattot*). But the wording of the prohibition may suggest that it is not wrong to follow the majority *if* one does not intend to do evil or pervert justice, in other words, if the person's motives are pure. This seems to contradict the authorial intention, yet it would be in full harmony with the rabbinic model of inquiry, which looks for the ambiguities of a written text to make it exact—to read a text as it is written and not as what the text *wants to say.* Thus one may read this passage without heeding the heavenly living *voice*, which supposedly wants to warn against majority judgments but then states that "one should incline after majority." So the very argument used in favor of the freedom of the written word against any intervention of the heavenly voice is already an innovative piece of reasoning extracted from the scripture, treated as *scripture* in the strongest sense of the word; that is, with no attention paid to the *spoken* intention. What can God do in such a case but smile and admit: *nitshuni banai* ("My children have triumphed over me")?[9] By writing down the Torah and leaving it in its sealed scriptural form, God has made himself—that is, his ongoing participation in the hermeneutic debates of his children—irrelevant. This is the first case of the "death of the author" as the master controlling the interpretation of the text, and the whole Derridean deconstructive method, which consists precisely of ignoring the authorial intentions for the sake of what really *remains* written, is comprised here in a nutshell.[10] When Truth is written down, it does not *say* anything. There is thus no rationale for "heeding to the heavenly voice."[11]

However, it would be too far-fetched to see in the preceding aggadah the "death of God" as pure and simple, as Slavoj Žižek does when he praises it in his essay "Dialectical Clarity versus the Misty Conceit of Paradox," a text particularly relevant to the topic of 'Talmud *and* Philosophy' because it draws the Talmudic reasoning into the very center of the formation of Western rationality:

> This Jewish legacy—in Lacanese, the passage from the big Other qua the abyss of subjectivity to the big Other qua the impersonal structure of the symbolic Law—found what could be said to be its most radical expression in the Talmud, in the story about the two rabbis who basically tell God to shut up.... No wonder this passage from the Talmud was endlessly exploited by anti-Semites as proof of the Jewish obscene-manipulative relationship to God! To cut a long story short, *what happens here is already the death of God*: once the act of creation is accomplished, God dies, he survives only in the dead letter of the Law, without retaining even the right to intervene into how people interpret his law—no wonder this anecdote recalls the well-known scene from the beginning of Woody Allen's (another Jew!) *Annie Hall*, where a couple waiting in line for cinema tickets debate a point about Marshall McLuhan's theory, and then McLuhan himself appears in the queue, intervening in the debate by brutally siding with the Woody Allen character.[12]

This intervention, as expected, does not win the argument for the Woody Allen character in the eyes of his female opponent. But Žižek is both right and wrong. This is precisely what one should not do: cut the long story short. The defensive practice of keeping God's living presence at bay is not synonymous with killing God or rendering him completely "inactive"; that is, "as good as dead."[13] God is *not* dead; rather, he is sublated in the original sense of the word *kathargein/aufheben*, as used by the Pharisee Paul, who was well versed in Judaism's long dialectical stories, of which Christianity formed for him simply the next chapter, with the Jewish law simultaneously preserved and deactivated. Just as monotheism is a historical religion, so does God's transcendence have a temporal aspect: he keeps his incontestable status quo, guarding the definite past perfect of the revelation, in which he had given us the Torah. However, because of the enormous "anxiety of influence" on the part of his human believers, he withdraws into virtual absence by leaving them with the freedom to read. Spinoza's vehement refutation of miracles as the proofs of God's existence as nothing but "taking refuge in the will of God, i.e., the sanctuary of ignorance"[14] derives directly from this unique tradition of mature and independent rationality—a "dialectical clarity"—which had emerged only on the condition of forbidding God to issue direct instructions.[15]

Commenting on the preceding fragment and similar ones in the Talmud, Robert Gibbs devised a formula that perfectly captures the rabbis' stance, simultaneously pious and agonistic: "disagreeing for God's sake."[16] The formula has two meanings. First, disagreement, or "sporting" different opinions, is not a matter of *sport*. It is not about the egoistic glory of a talented interpreter, boasting of his skills. Second, *for God's sake* is not *in God's name*: to speak in his stead as an immediate, participatory representative of transcendence within immanence is strictly forbidden.[17] *For God's sake* precludes any sacred empowerment of the interpreter, who would claim a privileged position in the hermeneutic community (Eliezer), but it also protects him from a total disempowerment, where it is only the "living God" who possesses the truth. The truth is no longer in heaven. It has been written, laid down in the form of the written word, open and accessible to all properly trained readers.[18] The truth is out there, not in the possession of the unapproachable transcendent deity but in the revealed text of the Torah, which—to paraphrase Saul Kripke's phrase—constitutes a rigid designator that fixes the reference of the rabbinic commentary without determining its content.[19]

The Kripkean rule—the more rigidly fixed the reference/designator, the less determined its description—is fully confirmed by the well-known words of Ben Bag-Bag from Pirqe Avot regarding the Torah: "Turn it and turn it, for all is in it."[20] Truth is given once and for all—but its content is open to an infinite discussion and commentary, which takes the form of the organized hermeneutic disagreement. Truth is one and revealed—but its meaning cannot be determined immediately and finally. Another quote from Pirqe Avot is Rabbi Tarphon's "You are not required to complete the work, but neither you are free to desist from it," which can be understood as praising the disagreement stage, which should be treated as autonomous, without the regulative idea of a consensus implied by the completion of the work.[21] Tarphon also describes the rules of the "dialectical clarity" required by the permanent dissent: his concept of the interpretive *work* dialectically intertwines *in*vention and *con*vention, the individualistic moment of agon and the communal moment of togetherness; newness and tradition. The sacred *work* of "disagreeing for God's sake" is envisaged as an interminable process, without beginning (relegated to the "radical past,'" which will be discussed shortly) or end (infinitely deferred and delayed, as Derrida suggested in his concept of the *différance*), passing constantly through all generations of commentators, past, present, and future.

This highly disciplined, positive freedom to comment is best illustrated by yet another passage from Pirqe Avot, in which Rabbi Joshua ben Levi says: "And the tablets were the work of God, and the writing was the writing of God, graven upon the tablets. Read not *charuth* (graven) but *cheruth* (freedom), for no man is free but he who labors in the Torah."[22] In the Ark of the Covenant, two sets of tablets lie next to each other: the original ones, which were shattered by Moses in his fury over the apostasy of Israel, and the new ones, called "free," on which the Law was written for the second time. In *Es gibt Geheimnis in der Welt* (*There Is Mystery in the World*), Gershom Scholem speculates on the metaphor of the two tablets as the central figure of the relationship between faithfulness, which rigidly fixes the commentator on the Torah, and freedom, which infinitely delays the consensual moment of ultimate understanding of its "descriptive essence": "Two sides of this conflict—he says—are best expressed by two phrases from the Talmud . . . which for the last two thousand years have remained alive in the Jewish tradition—'the freedom of the tablets' and 'the broken tablets,' which both lie in the Ark of the Covenant, i.e. within the same sacred sphere of Judaism."[23]

Thus, while the broken tablets symbolize the "Truth in itself"—which can never be reached as such—the graven-free tablets, which replaced the *original* ones, represent the free act of commentary that is offered by the "freedom of the written word" (*harut/herut*). This replacement shows the genius of *mediation* on which the Jewish tradition relies: the *lekh lekha* rule—"get thee out of here"—applied to the original revelation from which the finite mind has to "move away" to begin to *work* on its contents. Just as Abraham is told to leave the place of his origin, so are rabbis to distance themselves from the "strong light of the canonical" in order not to be blinded/traumatized/paralyzed by its immediacy.[24] The traumatic encounter with the Infinite must be defensively mediated if the finite mind is to survive it at all, for no one can face the Living God and remain alive. So, only in this manner, thanks to the defense mechanism of multilayered mediations, can "tradition be concerned with the realization, the enactment of the divine task which is set in the revelation. It demands application, execution, and decision, and at the same time it is, indeed, 'true growth and unfolding from within.' It constitutes a living organism, *whose religious authority was asserted with as much emphasis as is at all possible within this system of thought.*"[25]

This extreme assertion of the religious authority of the mediated/displaced origin, found in Bava Metzi'a 59b, is also expressed in the phrase of Emmanuel Levinas: "to love Torah more than God."[26] This is blasphemy only prima facie. This declaration not only is not blasphemous but also formulates the necessary condition of any *rational piety* in which reason does not have to abdicate in front of faith.

THE ULTIMATE DISAGREEMENT

But why is the possibility of disagreement (*mahloket*)—originary, irreconcilable, the potentially endless conversation of finite minds—such a crucial issue? The exclusion of God from the horizontal community of scholars who "incline after majority" and "do not heed to the heavenly voice" is prima facie a shocking act bordering on sacrilege—yet, on the other hand, when interpreted more soberly, it merely states the obvious: that the finite reason, if it wants to evolve at all and create its own tradition of rationality (i.e., secure a "true growth and unfolding from within"), must remove itself from the blinding light of the Absolute and seek refuge in the worldly realm of shadows, where, in the words of Emily Dickinson, you can "tell all the truth, but tell it slant / [because] the success in circuit lies." The slant and the circuit, which filtrate and diffuse the absolute light, do not prevent the participants of the hermeneutic community from "telling the truth," yet, at the same time, they incarnate the one truth into a multitude of carnal voices, each encumbered with its own slant/perspective, which turns what for God might be a single timeless utterance into a material plurality of winding narratives.[27] And once the one Voice translates into those polivocal stories, there is no turning back to any preestablished harmony: the disagreement emerges as originary.

Sergey Dolgopolski's *What Is Talmud? The Art of Disagreement* begins with the seminal question: "In particular, why does the Talmudic approach to disagreement as a goal in itself seem exotic and esoteric while Western philosophy's goal of reaching agreement in any discussion, intellectual or political, shapes common parlance?" Why, therefore, not take "the side of disagreement as an end rather than as a means"?[28] Indeed, why not? In fact, as I show in the next two sections, the originary dissent has not been as neglected or deemed as "exotic" as Dolgopolski claims. At least since Descartes, Western thinking has turned toward the framework of the finite rationality, which, historically speaking, was embraced for the first time by the Talmudic reasoning.

According to Dolgopolski, Talmud not only defends against the absolutist perspective of one voice/one truth, capable of superseding the democratic plurivocality, but also—most importantly—does not aspire to it, as is the case with philosophy, which inherited the Platonic obsession with the One, even if it was in the negative terms of an unattainable regulative ideal. The Talmudic scriptural reasoning admits only one *oneness*: there is *one* rigidly fixed tradition, inaugurated by the *matan Torah*, but precisely because the Torah was *given*, it cannot be univocal. The gift necessarily comes with a freedom to appropriate it, which cannot be immobilized and set in stone, as the sages insist when they say: read not "graven" but "free." The tradition, therefore, is like a sea of voices in which the apprentice must learn to swim in order to leave his own trace.

The phrase *sea of voices* derives from Harold Bloom, and the Talmudic practice of truth-making is indeed more akin to the Bloomian revisionistic agon of strong poets than to the veridictive procedures of philosophy, which, instructed by Plato, often usurps the divine transcendent vantage point of the ultimate truth. According to Susan Handelmann, the works of Bloom and Derrida, the two paradigmatic "slayers of Moses," clearly derive from the Talmudic lore based on the complex and ever-growing nexus of refutations, which knows no beginning and no end. While the Talmudic reasoning "slays" the authority of the origin (not only Moses but also God), it also infinitely delays/defers the final "truth-saying" or the *verdict* that would have ended the game of interpretation. Thus, just as "strong poets" wish to keep tradition/canon going in a creative manner, so it can generate ever-new "ephebes"—the rabbis insist on keeping the body of midrash living and open to "innovations" (*hiddushim*) against the veridictive absolutist closure, which, for the art of commentary, could only mean death. And just as the Derridean *différance* is emphatically *not* the Hegelian antithesis pushing toward the synthetic "end of story," so, too, is the rabbinic agon an ongoing invitation for new voices and perspectives to appear; it is not a stepping stone leading toward a future consent but a full affirmation of dissent as the ultimate expression of life—always *this* life, finite, singular, "thrown" into its world, opaque to itself. By drawing on the three thinkers who, despite belonging to Western philosophy, questioned its essentially Platonic setup—Heidegger, with his emphasis on the cognitive finitude as the critique of the post-Cartesian fully self-reflective subject; Derrida, with his promotion of *différance, ecriture*, and dissemination as the means by which language evolves and displays its potentialities; and Deleuze, with his diverse and polivocal "logics of sense"—Dolgopolski demonstrates the uniqueness of the Talmudic art of reasoning, which completely excludes any imitation of the divine absolutist perspective by making a priori impossible any infinite, identitarian, omniscient, and veridictive stance. For Dolgopolski, who in his analysis relies heavily on Canpanton, the fifteenth-century Sephardic rabbinic thinker, the rabbis who signed with their proper names are not real persons but synecdoches of what the former calls the "radical past"—the past that was not only not present but could never be made so essentially: they stand for "eons," the bits of the opaque space-time that were drawn into the orations in the form of tacit premises—a Talmudic version of the enthymemes, which "entail an inner element of an oration that is always spatially outside of its immediate language."[29]

The radical past, with its uncontrollable tacit premises, is thus the best synonym for the radical finitude that can never be sublated by an infinitist perspective of one truth: the inevitability of enthymemes and the opaque moment of the finite "throwness" that determines the perspective of a given eon and that is preserved in the Talmudic reasoning precisely as such—as impersonal abstract throwness/conditioning, which can never be overcome and which, precisely because of that, becomes an objective ground of disagreement. The commonsense stereotype of the ever-quarreling rabbis must thus be rejected because the disagreement is not taken merely as an expression of personal biases or emotional local colorings, as would be the case with Nietzsche's notion of perspectivism, which was motivated and fueled by the individual will to power. It is, to use Gibbs's witty phrase again, a disagreement taken up not for "sport" but *for God's sake!*—even if, especially with the exclamation mark, it also suggests a certain dose of the human—all too human—irascibility. Eventually, however, the Nietzschean personal bias is removed from the proper name of the rabbi, which stands here for the best-argued finite position that attempted to eliminate as many enthymemes as possible but that could not refute them all on ontological grounds. Carrying the work of refutation, which would dispel the doubts raised by the radically past tacit premises, is the task of every new adept student of the Talmudic school entering the "chain of the tradition."

> The Talmudic masters disagree if, and only if, there is a cause and this cause can be eliminated neither by correcting a mistake, nor by any voluntary act of agreement. The disagreement between parties comes neither from a logical mistake nor from a conflict of interests, but rather is constituted as a relationship between parties emerging as *permanently disagreeing eons* (or *multiple, finite eternities*) that refine and define each other due to the process of their disagreement. The disagreement in question is thoroughly impersonal and thus involuntary: Although it is represented by the personal names of the masters, those names no longer belong to

any biographical personalities, but rather designate eternal profiles that could always be manned anytime by anyone capable of understanding the disagreement, or "contemplating" it, to use Canpanton's term. The personal names of the parties in disagreement are no more than synecdoches for the event of disagreement itself. Again, because any oration is always already a refutation, the point of getting the refutation right consists not in agreeing with it, but rather in disagreeing with it intelligently.[30]

For this reason, every new intervention into Talmudic reasoning emerges via the refutation—the only point "worth making"—which exposes the limitations of the past orations due to their tacit premises on the grounds of a new set of tacit premises, which will become exposed in its own limitations only by the next refutation, and so on, potentially forming an infinite series of finite eternities.[31] "The disagreement contemplated in the radical past is no longer an intermediary point on the way to consensus, but rather is the fact of a radical past that, in order to remain so, challenges the student to speculate."[32]

The truth, therefore, emerges only on the basis of a dynamic double negation that can never close on itself. Despite the effort of the "maximized proximity" between the past oration and the present external judgment on the matter, the negation always preserves a gap, and this gap does not allow for any closure of the discussion. *Roma locuta, causa finita* is precisely the rule that does not apply here. God himself might have favored Rabbi Eliezer's position; even his opponents might have admitted that "he *is* the Halakhah," as if he were a perfect vessel (*keli*) embodying the ultimate true way, but this is not how things are done within the rabbinic discussion. Eliezer had to be excluded not because he was wrong but because he was "always right." Unable to play the mirror game of mutual refutations where all finite positions could be right, but also equally wrong, Eliezer aspired to incarnate the truth itself, which would end the game among the equals: the finite minds encumbered by their singular pasts, irremediably imperfect "vessels." Thus to capture the specificity of the Talmudic procedure of truth-making, Canpanton ventures a concept of the "inverted truth"; that is, a truth that can only be approximated via the refutation of its opposite:

> On the occasions when he [Canpanton] himself spoke of truth, he approached it rhetorically, rather than logically: "truth is recognizable

only through the inversion of it." The inversion in question leads not only to what is logically opposite or linguistically different; it primarily leads to what the truth rhetorically refutes. Inversion thus means nothing else but what is refuted. So for Canpanton, finding the refuted element in the truth becomes the high road to recognizing a given truth itself.... In Canpanton's own example, the truth about the proposition "This ring is of true gold," is not that "this ring is truly gold," but rather *the refutation of the ever-present but always implicit doubt that the ring may have been faked. Without such an implicit doubt, the oration "This ring is of true gold" would refer to a self-evident truth and would not be worth making*.³³

Thus only an oration that is not self-evident in itself and that implies a possibility of doubting and refuting is *worth being made*—and this, Canpanton and Dolgopolski insist, is a necessary condition of truth-making within the Talmudic reasoning. By contrast, Alfred Tarski's famous definition of truth—*"snow is white* is true if and only if snow is white" (or *"this ring is of true gold* is true if and only if this ring is of true gold")—although logically irrefutable relies on the statement that, in light of Talmudic requirements of innovation, would simply be not worth making. This, then, constitutes the main difference between the philosophical logic, which judges truth according to the criterion of self-evidence and, because of that, privileges tautologies, and the Talmudic reasoning, which implies rhetorical elements of contrariety, novelty, and curiosity, but, unlike the traditional rhetoric, shifts them into the very center of the truth-making procedure:

> Kant's definition of man—"man is a refuse"—thus also defines the student of Talmudic speculation, although not in any humanistic or moral sense, but rather in a rhetorical one: The student of the Talmud is "a refuse," in that he eliminates doubt, but doubt, in order to be eliminated, must first be found. He refutes an external judgment that, in order to be refuted and thus be further refined, must first be established. Disagreement is the internal element a student must seek in order to establish his external judgment and to refine it further, an element that, as we have seen, logic would fatally miss altogether.³⁴

Having found the decisive difference between the philosophico-logical and Talmudic rational procedures, Dolgopolski concludes: "The 'inverted truth' of Canpanton is thus neither logical in the sense of scholastics, nor expressionist in the sense of either Spinoza, Heidegger, or Deleuze.

Rather, it is of its own kind. It is Talmudic."[35] But as we shall see in the last section, the rejection of tautology as the model of truth that would simply be "not worth making" and as such would only be a waste of time is what, according to Hans Blumenberg, also characterizes modern science and, more generally, a modern style of thinking. It is, therefore, not an accident that Kant, a Western modern philosopher, defines man as a "refuse." The refutation of refutation, which never closes the circuit and preserves a gap between the best-argued position and the "truth in itself," is precisely the manner of the "finite thinking" that has discovered its "provisional" nature and abandoned the previous desire to imitate the Platonic art of infinite contemplation.

THE FATHERLESS WORD

The suggestion that the art of Talmud, although constituting a highly specific game, can form a paradigmatic point of reference for a "finite thinking"; that is, the late-modern Western philosophy finally ready to fully embrace its finitude and all of its materialist implications, yet without falling into the trap of atheism as the Nietzschean dissemination of perspectives, appears in Daniel Boyarin's *Sparks of the Logos*. By taking Jean Goux's *Symbolic Economy* as a polemical foil, Boyarin demonstrates that once the Father is gone—removed from the game as an unfair player capable of "trumping" all dissenting voices—the Talmudic word becomes "fatherless," no longer bound by the systemic limitations represented by the Father/Phallus/Logos as the triad governing the post-Platonic rationality, yet simultaneously bound by something else: the fixed reference to the holy text.

Boyarin's first move to demonstrate the "fatherlessness" of the Talmudic word is to show that the art of Talmud has nothing to do with what Western culture calls *interpretation*. While interpretation is a metacommentary that aims to reveal the system of meaning behind the text, midrash operates on the same level as the commented text to which it attaches itself on the basis of metonymy or, in Talmudic terminology, *mashal*, "likeness." "As the dominant mode of early rabbinic reading, it thus provides a direct contrast with allegoresis. In allegory (interpretation), a story is taken to signify a set of meanings—it is dominated, therefore, by the Jakobsonian sign of metaphor; in midrash, a story is placed beside another story, and connections or analogies between the stories provide mutual illumination of *understanding without paraphrase or translation into abstraction*. Its dominant sign is, therefore, metonymy."[36]

The metonymic rule further suggests that, within the Talmudic realm, the words themselves have no fixed significance: they are "virtual icons," marked with their material concreteness, which simply cannot be paraphrased by an interpretation attempting to abstract from them a steady meaning. The words, therefore, are material pictograms from which it is impossible to separate the meaning from the sign itself, just as it is impossible for Jews to separate matter and spirit, the finite *medium* and the infinite *message*. By paraphrasing Archibald MacLeish, a poet of the school of New Criticism, which strongly emphasized the iconic character of poems as material articulations of language, Boyarin could thus say that "the midrash does not mean, it *is*," implying that the words the midrash is made of must be taken in their radical finitude as inseparable entanglements of the imagistic concreteness: they can never assume an abstracted universal form (although Boyarin also finds MacLeish's formula to be not radical enough). By analogy with the economic processes of exchange, Boyarin claims that while the Western mode of interpretation grounded in *allegoresis* belongs to the stage of universal exchange based on the abstract medium of money, the Talmudic exegesis still deals with "bartered words," which also expresses the early-rabbinic resistance toward the global economy of the Roman Empire. Instead of exchanging words for words via the medium of universal abstract meaning, which allows for an exact paraphrasing of the original text, the rabbis exchange words for words on the principle of the material barter, which does not permit the distillation of an ideal value/meaning of any word. The words do not mean; they simply are what they are—and what they can be bartered for in a concrete transaction: "Early rabbinic interpretation, true midrash, barters without money, exchanges signification for signification, or places significations side by side, without positing a realm of abstract meaning."[37]

> Interpretation is the dominant mode of commentary in a culture within which value is expressed in terms of an abstract, universal, and in itself substance-free standard: the coin. By interpretation I mean virtually

all of our methods of formal response to texts by which the text is taken to mean something, by which meaning is extractable from a text and presentable, even if incompletely and not exactly, in paraphrase. Even the most extremely antiparaphrastic of western interpretative methods, for instance the poem-interpretation of the New Critics, still is infinitely more paraphrastic than midrash, which simply refuses to take even the text as verbal icon, preferring almost to read each word, and sometimes each letter, and sometimes the shape of the letter or even its serifs, as a virtual icon in itself. One way to bring this point home would be to insist that even according to those who would argue that "a poem must not mean but be" the poem remains at least partially translatable. With the modes of linguistic operation which are characteristic of early midrash in place, the text is simply untranslatable (something on the order of the untranslatability of *Finnegan's Wake*). Too many of the features upon which midrash founds its meanings are simply artefacts of the materiality of the language in its Hebrew concreteness.[38]

But it also means that the barter—an open horizontal exchange of goods/words whose value is never estimated *in abstracto* and then eternalized or "set in stone"—cannot have a Master who would arbitrate on the question of value by referring to the "universal equivalent," because this value does not exist apart from the concrete transactions. If the contrahents in question agree to barter, there is no point in discussing the bartered value any further. This is precisely how Boyarin understands the Bava Metzi'a fragment in which God himself is dismissed as a spurious arbitrator: "Midrash is the dominant mode of commentary in a signifying economy without the 'universal equivalent.' Widely known is the moment in Talmudic legend when God seeks to intervene in midrashic interpretation and is informed that he has no status because the majority of the sages disagree with his interpretation. *In commentary, at any rate, for the Rabbis, even the deity is not the measure of all things.*"[39]

The "bartered word" and bartering exegesis indicate that there is no system in terms of a "generalized form of value," pointing to the privileged status of Father/Phallus/Logos, which consists of holding all symbolic exchanges together in the form of virtual harmony, equivalence, and agreement: the "measure of all things." The symbolic economy of the midrashic art is different: by rejecting one Logos, which "gathers all" (as the word *legein* suggests), it is "no philology at all but rather a sort of misology."[40] Barter is a local form of exchange not warranted by the system governed by the privileged Master Signifier, constituting the sovereign exception outside the system. The meaning of the bartered word is not guaranteed by any transcendent Logos; it is essentially "fatherless"—even "godless"—and thus open to disagreement, which is originary, precisely the way it is envisaged by Derrida in his coinage of *différance* as an originary heterogeneity that is not just a negation of agreement or deviation from the virtual ideal represented by the Pater/Phallus/Logos who oversees and reconciles all into a systemic totality.[41] The original disagreement is a very different condition than a merely secondary dissent, always perceived as *privatio boni*, here understood as *privatio consensus*; that is, in purely privative and negative terms of "sin," Fall, "disjointedness," or *Un-Fug*.[42] Radical finitude goes hand in hand with radical materialism and the original condition of dissemination not to be condemned as a deviation from the harmonious ideal of universal consent or a Neoplatonic Fall from the One into the chaos of the multitude.

As Boyarin suggests in the final line of his essay, the "Not-All," the antisystemic position of late Lacan (as he admits, adopted by him due to the influence of what he saw as the tradition of Jewish materialism[43]), is indeed the natural metaphysics of the rabbis. As we have seen, Žižek agrees with this and, by drawing Judaism into the universal "passage from the big Other qua the abyss of subjectivity to the big Other qua the impersonal structure of the symbolic Law," he not only restores the eternal validity of the Jewish religion against the supersessionist claims of his opponent, John Milbank, but—in harmony with Boyarin's implications—affirms this validity also in meta-philosophical terms: as the necessary condition of rationality exercised by finite minds. Contrary to what Western philosophical tradition appeared to claim—that the paternal function of Logos/Big Other is necessary for the coordination of the symbolic sphere of exchange—the opposite is true: it is only when the sovereign *point de capiton* becomes loosened that the finite reason is able to move away from the "misty paradox" (which, according to Žižek, is Milbank's position: the impossible task of thinking in the full presence of the living God or what the latter calls grace) and assert itself within the "impersonal structure of the symbolic Law," which, at the same time, remains the *law*. The whole point of the "passage," therefore, is to avoid the nondialectical dualism of absolutism and relativism: the wrong transition from the providential supervision of Logos, the keeper of the absolute truth, to the nihilistic stance of posttruth as "anything goes" of the ever-changing *doxa*. The disappearance of the former, as narrated by the Bava Metzi'a fragment, does not have to lead to the anarchy of dissenting voices substituting truth with mere opinion—or the "return of the sophists" as advocated by Nietzsche, who saw it as a natural consequence of the final and irrevocable death of God. God is silenced but not dead. His authority may be withdrawn, contracted, in the state of *tsimtsum*, but it does not vanish completely. Instead of atheism, we may rather call it, again, a decentered theism.

In that sense, Talmud may indeed be said to anticipate many of the moves of modern philosophy, especially those concerned with creating a reliable sphere of human rationality. Long before Descartes and his refutation of *deus fallax*—the "devious God" of the nominalists portrayed by him as a capricious and manipulative demon—the rabbinic community refuted the living presence of God in order to establish a new conversation of humankind that, from this point on, will only take arguments from the equals. In that sense, Talmud is *before* philosophy as practiced in modernity: a shocking discovery that late-modern philosophical thought, gradually reconciling itself with the "finite thinking," has made in its Owl of Minerva startled hindsight.[44]

NOT HEEDING TO THE HEAVENLY VOICE: DESCARTES

I aim to prove that Boyarin's and Žižek's conjecture is right: once Western philosophy becomes a self-conscious "finite thinking," it begins to tread in the footsteps of the Talmudic masters and their decentered theism as a meta-philosophical position—starting with Descartes. The juxtaposition of Hans Blumenberg's seminal reading of Descartes in *The Legitimacy of the Modern Age* with Bava Metzi'a 59b reveals an intriguing analogy: an implicit continuation of the *lo bashamayim* argument in which Descartes *decides* not to listen to the "trumping" divine voice and, thanks to this decision, creates an autonomous space of reason. In that sense, Descartes, who gains distance from the arbitrary verdicts of the Nominalist *deus fallax*, thinly disguised as a "fictional" *genius malignus*, repeats the gesture of the Talmudic rabbis who achieve this distancing and thus a "breathing space" in the paradigmatic and foundational manner: as Blumenberg rightly points out, Descartes refutes the hypothesis of the malicious demon not logically but rhetorically—and yet, it *works*. In Blumenberg's view, therefore, modern philosophy is not free from the rhetorical element it constantly tries to exorcise; in fact, it is made possible by the Cartesian cut that gains freedom from the "all-trumping" and thus malignant omnipotence of the Nominalist "devious God," and, from this time on, becomes deaf "to the heavenly voice."[45]

It is hardly possible that Hans Blumenberg, despite his deep assimilation with German culture, did not know the "famous legend" that circulated among the milieu of German-Jewish thinkers. Although he does not mention it in his analysis of Descartes, one cannot avoid an impression of deep analogy. Just as God suddenly intervenes in the dispute of the rabbis and procures unwelcome miracles/exceptions that suspend the laws of the universe—the Nominalist God, *deus fallax*, enters the train of Descartes's methodical scepticism and subverts the laws of logic, rendering him helpless and unable to proceed. And just as rabbis reject the impossible argument from miracles (impossible because miracles destroy the framework of any rational argumentation), so does Descartes rebel against the "devious God," disguised as a "malignant genius," by stubbornly sticking to the last-ditch explanation of logic, which he sees as valid even for an omnipotent deity: "Even if I am deceived, I still exist—*ego sum, ego existo*!" According to the "theological absolutism"—the formation that grew particularly strong among the Nominalist scholastics, most of all William Ockham—God possesses *potentia absoluta*, which can create and immediately destroy, establish, and subvert anything and everything, including the laws of logic, which he is not obliged to obey. His only way to proceed is thus via *miracles*, which have just one justification behind them: *quia voluit*, "because He wanted it that way." In this theological game, which speaks the language of miracles and exceptions, God is the card that trumps all.[46]

By holding to the last voice of logic in the face of a *genius malignus* who is capable of deceiving us into a belief in the infallibility of logic, even if "in themselves" the laws of logic reduce to his arbitrary whim, Descartes does not refute the malign intervention on logical grounds because he admits that they may be nothing but a frail convention. Rather, in a manner analogical to the rabbis, who defend their game against the specter of the divine living presence threatening to destroy it, Descartes simply stops "heeding to the heavenly voice." He moves away from the vertiginous presence of the divine *potentia absoluta* and withdraws in the shadow of his own "provisional" finite thinking, which, as he claims, will be groping in the dark, proceeding slowly and with caution, step by step, by slant and circuit, relying on nothing but cautious logic—the same logic that the hypothesis of the malicious demon threatened to destroy and that, in fact, it *did* destroy as the way to achieve the absolute truth. Just as the "inverted truth" of Canpanton allows only for provisional results that can—and will—be refuted by the future participants of the Talmudic game, the Cartesian "provisional" thinking also never witnesses any truth directly and avails itself only of the method of refutation, from which it originated. The starting point of Descartes's positive reconstruction of being—a seemingly constative and triumphant *cogito, ergo sum*—has the structure of the provisional refutation of the refutation, or the "inverted truth": *Even if he deceives me, I still am* is a piece of reasoning that only refutes the doubt raised by the hypothetic existence of *genius malignus*. Can I reasonably doubt my being when there may be an omnipotent spirit capable of deceiving me on all fronts, the laws of logic included? Perhaps I could, but even while doubting or being deceived, I simply cannot doubt myself out of existence: the act of doubting proves the existence of the doubter. But what if I am deceived even about the rationality of this conclusion? This is also possible, but then the whole thinking would simply make no sense at all. We could obviously prostrate ourselves in front of the "misty paradox" and humble our reason, which would be only logical because it is the very logic of this situation that calls for the abolishment of all logic. But is this quietistic paradox—the abdication of reason deduced rationally, as in William Ockham—the only way to end this conundrum? Just as I cannot be doubted out of my existence, I also cannot be thought out of my thinking; once I claimed the tools of reason, which gave me my sceptical method, I will not end by granting to *deus fallax* the power to still my reasoning. I will go on, even if on "provisional" grounds, always full of doubt, finite and precarious, but—yes—*thinking*.[47]

This is what Blumenberg calls the moment of "self-assertion": the not fully logical act of the "provisional" decision to remain in thinking, now consciously opposed to the absolutist perspective that the "finite thought" no longer wants to imitate. More than that, due to the Nominalist crisis, which created the very idea of *deus fallax*, the finite thought finds any absoluteness apposite and hostile to itself.⁴⁸ For Blumenberg, Descartes is the first thinker to escape the snares of "theological absolutism": the Nominalist form of theism that followed the theocentric logic to the bitter end and created a "theological monster" who, instead of securing the existence of the world as its reliable creator, turned against his own creation and threatened to annihilate it.⁴⁹ Descartes's early-modern self-assertive rebellion against *deus fallax* clarifies again what Bava Metzi'a 59b explained long ago—that no "finite thinking" is possible in the strictly *theocentric* environment or, to use Derrida's idiom, that God must be *decentered* as *le Dieu en retrait*; in other words, removed from the systemic center if humans, the other pole of the covenant, are to assert themselves at all:

> Under the enormous pressure of the demands made upon it by theology, the human subject begins to consolidate itself, to take on a new overall condition, which possesses, in relation to ambushes set by the hidden absolute will, something like the elementary attribute of the atom, that it cannot be split up or altered. Absolutism reduces whatever is exposed to it, but in the process it brings to light the constants, the no longer touchable kernels [. . . .] The *ius primarium*, the primeval right to self-assertion, becomes comprehensible long before Descartes and Hobbes as the essence of modern age's understanding of itself—that is, as *the anthropological minimum under the conditions of the theological maximum*.⁵⁰

"Long before Descartes and Hobbes"—could indeed refer to the Talmudic "famous legend," in which the anthropological minimum asserted itself for the first time against the conditions of the theological maximum and, thanks to the self-assertive obstinacy of the rabbis, the theocentric tendency, always incipient in all orthodoxies, became—at least partly—defeated. This *decentration*, however, does not "kill" God in the Nietzschean manner; it occurs *within* the theological model, where it creates a "breathing space" of distance and respite (*Galgenfrist*), which occludes the terrifying face of the Living God and lets creation live—and think—in the conditions of the benign ("smiling") retreat/*tsimtsum*. Thus, even if later on Descartes restores God and God's good name (which excludes being a "deceiver"), this is no longer a theocentric argument: the deistic God of Cartesianism—essential only in the moment of creation but no longer a "necessary hypothesis" in the created realm "within our reach"—becomes relegated to the "radical past," which removes God from the central living presence but without rendering him "dead." God is not dead—he is merely, as in the motto taken from Rosenzweig, *refuted*.

But this is also the moment in which, according to Blumenberg, modern science is born, not out of the spirit of atheism but rather out of this peculiar decentered theism in which the existence of God becomes irrelevant and gives way to human self-assertion. Modern science, then, proceeds very much like the Talmudic reasoning: it gives up on the logical tautology as the eternal model of truth, stating only those hypotheses that are "worth making" from the pragmatic point of view, which it subsequently proves by the refutation of refutation and the procedure of the "inverted truth" (in other words, the principle of falsification according to which only the hypotheses that raise reasonable doubt can be called scientific); combines *in*vention of discoveries with the *con*vention of the received theories, which remain valid temporally, that is, until they are proved otherwise; and, finally, "inclines after the majority" within the community of scholars and its set epistemic paradigm. The fact that it resorts to the rule of the *experimentum crucis* in the procedure of first raising and then refuting the doubt is a secondary feature. Formally speaking, the Talmudic art of "exaction" and the scientific art of formulating the hypotheses as precisely as possible belong to the same lore of the "finite thinking" that proceeds slowly, provisionally, and with caution. Canpanton and Karl Popper could indeed shake hands.

VOIDING OF CHILD'S HEAVEN: LEVINAS

I once again return to Levinas's formula: "loving Torah more than God," which I take to be the best depiction of the rabbinic decentered theism as the necessary condition of the possibility of the "finite thinking": a metaphilosophical position allowing modern thought to pass "from the abyss of subjectivity to the impersonal structure of the law" or from the desire to imitate the divine omniscience to the horizontal exchange of hypotheses and refutations. In the short text under this title from *Difficult Freedom*, Levinas discusses the fictional diary published in Israel in the 1960s as *Yossel, Son of Yossel Rakover from Tarnopol, Speaks to God*, which presented itself as a document "written during the final hours of the Warsaw Ghetto resistance."[51] The concluding line of the "document," in which Yosel ben Yosel begins to understand that "the adult's God is revealed precisely through the void of the child's heaven [and] this is the moment when God retires from the world and hides His face" indeed reads as an uncanny parallel to the Cartesian *Meditations*:[52] "This accounts for the monologue's closing remark, in which Yossel ben Yossel echoes the whole of the Torah: 'I love him, but I love even more his Torah. . . . *And even if I were deceived by him and became disillusioned, I should nevertheless observe the precepts of the Torah.*' Is this blasphemy? At the very least, it is a *protection against the madness of a direct contact with the Sacred that is unmediated by reason.*"[53]

While the God of the infantile heaven can play tricks and perform miracles and thus taunt his childish believers, the "adult's God," whose direct voice the mature believer no longer wants to heed, is the giver of the Torah, which contains a self-sufficient "internal evidence of morality."[54] For Descartes, the point of certitude lies in the awareness of his own existence, which cannot be doubted away, even if the infinite mind of *deus fallax* plays tricks with our finite thinking. For Yosel ben Yosel, the certitude is the sacred text, which is the true unwavering divinity, the ultimate rigid designator. Thus even in times of the greatest despair, Yosel ben Yosel does not deplore the condition of the divine "occlusion" (*hester panim*) because it is precisely the possibility of this living dependence that makes him uneasy. This is not atheism pure and simple, although, as Levinas states: "True monotheism is duty bound to answer the legitimate demands of atheism."[55] It is, again, a *decentered theism* that rejects an emotional relationship with the living God as the paradigm of the religious bond and honors him only as the author of the Torah.[56]

To refute the living God, therefore, defines exactly the Jewish difference that protests against the desire to live in a state of dependence on the living God and be as close to his absolutist perspective as possible, which Levinas finds characteristic of Christianity.[57] What Rosenzweig attributes somewhat quixotically to Nietzsche—that he had to refute God the moment God became revealed—is rather the defining feature of Judaism as the religion of the absent God, *deus absentis* (withdrawn, retreated, contracted, concealed, occluded—whatever form this absence takes). But perhaps there is some truth in this seemingly exotic attribution:

Nietzsche, as a philosopher (or, rather, as long as he remained a philosopher), could not have thought in the direct contact with the Sacred. Hence the last line of Levinas's text: "Man can have confidence in an absent God and also be an adult who can judge his own sense of weakness" could just as well have come from the later meditations of Descartes, who has managed to put God at a safe distance and has begun to enjoy his logical procedures, always quietly aware of their provisionality.[58] Talmud *and* (modern) Philosophy may thus not be an impossible marriage after all: even if the latter has not learned directly from the former, it eventually discovered the same conditions without which the "finite thinking" could simply not go on.

AGATA BIELIK-ROBSON is Professor of Jewish Studies at the University of Nottingham and Professor of Philosophy at the Polish Academy of Sciences. Her publications include *Another Finitude: Messianic Vitalism and Philosophy,* and *Derrida's Marrano Passover: Exile, Survival, Betrayal and the Metaphysics of Non-Identity.*

NOTES

1. On the vastness of the commentaries on Bava Metziʻa 59b, see Rubenstein, *Talmudic Stories,* 314, where notes 1–4 contain a comprehensive list of the significant mentions of the story in the recent scholarly reception. See also Rubenstein's midrash on the legend on pp. 34–66, which very subtly points to the literary aspects of the story, usually omitted by those commentators interested mostly in the "Oven of Akhnai" as the best illustration of the Talmudic epistemology.

2. The phrase "finite thinking" derives from Jean-Luc Nancy's *A Finite Thinking,* which is mainly concerned with the post-Heideggerian evolution of the late-modern Western philosophy based on Martin Heidegger's rediscovery of human finitude as the factor determining the cognitive faculties of *Dasein.* In this essay, I intend to prove that the idea of the "finite thinking" existed within the Talmudic art of reasoning long before it became the explicit theme in Western philosophy, which, in accordance with Hans Blumenberg, I associate not with Heidegger but rather Descartes.

3. Scholem, *The Messianic Idea in Judaism,* 130–31.

4. Ibid., 132.

5. Bloom, *The Anxiety of Influence,* 99, 111, 128, 143. On the affinities between the rabbinic model of creating a *ratio* between the transcendent revelation and the immanent tradition and the Bloomian revisionistic agon creating a *ratio* between the poetic greatness of the dead precursor and the belated beginner/ephebe, see Bielik-Robson, *The Saving Lie,* 33–74.

6. This argument also figures very strongly in Rosenzweig's *Star of Redemption,* in which the divine absolutist glory can only be ascribed to those gods who never enter any

relationship with humans; that is, the pagan idols self-sufficient in their immortal "fullness of life," whereas the Jewish God, being relational, must choose a different idiom of self-expression, which, in Rosenzweig's openly Christianizing account, is a *bat kol*, the gentle voice of love: "The world of the gods always remains a world in itself, even when they enclose the whole world; then that world that they enclose is not on its own and with which God would have to enter into a relationship, but something that encloses him. So here *God is without a world*; or, conversely, if we wanted to characterize this representation as precisely a view of the world, this world of the life of the gods who remain among themselves would be—a *world without gods*. And with this we would have expressed the essence of what can be designated as a mythological conception of the world" (Rosenzweig, *Star of Redemption*, 42 [my emphasis]). The link between God's "defeat" as described in Bava Metzi'a and the Christian process of *kenosis*, which eventually leads to the "death of God," is also a theme of Slavoj Žižek's essay "Dialectical Clarity versus the Misty Conceit of Paradox," which will be discussed shortly.

7. The idea of the divine defeat is an integral moment of Judaic difference conceived most of all as the art of "arguing with God," which is shared by both scholars and popular commentators. For instance, by claiming that the book of Job is the climax of the Hebrew Bible, in which "Job has won, the Lord has lost," Jack Miles perceives God's "biography" as a didactic story in which "arguing with God" allows human participants of the covenant to mature and stand on their feet (Miles, *God*, 325). David A. Frank expands Miles's argument beyond the Tanakh and sees it also operative in the Talmud: "With this defeat, God falls silent; this is God's last argument in the Hebrew Bible. . . . In both the Hebrew Bible and the Talmud, God admits defeat in argument with humans. The arguing-with-God tradition ends with God's defeat in Job; God is not given direct authority in the Talmud, according to the Oven of Akhnai story. Argument between humans in the Talmud, absent the direct presence of the divine, and capable of hosting antinomies, does not have an ending point" (Frank, "Arguing with God," 81–82). According to Amos Rubenstein, the motif of "standing on one's feet" is what unites the book of Job with Bava Metzi'a 59b: "Yehoshua 'stood on his feet' and argued against the heavenly voice and the Gamaliel 'stood on his feet' to plead against the threatening wave" (Rubenstein, *Talmudic Stories*, 39).

8. See Derrida, "The Force of Law and the Mystical Foundation of Authority," in *Acts of Religion*.

9. According to Rabbi Tsvi Hirsch Chajes, a great sage from Brody, who commented on the Eliezer story in the standard Romm-Vilna edition of the Talmud, the verb *nitshuni* derives not from *nitsahon* (victory) but from *netsah* (eternity), so the phrase *nitshuni banai* should be read as "my children made me eternal." Instead of cherishing Hashem as a Living God (who, as Nietzsche rightly claimed, can always die), the rabbis turned him into an eternal Name, signing the one and only holy text.

10. This connection did not escape Daniel Boyarin, who perceives the Talmudic *intertextuality* as a precursor to Derrida's invalidation of authorial intentions: "The irony is that the hermeneutic conservative, R. Eliezer, the one who literally has God on his side, was excommunicated and exiled for his insistence that the Author controls the reading of His text" (Boyarin, *Intertextuality*, 36). See also Handelman, *Slayers of Moses*, in which she quotes Bava Metzi'a 59b and then relates it directly to the deconstructive practices of Derrida and Harold Bloom: "The boundaries between text and interpretation are fluid in a way which is difficult for us to imagine for a sacred text, but this fluidity is a central tenet

of much contemporary literary theory. The elevation of later commentary to the status of earlier primary text is one of the extraordinary characteristics of rabbinic interpretation, and involves a not so subtle power struggle" (Handelman, *Slayers of Moses*, 41).

11. There are numerous explanations for how the rule that, in Daniel Boyarin's words, "the majority of the community which holds cultural hegemony controls interpretation" (*Intertextuality*, 35) emerged, even though it seems to be such a blatant contradiction of God's words. Holger Zellentin, for instance, understands it as an element of the "rabbinic parody" or an ironic sense of humor subversive toward any, in Derrida's words, "mystical authority": "The passage in Exodus 23:2, of course, condemns precisely such 'inclination after the majority' to such an extent that the rabbis take the repetitive insistence as an invitation to derive the opposite lesson from the text" (Zellentin, *Rabbinic Parodies*, 218). The condemnation that goes too far and insists on repeating itself would thus be a pretext to do precisely what is condemned; that is, to follow the lead of Adam and Eve who were so abundantly instructed not to eat from the Tree of Knowledge that they simply felt invited to do so. This contrarian logic is also reflected in Paul's critique of the Jewish law as an inverted instruction on how to sin in Romans 7–8: "What shall we say, then? Is the law sinful? Certainly not! Nevertheless, I would not have known what sin was had it not been for the law. For I would not have known what coveting really was if the law had not said, 'You shall not covet.' But sin, seizing the opportunity afforded by the commandment, produced in me every kind of coveting. For apart from the law, sin was dead." It is precisely this "nevertheless" that would govern the rabbinic ironic logic of inversion.

12. Žižek, "Dialectical Clarity," 268–69.

13. "Such a Jewish art of endless interpretation of the letter of the Law is thus profoundly materialist, its implication (and maybe even true goal) being (to make sure) that God is (and remains) dead. This is why Christianity could emerge only after and from within Judaism: its central theme of the death of Christ only posits as such, 'for itself,' the death of God which, 'in itself,' takes place already in Judaism" (Ibid., 269–70). While the first part of the diagnosis, which points to the materialist character of the rabbinic reasoning, is right—the second, inferring from this a pre-Christian figure of the death of God, is far too hasty or is simply supersessionist. The Judaic rule of the "long story *not* cut short" found its best expression in Hermann Cohen's theory of subtle heteronomy, or "Sinai in our heart," which provides a historical perspective of gradual maturation: from the external moment of revelation, planting the seed of the Torah in human life, to the internalization of the teaching, from this time on evolving only within the community of finite minds: "The teaching is not in heaven but in man's mouth, in his faculty of speech and in his heart, and therefore also in his mind. It did not come to man from without; it originated within him. It is rooted in his spirit which God, the uniquely One, has put into man as the holy spirit, the spirit of holiness" (Cohen, *Reason and Hope*, 101).

14. Baruch Spinoza, *Ethics*, part 1, appendix, 113. This is perhaps also why Heinrich Heine, while obliquely referring to Spinoza, called modern Jews "the Swiss guard of deism": a position very close to what I call the decentered theism.

15. Also Peter Schäfer and Holger Zellentin emphasize the antimiracle (but also anti-Christian) thrust of the "Oven of Akhnai" narrative; while the former portrays Rabbi Eliezer as "an alter ego of Jesus" (Schäfer, *Jesus in the Talmud*, 49), the latter claims that "each of the miracles indeed ironically repeats a particular 'Christian' miracle and, most importantly, that using miracles in doctrinal arguments itself is a characteristic of late antique Christianity" (Zellentin, *Rabbinic Parodies*, 219).

16. In his vigorous apology of disagreement—"for God's sake!"—Robert Gibbs defends it against the theological monopoly of orthodoxy: "But, and here theology is not innocent, the need for these institutions for dissent and active disagreement, often arose because religion has seemed to insist on consensus, on orthodoxy and uniformity of opinion. Whatever we make of the Mishnah, for many in this room [and I had a pleasure to be there—A. B.-R.], the notion that disagreement is for God's sake may well seem paradoxical. And yet, for Jewish tradition it is not merely tolerated; it is central" (Gibbs, "Disagree, for God's Sake!").

17. This feature of the rabbinic reasoning is strongly emphasized by Jacob Neusner, who sees it as resulting from the passage from the prophetic ventriloquism characteristic of the "Scriptural modes of thought and expression [that] ignored or dismissed views contrary to one's own, which, often as not, were also represented as God's," to the rabbinic argument that engaged in a "logical inquiry [at the foundation of which] lay the philosopher's insistence that conflicting principles cannot both be right" (Neusner and Chilton, *Intellectual Foundations*, x–xi). At the same time, however, Neusner, who insists on the philosophical influence shaping the argumentative skills of the rabbis, admits the essential difference: "If then in Plato's dialogues, a name stands for a viewpoint to be set forth and argued out in the setting of a debate with a contrary viewpoint identified with a name, the Mishnah deserves comparison with those dialogues. And the one really striking difference is that while Plato's Socrates asks what, exactly, is justice, our sages of blessed memory occupy themselves with conflict over who owns a cloak that two persons claim or how to adjudicate possession of a sliver of land or the carcass of a gored cow" (Ibid., 9). The difference, therefore, consists in the blocking of the sublimatory act of abstraction that would lead to the "heaven of forms": not only is the Torah no longer in heaven but the whole thinking remains tied to the material earth, where it develops horizontally and creates a complex nexus of concrete cases.

18. The proof that the Talmudic reasoning is as strict as mathematics lies in another story, equally commented on, which describes the conflict between the school of Hillel and the school of Shammai. Here the "voice of the living God" also intervenes, but this time, it does not side with any of the rabbis involved. It says that *both* are right and, as such, it becomes accepted. This manner of dealing with the presence of the living God is a precise topological inversion of Bava Metzi'a 59b: the figure correlating one voice with the absence converts into the figure correlating presence with many voices, but their significance is the same. God can enter the rabbinic discussion either as a presence siding with all dissenting voices, but if he wants to side with only one voice, he must remain absent.

19. See Kripke, *Naming and Necessity*, 48–49: "A designator rigidly designates a certain object if it designates that object wherever the object exists; if, in addition, the object is a necessary existent, the designator can be called *strongly rigid* ... proper names are rigid designators." Following this definition, the Torah as the proper name of the Hebrew scripture would designate rigidly the necessary existent scripture before "purely qualitative descriptions" (Ibid.), which come only later and can never exhaust or replace the rigid designation. But if Kripke's theory aligns with the Jewish model of referring to the Torah, it might have been influenced by it in the first place. On several striking affinities between Kripke and Maimonides, see Fagenblat, *Covenant of Creatures*, 125: "A proper name designates an identity without imputing any descriptive essence to it."

20. Hertz, *Pirke Avot*, 5:25.

21. Ibid., 2:21.

22. Ibid., 6:2.
23. Scholem, *Es gibt Geheimnis in der Welt*, 47 (my translation).
24. The phrase, made popular by Harold Bloom, derives from Scholem's letter to Salman Schocken from 1937 and refers to the work of Franz Kafka as the most accomplished modern heir of the kabbalistic tradition: quoted in Biale, *Gershom Scholem*, 75.
25. Scholem, *The Messianic Idea in Judaism*, 131 (my emphasis).
26. I return to this theme in the conclusion.
27. On the claim that Moses heard only one barely audible sound, which the Hebrew alphabet designates as *aleph*, a beginning of all articulated speech, itself on the verge of silence, see Scholem, *On the Kabbalah*, 30. On the positive materialist appropriation of the anti-Judaic trope of "carnal Israel," see Boyarin, "This We Know to Be the Carnal Israel," in *Sparks of the Logos*, 24–58.
28. Dolgopolski, *What Is Talmud?*, 7–8.
29. Ibid., 94.
30. Ibid., 98–99 (my emphasis).
31. Ibid., 103.
32. Ibid., 102.
33. Ibid., 102–3 (my emphasis).
34. Ibid., 94.
35. Ibid., 103.
36. Boyarin, *Sparks of the Logos*, 157 (my emphasis).
37. Ibid., 145.
38. Ibid., 144.
39. Ibid., 144 (my emphasis).
40. Ibid., 161.
41. See especially, "Plato's Pharmacy," in Derrida, *Dissemination*.
42. As it is still in the case of Heidegger, whom Derrida criticizes in *Specters of Marx*, for his unreflected privileging of *der Fug* as the higher harmony of Being (Derrida, *Specters of Marx*, 27–32).
43. See Lacan, *On Feminine Sexuality*, 99.
44. I must emphasize again that what seems to be Žižek's major limitation—his insistence on "cutting the story short" and rendering the lesson of the aggadic fragment to the Nietzschean/Althiserian terms of "God is dead"—is precisely what does not allow for the passage he endorses. For, if God were *just* dead, there would be no justification for the Law to remain a law. Thus, even if God is dead as an author in terms of the authorial authority on what the text "wanted to say" (*voluoir-dire*, French for "to mean," which obviously did not escape Derrida's attention), God cannot be simply dead as the author in terms of the *giver* of the Torah, fixing it as the eternal source of the legalistic wisdom. Some of his authority, even if it is delegated to the "radical past," must be dialectically preserved. But Žižek, as is evident in his treatment of the "death of God" motif, is not fully free from the supersessionist bias: in this peculiar competition, the Christians always kill their God better!
45. Contrary to the cliché that insists on pairing Descartes's name with the absolutist view of truth that privileges logic over rhetoric ("if two men disagree, one of them must be wrong," which is the fourth rule of *The Rules for the Direction of the Mind*), Blumenberg reads the Cartesian story as the one akin to the book of Job or the Oven of Akhnai: the defeat of God as the arbitrary Absolute, who then becomes silenced, never to return *as the*

Absolute in Descartes's thinking, which then assumes a "provisional" character whereby logic becomes a main prop—a kind of logical halakhah as the instruction how to walk—but it is nonetheless a finite thinking, never to assume, imitate, or emulate the absolutist perspective. On Descartes's alleged triumphant absolutism in contrast to the rabbinic rhetoric, see Frank, "Arguing with God," 82.

46. As Blumenberg describes: "The God Who places no constraints on Himself, Who cannot be committed to any consequence following from His manifestations, makes time into a dimension of utter uncertainty. This affects not only the identity of the subject, the presence of which at any given moment does not guarantee it any future, but also the persistence of the world, whose radical contingency can transform it, from one moment to the next, from existence into mere appearance, from reality into nothingness" (Blumenberg, *Legitimacy*, 161–62).

47. See Descartes:

> The thought had come to me, that perhaps some God might have endowed me with such a nature that I could be deceived even about those things that appeared supremely obvious. But whenever this preconceived opinion of God's supreme power occurs to me, I cannot help admitting that, if indeed he wishes to, he can easily bring it about that I should be mistaken, even about matters I think I intuit with the eye of the mind as evidently as possible. On the other hand, whenever I turn my attention to the things themselves that I think I perceive very clearly, I am so thoroughly convinced by them, that I cannot help exclaiming: *"Let whoever can, deceive me as much as he likes: still he can never bring it about that I am nothing, as long as I think I am something; or that one day it will be true that I have never existed, when it is true now that I exist;* . . . *or that other such things should be true in which I recognize an obvious contradiction."*

Descartes, *Meditations*, 26 (my emphasis).

48. In his "Discourse on the Method," Descartes talks about the "provisional morality" as the essential part of the search for certainty undertaken by a finite mind: the will must be engaged in the pursuit of rationality, so it can go on, propped by the assertive moral attitude. His "provisional moral code" is thus necessary to foster the "finite thinking": "I thought I could do no better than to continue with the [occupation] I was engaged in, and to devote my whole life to cultivating my reason and advancing as far as I could in the knowledge of the truth, following the method I had prescribed for myself" (Descartes, "Discourse on the Method," in *Philosophical Writings of Descartes*, 1:124). Similarly, in *Meditations*, the will is also presented as the indispensable ingredient of the finite reasoning that must assert itself each time by warding off the specter of the "external influence," and as this power of self-assertion can actually measure up to God: "For although the will is incomparably greater in God than in me . . . nonetheless, when it is considered strictly as it is essentially in itself, *it does not seem to be greater in him than in me*. This is because . . . it consists purely in this: that we are moved in relation to that which the intellect presents to us as to be affirmed or denied, pursued or avoided, in such a way that we feel we are not being determined in that direction by any external force" (Descartes, *Meditations*, 41 [my emphasis]). And, as Descartes claims, once will and reason cooperate within the provisional morals/thinking, "all the true goods [are] *within my reach*." (Descartes, *Philosophical Writings*, 1:125 [my emphasis]). The image of the limited space "within my reach" is opposed to the infinite realm of absolute knowledge, which needs no *provisos* to know the truth and thus needs no will to maintain itself in the epistemological self-assertion.

49. "That such an idea of the absolute and its transcendence could achieve such a sustained influence on Scholasticism can only be understood as the repression of the humanistic element of the Christian tradition by its theological 'rigor.' Only when the indifference of divinity toward man had been thought through to the end was theology's immanent logic satisfied [. . . .] The world as the pure performance of reified omnipotence, as a demonstration of the unlimited sovereignty of a will to which no question can be addressed—this eradication even of the right to perceive a problem means that, at least for man, the world no longer possessed an accessible order." (Blumenberg, *Legitimacy*, 171).

50. Blumenberg, *Legitimacy*, 196–97 (my emphasis).

51. Levinas, "Loving Torah More Than God," in *Difficult Freedom*, 142.

52. Ibid., 143.

53. Ibid., 144 (my emphasis).

54. Ibid. A similar argument is made by Eliezer Berkovits in *Not in Heaven*, which presents the *lo bashamayim* principle in terms of the necessary mediation, which only the Jewish law can fulfill.

55. Ibid., 143.

56. The closest to the idea of the "decentered theism" as the *differentia specifica* of Judaism is Scholem's term *pious atheism*, which combines the moment of piety and its Kripkean "rigid designator" in the form of the Torah with the awareness of God's absence here and now; see Scholem, *On Jews and Judaism in Crisis*, 283. David Biale's elaboration of *lo bashamayim* as creating a tradition of "Jewish secularism" follows Scholem's intuition that "his secularism is not secular" (Ibid.) and develops "a contrarian argument: that many of the most avowed critics of religion, those we call secularists, could never escape the tradition they overturn" (Biale, *Not in the Heavens*, 176). The key to this paradox is that one does not have to escape the Jewish tradition in order to overturn it: the refutative agonistic moment of "arguing with God" is so strong that the greatest rebels become the holiest saints, and vice versa.

57. See Frank's remark, which connects the Bava Metzi'a aggadah with Levinas's position: "I believe the deeper reason why the majority rejects the divine voice as proof is the one expressed by Levinas: direct contact with the Sacred without the mediation of reason produces madness": a madness being precisely what Žižek calls "the abyss of subjectivity" (Frank, "Arguing with God," 81).

58. Ibid., 145.

2

Talmudic and Jewish Logo-Politics

ELAD LAPIDOT

אין סכין מתחדדת
A knife is not sharpened
Genesis Rabbah 69:2

Some conjunctions make a statement. The mere apposition of two terms, their plain placement next to each other, one with the other, one and the other, connected with *and* may suggest a community and story, or history, where none seem to exist—beyond, perhaps, the fact of belonging to the same language or only to language in general, to logos—and sometimes not even this. The word *and* suggests, displays and demonstrates, or *attests* to an already-existing union and coexistence, copresence of the two, but by this very display and unexpected force renders visible what has so far been near absolute nonconnection, coabsence without so much as the connection of disconnection, less than different: disparate and dispersed beyond all *and*.

This, or something like this, applies to philosophy and Talmud.

BETWEEN *T* AND *T*

Or we should write, rather, philosophy and talmud. The drama of this conjunction takes place between *T* and *t*, *Talmud* and *talmud*, a proper name and a concept. Sergey Dolgopolski already opened that space: "By the seemingly innocent omission of a grammatical article," the *the*, that is, the space between "'the' Talmud... as either a traditional source or a historical project" and "Talmud (without the *the*) as an intellectual project."[1] This was the difference between a historical project and an intellectual project, a difference between history and thought as different *projects*—both specific, temporally or historically identifiable undertakings, both, with or without *the*, properly named Talmud. To conjoin Talmud and philosophy on an equal footing or heading, an additional "seemingly innocent omission" or rather downsizing or reduction is required, by mere optics, from *T* to *t*, from name to concept, from thought as a project to thought as a discipline, like philosophy. Two concepts or forms of thought, philosophy and talmud, would be thus united or reunited in thought, and their conjunction *and* would be a connection of thought, a logical preposition, strictly speaking, no longer an indifferent *and* but some mode of conceptual synthesis. The only remaining perplexity would be that they—philosophy and talmud—were ever apart.

Yet the opposite seems to be the case. The conjunction of philosophy and talmud, historically and contemporarily, is far from obvious. Their conjunction *is* a statement. Whether two concepts or disciplines or modes or forms or configurations of thought, the space between them, the space of the *and* and the *and not* is not the purely conceptual, logical, or epistemological space. Rather than *philosophy* and *talmud*, their relation might be more appropriately designated as *Philosophy, Talmud*, two proper names connected by no article, no logical or grammatical relation, interrelated by sheer exterior, nonlogical space. Talmud and Philosophy would be the enigma of thought separated or dispersed by space of nonthought, it would be the question concerning the relation between Philosophy and Talmud as, to quote Dolgopolski, "traditions of thought."[2] The space of nonthought, where thought can be separated, where concepts and forms of thought may exist with no logical connection, not even *and*, would be the space or dimension of "tradition," a dimension of time or history, or, more fundamentally, a dimension of memory where thought exists in the plural, as projects or traditions of thought, for instance, Philosophy and Talmud.

For instance, and: What is the perspective from which these words are or may be spoken? From what point of view and what project or tradition of thought may the conjunction of Talmud and Philosophy be attempted? Is there a third, "neutral" or even comprehensive perspective? Wouldn't such a synthetic, synoptic perspective abolish and absorb the space of nonthought between Talmud and Philosophy? Does such a perspective have history or tradition? And who may claim to speak from and for this perspective? Who might be the voice of such a tradition? May I be that voice, may "we," that is, the collective epistemological and logical space in which this text may exist and speak, which can be tentatively identified as Western academic or scientific or something similar? All discourse on "traditions of thought" or "traditions of discourse" commits to self-identification.

From a neutral perspective, Philosophy and Talmud seem to be equally visible, accessible, and present: comparable. They are "commensurable and mutually irreducible ways of thinking," Dolgopolski writes.[3] Are they really equally present for us, these two traditions? Are they equally present in the locus of these words, the place in which their names, Philosophy and Talmud, are brought in conjunction? Dolgopolski's observation on the conditions or preconditions of observation—a phenomenologically foundational observation then, which marks a point of departure for his observation on Philosophy and Talmud, and for mine, walking here in his footsteps, in his "tradition," so to speak—is not the Talmud's visible and accessible presence but rather the opposite, an absence or concealedness, what he calls *"effacement"* of Talmud. For us, for our thought, Talmud, as a way or form of thought, exists in a certain mode of absence, effaced. All contemplation, observation, and theory of Talmud must essentially be a phenomenology of effacement, phenomena of absence.

One first obvious phenomenon of the absence of Talmud, of Talmud as thought, of Talmud from thought—our thought—is Philosophy, both in its manifest, evident presence and in its specific presence for us and in us, namely, as philosophy. In our epistemology, both conceptually and institutionally, philosophy is a synonym of thought: not *our* thought but thought per se. If Talmud, as a tradition of thought, is absent for us, it is from our thoughts that it is absent, and the site of this absence is philosophy. On the most evident level, the Talmud is absent from philosophy. Talmud is no topos and no locus for the thought and theory that guide our knowledge, not even our knowledge of Talmud. In "Philosophy and

Talmud," it is the former that is supposed to shed light on the latter, not vice versa.

It is important to remember that this felt presence of philosophy in our epistemology is not unproblematic, philosophically speaking. "Philosophy," if there ever was *one*, has shown itself in the twentieth and twenty-first centuries as a contentious and schismatic designation. Think of the chasm between "Anglo-American" and "Continental." Contemporary philosophy, like that of the Heideggerian school, has thus generated a discourse whereby the seeming presence of philosophy for us is the phenomenon of its real absence, the face of its effacement, so to speak, or that "philosophy" itself is the state of oblivion of thought. Could it be the same effacement as the Talmud's? Are Talmud and thought conjoined in oblivion? Heidegger might say that the self-oblivion of philosophy consists of forgetting itself as memory, a memory or tradition, forgetting Philosophy—genealogically and etymologically *Greek*. Is the invisibility in philosophy of Greek—and Latin, German, French, and English—the very effacement of Talmud from thought?

However, as Dolgopolski indicates, "effacement"—very much like Heidegger's "concealedness"—is "a dynamic process of the appearance of something at precisely the singular moment of its disappearance."[4] Like philosophy effaces Philosophy, talmud also disappears first not in philosophy but in its own appearance—for us. More precisely, the absence of talmud from thought takes place not as pure invisibility of talmud or nonexistence of any knowledge of talmud but as a specific knowledge, a specific perception and conception of the *singularity* of the talmudic way or form or tradition of thought, a specific perception of talmudic singularity, the talmudic kind of singularity, whereby this singularity has nothing to do with thought. I suggest that the specific perception of talmudic singularity, which effaces and renders absent for us talmudic thought, is the "Jewish." It is the Jewish, rather than Philosophy, that seems to be the main site of talmud's absence.

A better way of describing the relationship is to say that they are complementary sites. Tentatively and schematically, I suggest that "philosophy," understood as thought without tradition, memory, or language, pure logos transcending all difference, *universal*, is complemented in our epistemology by "the Jewish," standing for the singular as *particular*, in the sense of identity and difference beyond or before and outside all thought, logos and reason. The paradigmatic phenomenon of Jewish a-logical difference, Jewish particularity, is the Jewish human collective, understood as *ethnos*: the collective beyond or before thought, polis outside logos. It seems that it is within this category of Jewish particularity that talmud has been perceived by contemporary knowledge as the Talmud—as a central phenomenon of this particularity. From all textual and intellectual projects identified as "Jewish," it is indeed the Talmud, much more than the Bible or Kabbalah or Jewish philosophy or theology, that has been most identified with Jewish ethnic particularism and opposed to universalism and philosophy. Thus when philosopher Alain Badiou, a contemporary prophet of universalism, looked for a concise formula of contemporary Jewish particularism, he called it SIT: "the tripod of the Shoah, the State of Israel and the Talmudic Tradition," connecting Talmud to particularistic politics of Jewish race and state.[5]

Talmud's absence is present less in our philosophy's disregard or dismissal of Jewish particularity than in its affirmative epistemological performance. The very concept of "Jewish Studies" could be read as Western epistemology's translation, and thus equivalent and *substitution*, of "Talmud." Textual traces for this conceptual substitution, or supersession, can be found in the archives of the *Wissenschaft des Judentums*.[6] The foundational epistemological operation of the Science of Judaism, bequeathed to Jewish Studies, has been the de-epistemization of the Jewish: Jewish being and phenomena perceived paradigmatically not as forms of knowledge, theory, and thought but as *objects* of knowledge arising from non-Jewish, universal epistemology and thought, arising, ultimately, from philosophy.

It is this process of de-epistemization, de-logization, or effacement from thought that a more patient study could trace within the production and performance of Jewish Studies' Jewish Talmud, in Talmudic or Rabbinic Studies. It is there that talmud, as a way of thinking, is effaced by Talmud, as a tradition of thought, which is effaced by the Talmud, as a text, the paradigmatic perception of which shifts from logos to literature to history to document to manuscript, none of which function as media of thought but as phenomena of the nonthought that is Jewish being. Talmud is accordingly epistemologically present, *known* as a document of Jewish culture. Christine Hayes identified and criticized one point in this process, the shift of Talmud from literature to document, as "reductive historical analysis," which perceives and reads the text as a mere indication, a symptom or trace of "economic, political, national, and social" circumstances."[7] In perfect solidarity with this process are attempts to identify universal—philosophical—thought in Talmud *despite* its particular Jewishness, such as pointing at the way it deploys Aristotelian logic, for example. Within the category of "the Jewish," however, such attempts never escape some kind of apologetics, which, to avoid "triumphalism," veer into a harsher critique of Talmudic Jewish particularism, of Talmud *as* Jewish particularism. Such a critique presupposes itself as self-critique and thus more self-flagellating and more self-affirmative—the less Talmud, the more Jewish.

It is thus that the Jewish—Jewishness, Jewish existence, the human being, existence, and agency who understands and performs itself as "Jewish"—constitutes the presence of Talmud's absence for our knowledge and thought. This is not to say that Jewish existence has nothing to do with Talmud, or vice versa. On the contrary, what allows the one to operate as absence of the other is precisely a profound relation and intimacy, a relation of a certain deep and mutual negation, radical existential negation, something like the intimacy of enmity: "enmacy." This enmacy immediately suggests a complexity or paradox at the very heart of the notion of enemy, an enemy who, by the very radical existential *negativity* of their foreignness, would necessarily and essentially be always already present, in negative and in absentia, in the being of the self—such that the Jewish, as the absence of Talmud, would exist, in negative and in absentia, in the Talmud itself as its inner condition of nonbeing and disappearance and effacement, which would then be always already self-effacement. Would Talmud's effacement by the Jewish accordingly be Talmud's self-effacement as the proper phenomenality—mode of appearance, of Talmud—perhaps very much like self-concealment constitutes for Heidegger the proper truth of Being, its unconcealedness?

To start thinking in this direction or any direction toward Talmud as—a way, a form, a tradition, a mode, a configuration of—thought, and then toward Talmud and Philosophy, Talmud and philosophy, we must go beyond Talmud's absence, beyond the Jewish. More accurately, we must go beyond or rethink the configuration of philosophy and the Jewish as a *certain* contemporary configuration of thought and temporal-historical singularity, in which they appear as universality and particularity, universality *versus* particularity, mutually exclusive. Since this contemporary configuration appears paradigmatically as the opposition among thought, knowledge (*episteme*), reason, and logos (universal philosophy) on the one hand and historical collective human existence, ethnos or polis, polis as ethnos (the particular Jewish people) on the other, what needs to be rethought is the relation between logos and polis as present and familiar to us through the configuration of philosophy and the Jewish, or rather only the Jewish, as polis that breaks with logos. This rethinking needs to take the form of a logo-political critique or polemics against *our* universalism, that is, the notion and form of universalism that organizes our epistemology.

This self-critical exercise of what I wish to call *logo-politics* or *political epistemology* should, as already noted, take into consideration and make use of existing projects of logo-political self-critique in contemporary philosophy, such as Heidegger's, rendering visible the absence(s) that our present effects and effaces. This disclosed absence is the space and horizon, the *Nicht-Da*, where absents, like Talmud, may re-reappear. Beyond the Jewish and philosophy, a phenomenology (or aphenomenology, i.e., logos of a-phenomenon, of nonappearing) of Talmud must discover or recover, recall or remember talmudic thought not just as different or an alternative to the Judeo-philosophical, *ours*, but as rival, not to say *hostile*, logo-politics.

DISAGREEMENT

As previously mentioned, my contemplation follows a path that has already been charted by others. I mostly take inspiration from and struggle with—or, as the rabbinic saying goes, sharpen my knife against the knives of—Daniel Boyarin and Sergey Dolgopolski, or Dolgopolski *devei* Boyarin. It is to their conversation, their tradition—or, perhaps, to reference Dolgopolski—their "dance" that I wish to join via disagreement: disagreeing with or declining or even breaking the dance—is this still dancing?

Yet before the *dis-*, I state the agreement, or, rather, agreements; there are at least five, and they are fundamental. First, in both Boyarin's and

Dolgopolski's work, I read on different levels of explicitness the attempt to recall and read the Talmud as thought—a form, a mode, a tradition of thought—with its own specific configuration of the relationships between episteme or logos and polis, its own political epistemology or logo-politics. Importantly, both Boyarin and Dolgopolski engage with the highly specific and unique *form* of Talmudic discourse, the specific logics of its logos, the specific Talmudic "rhetoric," as they say, as constituting or performing eo ipso Talmudic politics before or beyond any Talmudic discussions pertaining to specific "political" themes, such as public institutions, the king, the courts, and so on. Second, this specific Talmudic logo-politics is asserted by both Boyarin and Dolgopolski as a logo-political act, in other words, not just as a theoretical, epistemological operation of suggesting another Talmudic model of logo-politics next to the more well-known, say, "philosophical" model but also as an act of opposition, resistance, or defiance, a political act of positing Talmud *versus* Philosophy. Third, their opposition to Philosophy is conducted as opposition to universalism, in the name of difference. Fourth, both Boyarin and Dolgopolski read Talmud beyond or before, which means against, the Jewish, at least in the most basic sense that they both are attentive to the fact that the Talmud hardly ever speaks of and never identifies itself or any of its many selves, "itselves," as "Jewish." This should be noted as a fact, which must nevertheless be interpreted as more than a unique feature of terminology and linguistic usage since the few mentions of "Jews" in the Talmud prove that the Talmudic selves know they are being designated as such *by others*, their nonuse of this designation for themselves must be understood not just as performance of difference but as an act or even project of logo-political resistance. Fifth, the consequence, which I more draw from than read in their work, is that contemporary efforts of recovering Talmudic logo-politics are required to assert themselves not only in opposition to Philosophy but, even more so, in—a much more complex and delicate—resistance to the Jewish.

These five elements in addition to a crucial sixth, the element of *effacement*, that is, a phenomenology of the effacement of Talmudic logo-politics by Philosophy and the Jewish, were assembled most explicitly and articulately in Dolgopolski's last book *Other Others: The Political after the Talmud*. I now wish to discuss my agreements and disagreements by taking a closer and unavoidably simplifying look at one of the book's basic lines of argumentation.

I focus on the book's central argumentative axis, which positions Philosophy and Talmud relative to one another, as two traditions and disciplines of thinking regarding their different relations to "the Political": "Talmud and philosophy as two commensurable but mutually irreducible ways of thinking the political that fruitfully can be brought into an explicit dialogue one with another."[8] The nature, conceptual possibility, and potential fruitfulness of such a dialogue remain open questions, considering that Dolgopolski claims that the two traditions of thinking the political have engendered two different political models or approaches, representing "two approaches to the experience of human existence [that] are mutually exclusive."[9] Mutual exclusiveness, however, seems to be a less favorable precondition for dialogue and more so for war.

A main thread in Dolgopolski's portrayal of Philosophy's political epistemology leads to a radical image of antidialogical destruction and extermination. The paradigm for this epistemo-political portrait of philosophy is a Kantian "subject of reason," a purely reasonable subject, whose pure logic supersedes all positive and empirically and historically given realities.[10] The collective existence, polis, or *earth*, to use Dolgopolski's geophilosophical terms, that arises from this epistemology is the "intersubjective space," a world of "isolated thinking subjects" where—in a dystopian vision echoing Hannah Arendt's critique of totalitarianism, Jean-Luc Nancy's critique of individualism and communitarianism, and Carl Schmitt's critique of liberalism—the total logic of "the industrial, postindustrial and informational" moves to supersede and to *efface* the political itself.[11] Dolgopolski is closer to Nancy and Schmitt than to Arendt because he identifies the historical paradigm of this supersessionist and eliminatory philosophical logo-politics in the paragon of liberal enlightenment, that is, universal humanism. Modern universalism is the deployment of philosophy's eliminatory logo-politics by means of the figure of "'the human' as a would-be common denominator capable of bridging all cultural, ethnic, racial, moral, sexual and geopolitical differences."[12]

Philosophy's antidifference politics, which Dolgopolski exemplifies in two modern thinkers who explicitly spoke *for* difference, Carl Schmitt (who, according to Dolgopolski, subjected difference to "political theology") and Jacques Rancière (who would have subjected difference to "political ontology"), culminates for Dolgopolski not just in assimilating and obliterating all differences under "the human" but, more radically, in denying and negating all *other*, nonassimilable kind of differences and positive identities, all "other others." As a paradigmatic "other other" that has been negated by modern philosophy's intersubjective, universalist logo-politics of "the human," Dolgopolski points at the modern figure of "the Jew," constructed by modern political epistemology as the negative counterfigure of "the human" and so preprogrammed for extermination. It is this twentieth-century event of extermination of the Jewish other others that would mark a limit and end of philosophy's universalist "human" politics, both a conceptual and a real historical end: "After what the Holocaust names, insufficiently, the human can no longer be automatically granted the status of a common denominator."[13]

Despite the precautionary qualification (*automatically*), the violence of the image summons the perspective not so much of a fruitful dialogue between Philosophy and Talmud, as rather of a *turn* from Philosophy to Talmud. If Philosophy's intersubjectivity effaced the political, this effacement is linked to the effacement "of the Talmud as the political," such that Dolgopolski suggests turning to Talmud not for the sake of "Jewish" Studies but for the fundamental sake of recovering the political itself, a non-self-effacing version of the political, "of which the Talmud might be the only surviving, or at least the only available, but in no way the only possible example."[14]

As noted previously, Dolgopolski recognizes the Talmud's political performance primarily not in any specific content but in the *form* of Talmudic discourse. Similarly to Boyarin, Dolgopolski discerns the formal specificity of Talmudic logos, in contrast to philosophical logics, in categories of literary studies. Both Boyarin and Dolgopolski analyze the Talmudic text as a genre of *literature*, deploying categories from Russian formalism, mainly Bakhtin. One may wonder whether philosophy and literature, as epistemological notions and domains, really or necessarily feature opposite or "mutually exclusive" discursive forms, or whether they are, as can be observed in the institutional epistemology of American academia, complementary. This would require asking about the epistemological meaning of knowing Talmud as and under the *scientific regime* of "literature," which, in contrast to "philosophy," seems to be constituted on a fundamental split between knowledge (literary theory) and its object (literary text), Talmud being paradigmatically allotted to the latter and so de-epistemized as a document of Jewish literature and culture. Here lies the bud of my *disagreement* or of the difficulty I identify in Dolgopolski's and Boyarin's phenomenology of Talmudic logo-politics. It seems that their accounts, at least at some central points, manifest a certain antiuniversalism that consists of asserting particularism; an assertion, however, that ultimately functions not as the negation but as the very performance of universalism.

In contrast with philosophical universalism, for which Talmudic singularity arises from Jewish particularity, as an illegitimate (ethno-) political break with logos, which thus must be banned from universal thought ("philosophy"), Dolgopolski and Boyarin point to Talmud as featuring an alternative logics, and thus logo-politics, of *difference*. The fundamental question concerns the nature of this Talmudic difference and, more specifically, its difference from philosophy. The difficulty shows itself in Boyarin's interpretation of Talmudic logics of difference with Bakhtin's category of "satire," which Boyarin identifies as a foundational feature of the Hellenistic culture of "rational inquiry as the way to truth."[15] He accordingly merges rather than distinguishes rabbinic and Socratic dialogues, both only *representing* difference and dialogue, while actually being "anything but dialogical, incorporating rather all voices into one single consciousness, that of the 'author,'" "Plato or the *stamma*."[16] Talmudic difference thus appears as the *inner* relation of a self to itself—"self-critical voice," "second-order reflection"—that is, as the very constitution of modern philosophy's "subject of reason."[17] This epistemology seems to correspond to Boyarin's logo-political interpretation of Talmudic difference as "diaspora," which does not counter philosophy's subject (the "human") but perfects it by liberating it from the last nonlogical contingency of territory, such that it is everywhere at home, Talmud being its "traveling homeland."[18] It is hard not to see in Boyarin's diasporic vision a paradigm of what Dolgopolski calls "the intersubjective space." According to this logic, the singularity of Talmud, like all other diasporas, is ultimately the empirical particularity of the individual, politically speaking, the *collective* individual, "the Jewish." For our epistemological system, beyond pure form, what Talmud says, actual Talmudic logos, would be a document of Jewish cultural difference, which for thought is a matter of indifference.

The same difficulty is ultimately presented by Dolgopolski's account, although his argumentation is explicitly antiphilosophical. Indeed, against philosophy's "intersubjective space," superseding and sublating any positive difference—and so any *politics*—by the universal logics of the reasonable subject, Dolgopolski describes Talmudic logo-politics as "interpersonal," which he defines as "a way of thinking and acting in society that both involves a multiplicity of positions and does not involve any rigid connection between any position and any individual who performs it."[19] "Interpersonal" space would avoid both communal and individual totalitarianism. It would be a logo-political space without a transcendental subject, seemingly without an "author" but of an essential multiplicity of "positions," of "personae." Both notions, "position" and "person," suggest an aspect, perspective, face, or hypostasis of a certain *whole*, that is, the totality of a literary unit, which Dolgopolski's Talmudic readings most often perform as a theatrical play, with various "characters."

Thus Dolgopolski describes Talmudic logics underlying interpersonal multiplicity as logics of *refutation*, in which "positions can stand only in their mutual contradistinction," that is, connected through disagreement.[20] However, as Dolgopolski emphasizes, in reference to Boyarin, Talmudic disagreement does not aim at "cultivating arguments for argument's sake or remaining genuinely open to an unknown truth that it is the goal of the discussion to attain. The new Babylonian dialectics contributes to the reaffirmation of the authority of the traditions of the past."[21] If Talmudic dialectics has no author, it is nonetheless subject to an *authority*. This authority is typically present in or through the Mishnah; however, it is present in a mode of absence, of open and uncertain past such that disagreement—refutation and counterrefutation—is subjected to the task of establishing the "truth of tradition," in other words, by way of remembering. Stating that in Talmud, "rational thinking becomes subservient to the task of memory and of remembering," Dolgopolski asserts the given positivity of Talmudic tradition versus pure, autonomous reason of Kantian epistemology.[22] However, just as Kant's transcendental reason is ultimately united by the individual *I*, the "*subject* of reason," in

Dolgopolski's account, the positive authority of tradition subjects all differences to an ultimate unity: all disagreement remembers. Rather than interrupt or break universal logos, Talmudic dialectics would perfect it, enhancing a static, Kantian state of reason to a dynamic, Hegelian spatiotemporal event, which Dolgopolski describes as "carnival" or "theater" but more often as "dance," a "dance of memory."[23]

As in the case of Boyarin's satiric diasporism, Dolgopolski's carnival of remembrance also features a Talmudic logic of difference that is nonetheless generative of a higher form of a unified system of reason—a subject or state. Talmudic logo-politics emerges as the universal pure form for the space between different interpersonal carnivals, other "Talmuds," which would ultimately be an intersubjective or interstate space, readily evocative of the international nation-state system arising from our current epistemo-politics. This universality of pure talmudic form, however, implies the extreme particularism of the Talmud's actual content, which would be contingent on and indifferent to universal thinking—a "Jewish" culture. Talmudic logics ("talmud") would render Talmudic logos ("the Talmud") indifferent for thought.

To further articulate the difficulty identified in Boyarin's and Dolgopolski's groundbreaking phenomenologies of Talmudic logo-politics, and to begin pointing at the alternative direction I propose, in the next section I revisit one of the two thinkers that Dolgopolski presents as paradigmatic for modern philosophy's politics, Carl Schmitt. Despite Dolgopolski's critique of Schmitt, Schmitt's political theology and state theory seem to offer an intensive confrontation with the same fundamental difficulty that I analyze, such that it may provide a helpful conceptual framework for approaching Talmudic political epistemology. Certainly, any explicitly logo-*political* investigation must acknowledge and address the paradox or scandal of referring to "the crown jurist of the Third Reich" as a gateway to Talmud.[24] Indeed, far from wishing to blur this *skandalon*, I think there is here, on the contrary, a central, extremely sensitive and difficult point, too complex to be appropriately analyzed here, that touches and renders tangible the stakes and dangers of searching for Talmud contra the modern Jewish. Such a quest is obligated to confront—and open new perspectives for the confrontation with—the historical forms of the anti-Jewish.[25]

EVIL

Schmitt's basic intellectual project, as he characterized it in his famous essay in *Political Theology* (1922), was, in essence, logo-political. Schmitt called it a "sociology of juridical concepts."[26] By this term, he did not mean the empirical study of social conditions giving rise to legal notions. What he meant was the relation between, on the one hand, *socio-logy*—the fundamental logos of society, its "metaphysics" or, as Schmitt says in a later text, its "concept of truth"—and its legal and political institutions, on the other hand.[27] Schmitt's basic interest was in the relation between society's logos and its polis. Significantly, metaphysics is, in Schmitt's perspective, sociology, and the political appears as the *juridical*, Schmitt's most intimate element, which is the proper logos of the polis: not politi-logy, science of the political, but law, nomos, as the very logos that *is* the polis. "Sociology of juridical concepts" is, accordingly, the interaction between two types, forms, or events of logos, the metaphysical/social and the political/juridical, which are related but separated and feature a radical split or break in logical totality. It is this break of logos that stands at the center of Schmitt's thought.

His initial observation in 1922 was of a fundamental logo-political break in the society of "modern Europe." In contrast to critical visions of totalitarianism in the age of reason, Schmitt pointed to a significant dissociation between modern Europe's political organization and its thought, a break between European *Staatslehre*, which is not only theory or science but also doctrine, art, and practice of the state, "the juridical," and the specific European metaphysics from which this doctrine, according to Schmitt, arises—"theology." Schmitt understood this modern rupture between the state's logos and its underlying theo-logos to be a detheologization of the essentially theological, an operation and event of "secularization." This is the logo-political meaning of Schmitt's most famous dictum in *Political Theology*: "All significant concepts of modern state doctrine are secularized theological concepts."[28]

The crucial element in Schmitt's observation was highlighting how this logo-political break is constitutive for the state's most intimate logos, that is, for its nomos, its *Recht*, modern state law. Against jurists such as Hans Kelsen, who identified between the state and its law, between the state law and the state as a "state of law," *Rechtsstaat*, a systematic, self-contained normative totality—which is how state law constitutionally defines itself, de jure—Schmitt's 1922 essay indicated how state law is de facto founded on a *break* with law, norm, and logics. As *positive* law, modern state law draws its validity from no law or norm, reason, logos, or truth but—similarly to Dolgopolski's "tradition"—from absolute authority. Schmitt quotes Hobbes: "*Autoritas, non veritas facit legem*": "It is authority and not truth that makes the law." Absolute authority, seen from inside of the legal system that it makes, from inside state law, appears as its *exception*: as the ultimate power that is *not* subject to the law—"the sovereign." The state sovereign is thus an *a-legal, a-logical* being, it is no institution or corporation but a "person," by which Schmitt does not mean, like Dolgopolski, a position within a discourse but rather an individual, nonincorporated body, *physis* arising from no idea, reason, or logos, which can thus be the absolute origin of law, as a "personal command" (ibid., 36). The sovereign act, which founds the logical structure of state law, is thus absolutely nonlogical; it follows from no norm or discussion, inferable (*ableitbar*) from nothing, arises from nothingness, *aus einem Nichts*, an absolute act ex nihilo, which Schmitt famously terms *Entscheidung*: "decision."[29] "Decision liberates itself from all normative bind and becomes in the true sense of the word absolute."[30]

Five years later, in 1927, Schmitt extended his observation of this a-logical logo-politics from the specific political organization of the modern European state to the very essence of politics, to "The Concept of the Political."[31] In this essay, Schmitt defined the polis, the "political" collective or group, as a grouping that, whatever the constitutive logic and norm of its internal association—religious, ethnic, national, moral, and so on—defines itself in contradistinction to another, *foreign* group, whose foreignness is identified by the first group as constituting a radical *opposition* to and *negation* of itself. The relation of "opposition" and "negation" suggests logics. Schmitt's point was, however, that whatever the original, internal logos of the grouping may be, the opposition with the external foreign becomes *political*, an opposition with something external and foreign, when it detaches itself from any logos. Thus political negation is no longer logical or normative but *existential* or ontic, "*seinsmäßige* negation of another being [Sein]."[32] Political opposition is, for Schmitt, essentially and paradigmatically—if usually only potentially and virtually—*war*, a *polemos* that is no "polemics," no "discussion." War does not contrast logical entities or discursive "positions" but rather physical bodies in a negation that is not epistemological but ontic: a negation not of refutation but of "physical death." The polis lives in view of its death, which appears in the famous Schmittian figure of the *Feind*, the "foe," the political enemy. The identification of the foe, which is *at once* a declaration of war and a declaration of independence, and, eo ipso, the constitution of order and law is a *sovereign* act, which follows from no norm, reason, or logic. It is pure *decision*. The modern *state* would be an accomplished form of a-logical polis because the ultimate definition of the state collective, as well as the boundaries of its authority and law, follows no reason but the arbitrary, physical, and geographical border. A modern state exists as an individual political unity not by virtue of its conceptual legal singularity but rather by virtue of its separate geographical *territory*.

Any attempt, like Dolgopolski's, to present Schmitt's thought as representative of modern universalist humanism would have to account for the fact that Schmitt did not *criticize* and did not propose to repair or bridge the break or rupture of logos that he observed as constitutive to politics and even more so to the modern state. On the contrary, it is this break, manifesting itself as initially noted in the modern dissociation between politics and metaphysics, in "secularization," that Schmitt asserted as the heart of the forgotten metaphysics, that is, *theology*, which he thus proposed not as refutation but as a legitimate authority and foundation for the a-logics of Western politics. There would be a logos of the political break of logos, and this logos is the theo-logos, such that *theos*, God, would stand for the end of logos and the beginning of polis.

At the end of logos and the beginning of polis stands God or, rather, the discourse of God, theo-logos, which enacts or represents or simply *is* God in absence. Theology takes place in the absence of God. It is, in fact, the absence of God and not God's omnipresence or omnipotence that is at the heart of Schmitt's theology. Schmitt's theological reflections say nothing of God. His theological passages, such as *Roman Catholicism and Political Form* (1923), focus not on God's presence but on human institutions and politics as performing God's absence, paradigmatically his representation through the Catholic church.[33] The most crucial aspect of theology for Schmitt, which turns God's absence into the condition or element of politics, pertains not to God but to the "nature of man" and its social implications. Schmitt's theology is primarily social anthropology. Its fundamental logos, as Schmitt initially learns from the Catholic contrarevolutionists, is that human nature is sin. Man is by nature *evil*.[34]

What is evil "by nature"? That human nature is evil means human evil does not lie in any specific bad mood, evil state of mind, or malicious intentions to do "bad" things. On the contrary, it means that people do evil even and precisely when they have good intentions. In other words, evil as human nature and sin as a human state designate a condition in which human beings are—or, socio-anthropologically speaking, humanity is—unable to be and do good, precisely due to their good intentions, due to the humanly good reason, knowledge, and logos. Under these conditions, humans are in their essence and being, in their physical existence a *seinsmäßige* negation of the good, or a *foe*. The *sociological* consequence is that any attempt to enact and institute the good, to create a good order, society, and law, must assume a foreign collective, which by its own logic, society, and law, by its very essence, being, and best behavior is its enemy, its foe: enmity thus beyond any logic, dia-logos, and discussion, beyond any possible understanding. Evil is the human condition of essential, structural war. "The fundamental theological dogma of the evilness of the world and man leads, just as does the distinction of friend and enemy, to a categorization of men and makes impossible the undifferentiated optimism of a universal conception of man."[35] Theology would accordingly be the logos of the break of logos and, so, of the *seinsmäßige* "division of men," as Schmitt says. "A theologian ceases to be a theologian when he no longer considers man to be sinful or in need of redemption and no longer distinguishes between the chosen and the nonchosen."[36] Theology would be the logos of the political.

What follows from this "political theology" (in fact, a pleonasm), which is thus informative for any contemplation of talmudic versus philosophical logo-politics, is a powerful critique of universalism. The greatest threat, the greatest *evil* in the human condition of *essential* evil is to declare evil itself a foe. Declaring war on evil is always already the victory of war, the victory of evil. As Schmitt shows, declaring war on evil is declaring war on war, a war on the distinction between friend and foe. This war on human division—hence on the political itself—must be declared in the name of human unity, in the name of *humanity*. War on war is a war on polis in the name of logos: peace, justice, reason, progress, civilization, and God or Christ. It is a *just* war, a crusade. As a war, however, this just war on war, *human* war on war necessarily has a foe, who must be identified, declared, and fought against as *inhuman*. Just war is, Schmitt observes, necessarily a war of *Vernichtung*, of annihilation and extermination. "The war is then considered to constitute the absolute last war of humanity. Such a war is necessarily unusually intense and inhuman because, by transcending the limits of the political framework, it simultaneously degrades the enemy into moral and other categories and is forced to make of him a monster that must not only be defeated but also utterly destroyed."[37] It is again in Hobbes that Schmitt finds "the correct recognition that the conviction of both parties about the true, the good and the just leads to the most terrible hostilities, ultimately also to the *bellum* of all against all."[38]

The basic, *universal* politics that arises from Schmitt's theology is accordingly antiuniversalism: the politics of maintaining human division, maintaining foe and war by keeping separate polis and logos, politics and reason, knowledge or truth. This concerns the basic nature of human praxis, the basic human act underlying all politics: an act that breaks with logos, that is, decision. The fundamental decision is the decision on the decision: theology. Theology would be the logos of decision, that is, a-logical logos, a truth or revelation that is not inferred, proven, or justified but positively declared: dogma.[39] Similarly, the logos of the polis is a logos of decision: "the juridical" not in the sense of the normative and the legal but in the sense of the judicial, the judgment, a decision by no reason but on authority. "Such a decision in the broadest sense belongs to every legal perception. Every legal thought brings a legal idea, which in its purity can never become reality, into another aggregate condition and adds an element that cannot be derived either from the content of the legal idea or from the content of a general positive legal norm that is to be applied. [...] In every transformation there is present an *auctoritatis interposition*."[40]

Schmitt provides no systematic or detailed description, even in outline, of the specific historical doctrines and institutions that would have arisen from this theo-logo-politics, which, following his thought, could function as a hermeneutical key for reading the history of Roman Catholicism.

Catholic antiuniversalism, a paradoxical universal antiuniversalism, opposition to universalism in the name of universalism serves Schmitt first and foremost, as noted previously, as the raison d'être or the irraison d'être of the modern state, the consummated polis founded on the division between polis and logos: *autoritas, non veritas facit legem*. For Schmitt, this division of power from truth ensures the essential nonuniversality, the essential individuality or particularity of the state, singularity without reason as a limited authority on a limited territory, which can therefore fight only limited wars on limited foes for limited causes. The great achievement of modern state doctrine, according to Schmitt, was to institutionalize the political world as a *pluriversum*, a plurality of sovereign states. State doctrine, which perfects the political idea, is a logo-politics of difference. Each state maintains law within: a state law in which evil is legalized and is criminal, not foe. Politics and war are kept outside, between states in a paradoxical state of interstate law, a law on war, the fundamental purpose of which is to ensure that war is *not* legalized, so that the enemy—a mass murderer—is never criminalized, never *brought to justice*.[41]

Whence arises Schmitt's own foe, his own war—and politics. If the crusades and religious wars were the premodern foe of the political, the evil faced by the modern state, the modern figure of radical evil, the foe of the foe, and so of Schmitt's *Political Theology*, is the modern opposition to the *theo-logo-polis*. This is not "secularism" per se because secularism does not eliminate but rather presupposes theology, so that the modern state, as noted previously, could be seen as the very reality of secularism.[42] Antitheology abolishes God and Evil, reunites logos with polis, and so, for Schmitt, abolishes politics and declares war on war. Schmitt recognized two basic forms of modern antitheology. First, *anarchism*, or *revolution*, is a programmatic and explicit anti-theo-logos. It denies God, asserts human reason, and fights the state. This antitheology, however, still takes the form of theology. For political theology, revolutionary antitheology is not absolute, *seinsmäßige* negation, not a *foe*. Political theology and anarchism still have something in common. Schmitt claims that Bakunin, Lenin, and Mao "knew what they were doing."[43]

The real foe of Schmittian political theology is not anarchism but *liberalism*. Liberalism does not negate theology *logically* but rather ignores theology, negates it ontically—*seinsmäßig*. Liberalism exists in a world of evil, a political world; it exists *as* worldly evil, as a state, the liberal state—but without knowing it. Liberalism, Schmitt says, has neither theology nor a theory of state.[44] In other words, liberalism completely ignores the break of logos. There would be a liberal *illusion* of universalism very similar to the one criticized by Marx. Liberal metaphysics is physics, natural science; its politics is police and policy of neutrality and depoliticized technology. It sees no decision, only "eternal discussion"; no sovereign, only legal system. The foe of liberal politics, which declares itself "nonpolitical," is consequently *politics*. Liberal distinction between friend and foe is a distinction between nonpolitical and political. Liberal wars are wars on war, *imperialistic* wars in the name of peace and humanity, necessarily taking the form of *Vernichtung* crusades with limitless technological power.

In the 1920s and 1930s, Schmitt fought his war against this evil in the name of the state. In his later years, he still understood the evil of both revolutionary and liberal universalism as an imperialistic abuse of the state system.[45] But is imperialist universalism an abuse of the sovereign state? If the state is a limited, individual, and particular polis, has not its discourse and logic, its modern state logos been essentially humanistic and revolutionary, essentially universal? Are not modern state and modern reason interlinked, as Dolgopolski argues? Schmitt's account seems to indicate that they are: sovereignty is the state of an absolute self, a self-identical and self-sufficient individuality, an individual totality, which is the very condition of the perfect system of reason and law, the perfect autonomy. It seems that the sovereign state *must* understand itself as a *Rechtsstaat*, a state of law, which stands for universal human values, such that its—territorial—limitation is indeed purely contingent. State logos is in its essence total and universal, precluding any logo-political break. It is therefore the same difficulty that arises from both Schmitt's antiuniversalist state and Boyarin's and Dolgopolski's antiuniversalist Talmud. Both accounts feature a logic of difference, of a supposed break in universal logos, which nonetheless generates perfect individual subjects, perfect individual selves, who, precisely because they are liberated from universality, are no longer subject to anything but their own law, hence absolute. If I subscribe to Boyarin's and Dolgopolski's attempt to identify a Talmudic logo-politics that would present an alternative to universalism, I also acknowledge the paradox of the logic of difference as it transpires in Schmitt's political theology of the sovereign state.

In late Schmitt, there is a brief and undeveloped point at which I believe he saw a way out of this paradox. In the 1963 preface of *The Concept of the Political*, Schmitt acknowledged the intimacy of state and imperialism, be that the intimacy of "abuse." Accordingly, against the evil of liberal imperialism, he could no longer suggest a dogmatic logos of separation between polis and logos, a logos *of* a-logos, a theo-logos. He could no longer assert theology against imperialism. Instead, Schmitt evoked a more radical break of logos, which he proposed by way of a postmodern observation: "The time of the systems is gone."[46] The end of the system signifies the end or break of logos in its basic coherence and unity, namely, in its basic faculty of generating a totality of meaning and signification, a break of logos as indication, revelation, and dogma, which may serve—even by abuse—as a principle of sovereignty. Schmitt named two ways to perform this break. One was "historical reflection," which is what he did in *Der Nomos der Erde*.[47] The second one, "contrary to it," he wrote, was "to leap into aphorism," that is, broken and fragmented logos, which, he added, "for me, as a jurist, is impossible."[48] It is the *possibility* and perhaps the historical actuality of something like aphorism as a logo-political principle that I wish to contemplate now through a phenomenology of Talmud.

EXILE

I start by restating the basic logo-political plot that I find helpful to elicit from Schmitt. His political theology, as already noted, is a logos of the *absence* of God. This logos of absence—the absence of the object or reality or being to which the logos, as theo-logos, refers—is eo ipso logos of logos or discourse on the knowledge of God in God's absence. Theology of absence is epistemology, an epistemology of absence, which is another pleonasm, insofar as epistemology is logos, or knowledge, *of* knowledge; that is, by definition epistemology is always at a distance from and in the absence of the *object* of knowledge, in the absence of Truth. Schmitt shows this absence of God or Truth—theology or epistemology—to be the very element of the political. The political would be the enactment and performance—in the broadest sense, knowledge or consciousness—of

God or Truth, of the "Universal," *as absent*; politics would be the performative disruption of logos, a disruption that is nothing but logos itself *as* performance, that is, not as perfect substance but as a not-yet-perfected event. The greatest challenge of political theology or epistemology, of logo-politics, is to maintain the tension of presenting absence (of God, of Truth) without abolishing either presence or absence.

Schmitt's Roman Catholic legacy, as it shines through his work, institutionalizes the logo-political tension through the separation between—and cohabitation of—church and state as two separate polities with two separate logoi. I mentioned previously how Schmitt's work problematizes the logo-political performance of the state, whose sovereignty structurally tends to transgress its limits—tends to the evil of imperialism. It is important to ask to what extent the same problem may be also demonstrated with respect to the church, which, according to Schmitt, performs the presence of absence by way of *representation*.[49] Be that as it may, I suggest that Talmud may be contemplated as performing the same fundamental logo-politics of absence—in a fundamentally different way. My comparative observation is that Talmudic logo-politics does not primarily perform the break as a separation between two polities with two logoi but as a break in the very being of polis and the very being of logos. Talmud is the performance of logos as text and polis as exile. Accordingly, talmudic logo-politics is a counterperformance both to the perfectly universal logos of philosophy and to the perfectly particular Jewish state.

What is Talmud? Be it logos as thought (talmud), it is *essentially* Talmud, a thing or being, logos as text. I contend that this text is not just logo-political—not just logos underlying a polis or the political—but is itself a logo-political unity, a logo-*polis*, the performance and being of a polity. Talmud is not just logos but also the relation of logos to logos and, more specifically, the performance of one logos (Mishnah) by another logos (Gemara).[50] This interlogos, or intertext, even if it does generate a certain identity or self, a certain Talmudic self, is, however, no "self-reflection." It rather features something like the broken relation that Schmitt observed between modern metaphysics and law.

The question of Talmud is accordingly eo ipso the question of Mishnah—and in a certain way, the obverse is true. The Talmud exists in the element of the Mishnah. Mishnaic logos constitutes the basic environment and fundamental logical features of all Talmudic logos. Despite the attempt to reinscribe the Talmud in thought, as talmud—or rather for the sake of this inscription, which must take the Talmud in its singularity—it is crucial to note that the discursive constitution of the Talmud, the Mishnah, as a discourse, does not feature the formal, logical characteristics of the philosophical, metaphysical, theological, scientific, or even literary discourse but rather of what Schmitt called "the Juridical." As obvious as this may seem, it is nonetheless an epistemo-politically challenging acknowledgment because "legalism" is the reproach on account of which philosophy has often and typically excluded "the Jewish" from thought. As Kant famously said: "Jewish faith, in its original setting, is a compendium (*Inbegriff*) of mere (*bloß*) statutory laws," wherefore "the Jewish" is neither a religion nor a church.[51] No doubt, the specific perception of the juridical as "statutory laws" better describes Maimonides's Mishnah than the Talmud's Mishnah, as Dolgopolski showed.[52] But the categorical rejection of the legal and juridical as the foundation of Talmud seems to have been constitutive for apologetics of "Jewish thought," which tended to focus on Jewish philosophy and Kabbalah.[53]

In characterizing the Mishnah as "juridical" and not "legal," I break with the apologetics and do not, for instance, assert, against Kant, the rationality and order of the Mishnaic legal logos. On the contrary, I accept Kant's description of "statutory laws" as a raw, naked—"*bloß*"—form of reason, an undeveloped or broken mode of logos. In fact, it is due to its Mishnaic constitution that Talmudic literature may be contemplated as a phenomenon of disrupted logos. I am thinking of all the basic features of the Talmud as logos, discourse or text, that instead of consolidating or remembering its literary unity, as Boyarin's and Dolgopolski's accounts suggest, rather *fragment* or dismember it: a multiplicity of tongues, authorities, and voices; the lack of author; and, most fundamentally, the lack of logical or narrative continuity and unity. These are the features of a fragmented logos, which lack the inner unity of a self-identical self, of a "subject of reason," which may be embodied as the "author," as "Jewish." Mishnah structures Talmud as a logos with an entirely external unity, the unity of the page, a *compendium* of separate independent fragments or "aphorisms," as Schmitt imagined logos to be after "the time of the systems." As "a jurist," he thought aphoristic logos was "impossible." By "jurist," however, Schmitt must have meant a *Rechtswissenschaftler*, a "scientist" or *scholar* of law since aphorism seems to be the basic form of juridical logos. It is as law that the Mishnah structurally sets Talmudic logos in the mode of interruption, as "a very strange book indeed, a unicum even on the rabbinic scene, a fortiori in world literature, one composed of many and disparate elements, all 'mixed up' with each other."[54]

I continue contemplating the Mishnah as the Talmud's basic juridical logos in agreement with Kant and Schmitt, who identify law, imperfect logos, as the proper logos of the polis. Kant's full observation is that "Jewish faith, in its original setting, is a compendium of mere statutory laws, *on which a state constitution was founded*" (my emphasis). The Mishnah, as law, is the constitution of a polis, a *politeia*.[55] This is what makes Talmud, a broken logos, properly logo-political. However, Schmitt's work has also demonstrated that the polis, instituting the break of universal logos, what he called "evil," precisely as *institution*, as a "state," essentially tends toward self-absolutization and self-totalization, thus threatening to become the ultimate figure and source of evil, "imperialism." Finding that Mishnah, the basic logos of Talmud, is juridical is therefore insufficient for establishing the nature of the logo-political break performed by the Talmud because the juridical break of logos is also the basis of the Roman Empire, the Roman Catholic Church, and the modern state. The crucial question concerns the precise identity and nature of the polis for which the Mishnah is the basic law and logos.

I suggest that the Mishnaic polis is the Talmud. In fact, as noted previously, Talmud is one logos, Gemara, acting on or performing another logos, Mishnah. Talmud is action on Mishnaic juridical logos, an action on the authority of Mishnaic law. In this sense, the Talmud may be said to be praxis on the basis of Mishnaic constitution and, so, a Mishnaic polity. If the Mishnah is logo-political, the Talmud is a logo-*polis*. This is the sense by which I subscribe to Dolgopolski's description of "the political" in the Talmud not just as logos or text but also as actual *performance*—dance, play, theater, carnival. The fundamental Talmudic political performance of the Mishnaic law does not, however, proceed by way of *application*, that is, the realization of the juridical logos in the realm of things, the *fulfillment* of the law (πληρῶσαι) in a Jewish subject, or—at least not primarily—by way of establishing or remembering the law, as Dolgopolski argues. This is a description that better fits the concept of *mishnah* (literally, "repeating, reiterating, reciting"). Talmudic actualization of Mishnaic law seems to paradigmatically take the form of what Talmudic discourse typically considers to be the fundamental mitzvah, both law and practice, namely, the very praxis of *talmud*, or Aramaic Gemara: the praxis of something like "study."

Talmud is, accordingly, the practice of law as study. More accurately, Talmud puts the law into practice by performing the act of study on the law, which, without suspending the law, turns it into an object, an element, and a medium of study. Gemara is in this sense the translation of nomos in *torah*. Talmud performs Mishnah as torah. Mishnah-based study, talmud torah, takes place in the element of the law and as performance of the law, such that its study is *studium*: never pure theory but self-application, essentially praxis. In Talmudic discourse, talmud is not just "study" of Torah but typically עסק התורה, the concern, business, or work of torah. This, as mentioned previously, may be deemed as the paradigm or principle of Mishnah-abiding praxis, which functions as the constitutive principle of the Talmudic polis, hence a state of study.

The question of the Talmud's essence is accordingly the question of the nature of Talmudic "study." Its basic function, as noted, is to translate nomos into torah. In other words, Talmud acts on the law, a fragmented, imperfect logos, but instead of immediately fulfilling it—and thus healing and perfecting it as a direct, uninterrupted reference to the immediate reality of life, life beyond logos and law, "Jewish life"—Talmudic study enacts law *as* the imperfect, ongoing logos that it is. Talmudic study renders Mishanic law visible *as* logos. Talmud thus employs on the Mishnah the basic operations of logification, of turning or re-turning immediate data into discourse, image to concept. There are first and foremost the operations of question and negation, which Dolgopolski identified in the rhetorical forms of refutation and disagreement. But disagreement remembers, and refutation, or *relative* negation, as Hegel showed, is the very act of absolutization. In performing Mishnah as *imperfect* logos, Talmudic studium seems to deploy operations of question and negation more specifically and radically on the very logical quality of Mishnaic logos, that is, questioning or disrupting it *as* logos. In other words, Talmud questions—and thus renders visible or establishes—Mishnaic discourse not only and not paradigmatically as indicative or *dogmatic* (not just by objecting to what Mishnah says); rather, Talmud also questions the very signification and signifying function of Mishnaic logos. Talmud, as the translation of nomos into torah, translates or returns indication to signification, words to signs and letters.

A common procedure for this purpose, already featured in the Mishnah, is the representation of direct (immediate) through indirect (mediated) speech, namely, *the quote*. The quote produces the double effect of enacting law as broken logos. First, it fragments the unity of logos, an effect not of remembering but of dismembering logos. This rupture in logos as logos interrupts the fundamental logical operation and unity of signifying, of referring to and rendering visible an object or concept and so creating some representation, perception, or realization (in Husserlian terms: *Anschauung*, "intuition") of having a meaning. This interruption of signification, of object-intuition, however, creates, as a second basic effect of talmud, another intuition or visibility, namely, of the *sign* itself. Talmud exposes the law as words in language. Here, *words* means neither the "signified" (not meanings or concepts) nor pure "signifiers" but rather signifying *things*, which have not only a semantic being but also a real, physical existence: letters. Talmudic translation of law into logos, of Mishnah into Torah, then, enacts law not exactly as logos but—in Derridean terms—as *gramma*, that is, as writing or text, as the individual corpus of the Mishnah. Talmudic performance thus "fulfills" the Mishnaic law in the sense of realizing and materializing it as logos, by solidifying its signs not just as moments in time but also as things in space. Referencing Dolgopolski, Talmud thus generates not only memory but also *earth*. In Talmud, the Mishnaic juridical logos becomes a real and actual site for its own interpersonal performance, the site of its Talmudic polis.

It is in this nonmetaphoric, *literal* sense that Talmud may be described as a "traveling homeland" in the sense that the text is the real, physical place of the Talmudic polity. The reality of this polis would be the reality of its sign, whose signification (its function of referring to and indicating or naming some "thing") was interrupted, broken, or suspended. "Traveling homeland" would therefore mean not that Talmudic polis is everywhere "at home," as Boyarin's notion of *diaspora* asserts, but rather that Talmudic polis has its sole place in Talmudic text, is thus nowhere, in no real place "at home." Talmud is the logo-polis of exile. This exile is universal because it is exile not only from a specific land but also from the very dimension of extratextual territory, namely, from the perfection of logos and meaning as an immediate, sovereign presence, as pure intuition and bare life. Talmud is exile not just from Judea but also from the Jewish. The singularity of Talmudic deterritorialization requires further patient analysis.[56] Its *exilic* operation would need to be distinguished from diaspora as well as from Gnostic *Entweltlichung*, which, based on Hans Jonas's analysis, does not exercise exile from all presence but rather causes a shift, switch, and turn from worldly to otherworldly presence.[57] This line of contemplation would further allow—and require—a clearer perspective on the Talmudic polis as a historical logo-political project of universal exile in relation to Rome as a project of universal state and presence, a project of Empire.[58] Additional focus should be directed toward the aforementioned relation between the two different logo-political responses to Roman imperialism that are the Roman Catholic Church, instituting a separation of powers, and the Talmud, instituting something like underground opposition or resistance, world polis in exile.

YISRAEL

Taking a more specific look at the Talmudic text, I return to the question of Talmudic political singularity, that is, the question of the Talmud's people, and, more specifically, the question concerning the exact logo-political nature of this singularity in relation to the Jewish and particularism. I previously noted the absence of "the Jewish" as self-naming in the Talmud—but what's in a name? In what way is "the Jewish" categorically different from, say, "Yisrael," one of the more common names used by Talmudic discourse for designating its political self?[59] Significantly, there is no Talmudic tractate dedicated to "Yisrael" or to determining other basic categories and issues regarding the Talmudic self. There is no Talmudic constitution. Insights gained from Schmitt's work emphasize the significance of a tractate dedicated to the Talmud's foe, *avodah zarah*, which I suggest as a central topos for examining the Talmud's logo-political understanding of itself and for the reading of which I now provide a few reflections.

Avodah zarah, literally foreign work, worship, performance, or praxis, functions in Talmudic discourse as a Schmittian concept for the foreignness that constitutes an existential, ontic negation of the Talmudic self.[60] Not only is avodah zarah punishable with death, but the foreigners in Mishnah Avodah Zarah are considered potential murderers.[61] Maimonides could thus posit the prohibition on avodah zarah as being "against all of the mitzvot," such that "Yisrael who performed avodah zarah is like a goy."[62] In modern discourse, this ontic negation was transposed into the logo-politics of "the Jewish." R. Adin Steinsaltz's *Introduction to Tractate Avodah Zarah* describes avodah zarah as "the complete negation of the Jewish essence."[63] Similarly, in Jewish Studies, avodah zarah is typically understood as dividing between "Jews and non-Jews."[64] I claim—or rather indicate elements for the claim—that this is a paradigmatic instance of *effacement* of Talmud by the Jewish, an effacement that is connected to the very understanding of avodah zarah or, more fundamentally, to the very reading or even perception of the words עבודה זרה, namely, to the understanding—and the translation—of these words as a name for *idolatry*.

According to scholarly research, the Mishnaic term *avodah zarah*, which, before naming anything, signifies "foreign work," can be read in relation to and *as acting on*—that is, interpreting and replacing or *refuting*— the proper biblical term for idolatry: the worship of *elohim aherim* (אלוהים אחרים), "other gods."[65] Notably, the postbiblical transformation of this notion, for instance, in the Mishnah's contemporary Tertullian, into the category of *idolatria*, literally meaning "the worship of small images", removes the direct reference to "other gods" and thus *all* reference to the master referent "God." The category of idolatry accordingly transforms the prohibition on "other gods" to a preclusion of and prohibition on any direct reference to God as the paradigmatic referent, the paradigm of paradigm, the paradigm of *idol*: of idea, form, and *image*. Idolatria signifies and precludes the idolatry of theology, of the discourse on—and, so, the cult of—the object "God" as the Object-God. The Mishnah also speaks of avodah zarah as the worship of images.[66] The concept avodah zarah, however, effects a further refutation or suspension of the notion of "idolatry." It suspends not only the reference to the object "God" as the master image but also the reference to the *idol*, to the object "image" itself. The category avodah zarah thus performs a radicalization of the prohibition effected by the category *idolatria* by instituting the idolatry of "idolatry," that is, the idolatry of seeing the problem of idolatry in the identity of its object, rather than in the—foreign—quality of its praxis (*latria*).[67] Consequently, the category of avodah zarah signifies and precludes the cult of objects, primarily in the foundational praxis of objectification, namely, doxic or indicative discourse, perfected logos. The negation of avodah zarah is the interruption, suspension, and *performance* of logos as event and verb, as ongoing signification—signification without perception, or Talmud.

The basic project of Mishnah Avodah Zarah is to suspend the image, beginning with the image of the suspended image, the image of "avodah zarah." The Mishnah does this by suspending any notion of avodah zarah as a foreign substance and retrieving the ontic opposition effected by the category avodah zarah, that is, the contrast between the avodah zarah praxis (the foreign) and the Mishnaic praxis (the self), from a substantive, static being to the process of signification, from perfected to imperfect logos. The Mishnah transforms the sociopolitical opposition caused by the prohibition on avodah zarah, which is the foundational principle of its political project, from the physical, absolute negation of war (as the Bible prescribes in relation to worshippers of "other gods") into a dynamic configuration of relative tensions and negotiations, from polemos to polemics. This is done foundationally through the inscription of avodah zarah as a legal category within Mishnaic law and thus as an institution of the Mishnaic polis. The first provisions of the Mishnah institute and regulate commerce and the limits of commerce with avodah zarah practitioners. These practitioners are not referred to as "evil" (ontically negative) but as שוטים ("fools"), the epistemically negative with whom the Mishnah stages polemic dialogues.[68]

Mishnaic laws on avodah zarah thus constitute what Moshe Halbertal called a "neutral space," which he described in Enlightenment terminology as a "common ground of humanity and citizenship shared by all regardless of their particular historical identity."[69] According to Halbertal, this neutral human polity would suspend the political significance of communal particularities and suspend the significance of the political by referring it to "the real," such that Mishnaic law would do nothing more than "reflect a reality of two communities, Jewish and pagan, entangled with one another, within the Hellenistic cities of the land of Israel."[70] In this context, Halbertal's suggested perspective of the enlightened "neutral human" recalls Schmitt's critical observation on the intimacy between liberalism and imperialism since, in this Hellenistic context, creating a neutral space for the coexistence of "entangled" Jews and pagans, and others, was the project of imperial Roman law.[71] Halbertal acknowledges that the Mishnaic category of avodah zarah does not limit or relativize but rather *universalizes* the application of the biblical prohibition on idolatry.[72] The neutrality of the space generated by Mishnah Avodah Zarah is the universalization of the *Mishnaic* or, to use Halbertal's categories, "Jewish" space. Because of the operation of logification and deontologization— and so universalization—carried out by the category of avodah zarah, the Mishnah can be interpreted as an imperial Jewish, not Roman, project in which "the Jewish" presents itself as the neutral, "the human," which may therefore generate the common space—a Jewish State—of Jews and pagans, of Jews and non-Jews, who, in this configuration, would represent the nonneutral and nonhuman.

I suggest that it is as *resistance* to this potential imperialism of Mishnaic logification of antiidolatry law, as resistance to Halbertal's "Jewish" reading of the Mishnah, that we can read the Talmudic performance of the Mishnah. This is the second element of my claim that the Jewish reading of Avodah Zarah effaces the Talmud: a basic Talmudic operation on Mishnah Avodah Zarah consists of interrupting and breaking the Mishnah's seeming neutrality by shifting the problem of avodah zarah, of the foreign objectifying praxis from the foreign to the self or, more accurately, by interrupting the objectification of the *difference* between foreign and self—by rendering visible and suspending the image of the anti-Talmudic Foreign vis-à-vis the image of the Talmudic Self.

I emphasize here the discursive process set in motion by the first Gemara Avodah Zarah, which begins by questioning the most fundamental identity of the Mishnaic self as text: its orthography.[73] The Talmudic performance undoes Mishnaic neutrality by reconfiguring the relation between the anonymous, direct-speaking Mishnaic law and avodah zarah practitioners—goyim—as a political opposition between the named entities "Yisrael" and "The Nations of the World." The naming is followed by imaging, an eschatological vision based on Isaiah 43:9, in which Rome and Persia, the literal Nations of the World, the two world empires, are presented not as idolatrous but as fully subscribing to the same fundamental praxis that defines the Mishnah's rabbinic polis *against* the foreign praxis of avodah zarah. The empire is imagined as being based on the praxis of *torah*, עסק התורה, through the people of Yisrael. This vision demonstrates or renders *imaginable* how the Mishnah could function as the constitutive logos for an imperial polis. Yet what renders this imperial performance of the Mishnah "foreign" to the Talmud and Talmudic Yisrael is, according to the Talmudic vision, the adherence of the Nations of the World to the principle of the absolute, sovereign ontological "self"—their own selves, Yisrael's self and the separation thereof. The Talmud conceives of avodah zarah as the praxis of the collective "self" (לצורך עצמכם, "for the sake of your [common] self").

By contrast, the logo-political singularity of Talmudic Yisrael would not arise from its sovereign individuality, its absolute particularity, its perfected existence as a substantive self. On the contrary, the singularity of Yisrael would consist of rejecting absolute sovereign selfhood, which goes hand in hand with resisting all perfected systems of logos and meaning. Yisrael's singularity is linked to the semantic imperfection of the Talmudic logos, the Torah, as *gramma*, a signifying thing, which, as noted in the Talmudic narrative, cannot be comprehended by a concept but only indicated as "this" (זאת).[74] Talmudic Yisrael thus emerges as the universal project of exile of the political self from a territorial presence to the homeland of text. Therefore, it can be concluded that the ultimate foe of the Talmud, whose negation would ontically define the Talmudic self, is not Rome and Persia or any other "foreign" nations but the Talmudic self—Yisrael—in its nonexilic mode of substantive particularity. The ultimate foe of the Talmud, with whom the Talmud stages no polemics and who can thus be said to be the Talmud's actual ontic negation and ultimate avodah zarah, may be designated as "the Jewish."

ELAD LAPIDOT is Professor of Jewish Thought at the University of Lille, France. His publications include *Jews Out of the Question: A Critique of Anti-Anti-Semitism*; Hebrew translation with introduction and commentary (with R. Bar) of Hegel's *Phänomenologie des Geistes*, vol. 1; *Heidegger and Jewish Thought: Difficult Others*, edited with M. Brumlik; and *Être sans mot dire: La logique de Sein und Zeit*.

NOTES

1. Dolgopolski, *What Is Talmud?*, 7, 1.
2. Dolgopolski, *Other Others*, 8, 200, 209.
3. Ibid., 8.
4. Ibid., 2.
5. Badiou, *Polemics*, 230. For a critical analysis, see Lapidot, "Jew, Uses of the Word." But see Badiou's less-known self-correction in his exchange with Ivan Segré in Segré, "Controverse sur la question de l'universel" and Badiou, "Discussion Argumentée."
6. See Elad Lapidot, "On the Translation of Philosophy."
7. To the effect of effacing "the special characteristics of rabbinic texts," see Hayes, *Between the Babylonian and Palestinian Talmuds*, 8, 5, and 9, respectively. It should be noted, however, that Hayes understands the task of her reading of the Talmud, in the occasion tractate Avodah Zarah, as gaining "insight into the rabbis' view of Jewish-Gentile relations in Palestine and Babylonia" (30), that is, Talmud as a literarily complex perspective on Jews.
8. Dolgopolski, *Other Others*, 8.
9. Ibid., 92.
10. Ibid., 28.
11. Ibid., 31, 1.
12. Ibid., 9.
13. Ibid.
14. Ibid., 4.
15. Boyarin, *Socrates*; understanding "satire" "in the sense of *satura*, a mixture of things that don't belong together, of things that contradict each other, not as a censure of immorality" (27), what Boyarin terms the "seriocomical": "we find the *same* rabbis as the producers of all that is ethical, religious, and fine in the tradition and as being involved in wild aggadic narratives that so sharply disturb and disrupt the picture of the rabbis as objects to be imitated and indeed the picture of the Torah as eternal and holy," 22; ibid., 29.
16. Ibid., 31.
17. Ibid., 32.
18. Boyarin, *A Traveling Homeland*. For a more detailed critique, see Lapidot, "Deterritorialized Immigrant."
19. Ibid., 30.
20. Ibid., 62.
21. Ibid., 32.
22. Ibid., 11.
23. Ibid., 91, 188, 94.
24. Frye, "Carl Schmitt's Concept of the Political"; Gross, *Carl Schmitt und die Juden*.
25. I developed this question in my last book, *Jews Out of the Question*.
26. Schmitt, *Politische Theologie*, 47.
27. Schmitt, "Das Zeitalter der Neutralisierungen und Entpolitisierungen," in *Der Begriff des Politischen*.

28. Schmitt, *Politische Theologie*, 43.
29. Ibid., 38.
30. Ibid., 18.
31. Schmitt, *Der Begriff des Politischen*.
32. Ibid., 31.
33. Schmitt, *Römischer Katholizismus*. In this sense, "Political Atheology," a title that Dolgopolski, on Boyarin's suggestion, contemplated as expressing his distance from Schmitt, could also describe Schmitt's own project (see Dolgopolski, *Other Others*, x).
34. Schmitt, *Politische Theologie*, 61–63; *Der Begriff des Politischen*, 55–63.
35. Ibid., 60.
36. Ibid., 59.
37. Ibid., 34–35.
38. Ibid., 60.
39. Schmitt does not explicitly analyze the theological form of the dogma. He does, however, comment on his great source of inspiration, Donoso Cortés, that "in his systematic train of thought there was an effort to be concise in the good dogmatic tradition of theology" (*Politische Theologie*, 66), a description that may apply to Schmitt.
40. Ibid., 36–37.
41. Schmitt, "Vorwort," in *Der Begriff des Politischen*, 9–11. See also Lapidot, "Prisoner-of-War."
42. Cf. Schmitt, *Politische Theologie II*, 72.
43. Schmitt, *Der Begriff des Politischen*, 12; *Politische Theologie*, 70.
44. Ibid., 57.
45. Schmitt, "Vorwort," 15: "The revolutionary abuse [*Mißbrauch*] of concepts of a classic legality."
46. Ibid., 16.
47. Schmitt, *Der Nomos der Erde*.
48. Ibid., 16.
49. Schmitt, *Römischer Katholizismus*, 14.
50. I consider Mishnah and Gemara as two logoi, two regimes of discourse, which, even if they do determine the dominant and defining features of two textual corpora, respectively, are nonetheless not neatly separate between these corpora but are present in both.
51. Kant, *Die Religion*, 125.
52. Dolgopolski, *Other Others*, 144–55.
53. See the critical discussion of this tendency in the work of Gershom Scholem, as recently offered by Raz-Krakotzkin, *Toda'at Mishnah, Toda'at Mikra*.
54. Boyarin, *Socrates*, 23. This raises the question concerning other rabbinic textual corpora, which are also edited in the form of compendium but are less obviously "juridical" than the Mishnah, such as midrash.
55. Or, as Ron Naiweld describes it, "an imagined political regime"; see his "The Rabbinic Model of Sovereignty," 409.
56. See Dolgopolski, "How Else Can One Think Earth?"; Lapidot, "Deterritorialized Immigrant."
57. See Jonas, *Gnosis und spätantiker Geist I*; *Gnosis und spätantiker Geist II*. See Lapidot, "Gnosis und Spätantiker Geist II."
58. For a recent discussion of the Mishnah as a juridico-political project inscribed within the imperial context, see Naiweld, "The Rabbinic Model of Sovereignty." Naiweld

suggests that "the imperial model can [...] be regarded as the infrastructure of mishnaic politics," 415. In contrast with my contemplation of Talmudic polis as a universal counterimperial project, however, Naiweld observes that Mishnaic rabbis "did not conceive their Israel as a universal political entity but as a particular one" (416), such that their "resistance" to Rome would have proceeds for the cause of particularism.

59. I use the orthography "Yisrael" rather than the more common "Israel" to interrupt and destabilize the indicative force of this sign and render it visible as a sign.

60. Zohar, "Idolatry," indicates that the "foreign" of avodah zarah means not just "other" but also "illegitimate." See also Zohar, "Partitions around Common Public Space," speaking of the "extreme demonization" (155) of avodah zarah practitioners, which "justifies negating their existence" (156). By contrast, Naiweld interprets the Mishnaic category of avodah zarah as introducing the rabbinic "god to the imperial system as one other god—the best for those who believe in him, and simply 'other' or 'foreign' for those who not." Naiweld, "The Organization of Religious Signs."

61. M. Avodah Zarah 2:1.

62. Maimonides, Moses, 1135–204. Mishneh Torah: Hu Ha-Yad Ha-Ḥazaḳah. Jerusalem: Mosad ha-Rav Ḳuḳ, 2:7–8.

63. Steinsaltz, "Hakdama LeMasekhet Avodah Zarah," in *Talmud Bavli: Masekhet Avodah Zarah*, 7.

64. See, for example, Hayes, *Between the Babylonian and Palestinian Talmuds*, 24; Furstenberg, "The Rabbinic View of Idolatry," 366; Gvaryahu, "A New Reading," 207.

65. See Naiweld, "The Organization of Religious Signs"; Zohar, "Idolatry," 66.

66. M. Avodah Zarah 3:1–3; Gvaryahu, "A New Reading," 221.

67. Zohar refers to the "consciousness of the worshipers" ("Idolatry," 75). From here arises the linguistically unique rabbinic use of the expression *avodah zarah*, as observed by Zohar, "designating the object of the action (what is worshipped) through the form of the verbal noun (the worship)" ("Idolatry," 65).

68. M. Avodah Zarah 4:7, 3:4.

69. Halbertal, "Coexisting with the Enemy," 163.

70. Ibid., 159.

71. See Naiweld, "The Organization of Religious Signs": "The problem of cohabitation of Jews and Gentiles was an imperial one." Naiweld thus lays the ground for a reading of Mishnah Avodah Zarah in the context of the Roman Empire and as a project *within* the imperial order.

72. Ibid., 161.

73. B. Avodah Zarah 2b.

74. Ibid.

3

But I Say

The Political (Dis)appearance of the Past in Rabbinic Citation

SERGEY DOLGOPOLSKI

"But I say..."
MATTHEW 5

"But I say..."
(PALESTINIAN TALMUD SOTAH 7:1)

INTRODUCTION

And the reading of the Shema [can be pronounced in any idiom.[1]][...] Rabbi [Yehudah the Prince] said: But I say, the reading of the Shema[2] shall only be pronounced in the Holy Tongue.[3] Rabbi Levi son of the Tailor went to Caesarea. There he heard voices reading Shema in [a] Hellenist [tongue, i.e., in Greek]. He demanded to stop doing that. Rabbi Yose said: This is how I say: What, the one who cannot read from Aramaic, should not be reading [the Shema] at all? Rather, [such person] can fulfill his/her duty in any tongue he knows [to read]! [To which] Rabbi Berakhiah[4] responded: Behold, the Esther Scroll: If one knows to read it in both Aramaic [lettering] and in the babbling tongue [= Greek],[5] one does not fulfill one's obligation, except in Aramaic lettering. Rabbi Mannah[6] said, About the Esther Scroll: if one who knows how to read it [in] Aramaic lettering and to babble it [in Greek] one can only fulfill his/her obligation in Aramaic lettering; but if one knows only to babble [in Greek] one can fulfill his/her obligation by babbling [in Greek] and similarly [such person] can fulfill his/her obligation in any other babbling. (Palestinian Talmud Sotah 7:1, 21b)[7]

The sequence in this excerpt is as follows: a citation from the Mishnah; a self-citation of Rabbi Yehudah the Prince to counter the Mishnah citation; an exemplary act of a confrontation between two self-citers—a visiting rabbi in Caesarea (Rabbi Levi), who represents Rabbi Yehudah the Prince's self-citation, and the local rabbi, Rabbi Levi, son of the Tailor, who retorted the visitor with another self-citing; Rabbi Berakhiah's citation to lessen the scope of Rabbi Yose's lenient rule by reducing it to an exception (for Greek); Rabbi Mannah's citation to extend the scope of the exception (beyond the "Greek" tongue alone).

The excerpt is from the corpus of the Palestinian Talmud (PT), the production of rabbinic schools of rhetoric in Tiberias, Caesarea, and Sepphoris between the third and fifth centuries and its rabbinic interpretations through the Middle Ages to the modern period. A complication lies in the fact that this text also belongs to the living corpus and tradition of thought about how memory can tame oblivion. It is a *living* tradition of the struggle of memory with oblivion, which the copula *and* severs and dissects. Copulating and diverging traditions of thought among the schools of philosophy (academies) and schools of the Talmud study (yeshivas) result from this dissection. One result is a sense of two or more traditions with different antecedents. The tradition of philosophy sees itself as continuing and interpreting the schools or academies of Plato and Aristotle, including their antecedents, the pre-Socratics. In this way, the schools become the beginning of the tradition, even if they emerge *after* their posited antecedents. Similarly, the tradition of the two Talmuds interprets the rabbinic academy in Yavneh in the late first through second centuries, leading to the Yavneh academy's distant, 3rd century product the Mishnah (a unified composition, codex, or testament for another divine law in conjunction with Scripture). In this way, the academy in Yavneh also becomes the beginning of the tradition, even if the tradition emerges from Yavneh's posited antecedents: the Scribal and Priestly traditions of the Holy Writ or Scriptures and their exegetical interpretation, midrash.[8] In both cases, a beginning (the Platonic or rabbinic academy, respectively) comes after its antecedent.

Structural similarity among traditions with beginnings that produce their own antecedents from the past suggests a commonality in their relationship to the past. Both the rabbinic rhetorical schools after Yavneh and the philosophical schools after Plato's academy in Athens (as well as in Egyptian Alexandria or Phoenician Palestine and Syria, up until these schools' closures with the advent of Christian Rome) posit beginnings that produce their antecedents from the past.

The complexity and stakes of this relationship to the past require careful consideration. That consideration, however, should advance without putting forward yet another specter of a common beginning (neither a "new" nor an "other"), even if some commonality might exist.[9] One candidate is the "archaic" struggle that memory and remembering launch against the never-ending onset of oblivion.[10] Rather than accept the premise that this archaic struggle against oblivion constitutes a common antecedent for the rabbinic and philosophical schools, the guiding question in rethinking the copula of these traditions should be how to situate each school within that archaic struggle as an ongoing process that implicates the beginnings of each one. In the following pages, I approach the preceding excerpt from the PT with this question in mind.

E-FACING OBLIVION

One way to think through the powers of copulation between the rhetorical schools of the PT and the philosophical academies is to situate both vis-à-vis the "archaic Greece" (Marcel Detienne) of taming oblivion and "mastering truth."[11] According to Detienne's reading of Hesiod, the "masters of truth" are the Muses who help humans sing the laudatory song for the past in order to tame the ever-arriving oblivion. Muses can do this, but they can also inspire praising of the past by making the past pleasant. In the second case, oblivion proliferates in pseudolaudation and pseudoremembering. The Muses' mastery lies in their ability to go in either direction, and no one else can determine their chosen path. The sweeping power of oblivion is the river of *Lethe*, and the "truth" under the Muses' control, *a-letheia*, is a privative term from *lethe*. What other languages describe with positive or primary terms (*truth, veritas, Wahrheit*, etc.) is here only a privative: the act of taming the waters' current. This explains the "archaic distinction" between forgetting and its attempted interruption—the "truth." I borrow the coinage from Jan Assmann's term "Mosaic distinction," which is discussed shortly.

To follow Detienne's argument further, the archaic distinction shifts over time into a "platonic distinction" between "what-is" and "what-seems-to-be." The resistance to the waters of Lethe is achieved with the search for "what-is-the-case-in-each case" as opposed to "what-seems-to-be-the-case-in-each-case." "Mastery" moves from Muses to "lovers of wisdom," who persist in this search. Thus the positive assertion of "being" replaces the privative nature of one's resistance to the waters of Lethe, the displacement of the distinction between oblivion and memory by a distinction between being and seeming-to-be.

Thinking through the copulation of the PT and philosophy in view of oblivion needs to account for another distinction, Jan Assmann's "Mosaic distinction" as well.[12] This is the distinction between appealing to multiple deities by calling them multiple names and evoking the exclusionary deity. The name of the exclusionary deity, the tetragrammaton or, per the English rendition, "G-d," is graphic—indeed, glyphic. It defies any evocation through laudatory singing or speaking. The tetragrammaton of the glyphs-to-have-become-letters spells the divine name, which, according to the rabbinic tradition, a human is not to (or perhaps even no longer able to) vocalize. Under the Mosaic distinction, the parallel of *lethe* is in שכח, in the primary and assertive sense of "leaving," "letting go," and "ceasing to care"—as distinct from the secondary and privative sense of obliviating or forgetting.[13] One is not "to let go" of the tetragrammaton and his teachings but rather is commanded to "remember" the tetragrammaton the way one remembers (or forgets) things (including deities) in the world. Similarly to *lethe*, שכח features the primary operation, which, in turn, renders both the agency of memory and its content (false or true) a secondary product. The operation of (not) "letting go" remains fundamentally primary; *even* for human beings confronting the exclusionary deity of Assmann's distinction, the primacy of positive memory is constantly stressed. Unlike Detienne's Muses in Hesiod, the exclusionary deity of Moses commands: Do *not* "let go" of "my commandments" more foundationally than "to remember" these commandments in their procedural specificity. Yet in the rabbinic school in Caesarea, the proper procedures of "remembering" the tetragrammaton in and through action are coming afore and taking precedence. If the destroyed Temple could have been the Place where the Name of the tetragrammaton is not let go (the primary operation), in rabbinic schools outside of Jerusalem, after the Temple, the Name of the tetragrammaton must be "remembered" through remembering and observing the proper procedures.

The result is that in the rabbinic schools, the secondary task of memory and remembering takes precedence over the primary task of not "letting go." More precisely, the rabbis consider themselves to be united in the endeavor of not "letting go" of the Name, while they actively polemicize among themselves about the proper procedures (*ius*, הלכה) for remembering the Name by acting properly in a given locale, so that G-d will not let go of them.

The teachings of the rabbinic school in Caesarea are far not only from Jerusalem's Temple but also from Hesiod's Lethe. If lethe is a constant thread to forget, the rabbis take for granted that the divine law cannot be let go of, cannot be forgotten. The tetragrammaton triumphs over lethe and grants his adherents the inability to forget. Their challenge, however, becomes to remember. Rabbinic polemic about procedures of remembering by and through action ensures that the law of G-d is not let go of. In other words, "not letting go" becomes necessary but insufficient, while remembering procedure, in a noncontestable way, becomes both necessary and impossible.

This complexity of relationships between the (non)forgettable law of the past and the impossibility of remembering it without polemics allows us to think more precisely through the copulation of rabbinic and philosophical traditions—or, rather, the "tradition of tradition" that each constructs for itself.[14] Achieving precision requires reading the preceding excerpt from the PT slowly.

LIFTING "AND," READING SLOWLY

I do not use the phrase *slow reading* loosely. What does *slow* mean in relation to *close* and *distant* reading? "Distant reading" (Moretti) emerged in response to "close reading" (Wimsatt and Beardsley), yet the common denominator between the two is a stable "distance."[15] The proximity of the close reading means the "authorial intent" is an inner part of the read rather than the starting point defining the read from the outside. The loss of this proximity of intent in the distant reading means that the "intent" is no longer attributed to a person, an author. Rather, such a depersonified intent becomes attributed to and determined by vocabularies in masses of texts united by geographical and chronological principles. The proximity locks the personal "intent" of the "author" in the text. Distancing depersonalizes the intent while still locking and stabilizing the intent in the texts framed in the chronological and geographical terms. In contrast to either of these ways of stabilization and stability, the slow reading deals with speed and timing—more concretely, with the time and speed of appearance and disappearance of the past that a reading creates. These two processes advance simultaneously and as one. I describe the complexity of that dual-singular movement—and its speed—with what I will call *e-facing* the past in citation, a process of both giving the past a face and erasing the past through that very face-giving. Reading e-facing corresponds to a slow reading as a reading putting this double process on display. The past in question is that of citation, the speed is of the simultaneous appearance and disappearance of that past, and the reading able to address that elusive past of citation is "slow reading."

The objective is to reclaim the significance of a site of citing, the PT, for the developed horizon of the question of citation in the tradition of thought in philosophy, even as the PT remains irreducible to that horizon. Conversely, this chapter engages the intellectual resources of philosophical or literary-critical analysis of citation to shed light, and more specifically to shed darkness, on the PT so that this archive can display—in the dimmed rather than bright light of philosophy—a new view of the problem with citing the law of the past.

DEPARTING FROM MODERN SUBJECT

To begin with, let us examine Derrida's analysis of the limits of citation in his reading of Blanchot's "An Account?" ["Un Récit?"] Derrida claims that a survivor of the event cannot be a witness because the personal experience of an "I" who survived an event can only repeat the experience rather than provide a legally acceptable testament of the event without losing the personal sense of event and thus losing the power of having witnessed it altogether. The problem lies in the fact that always a singular experience, the personal witness does not translate into the universal language of testimony and therefore cannot become testament either. This is similar to Benveniste's analysis of the difference between the survivor and the witness. For Derrida, the survivor can only repeatedly survive the event always singularly and always for the first and only time. To use Benveniste's terms, the survivor of the event is *superstes*, the one who survived and accounts for the event without having ever attended it in the way that a *testis*, a third-party witness, could have.[16] Can a law officer (a prosecutor or judge) take a *superstes* seriously? Can such an officer see anything there except a story that has been lost or forgotten? Can a modern historian regard a *superstes* as a valid historical source?

The excerpt from the PT diverges from this modern context. In "But I say" the "I" might be a *superstes*. Yet there is neither the expectation nor the problem of this "I" having personally lived through a story that took place in the past before the eyes of a third-party witness, or *testis*. The "I" in "But I say" is not the modern "I" that survived a personal event, which that "I" cannot help but only live over and over without letting the event become the story of the past. And yet this "I" of the PT offers a testimony to the law and expects that this testimony will be accepted as a definitive testament—even if, as we will see, there is a clash of such expectations.

What does it mean, then, to self-cite or, more generally, to cite a law with the help of such a nonmodern "I"? In the modern context, self-citing—the citing of "my" own experience—is a form of a more general practice, that of citing (grasping, capturing) what was (said) before. In "But I say," the relationship reverses. Self-citing, or asserting that what *is* said is said *by me*, is the core and secret power of any citing. How so?

Self-citing in "But I say" can reveal something important about nonmodern citing more generally. A simple act of presenting a rule or exemplary act as self-citation gives the rule or example more power than a simple pronouncement or performance could have. The power is in emphatically asserting that which, as a result, no longer needs to have been imagined to have been already said or performed in the past; yet it still exerts the power of having come from the past. In the terms of Derrida and Blanchot, such citation would come from the past of the never-ending "personal" event. In the PT, by contrast, it is a citation of an event that "I" am not to be assumed to have "personally" survived: a past that does not even purport to amount to story or history. In this context, *superstes* is the privileged *testis* to the law—a reversal, indeed a subversion, of the former problem of *superstes*, the only survivor as an insufficient *testis*. Instead of testifying as a *testis* to report as a third party what has been observed, in "But I say," testifying is living up, that is, surviving the law, without necessarily having "lived it" at any particular point in the past. Such a *superstes* to the law is closer to the law's *martyr*: a role not always requiring to die testifying but always meant to live the law of the past by making it both public and present by the power of having come from the past, in which "I" neither has nor is expected to have a story to tell. If for Blanchot the law is on the site of the story, for "But I say," the law is on the site of the event of the past, which is not "mine" at all.

To appreciate the importance of this difference between the two modes of witnessing is to situate the PT excerpt in the framework of the following broader distinctions: the archaic Greek distinction between the human default—oblivion—and the challenge of being human as that of fighting against the powers of oblivion, the replacement thereof by a Platonic distinction between what is and what-seems-to-be, the Mosaic distinction (Assmann) between the one ineffable and the many effable G-ds, and the Roman distinction between procedural law (*ius*) and the law of the nomos or fate. These distinctions provide a lens through which to appreciate the differences between modern modes of witnessing and the witnessing in the PT with greater precision, to free up the witnessing in the PT from confusing it with modern attribution of the witnessing to the personal experience of the "I."

The power of the law as testified in the PT is the power of the past, which is, however, not quite a power of either story or history, if the latter means an account of "what was" or "had been" in the past. The power of the law comes from the past as past, not from what took place therein. That is to say, in the PT excerpt, laws reach their followers from the past but are available only in the present and only as citations—references to an antecedent source of authority, which, however, has not and never had any other presence.

Can citing laws in the present, then, fully encapsulate the law of the past even if and precisely because this law does not necessarily concern "what was"?

To slow the reading even more, the preceding excerpt is not unlike the Sermon on the Mount in Matthew 5, directed, as the latter is, against Pharisees and Scribes. "We hear [from them] . . . but I say."[17] What this means, however, is not only or primarily that the Sermon on the Mount is one of the earlier forms of what would become a rabbinic debate[18] but rather that citing the law by citing oneself, "self-citation" was—in either real or idealized Roman Palestine—a form of establishing an authority in a locale. So acts Rabbi Yehudah, the Prince in Yavneh, the only self-citer in the entire Mishnah, which he "edited" or "composed," as does Rabbi Yose, laying claim to Rabbi Yehudah's authority not only in Yavneh but also in Caesarea. So, too, does Rabbi Levi, son of the Tailor, who defends his local authority in Caesarea against Rabbi Levi's intrusion (done as it is on behalf of Rabbi Yehudah the Prince). In short, to self-cite is to claim one's authority in a locale. The same can be said of the Sermon on the Mount.

POWERS AND APORIAS OF SELF-CITATION

There are many more and far more crucial powers involved in self-citation. In addition to claiming or stabilizing local authority, it also reveals a deeply unstable nature of citing the law of the past in the first place. Both the fragility and necessity of self-citing in a locale reveal something important about any individual citation or testimony of the law, be it in the form of a cited rule or of performing, or accounting for, an exemplary act. An exemplary act or an act of martyrdom in either the broader and weaker sense of testifying the law through publicizing (and, in particular, self-publicizing) one's deeds or the narrower and stronger sense of dying for the sake of such public testament is even more obviously an act of a self-citation. The logic of self-citation suggests that I act in a certain way to exemplify a certain law.[19] Martyrdom as a testament is thus always a form of saying, "But I say." Less obviously, but no less strongly, the mere act of citing the law in the form of a rule in public is also an act of citing oneself. For, after all, there always is an individual, a testifier. Even if that individual can omit an explicit part of self-citing ("But I say"), it is always this particular individual who puts themself on the line in citing the rule.[20] Applicable to any citer, self-citer included, citation and self-citation are never establishing the law on behalf of the citer's will. Rather, rhetorically and politically, self-citing means that what I say is not really my own invention; rather, it is a citation and thus a law of the past of which I have an account that is different from others' accounts. Testifying—thus self-citing the law in the form of rules or exemplary acts—is therefore fundamentally and always a citation of the law of the past, both in its affirmation of that law and in its negation of other accounts.

The conundrum of this citation is closely tied to whether the account, the citation, is a repetition of an already-given account or whether it is an account of something that cannot be accounted for. If the latter is true—or if it is at least a looming possibility, that is to say, if citation is (or can always be) the first and only affirmation of the law of the past—then that law cannot have any other account, any other form of presentation of making itself present.[21] This question of the (im)possibility of citation as repetition (in Derrida and Blanchot) remains important. Yet there is another and no less pressing question: What gives the citation power in the first place, that is, regardless of whether this citation is or is not repetition? What is and whence comes the power of words or acts as citations in the form of "But I say" (or, by extension, "I say"—the "But" always implied)? What power or authority do these words and acts gain, as compared to the same words not introduced as citations, that is, to the same bare words and acts if they emerge or act without the power of "But I say"?[22] The question, in other words, is not whether a citation, an account, is a repetition, an account of that for which one cannot account according to the very logic of the law. Rather, the question is how the possibility of an answer to that question (whether it is yes, no, or there-is-no-way-to-know) emerges in the first place. Part of this larger question is universal and can be expressed numerically, even if not digitally. The first is never the initial ordinal number, for there is no first before there is second. The second is thus the first number, the first possibility of counting. What comes second is first. This numerical paradox has some less abstract expressions: the "Old Testament" in Christianity is only the "old" by virtue of positing the "new," so that the new or ordinally second testament becomes the "first," without which there cannot be the ordinally first—"old"—Testament either. Yet beyond that numeric and therefore impersonal conundrum, there is a more personal one. This concerns the individuality, personality, and livelihood of a witness, with the possibility for *this* witness to be accepted as a *martyr* of testimony and ultimately of a testament. As a result of that acceptance, from the witness of a witness as testimony emerges a "testament"—the unchangeable and unavoidable "last will," one that the-witness-to-have-become-testament casts on the judges and audiences alike.

This series of aporias reveals a deep instability of citing the law of the past in any testimony, citation, or self-citation, despite and regardless of the express purpose of such citation to stabilize authority in a locale (whether Rabbi's Yavneh in the Mishnah, Rabbi Yose's [and Rabbi Berakhiah's] authority versus that of Rabbi Levi in Caesarea in the PT, or of Jesus of Nazareth on a Galilean mountain in Matthew versus the Pharisees).

PALESTINIAN TALMUD: MORAL COMPASS IN SEAS OF MEMORY?

The characters in the PT deal with a law that exceeds and precedes the moral order. For example, we can refer to this order as the "moral compass," always (and presumably, always only) pointing to the "north pole" of the "universally good." A witness (*testis* and *superstes* alike) to offer a testimony, acceptable by judges as a testament, commits an action that extends beyond and exceeds the moral order of an individual action. It is presumably always perceived as "good." As accepted (not only *offered*) witnesses, testaments exceed their agents; the "will" of a "testament" has an influence beyond the ones who committed or commissioned that "will."

The PT characters' acts of testimony exceed the legal order as well, for the power of the law is not controlled by the legal process either. Rather, for the characters, at least, that power comes from the past—the past as a form—rather than from a past as presentable or representable, citable, recitable, or accountable for.

These acts of testimony exceed the order of reason as well as of myth and the premythic ecstasies. And yet there remains an all-important difference in the structure of testimony in the PT. The laws that characters are testifying are not their personal or individual recollections, nor are they personal events that one either can or cannot account for. These testimonies engender memory of the law rather than any recollection, rather than any account of any personal past. Instead, the PT affords the personality of the testifier a much greater but also much less central role.

In a (not so rare) extreme, the testifier may even testify by and through their death, but the testament is always a rule or an exemplary act, not a personal experience (either recalled or evoked).

As compared to a personally experienced and accountable/unaccountable past with a certain, however elusive "content," the PT deals with the past *as past*, with the past as a *form*. This is not an empty form. As past, past cannot have any present and thus no (presentable, accountable for) content either; yet it has power. The effort of "But I say" is that effort, that power of the past as pure form and pure power at the same time. The danger of that effort, however, is that the presentation, presencing, making the past present can undermine the very power of it as the past. Instead of an aporia of an account that tells no story of the past, there emerges an aporia of the power of the past, which is only palpable through the present but which is in constant danger that its presentation will void its very power of the past.

With this consideration of citation and testimony, I outline the structure of the broader question of citation in relation to this chapter's questioning of the hitherto dominant "tradition of traditions," which separates the traditions of philosophy, theology, and rabbinic thought in (the) Talmud.

THE PALESTINIAN TALMUD: CITATION BETWEEN THE TRADITIONS

This broader question takes me to three different contexts in critical thought and scholarship where this argument has purchase: the concern with citing the law of the past, with political philology, and with the scholarship on the PT. I articulate the relationships between the three. One might simplistically see the first context as a theme or guiding question for my argument, that of citation. The second might be seen as a theoretical framework ("political philology," to be explained shortly) in which one deals with the question of citation, and the third, the PT, as a particular archive of texts that one approaches with this question and theoretical framework in mind. I describe a more complex and less linear nature of the relationships among the project of political philology, the scholarship on the PT, and the question of the citation of the law of the past.

I begin with political philology. Conceived in Gramsci's *Prison Notebooks* and more fully described in Geoffrey Waite, political philology is a way of critiquing a hidden inversion (metalepsis) of cause and effect in matters of thought, theory, and ideology.[23] Political philology regards such inversion as a broad (and well-hidden) ideological mechanism that may but does not have to engage explicit religious themes. Yet there remains an intimate and elided relationship between political philology and theology. Even when directly approaching religious themes, political philology has regarded the Christian theologeme of the possibility of a "new testament" to the law of the past as an object of critique that is taken for granted. That tacitly shaped the main thesis of this critique. The thesis was of the hidden reversal (metalepsis) of effect and cause along the lines of the theologeme of relationships between the two testaments. Thus the Old Testament (OT) *seems* to foreshadow the New Testament (NT), but *to the critical gaze of a political philologist*, the NT is a prerequisite for the OT to exist. The NT *seems* to be the effect but *is* the cause of the possibility of the OT to come to being. In this view, only the political-philological critique can lay bare the metalepsis. In other words, metalepsis cannot be practically undone, nor can relationships of cause and effect be restored except by the "political-philological" revolution. More prominently, a political philologist applies this critique of the cause-effect metalepsis to the theme of body-mind relationships, especially to what Geoffrey Waite criticizes as "visceral reason," or an ongoing, tacit inversion of the cause-effect relationships between the viscera and rational thinking and knowing. This applies to thinking through the relationships between past and present: the political philologist would argue that, just as thinking falsely ascribes itself to the viscera, so, too, does the present falsely ascribe itself to the past. For thinking through the relationships between the past and its presentation in citing, political philology is heuristic in discovering a hidden inversion in which the present (the citation of the law of the past) threatens to subjugate the past (from which this citation purportedly stems): the present presents itself as secondary to the past, yet the present is tacitly controlling the past—a control against which the political philologist calls for revolt.

The broader theme of the critique of visceral reason in political philology obscures a less prominent but much more crucial dependence of political philology on the Christian theologeme of the two testaments. A political philologist might see the relationship between the OT and NT as only one example of metalepsis, considering visceral reason and other broader topics to be the primary ideological battlefield against metalepsis. This would make metalepsis of the OT and NT only one outcome of the broader and more foundational metalepsis of all ideologies. But it is no less plausible that the political philologist repeats the symptom, reversing cause and effect. It is no less plausible that the metalepsis of the OT and NT is the *primary* metalepsis of all ideology, the hidden cause of all others. Once we commit to this heuristic shift in the political-philological way of thinking, it becomes increasingly relevant as a theoretical framework for our inquiry into citation in the PT.

The PT affords a clearer vision both of the theologeme of a new testament at work—intimating a broader and more self-critical view of political philology as a way of thought—and of the critique outside the confines of theology (even if it is still within the confines of the theologemes developed throughout theology's history). This leads to my third but no less important concern: the archive of the PT.

I approach the PT as an archive of text and thought in a programmatic disconnection from the traditional lines of its reception, which continues to influence both the traditional and academic study of the archive. In such a radical move against the lines of its reception, the PT displays and articulates a new complexity of the problem with citing the law of the past. It does so in a way that provides a new view of both the traditional Christian notion of the NT and a broader theologeme of the possibility of producing a new testament to the law of the past—without consigning the law of the past as the old law. The PT, in other words, necessitates a new political philology.

The relationship among the three contexts is thus not a linear one among a theoretical framework, a text, and a theme. Rather, the three elements form a counterpoint that structures the question of citing the law of the past. The PT offers a fresh perspective on the question of citation as the question of the very impossibility and necessity of citing the law of the past. The matter extends beyond the question of how to cite the law of the past without dismissing the past as "the old law"; for the citing and the testifying are, by definition, always new. The larger question is how to cite the law of the past without undermining the very nature of the past as past, that is, as distinct from the present.

POLITICAL PHILOLOGY BEYOND POLITICAL THEOLOGY?

At this point, the question is: Can the PT, as an archive of text and thought, open up a view of a political philology that frees itself from the political theology of metalepsis of the "Old" and "New" Testaments instead of reducing the role of critique to laying bare the metaleptic logic of relationships between the OT and NT?

From such a triple counterpoint arises the foundational argument structure of this inquiry. I introduce the question of citing the law of the past by situating this question in a broader theoretical context, which encompasses political philology. This context is the dogmatism-relativism dilemma rather than a viable and broadly recognized third way: philosophical transcendentalism. This theoretical context supports the argument that citing the law of the past in the PT and beyond offers another third way out of the dilemma. The context locates political philology as a version of transcendentalism and solidifies the question of the limits of political philology, in connection with the limits of a transcendentalist inquiry. I consequently reintroduce the PT as an archive that, in the context, displays the complexity of relationships between citing the law of the past and the power of the past *as* past from which the law draws its authority and legitimacy. Finally, I reformulate the result as an entrance to a new political philology: the political philology of the PT. The central question, then, is: How does a law, which always comes from the past, relate to the citation of that law as a source of authority in the present? The complexity of this question requires at least a preliminary theorization. The past *as* past is not simply distant. It is also never fully translatable into a presence, never has a face, and is never even on the horizon. It always lies beneath or beyond what one can see. The past cannot be forgotten, nor can it be readily recalled. If it could be recalled, it is not the past but only a presence looked at from a distance and thus determined as stable and determinate—something with a face that *is* known or recognized, or else is too fearful to be seen. In contrast, the past as past is a faceless depth, and any face it appears to wear can only hide it, masking that obscurity by what is read in that face. In short, the problem with the past is that qua past, it cannot be remembered, recognized, or known as a present. But it cannot be forgotten, either; a faceless past constantly takes on faces. These taken-on faces are nothing but citations or, more substantially, the witnesses who testify with these citations, so that, once accepted, these citations can become testaments. They are also the faces or characters of the rabbis in the PT. Citations are faces claiming to testify for the testament of the faceless past.

What does it mean for the law to come from a faceless past, from a past with no properly determinate or recognizable face—not even from the past of a person, as was the case in Blanchot? If the law always comes from the faceless depth of the past, any citation of the law as a source of authority always gives that law a face value, thereby *e-facing* the past—giving it a determinate face and undoing the (authority of the) law at the same time. The word and term *effacement* names the process in which the faceless depth of the past is masked in and by the attempt to make (*facere*) it up as a face, that is, to present the law of the past as a face value. *Effacement* is a dynamic process of evanescence and (re)appearance of the law in a testament to the faceless past in the *en face* of the law. Such is the dialectics of effacing the past by citing it as something present.

In light of this problem, the text in the PT displays a new way of addressing the law of the past—or, perhaps, a way of addressing the past that has been forgotten and needs to be remembered. As a result, the text displays a new—or, again, forgotten—paradigm for the political act as an act of engaging with and disengaging from the citations and self-citations of the law of the past.

How does this presentation or presencing of the past work? What are the specific details involved in the processes of e-facing?

The citation of a law as a source of authority either creates the law in the form of a rule or exemplifies it in the form of an act. Both cases occur in the present and give the past law a determinate face value.[24] Such a formulation is a testimony. Once accepted, it becomes a testament to the power of the law. One can produce such a testimony as a witness—for example, by reciting or retelling the rule or by performing an exemplary act, as in martyrdom. A sample citation of the past in the form of a rule is: "But I say, the reading of the Shema shall only be pronounced in the Holy Tongue" or "[One] can fulfill his/her duty [to recite the Shema] in any tongue he knows [to read]!" Such rules are formulated in the present tense—*must* or *is*, *shall* or *can*—and, more importantly, are presented (cited) "here and now"—in front of or by an adept. For such an adept, the citation or self-citation becomes *the* valid representation or presentation; the presenting, or "presencing," of a law sanctified or legitimized by having come from the past either by way of divine revelation or through the authority of previous generations, cited or self-cited right at the scene. Such citation is naming—and facialization, e-facing—of the faceless depth of the past. Similarly, in an exemplary act or an act perceived by the actor or audience as exemplifying a law of the past (e.g., by reciting the Shema in the Holy Tongue only), the practitioner is not only enacting the law but also exemplifying it, that is, citing it, translating it into the present time of a practical action that performs or delivers an exemplary act as a citation of the law of the past.

Both rules and exemplary acts are forms of testimony of the law and, as such, once they are accepted, they result in a codified form or testament of the law. A testimony implies a witness. Inclusion in a testament additionally involves the approval of their testimony if it is to become a part of the codified law. However, the temporality of testimony and testament is problematic. Both rules and exemplary acts transform what comes from the depth of the past into the determinate face value at the present—either the immediate present or a remote, historical, but determinate past, defined from the viewpoint of the present. The law of the past inevitably becomes lost, that is, *e-faced* in its citation, buried in a testimony and a testament. The temporality of a testimony or testament is precisely that of translating the law of the past into the present, into a set of narrated rules or exemplary acts. The Gospels in the NT or the codex of rabbinic law in the Mishnah consist of such translations.

This complex temporality involves an ongoing contravention of the content of a citation, on one hand, and its authority or legitimacy, on the other. The content is in the present, but the authority is in the past, and that authority does not quite make it into the "here and now" of the citation, not even in the bold act of self-citing. Rather, authority must remain in the past and retain its aura in order to be what it is: an authority legitimizing the citation at hand. It is precisely the aura of having come from the past that gives the citation the force of a testimony and, consequently, of a testament. The temporality of citing the law as law thus involves a paradox. The past must *remain* the past in order to authorize the cited law in its *modus* of the present. Yet citing law in the present *departs* from the past, thereby leaving behind the past and the authority it generates. The paradox is that authority comes from and must remain in the past, yet the citation it authorizes must be in the present, dangerously detaching itself from its own authority.

RESPONDING TO THE PARADOX OF CITATION

Both traditional and modern responses to these contravening moves in the temporality of citation, testimony, and testament vary. They range from dogmatism (bluntly and blindly equating the law with a given set of rules) to relativism (no less bluntly denying any legal force to a rule except for the force of either convention or imposition, often dubbed as a *social construct*) to transcendentalism (which moves from an exemplary act to a universal law—or the "maxim of your will," as Kant puts it, which one's acts are always to exemplify).

For a dogmatist, a rule or exemplary act is a given. The dogmatist can, of course, look for a justification for the rule. She often questions the accuracy of its rendition, but she would not question the axiomatic validity of there being a rule—"here and now"—that one must always follow. In the contravening temporality of a testament, the dogmatist takes the side of the present and misses—more precisely, dismisses any significance of—the past, unless that past translates into a form of the present, into *praesens historicum*, that is, the present pushed back to a previous point.

A relativist stands on the other side of the contravening temporality of a testimony or testament. For him, any given rule or exemplary act is not a dogma to accept but is "merely" a circumstantial result of its historical production—as relative as these circumstances might be and as no longer obligatory to follow as the resulting rules are. Instead, the rules can be denied, played with, or changed. The relativist recognizes that the "historical" past creates the rules and that these rules therefore are only and always relative. However, the relativist is not as far from the dogmatist as he might seem.[25] Not unlike the dogmatist, the relativist can only consider a historical past, *praesence historicum*, a present that simply was happening earlier. This present has nothing to do with the faceless depth of the past. The relativist, like the dogmatist, does not appreciate the past *as past*; he reduces it to a mode of the present, a present in the past. Both positions, however, remain radically blind to their similarity in losing the sense of the past as past, the faceless past of the law.

The position of the transcendentalist is a much more modern phenomenon than that of the dogmatist or relativist and is secondary to them. By *secondary*, I mean that transcendentalism is a response to the dogmatism-relativism conundrum that purports to overcome the conundrum. Transcendentalism initially takes shape by polemically dismissing both dogmatic and relativistic points of view. A transcendentalist is primarily interested in her individual experience. She differentiates and distances herself from both the dogmatist and the relativist by realizing that her experience is neither dependent on her nor defined by anything beyond her. The term *transcendental* describes what is fully within the limits of her experience (unlike what is "transcend*ent*") but also what is both independent of and definitive for that experience. In the area of practical law, this translates into Kant's "categorical imperative," which calls "you"—an individual—to act in accordance with a "general legislation" that is neither dependent on "you" nor imposed on "you" but is rather discovered by "you." That discovery must be exemplified—every time anew—by "your" action. Such an approach is not dogmatic because it does not accept any pregiven ("positive" or "imposed") rules simply because they are pregiven. Neither is it relativistic because it does not treat the rules on which you are acting as historically circumstantial.

Because the transcendentalist dismisses the relativists and dogmatists because of their presupposition that the law is pregiven, or "positive," whether absolute in dogmatism or constructed in relativism, she breaks with the past as a source of legitimacy for any given rule, exemplary act, or citation. She rejects any sense of the authority in a testimony or testament. And yet, in refusing any pregiven rule, the transcendentalist still embraces the idea of an exemplary act. Even though the transcendentalist resists cited rules because they come from the outside or "by imposition" (such an "outside" is also how the transcendentalist categorizes the past), the categorical imperative of the transcendentalist still follows the logic of the exemplary act. Her acts must still exemplify rules, or "maxims," and her "will" must still accord with the maxims exemplified; otherwise, her action would lose legitimacy. The valid or legitimate maxims are transcendental by definition. They do not depend on the personality of the transcendentalist because these maxims must be able to be "a foundation of general legislation," and that is possible only if they are not imposed from the outside. In other words, the maxims should neither be transcendent nor arrive from the transcendent. Instead, the transcendentalist must generate the maxims, rules, or "principles" by creating exemplary actions, which are not self-citations.

Moreover, while distancing herself from the other two positions, the transcendentalist unthinkingly retains a commonality with them: all three do not engage the past as such, the faceless past of the law, a past that must but can never be cited or become present. All three positions cannot engage with the law, which always comes from the faceless past.

Are there any other positions or resources beyond these three? The question is precisely ours: How else could we approach the faceless past of the law?

LOSING THE PAST

The fundamental insensitivity of dogmatism, relativism, and transcendentalism to the faceless past, as the *primary* element of the law, stems from the centuries-long tradition of legal interpretation; shared as it has been in different versions and variations, in both rabbinic and Christian traditions of thought. In both traditions—or, rather, in how they have been read and have understood themselves in their "traditions of tradition"—it has been assumed that there is a fundamentally unproblematic possibility of testifying to the law; that there is a testament to that law, a document or exemplary act; and that the very existence of the possibility of giving/receiving a testament to the law is beyond question.

The PT calls for questioning this assumption. To hear this call, one approaches the PT as a paradigm for thinking about the law as coming from the past, a paradigm that can be articulated and displayed by putting the arguments in the PT into a conversation with the dogmatic, relativistic, and transcendentalist ways of approaching the law.

It is within this threefold philosophical contextualization that the focus must shift toward the PT in its relationships to the NT and, by the same logic, toward relationships among the late ancient discipline of thinking (displayed in PT) and the two relatively new disciplines, political philology and political theology. Arguably, the two later disciplines grow from and still position themselves within the system of coordinates charted by the set of differences among dogmatism, relativism, and transcendentalism, particularly because the latter, formulated in Kant's three *Critiques*, set the standard for modern critical thinking. The current task is to go beyond this system of coordinates and explore new ways of understanding how an action in the present is possible based on law that comes from the past *as* past.

As suggested, there is a traditional theologeme at stake here. Working against the grid of this theologeme informs the heuristic path of developing a new political philology, based on the PT. A version of metalepsis of the OT and NT, this theologeme is "suspension." It is perhaps best known through the doctrine of supersessionism: the NT "supersedes" the OT, love and charity supersede the literalism of the Mosaic law, and "Israel in spirit" supersedes the "Jews" as "carnal Israel." The OT thus becomes both valid and deactivated, and the NT suspends and cancels but does not undermine the OT. Needless to say, any critical understanding of supersessionism must come from a critique of its conceptual node: suspension.

In moving beyond the traditional theologeme of suspension and away from supersessionism, we must articulate a broader concept of *a* new testament. That means treating *the* NT as *a* new testament rather than as the conceptual model for the relationship between old and new. It also means rereading and reevaluating the approaches to any new testament that the PT may display.

I approach this broader concept of a new testament by articulating the complex and never-fully-transparent temporality of effacement; the temporality of e-facing. The complex temporality of effacement is a more general foundational starting point through which to approach the problem of the e-facing law of the past.

A more complex and precise sense of effacement as e-facing means moving away from predominant ways of thinking of the relationship between the law and a testament thereof; in particular, between the two testaments, "Old" and "New." It also moves beyond transcendentalism by foregrounding an all-too-static nature of the latter—its perhaps all-too-quick yield to oblivion. Thinking the law of the past as past, in the traditional and more static terms of suspension or supersession (from which transcendentalism is not exempt either), both elides and produces its own foundation—a foundation that is a more dynamic process of the effacement of the law of the faceless past in its testaments in the present. In self-citation, the law e-faces itself, and this dynamic effacement is absent from the stabilizing efforts of dogmatism, relativism, and transcendentalism. The never-stable, always problematic possibility and impossibility of citing the law of the past calls for a critical evaluation of the complex process of effacement of *an* and *any* new testament, including the NT, as this process is displayed in the PT.

"But I say" displays just this: the impossibility and inevitability of citing the law of the faceless past. The plurality of parties involved in every "But I say" and the seeming marginality of "But I say" in the PT, along with the univocity thereof in the Sermon on the Mount, may make the tacit work of e-facing the faceless law of the past more palpable—and programmatically less certain—than can any personal (individual or collective) testimony to the past or the law. The past cannot be located through appealing to it, citing and self-citing in a locale neither in Caesarea nor on the Galilean mountain, let alone on the streets that Blanchot's "Account?" described. Nor can these localizations of "But I say" be avoided. The result is that the stability of localization can never be taken for granted, not even if one contravenes it by haptically palpating the dynamic act of e-facing, which is built in, and operates contrary to, any localization in every and all "But I say."

What are we left with? The polemical "But I say" of self-citing is more assertive than the suspension of the possibility of an "account" (Blanchot, Derrida) of the experience of the event a modern subject-agent (either individual or collective) of either passion or action lived through as a *superstes* of that event. It is less assertive and less exemplary than a transcendentalist oblivion of the memory of the past in and by the "maxim of my will." Reaching beyond and looking ahead of these two poles of modern subjectivity of the subject-agent, "But I say" does not fall back on the dogmatic view of a full commitment to the testified law. Nor does it sink in the torrent of relativizing any testament to the law of the past by reducing it to the circumstance of a historical present in a given moment. Escaping the unaccountability of modern subjectivity as well as the excessive assertiveness of a transcendentalist account of "my/our will," the polemical testament of "But I say" lands neither in dogmatic nor in relativistic dispositions of thinking and acting. The call of "But I say" is that to the law of the faceless past which we, to whom "But I say" is addressed, must face.

In that, "But I say" describes no beginning, neither the new nor the other; neither in "philosophy" nor in the "Talmud," if we think of these two in the context of the traditions of their traditions. Rather, the suspended testament to the law of the past can only be manifested in a place where there is articulation, where thinking and acting advance under, instead of, behind, and beyond the space and time controlled by the copula "and." Under, before, beyond, and instead of the copulative *and* the "edifice of the logos" lurks the faceless past, which can only be faced through the gap, that is, through the lens that removing the edifice of the *and* can create. To suspend the edifice of the logos in rethinking the traditions of philosophy and Talmud is, therefore, to remove the *and* but to close up neither the gap nor the abyss behind these two traditions that the gap opens up.

To lift the *and* without closing the gap, to face the past without e-facing it into the present, and to read the PT as a way of rereading the relationships between Talmud and philosophy—an intertwinement of these three horizons of thought projects what becomes the next step on the way back to other futures of the traditions of (the) Talmud and of philosophy.

Where will these pasts and futures go? What are the next steps in rethinking the traditions of the traditions of Talmud and philosophy in light of their shared abyss of citing the past? From the preceding arguments transpire six interconnected nodes for charting the next steps in thinking of and through the abyss.[26]

1. Powers of citing the past. The basic structure of authority in any citation as a testimony to the past in light of the future is the structure of self-citation. One cites oneself, launches an indirect speech rather than speaking directly, and thus gauges by that an authority stemming from the past (even if it is the immediate past of oneself).

2. A history of forgetting. The Palestinian tradition of self-citing belongs to the *longue durée* of the history of forgetting as the primary operation in the human condition. Common to both Talmud and philosophy, this long duration is lost from view, screened by a perspective in which memory becomes the primary operation and forgetting recedes to deviation.

3. Slow reading. Slowly reading rabbinic and philosophical texts involves renegotiating the traditions of the texts' traditions. This means returning the PT to the broader history of forgetting, rather than limiting the PT by the tradition of its later rabbinic reception or construction.

4. Beyond the modern subjective past. The relationship to the forgotten, remembered, and cited past in the PT exceeds the horizon drawn by the impasses of reciting/narrating the past by the modern subject, either individual or collective.

5. E-facing. The concept of e-facing—simultaneously facing and effacing the past in a testament—is a dialectical relationship to the past in citation that a slow reading of the PT in the broader scope of the history of forgetting can help display.

6. The abyss. Behind the self-citation in the PT (unlike the self-citation of the modern subject), there is no beginning, a consequence that calls for a reconsideration of any pursuit of a beginning in the traditions of philosophy and Talmud.

In light of these factors, the two traditions enable the critical adoption of each other's traditions of tradition and discern the abyss of forgetting that opens up behind the /and/ of their mutually incurred self-separation.

SERGEY DOLGOPOLSKI is Professor in the Departments of Jewish Thought and Comparative Literature, and Gordon and Gretchen Gross Professor of Jewish Thought at the University at Buffalo, SUNY, and author of *Other Others: The Political after the Talmud; The Open Past: Subjectivity and Remembering in the Talmud;* and *What Is Talmud? The Art of Disagreement.*

NOTES

1. I would like to thank Bruce Rosenstock and Zvi Septimus for a series of productive conversations about the materials and problems this chapter addresses.

* I render the biblical tetragrammaton as "G-d" to perform graphically what the argument in this chapter does theoretically. This is, in part, to make visible the middle ground between forgetting and remembering, as discussed in this chapter. The rendition highlights a graphic, indeed glyphic—rather than acoustic, phonetic, or descriptive—energy of the biblical four-letter name. This glyph (rather than an alphabetically expressed word) is traditionally forbidden/impossible to pronounce. That also means that one could not or should not reduce G-d to a word that can be deciphered and read or used to describe things. What remains, then, is a bare theophany of the glyph. If remembering means memory for either words or describable things, in seeing the glyph, there is nothing to forget, for all is right there; yet there is also nothing to remember, for the glyph neither spells a word nor describes a thing. Of course, there can be both remembering and forgetting, but only under an older—say, Egyptian—assumption that things and glyphs are the same. Since the glyph offers no description, it escapes the either-or of memory and forgetting of describable things. However, existing in the world of the describable is not all there is: beyond remembering and forgetting of that which can be described, there looms a danger of total obliteration, not only of things but also of the human. The glyph protects against that looming obliteration, the full oblivion by the bare energy of its graphic form. The glyph meets the eye but escapes the tongue, thereby letting neither the human nor the world of things sink into obliteration. As recorded in m. Sotah 7:1.

2. "Listen, Oh Israel," Deut. 6:4.

3. P. Sotah 7:1. Verbatim.

4. Rabbi Berakhiah cites a rule about the public reading of the Esther Scroll. Citing him here restricts what would otherwise be too broad a lenience of Rabbi Yose by limiting reading in other tongues only to those who cannot read in Aramaic lettering and in the Holy Tongue.

5. The expression "babbling tongue" in reference to the Greek is supposed to lend a dismissive tone to the justification of the Aramaic lettering.

6. Rabbi Mannah supports Rabbi Berakhiah's argument by citing a similar rule about a public reading of the Esther Scroll while also broadening the exception to include other tongues, beyond "Hellenistic," thus denying the latter any singular role or importance.

7. p. Sotah, 7:1 21b; cited and translated from *Talmud Yerushalmi according to MS. Or. 4720 (Scal. 3)*, 933.

8. The midrash presents itself as emerging from, rather than coming in conjunction with, the Scripture.

9. I refer to Martin Heidegger's distinction between the "first beginning" in pre-Socratics, to "new beginning" in Kant, and to Heidegger's "other beginning," in which he comes back to the pre-Socratics to find a better future for both philosophy and society.

10. Although widely accepted, *archaic* is a figure of a complex dialectics of antecedent and beginning. A beginning always has an antecedent. For example, on a standard account, *pre-Socratics* is an antecedent from which begins Plato's philosophy. So, too, on Detienne's analysis (see n. 11), the "archaic" struggle with oblivion is an antecedent, on the base of which begins Platonic philosophy. The rhetoric of *archaic* or *presocratic* describes an antecedent against which philosophy (or, on other accounts, "civilization") begins. Such beginnings both create and appropriate their antecedents (pre-Socratics versus Plato, archaic versus civilization, etc.). The task is to bypass such an appropriation and ask about the relationships the philosophical and rabbinic rhetorical schools have with that allegedly *archaic* struggle against oblivion. The copula only reinforces

such appropriations of antecedents by beginnings. Bypassing such an appropriation can bypass the copulation as well. The copula only reinforces the dialectics between beginning and their always-retroactive antecedents. The critique of the copula is thus to open up a space (quite possibly the abyss) between the beginnings and the antecedents of both rabbinic and philosophical schools.

11. Detienne, Vidal-Naquet, and Lloyd, *Masters of Truth*.

12. Assmann, "The Mosaic Distinction."

13. The matter is not with זכר, the remembrance of the G-d of Israel, but rather with שכח, "letting go" of the Torah and its commandments: "Do not let my Teaching go, let my commandments preoccupy your heart constantly," to interpret Proverbs 3:1. Even stronger, שכח, as "letting go," appears as "erase any memory of Amalek under the heaven, do not let go" (Deut. 25:19). The interpretations of these verses highlight the assertive or at least neutral—rather than either privative or negative—sense of שכח as "letting go." This stands in affinity with the also assertive or neutral, rather than negative, powers of *lethe* and in distinction from the inevitably privative and thus negative sense of the English *forget*, the German *vergessen*, or the Latin *oblivisci* ("obliviate"). The primary operations of *lethe* and שכח thus come together in contradistinction from secondary (privative) operations of forgetting and oblivion. The nature of this operation disappears when one considers the agency of memory primary and that of forgetting secondary. Assmann predicates his notion of mosaic distinction on remembering the G-d of the Bible to the exclusion of "other G-ds." In this, the commandment of "not letting go" escapes the plane of opposition between the exclusionary "monotheism" and inclusive "polytheism" charts. This, however, is beyond the scope of this chapter.

14. Following the terminology of "traditionis traditio" in Granel, *Traditionis Traditio*.

15. Moretti, *Distant Reading*; Wimsatt and Beardsley, "The Intentional Fallacy."

16. I refer here to Benveniste's analysis of *superstes* in opposition to *testis* as well as to the evocation of this analysis in Carol Ginzburg's discussion of relationships among history, memory, and forgetting. Benveniste and Palmer, "Religion and Superstition"; Ginzburg, "Just One Witness."

17. For our purposes, the Sermon on the Mount involves polemics and a claim of authority in a locale against Pharisees and Scribes by contravening their citations of the law with a self-citation. Contrary to a later form of relationship between the Old and New Testaments, this self-citation does not attempt to introduce a new testament by consigning the law of the past to "old" law. The formulation *ancient* (ὅτι ἐρρέθη τοῖς ἀρχαίοις) in Matthew 5:21 is far from "you have heard said" (Ἠκούσατε ὅτι ἐρρέθη) in Matthew 5:43. "But I say" goes against what "is heard" and only consequentially and potentially against the "ancient" antecedent. The *before* to which "But I say" responds is as *earlier*, as it is concurrently "other" or "heard." "But I say," by definition, is "new," and what "I" responds to is, by definition, "old." The only question is, how old: Is what "I" speak against only another presencing/presenting/citing of the "original" law of the past? Is "But I say" a break with that very past? Is it possible to determine a clear difference between the first and the second? Arguably, such a difference becomes stronger once Matthew is included in the framework of the NT.

18. I thank Zvi Septimus for the suggestion. I would emphasize that self-citing, if taken as an earlier form of rabbinic debate, both retains and becomes marginalized in rabbinic literature, even in the PT. Perhaps both that retention and that marginalization are due to the self-obvious vulnerability of an authority to have come from a "mere" act of

self-citing, as well as to the hidden centrality of self-citing in any act of citation, even if it presents itself more readily as a citing of a statement of another authority from the past or (of more interest in this chapter) of the law of the past.

19. Kant's categorical imperative to "act in such a way that the maxim of your will can be a foundation of general legislation" falls into that broad category of self-citing as well.

20. On a literal level, in the testifying, the self that one puts "on the line" can even be his testicles or her womb; the very viscera of procreation.

21. See Derrida and Ronell, "The Law of Genre."

22. The question here is not one of a universal or tautological performativity of "I say" as always confirming its truth, if truth means "correspondence" between words and (f)acts. Rather, the question is that of an individual and personal affirmation of a testimony, for which the witness is personally responsible in juxtaposition to all other witnesses and to all others who do not or fail to provide witness, to testify by putting their lives, honors, or names on the line.

23. White, "A Short Political Philology."

24. Citation therefore never ends, which both parallels and differs from Lyotard's notion of excitation.

25. The position and task of the deconstruction is no more and no less than to show the antinomian impossibility of these two positions. Whereas it is very common for professional historiographers to position themselves within Nietzsche's dichotomy between (relativistic) critical history/genealogy and (dogmatic) monumental history, identifying with one horn of the dilemma does not avoid the structure of dogmatism.

26. The trajectory outlined at the end of the chapter anticipates a book-length project, to which the chapter would serve as an introduction.

4

Pragmatic Points of View
Kant and the Rabbis, Together Again

JAMES ADAM REDFIELD

לעושה נפלאות גדולות
For Lorraine Daston

*Lack of knowledge of human beings is the reason
that morality and sermons [Kanzelreden],
which are full of admonitions of which we never tire,
have little effect.
Morality must be combined with knowledge of humanity.*
KANT, LECTURES ON ANTHROPOLOGY (transcript attributed
to Friedländer, Winter Semester 1775–76)

UNJUSTIFIED MARGINS

In a volume on philosophy /and/ Talmud, which aims to go beyond the historical one-way street from the former to the latter, the name *Kant* looms largest as a roadblock or a detour sign.[1] Due to the influence of neo-Kantianism on the philosophy of Jewish law (halakhah),[2] systems of Talmudic logic and their methods of textual analysis[3] are widely associated with Kant—even if they do not reflect his thought.[4] There are faster routes to a new relationship between the terms *Kant* /and/ *Talmud* (or, in the present case, a related more obscure branch of classical rabbinic literature). Another roadblock at this Kant/Talmud intersection is the prevailing emphasis within neo-Kantian halakhic theory—no less than among Kant scholars—on the thought of Kant's *Critiques*. Until recently, the work Kant began before his critical period (especially his anthropology lectures, which ran for twenty-four years, culminating in *Anthropology from a Pragmatic Point of View* (1798), his bestseller in his lifetime), received little attention. Most attention on the precritical Kant was centered around his connection to the *Critiques*.[5] Both of Kant's afterlives, then—a focus on his critical turn, and modern Jewish legal theory's readings of the Talmud through the lens of avowedly Kantian transcendental logic—have marginalized the Kant of the *Anthropology*, just as they have marginalized anthropologies that could be recovered from the classical rabbis by way of Kant. Historically, it is not difficult to situate both margins: Kant's *Critiques* are far more central to modern philosophy, just as halakhah plays an outsized role in the modern reception of rabbinic sources. Yet by placing the margins of not only the philosophical but also the Talmudic canon side by side, and scribbling across them, a new sort of conjunction will hopefully begin to emerge.

To that end, this chapter juxtaposes the spaces of German Enlightenment anthropology and classical rabbinic thought figured by Kant on one hand, and the Roman-era rabbinic discourse *derekh erets* ("the way of the world") on the other. I propose that Kant's approach to anthropology (his "pragmatic point of view"), and his way of integrating it with morality, is selectively analogous to how *derekh erets* discourse was also used to reflect on the relationship between rabbinic anthropology, in a philosophical sense, and moral norms.[6]

I begin by mapping a triangle of concepts within Kant's system: the "pragmatic," "prudence," and "character." The way in which Kant defines and interrelates those terms illuminates his distinctive view of the relation between anthropology and morality. I proceed to mark the spot on this map where Kant's "pragmatic point of view" appears to build a bridge from anthropology to morality (but without crossing it). The two branches of his thought remain distinct in principle, but he gestures toward how they could be related.

Having come to the point where Kant stops—the crossroads of anthropology and morality—I analogize this corner of his system to the same conceptual intersection in the rabbis' discourse of *derekh erets*. Here I argue that the way in which the discourse of *derekh erets* relates anthropology with morality may be productively analogous to how Kant's "pragmatic point of view" does so as well, especially because Kant's approach touches on a major unresolved question in the scholarship on *derekh erets*: How did the rabbis conceive of the bond between morality and what they labeled *derekh erets*: an expansive term with at least eight distinct senses? In particular, since *derekh erets* often designates the natural or the normal, as opposed to the normative, how did early rabbis envision the relationship between those poles of their discourse? Did they imagine a hierarchy or progression between the two? Is the moral sense of "*derekh erets*" the foundation of all its others? Yet the term also indexes what we would call *anthropology*: social norms and patterns of human conduct, which cannot be universal or absolute. Why, then, have modern scholars read *derekh erets* as the basis for *all* rabbinic morality; whether a version of natural law, a broad term for any and all "value-concepts," or the residue of a primordial, universal Jewish-Christian piety?

Rather than privilege a few instances of *derekh erets* or strain its meaning through another theology, I reanalyze this discourse as a whole, in early Palestinian oral tradition, by developing my analogy with Kant's "pragmatic point of view." I argue that the way in which Kant's "pragmatic point of view" bridges anthropology and morality can clarify how early *derekh erets* discourse incipiently relates those domains. I conclude by reviewing what this analogy to Kant contributes to our study of early rabbinic thought (leaving it to philosophers to explore the reverse: what a marginal discourse of rabbis in Roman Palestine could have taught the sage of Königsberg). Throughout, I reflect on the value and limits of this methodological experiment: *analogical reconstruction*, or conceptual translation, that is, using one system of thought to fill gaps in another.

THE CHARACTERS OF KANT'S PRAGMATIC ANTHROPOLOGY

Kant certainly does not advise leaping directly from the *Is* of anthropology to the *Ought* of morality. As his understanding of the latter develops—marked by the first *Critique* (1781) and the *Groundwork* (1785) but also by lectures on moral philosophy throughout his career—he tends to stress that on the contrary, in terms of human agency, there is a gap between anthropology and moral philosophy. Morality is the space of law and freedom; anthropology is empirically conditioned, which constrains agency. Kant presents his anthropology as a species of applied morality or as a proving ground in which to test out moral norms—not as a basis *for* morality.

Recent studies, however, have bridged that apparent gap in Kant's system by showing how his anthropology extends morality "downward," so to speak. Rather than the pure, rational, abstract morality of the agent of the *Groundwork*—the morality of an agent that "does not borrow the least thing from acquaintance with him (from anthropology) but gives to him, as a rational being, laws *a priori*"—these studies show that Kant also needed an "impure," practical, and embodied anthropology, in order to apply the moral *a priori* to *a posteriori* knowledge of actual human beings.[7] Rather than limiting the normative program of his anthropology to either a retroactive application of moral laws to specific cases or an instrumental "doctrine of prudence," Kant stresses that one must observe humanity to teach and internalize morals.[8] His observations of moral character in all its forms, including anthropology, are always already "value-embedded."[9]

This mediating role of anthropology concerning moral norms is reflected in Kant's uses of the label "pragmatic" as well as his gossipy, offensive, eclectic, "popular," and original tributary of what looks more like cultural anthropology today: his lectures/textbook unit on "characteristic features" (*Charakteristik*).[10]

I do not use the term offensive lightly when describing this part of Kant's course and writings devoted to the characteristic features of different human types. Like other areas of his work where his anthropology arose (especially his aesthetics and racial theory), others have long, widely, and rightly noted that Kant's racism is strongest, or at least most obvious, in this domain of his thought. Nor am I persuaded by strenuous efforts to reinterpret him or argue that he changed his mind. Thus, as I pursued my analogical reading and borrowing of several concepts from his anthropology, I was led to reread it in the opposite direction: against the grain of his *Charakteristik*, as I reexamined the historical archive and context where Kant formulated his racial anthropology. This yielded another essay, critically rather than experimentally oriented, responding to literature on the racism of Kant's anthropology and its implications for how and why we read Kant today.[11] I hope that readers of this chapter and my essay will arrive at a creative antagonism between the two, using the essay to critique this chapter, just as they reread this chapter in order to seek the proverbial baby of Kant's anthropology in its vile bathwater. Since the goal of this chapter, read for the first time on its own, is not to probe Kant's system per se but to read his anthropology selectively in order to rethink an analogous area of rabbinic discourse, I ask readers to suspend the valid but irreconcilable axiom that it is problematic to do anything constructive with his anthropology without critiquing it.

Beyond this temporary and tactical suspension of the claim that Kant's racism causes major problems for his entire system—as often argued, including by my other essay—I would add (without yet being able to prove against myself) that it is legitimate to borrow concepts from the racist system he built without accepting all of the uses to which he put those concepts. In this case, I argue that his anthropological concept of "character" can clarify a lacuna in the early Palestinian rabbis' own way of thinking, without using Kant's concept to foster universalism or a hierarchy of character types, as I think he does. On the contrary, by exploring differences arising from translating Kant's concept into a rabbinic mode of thought, I question his uses of his own ideas.

A second objection to this enterprise concerns the rabbis' idea of *derekh erets*: that it, too, is universalist, hierarchical, and even racist, at least in their uses of it, and so it has the same contaminated and contaminating potential in their thought (as well as the same need for parallel critique and more patient dialectic) if it is to be translated. While there are a few passages in rabbinic texts where the function of the term *derekh erets* might support that objection, none of them are from the early period covered here—in this corpus, the rabbis are more vague about the borderlines of race and ethnicity (or ethnic/racialized religion) they drew in the Babylonian Talmud, Palestinian midrash, and even in some early legal texts. Early *derekh erets* discourse often seems to be addressed to Jews and proto-Christians, specifically to pietists and circles of the sages, as its ethical norms and rules of protocol would be unintelligible in other contexts. Yet the discourse also questions humanity in its universal form—those who suffer and strive in the raw world of death, sex, and labor—without erecting a Jew/Gentile boundary. If there is an antagonism here, a need to critique *derekh erets* in terms of rabbinic "racism," it would have to be the antagonism between earlier (Tannaitic) and later (Amoraic) sources, requiring a comparative study of another kind, which also does not exist.

As the Talmud says, *gufa*, "the body": now back to the matter at hand. The first task of this analogy is to show how scholars have rediscovered the very narrow bridge that Kant built between anthropology and morality; one we will recross when we come to the same gap in the early discourse of *derekh erets*. After clarifying Kant's definition of "pragmatic" and the moral theory he buries in that definition, I explore how Kant's projected synthesis between anthropology and moral philosophy takes shape in his observation of humanity's "characteristic features" and the concept of "character" that stands behind them. Those key terms (*pragmatic, prudence, character*) draft his faint blueprint for the relationship between anthropology and morality.

The Pragmatic World

Kant defines pragmatic both negatively and positively.[12] In his negative definition, he opposes it to alternative ways of doing anthropology: physiological and scholastic/speculative. Physiological anthropology, in Kant's historical context, was mired in the material basis of thought: "sources of the phenomena" that we experience.[13] It did not even rise to the level of empirical psychology (the closest thing to anthropology, in Kant's view), instead remaining a popular anatomy that tried "to give itself a comprehensive character with the name 'Anthropology' or 'Philosophy.'"[14] Kant's immediate target here was Ernst Platner, whose *Anthropology for Physicians and Men of Worldly Wisdom* (1772) appeared the same year that Kant began teaching the subject, occasioning his famous programmatic letter to Marcus Herz (1773). Rejecting Platner's "subtle and, in my view, eternally futile inquiries as to the manner in which bodily organs are connected with thought," Kant envisioned his own anthropology as a study of "phenomena and their laws" and "the sources of all the [practical] sciences" (my emphasis).[15] He sought what is particular to human experience in human nature, not in human anatomy.

Similarly, Kant opposes "pragmatic" to scholastic/speculative anthropology (which he also associated with Platner). He distinguishes the two in terms of their sources and purpose.[16] Platner et al.'s sources were things of *nature* that they misinterpreted as causes of human conduct. Their purpose was abstract cognition of those causes.[17] Kant's textbook example—explicitly attacking Descartes but, implicitly, Platner—is the faculty of memory. It is all very well to meditate on "traces of impressions remaining in the brain," but this "theoretical speculation is a pure waste of time," for one "does not know the cranial nerves and fibers." Even if one did, one would not be able to use this knowledge to modify those impressions. If, however, one studies what is known *by observation* about the faculty of memory in order to "enlarge it or make it agile," knowledge becomes "pragmatic." Pragmatic anthropology is thus distinctive in both its sources—direct observation of humans—and its purpose: to apply knowledge of human nature, derived from such observations, back to human behavior. Hence the two-way traffic between anthropology and moral philosophy resurfaces *within* pragmatic anthropology itself. One observes human conduct in order to derive not merely its empirical regularities but also a clear picture of the human agent to whom moral laws must apply. Anthropological observations have normative value: they shape the scope and application of morality, even though morality per se does not depend on them. This is where Kant's "pragmatic" domain verges on an "impure ethics," without becoming relativism.

Kant's positive definition of "pragmatic" hinges on the specific sphere where he sees anthropological knowledge not merely as an accessory to moral laws but also as bearing a normative force of its own: the sphere where it shapes knowledge of ourselves and others as well as our conduct. He calls this sphere "the world," as opposed to the "school" of his scholastic competitors. The human being, from a pragmatic point of view, is a "citizen of the world" (*Weltbürger*). Anthropology avoids egoism by teaching us to see ourselves in relation to our species as a whole and avoids anthropocentrism by linking our species to the nonhuman world. At the same time, by teaching us what is distinctive about our nature as humans, anthropology fulfills our "final end" (*letzter Zweck*) by leading us to the self-knowledge of which we are uniquely capable. Anthropology, therefore, "deserves to be called knowledge of the world" (*Weltkenntnis*), rather than knowledge of humans as merely one among many "creatures of the earth."[18] Anthropology is not called "knowledge of the world" because humans *are* the world but because it helps us to be *in* the world as the hybrid natural/moral beings ("earthly being endowed with reason") that we are.¹⁹ It acts on us pragmatically by redefining what counts as useful knowledge ("not merely for the school but rather for life") and widening the scope of our self-knowledge beyond "noteworthy details" to "the relation as a whole in which they stand and in which everyone takes his place": in a word, the world.²⁰

What good is this pragmatic self-knowledge? Kant's answer is hard to grasp because it is practical rather than theoretical, yet it is not merely instrumental. When we develop his pragmatic point of view, we aim to "use" others for prosocial rather than selfish ends: the "pragmatic predisposition [Anlage]" is to "use other human beings skillfully for [one's] purposes."²¹ Out of context, this definition of anthropology seems to be the self-interested study of Others—a fear that haunts the modern field.²² In context, however, it simply places the pragmatic between two other predispositions: the "technical," the exercise of skill, and the "moral," or the exercise of pure reason. Kant argues that we must develop our ability to "use" one another to moral rather than merely instrumental ends and for the collective good: "to come out of the crudity of mere personal force and to become a well-mannered (if not yet moral) being destined for concord."²³ Here, again, the pragmatic stands between raw skill and pure morality. It is a form of practical reason that is adapted to living with others. The pragmatic is a mode of self-cultivation concerning others (a sort of "people skills"), directed to fulfilling our telos as members of the human species. In pragmatic anthropology, as in education generally, we can learn to "use" others to more fully become, as individuals, what we already are as a species: social beings.²⁴

Prudence between Anthropology and Morality

This triad of *technical*, *pragmatic*, and *moral* abilities in the 1798 textbook is mirrored in the program for Kant's anthropology that he had already outlined in his 1773 letter to Herz. He defined pragmatic anthropology, or "knowledge of the world," as "a very pleasant empirical study [*Beobachtungslehre*]," which he aimed to turn into a "preliminary exercise in skill [*Geschicklichkeit*], prudence [*Klugheit*], and even wisdom [*Weisheit*]."²⁵ From a developmental standpoint, he suggested, the pragmatic is situated between these other predispositions: we use our hands in nature and other people in society; whereas, in morality, we submit to a "law of duty."[26] Each predisposition marks a different stage in human progress. Yet within the middle stage, as we cultivate our pragmatic predisposition, individuals work on refining all three abilities. In this effort, again, the middle term is the crucial mediator: prudence is at once the supreme technical skill and the art of practical wisdom. "All pragmatic doctrines are doctrines of prudence, where for all our skills we also have the means to make proper use of everything."[27] Prudence is not the pure morality of the *Groundwork*, but it is not normatively null either. Prudence elevates skill, and verges on wisdom, by making all of our human abilities useful, not unlike Aristotle's "practical wisdom" (*phronēsis*), in contrast to theoretical wisdom (*sophia*).[28]

This mediating role of prudence accounts for Kant's conflations between prudence and skill, as well as for places where prudence brushes up against the pure realm of moral reason. As he said about his textbook: "If we are to speak of a book as an *opus* [...] then its end can be defined from a threefold point of view: how the human can become 1. more shrewd [*gescheuter*], 2. more prudent [*klüger; geschickter*], and 3. more wise: i.e., from a pragmatic, technical-practical, and moral point of view.—*The pragmatic point of view is the one [on the] basis of which the others are formed.*"[29]

Here, skill (the technical predisposition) seems to change places with prudence (the pragmatic one). The pragmatic is identified with shrewdness, a "lower" exercise of practical reason than prudence: "A shrewd human being is one who judges correctly and practically, but simply." Yet from a pragmatic point of view, "experience can *make* a shrewd human being prudent," turning a shrewd mind into a more versatile one.[30] This is essentially the viewpoint of an educator, who focuses on what a person "*makes* of himself[31] as a free-acting being, or can or should *make* of himself."[32] Insofar as it helps us to integrate all of our predispositions, the pragmatic integrates these stages of practical pedagogy even though, in Kant's system, they correspond to starkly distinct ways of exercising our will (skill/prudence to *nature*, morality to *freedom*).[33]

Just as prudence interchanges with skill, it also brushes against the "higher" term in the triad of the pragmatic point of view: morality. Indeed it has recently been argued that Kant attributed independent or semi-independent moral norms to prudence apart from his autonomous laws of pure morality.[34] These prudential norms seem to be grounded in both pursuing one's happiness and acquiring and applying useful knowledge of other people.[35] These norms may indicate crucial areas where Kant's anthropology converges with his moral philosophy, suggesting that Kant's pragmatic and pedagogical interests in human nature and society bear normative implications that *cannot* be expressed as rational imperatives or a "universal moral law." Prudence is, rather, a response to a human relationship: "Skillfulness is directed toward things; prudence, toward human beings." For example, "The watchmaker is skilled if he makes a perfect watch; but if he knows how to bring it to the customer quickly because he repairs it according to fashion, then he is prudent." Furthermore, because human beings make things, and things are made for them, to gain prudence ("knowledge of the human being") is to gain the most important skill of all: the skill of "using" human beings, and through them, of using things.[36] Again, this "use" of people is not instrumental or self-interested; its end is the good of the species: happiness. Prudence is not founded on rational principles, and it is not quite wisdom (the use of reason to "judge about the true worth of things"). However, prudence does "use and apply" what one learns about humanity for constructive human ends. Like skill with things (technique), the end of cultivating this skill with humans (prudence) is our "well-being" in life.[37] Prudence, as the normative function of the pragmatic point of view, refracts knowledge of the human world back onto the human world—approached as an end in itself.[38]

We have reviewed what pragmatic anthropology is knowledge of (the human world), what it teaches (how to use things and people as we make ourselves civilized), and what its good is (happiness in the world). But what methods can we use to obtain knowledge from others and use it to remake ourselves, in a civilized world, so that we progress toward happiness as a species? In short, how can we become prudent? According to Kant, the best way is through "observations of others"; a method similar to what anthropologists today call "participant-observation."[39] It is not enough to "*know* the world"; one must also "*have* the world" (*die Welt haben*), for the former "only *understands* the play that one has watched, while the other has *participated* in it."⁴⁰ No less than the pulpit's didactic morality, the practical morality of pragmatic anthropology is useless as mere theory. However, Kant sees pernicious obstacles to accurate participant-observation (not to mention self-observation), especially the obstacle that "in the field," so to speak, we encounter people under empirical conditions that have shaped their behavior into habit (second nature) rather than human nature, the object of pragmatic anthropology.⁴¹ We observe society, not humanity. To access human nature, therefore, a pragmatic observer must look not for habit but for *character*.

Two Senses of Character

Like prudence, Kant's character (*Charakter*) places pragmatic anthropology squarely between empirical and moral views of human nature. In its singular, indivisible sense ("character purely and simply"), character is the individual's capacity for practical morality.⁴² In this sense, we say that someone "has character" in general. They adopt "definite practical principles" and resolve to follow them rather than to "fly off hither and yon, like a swarm of gnats."⁴³ Those principles adhere to "the formal element of the will." At its origin, then, character is no less lawlike than the morality of the "good will" in the *Groundwork* (although with prudence, the universal form of character is more negative maxim than categorical imperative).⁴⁴ Moral character, in this indivisible singular sense, is what any human being "is prepared to make of himself." In other words, moral character is the fulfillment of an individual's "pragmatic" predisposition: the moment of epiphany when one internalizes principles that one has learned from experience as an invariant "property of the will."⁴⁵ As Kant says, "Like a kind of rebirth, a certain solemnity of making a vow to oneself," moral character is not natural or innate but "acquired."⁴⁶ When this fit between the empirical individual and their rational principles is strong, practical morality manifests as active, internal, self-consistent "conduct of thought" (*Denkungsart*) and not passive "sensibility" (*Sinnesart*).⁴⁷ Moral character, in this absolute singular sense, is an exercise of rational freedom to transcend one's empirical character. Through character, one is not born, but becomes a human.

That said, Kant is curious about humans' various and relative empirical characteristics. His anthropology teaches prudence: how "citizens of the world" should interact with *other* people for mutual happiness. This requires not only inner certainty about what one ought to become but also observations of humans as we are. To that end, the second half of Kant's textbook, on "that which is characteristic" in humanity (*das Charakteristische*), spans four scales of analysis: person, sexes, peoples, and species.[48] Whereas the framework for the first half of his course was empirical psychology, focusing on inner qualities or faculties using methods of self-observation, in this highly original unit on empirical "character" (*Charakteristik*), Kant adopted the opposite approach. He systematized his observations of what can be known of human nature "from the outside,"[49] echoing his distinction in the first *Critique* between such "empirical character (sensibilities)" and inner moral character.[50]

As Munzel shows, Kant aspires to turn the former into the latter, integrating empirical with moral character. He aims for a "synthetic unity" where morality is the basis for culture without substituting for it.[51] Yet in this "popular" mode of his anthropology course, he seems to bracket that lofty goal, simply displaying a range of human characters under passive categories such as "temperament" (*Temperament*), here equated with "sensibility" (*Sinnesart*), in other words, the very opposite of the principled *Denkungsart* of moral character.[52] His course on *Charakteristik* surveys the flux of human actions and reactions in an externally conditioned cosmos. It seems to contrast human types in a protobehaviorist way: as patterned responses to stimuli, regulated by inner motives (desire, inclination, will, or weakness). His ideal of the rationally self-governed individual moves to the wings. At center stage is human difference, not unity; under the sign of nature and necessity, not reason and freedom. This self-consciously "popular" program appealed to a taste for the varieties of humankind in provincial Prussia, and here, Kant dabbles in doctrines like the four humors or physiognomy—albeit limited to "observed effects" rather than causes, to intuitive "illustration and presentation" rather than concepts.[53] This part of his course resembles what many college students still seem to expect from their anthropology courses: classification and anecdotes about the varieties of humankind in terms of how we typically feel, appear, and act.

Pragmatic Normativity: Prudence and Character

Kant's *Charakteristik*, however, is more deeply "value-embedded," more closely intertwined with morality, than it may appear. This part of the course, in both textbook and lecture formats, shows Kant repeatedly lining up both aspects of prudence with character—also in the second, empirical sense of *character*. Prudence, as the skill of "using" or getting along well with people in the world, is well served by studying human features that are hard to understand or that cannot be understood in rational terms. Physiognomy, for instance, is a useful proxy for moral character. What we observe of someone's face and gestures "makes us suspicious even before we have inquired about his morals"—and there is something to our intuition. It cannot be expressed systematically according to a rational rule, and, therefore, physiognomy cannot teach us to predict how people actually think. But it can still cultivate our "taste [...] in morals, manners, and customs, in order to promote human relations and knowledge of human beings."[54] Similarly, prudence as a form of social normativity, directed to the welfare of the human world—ultimately, to the happiness of our species—has much to learn from empirical character. Rather than the origins of national characters, for instance, pragmatic anthropology can teach prudence on a geopolitical scale: what each nation can "expect from the other and how each could use the other to its own advantage."[55] Finally, on the scale of the human species, prudence joins empirical character at the point where our "use" of one another has a civilizing effect: education. Conceding that it cannot be *proven* on the basis of certain knowledge about human nature, Kant reaffirms his faith that, through education, humanity can progress to happiness (becoming "the creator of its own good fortune"). By way of "prudence and moral illumination," he insists, each person can be "*educated* [*erzogen*] to the good."[56] Here again, prudence brushes against morality just at the point where norms enter society: education in practical morality, the pragmatic domain par excellence.

So Kant does grant an important role to anthropology, the empirical study of character, within prudential norms. By studying human beings, we can make better use of others and move incrementally toward happiness, removing obstacles to our natural development and opting for more evolved forms of social organization that benefit the species.[57] It is hard to see, however, how an education in human *characteristics*—in the plural and empirical sense—could relate to the formation of moral "character" in the singular, indivisible, and lawlike sense. The chasm between morality and anthropology still looms: anthropology is normatively null if not an obstacle in its own right. Like a preacher who tries to "deduce morality" from history, it is a natural human tendency to *try* to establish moral principles on the basis of culture. But, Kant maintains, that impulse is entirely backward. We should reform our culture in the image of moral rules, established on the basis of reason.[58] How could anthropology offer these? If anything, it risks turning a student into a man without qualities: a mere "*imitator* (in moral matters)" who derives his moral character from the study of others rather than "a source that he has opened by himself."[59] The study of *characters*, using outer traits and sensibilities, opposes moral character as one's own inner "conduct of thought." The "rules" that Kant derives from his observations are useful regularities of human conduct, not a substitute for moral principles.

Despite that obstacle to reconciling morality and anthropology in Kant's system as a whole, within his pragmatic point of view, he does sketch a tentative bridge between the two. I believe that is what he means when he (reportedly) says that "morality should be combined with knowledge of humanity." If *ought* implies *can*, as it does, then one must observe what humans *are* (our nature) in order to know if we *can* do (in the pragmatic world) what we *should*. This is entirely different from trying to justify our actions *a priori*: empirical and moral characters are distinct in principle but coextensive in reality. Therefore, the normative role of pragmatic anthropology is that it can teach us to modify our empirical character in accord with prudence. "Everything that bears no relation to the prudent conduct of human beings, does not belong to anthropology," and vice versa: "Only that from which a prudent use in life can immediately be drawn, belongs to anthropology."[60] The prudent is not the good, but, within our social world, it does have normative value. It serves as a check on morality's penchant for inflexible, egoistical, abstract, or inapplicable laws. Prudence helps us to live in a civilized way by facing our nature as we are: normativity *in medias res*.

Analogical Interlude

Having mapped the relationship of anthropology and morality within Kant's "pragmatic point of view," we can draw an analogy to rabbinic *derekh erets* discourse that stands to clarify a central issue about the latter. But first, a word on analogy. Analogy is not homology. Analogical reconstruction does not reduce concepts to one another, let alone conflate systems of thought. Rather, the premise of this analogy is that one relationship (gap, inconsistency, contradiction) in one system can appear in a new light (be "reconstructed") by looking at another system of thought containing a formally similar relationship. Just as we define a difficult word in one language by translating it into another language ("In German, one would say..."), thereby comparing sets of pure *relations between* terms in the two systems (rather than the terms' original etymologies or decontextualized dictionary meanings), so, too, can we clarify a difficult relation between concepts by translating it into another relation between concepts. We are not obliged to know either "language" (system of concepts) perfectly as a whole (as if that were possible). Nor must we capture the conceptual relation in the target "language" perfectly. Rather, like any good translation, analogy helps us to reflect on a relationship between elements in our source(s) by exploring something that is, in some sense, like it. When the two systems of thought do not correspond, valuable questions can be asked about why they do not and can help to clarify our original problem ("That aspect of the analogy does *not* hold for this system, because..."). Like translation, analogy enhances meaning not despite but because there is never a perfect fit between the original and the target. In fact, friction between partly mismatched, partly congruent concepts can emphasize the contours of the wholes where they are embedded.

In this case, our analogy is between (a) the anthropology/morality relation in Kant's "pragmatic point of view"—which relies on his concept of *prudence*, his study of empirical human *characteristics*, and his idea of moral *character*—and (b) a parallel set of relations within the discourse of *derekh erets*. This rabbinic discourse also treats anthropology (in the general sense of a theory of human nature); it is also empirically grounded in the observation/description of humanity, and it also offers (men, normatively) an education in moral skills.[61]

I suggest that the conceptual structure of Kant's anthropology is further *like*—that is, formally analogous to—the conceptual structure of *derekh erets* discourse in one area where *derekh erets* is notoriously opaque. By setting up an analogy between the two systems, we can reconstruct that difficult area. The difficulty is in the relationship between the moral aspect of *derekh erets* and the rest of this term's myriad meanings. *Derekh erets* clearly involves morality, but not in a consistent or comprehensive way. Efforts to cherry-pick prominent instances, thereby imposing the interpreter's theologies on the early rabbis' conceptual system, have not done justice to the discursive integrity of *derekh erets* as a whole. On the contrary, there must be some relationship between the vast majority of this term's mundane, nonexplicitly moral instances, on one hand, and the passages where it reveals a fundamental, even cosmic moral order, on the other. That relation, however, has not been—and perhaps cannot be—uncovered from within the discourse itself: every philological analysis, however scrupulous, has ended with a leap into the scholar's own theology at precisely the point that he tries to explain how these senses of *derekh erets* fit together.

However, if we examine several ways in which derekh erets is *like*—formally analogous to—Kant's "pragmatic point of view" on human nature, we will be better positioned to see that they resemble one another in this respect as well. Like Kant, the early rabbis who formulated and transmitted *derekh erets* were concerned with the relationship between anthropology—the *Is* of human nature and the empirical, observed regularities of human conduct—and morality: the *Ought* to which those observations should be applied and which, at a deeper level, is the very law of their existence. They did not state that relationship explicitly with reference to *derekh erets*, but there are enough interconnections among the different uses of this term to show us how they may have done so—if we turn a Kantian "pragmatic point of view" on their sources.

DEREKH ERETS: ANOTHER PRAGMATIC POINT OF VIEW

As we recall, Kant's central category in his triad of human predispositions and abilities is prudence, which is fully coextensive with pragmatic anthropology in general: both subject matter ("the prudent conduct of human beings") and application (a "prudent use in life").[62] Hence, the empirical evidence that Kant saw as worth collecting, and what he sought in it, is also defined by prudence. "For we study human beings in order to become more prudent, which prudence becomes a science."[63] The procedure of empirical anthropology is to study characteristic features of humans (by categories like sex, race, nation, etc.) in order to find regularities of their conduct. Then pragmatic anthropology, informed by prudence (the skill of knowing how to "use" other people for the common good), draws consequences from those regularities about how to live in the world in a more civilized way. This is the normative function of prudence: it establishes what we are capable of becoming as individuals in society, based on observations of how human beings typically think, feel, and act. Prudence thus plays an essential role in mediating anthropology (the study of what people make of themselves in the world) with its empirical basis (the observation of human characteristics and regularities of conduct).

The normativity of prudence is not morality. Morality comes from a law (rather than from observed regularities); it is solidified as an individual's inner conduct of thought (rather than as sensibility and temperament); and it results in having character (not merely in sharing characteristics with other humans who occupy the same particular categories). Yet prudence also mediates the pragmatic aim of anthropology (educating us to live in the civilized world) with the, systematically speaking, separate province of morality (because we need to know about our characteristics and behaviors in order to determine whether we *can* do what we *should*). Prudence thus confronts human nature as the limit of human freedom. It shows practical morality what it has to work with: only laws of moral character that are "joined to knowledge of humanity" can be called practical and not merely theoretical.

Derekh erets plays an analogous role to Kant's prudence in both respects: it mediates between rabbinic anthropology and its empirical basis as well as between empirical and moral human character. First, like prudence, *derekh erets* is both a means of self-observation and an end of rabbinic anthropology. It describes norms of human conduct and applies those norms usefully to our conduct, becoming a branch of study unto itself. *Derekh erets*, in its sense of manners or know-how (see app. item 7), is analogous to Kant's *Charakeristik*.[64] It encapsulates typical patterns of human thought, emotion, and action. It is also like Kant's prudence because it documents human characteristics with a pragmatic final end (*Endzweck*/telos): to help a rabbinic student live well in the world by aligning his conduct with those patterns. That is the term's most-common sense (app. 7): it covers a range of norms in every sphere of life, from the privy to the bedchamber, study house to Roman road. In this sense, *derekh erets* is the precondition for life in society: early rabbinic sources do not forbid contact with Jews who are unlearned in the oral Torah, but they do insist that "he who does not have [i.e., know] Scripture, Mishnah, or *derekh erets* is not of the settled world,"[65] just as later sources enjoin rabbis to forswear any traffic with such individuals.[66] Much as Kant described pragmatic anthropology as useful "knowledge of the world," for would-be "citizens of the world," *derekh erets* served as rabbinic grounds for membership in a universal society (*yishuv, oikoumenē*) that it conjured into being. Much as *Weltkenntnis* was aimed at better living as a *Weltbürger*, rabbis promoted *derekh erets* as a mode of empirical inquiry that projected, and so created, a normative social horizon: an education in something like "prudence."

As a collection of observations on humanity, with a prudential normativity, *derekh erets* became a telos of rabbinic anthropology: an integral subdiscipline. It was taught and transmitted as its own area of study (see app. item 8), composed of such norms. It was a less-vaunted part of the curriculum than Scripture or Mishnah (e.g., one *could* teach "rules of *derekh erets*" in a state of minor ritual impurity, but not those subjects).[67] Yet it was not fully distinct from other sets of legal or nonlegal norms, in rabbinic tradition or in Scripture. Rabbis derived *derekh erets* rules exegetically, reading Scripture as a participant-observer of human nature like themselves and articulating normative conclusions on that basis with formulas such as "Scripture comes to teach you *derekh erets* from the Torah" (citing a verse as a rule of conduct).[68] Alternatively, they invoked *derekh erets* as "best practices" (see app. item 5) to apply a rabbinic law or to interpret a law in Scripture. For instance, attributing meaning to the redundancy "hunteth and catcheth" (*yatsod tsed*), they extended a hunter's obligation to cover the blood of his prey with dust (Lev. 17:13) to the slaughter of domesticated animals: "It is best practice [*derekh erets*] that one should eat meat only with this preparation."[69] The term here cannot mean simply "good manners": at stake is the scope of a commandment.

Derekh erets includes the "skill" of applying Scriptural norms in life, just as Scripture can teach about, or speak in the language of, *derekh erets*.[70]

Social norms and the observation of everyday life also intersect within the concept of *derekh erets*. Many rabbis assumed that if we know how people normally talk or act, or what normally happens in our world (see app. item 6), it might clarify how we should apply norms in Scripture or earlier rabbinic traditions. They sometimes invoked that very assumption to apply those inherited norms more strictly. For instance, because the "usual way" (*derekh erets*) for a man to be angry in his household is to attack ("cast his eyes upon") its youngest member, when the Israelites challenged Moses, they upended this social norm by attacking its most senior member. They had violated the social hierarchy between great and small (reading "the people did chide [*vayyarev*] with Moses," Exodus 17:2, as "the people *made themselves greater than* Moses").[71] Therefore, they "transgressed [*averu 'al*] the line of justice." It is not that they did something wrong or immoral, a priori, but they misapplied a social norm that could have been applied less wrongly or even constructively. *Derekh erets* is not a prescriptive norm here; the rabbis mean that it is more normal for a man to abuse his children than the reverse—not that it is good! Rather, *derekh erets* here is a social "rule of thumb" for narrowing a general rabbinic norm.[72] Conversely, rabbis used the same assumption to relax their inherited norms. In these cases, their source's "manner of speaking" (app. 6) need not be taken literally. For instance, Scripture says to recite Shema "when going on your way," but this refers to the time when one *normally* goes out, not literally during one's daily commute.[73] Hence "Scripture spoke [only] *derekh erets*"—i.e., "[only] in a manner of speaking." Like the formulas "Scripture spoke *only* of the present" and "Torah spoke according to human language," the notion seems to be that ordinary language use can restrict or expand a norm beyond how it was literally formulated.[74] (The formula also functions this way in nonlegal contexts to designate, e.g., items in biblical stories as *ab*normal or *un*usual—thus implicitly marking the boundaries of what *is* normal in nature or society.)

All four of the preceding functions of *derekh erets*—"best practices" for applying inherited norms (5); "normal" aspects of language, nature, or society (6); "know-how"/"people skills" and the norms of conduct based on them (7); and a body of such rules (8)—bear a normative aspect analogous to Kant's "prudence." Like prudence, *derekh erets*, in all four of these senses, is a way to study human nature, derive norms from it, and navigate such norms in our world. It is an expertise in navigating between the norm and the normal.

The Problem of Morality

The great difficulty within the discursive structure of *derekh erets* is its relationship to morality. This difficulty arises because none of the previous senses of the term are moral in a deontological sense of good and bad, right and wrong. Nor are they moral in a more specifically Kantian sense: absolute, autonomous norms that we, in an exercise of our rational freedom, internalize in the form of our character and conduct of thought. Rather than moral character, in an absolute and universal sense, the normativity of *derekh erets* conjoins nature, human nature, and society. Rather than deontological, the normativity of *derekh erets*, like that of "prudence," is pragmatic. It concerns the contexts where norms are applied and the room for maneuver that one has in adjusting a given norm to its context. Furthermore, such contexts are overwhelmingly anthropocentric (even if some norms at play in them are emanating from a divine text). The autonomy of Kantian moral law is not prominent, nor is there a clear hierarchy between human and divine norms—no explicit grounding of human morality in divine will and law. The worst sanction for violating norms of *derekh erets*, exclusion from society (the "settled world"), is a social sanction administered by people—not a moral sanction administered by God.[75] Perhaps the early rabbis were indeed a bit Kantian, but were they so Durkheimian as to elide that distinction?

Additional senses of *derekh erets* bear no moral connotations either: natural death (1), intercourse (2), and literal work (3). On the contrary, the first two, originally biblical senses of the term, are explicitly amoral. "Natural death" is defined by *opposition* to death for moral reasons (*karet*, premature death by God's will).[76] As for sexual intercourse, already in Genesis 19:31, the biblical source for rabbinic *derekh erets* is a fact of nature: "Our father is old," says Lot's daughter, "and there is not a man in the earth to come in unto us after the manner of all the earth (*kederekh kol ha'arets*)." What the daughters then do with Lot may or may not be moral (perhaps because that phrase scans as an explicit justification, many readers are remarkably easy on them).[77] Regardless, *derekh kol ha'arets* is not a moral term: it simply means that sexual intercourse, like death, is universal and natural for all creation. In the rabbinic canon, too, *derekh erets* in the sense of sex has nothing to do with morality per se. It is listed (with sleep, pleasure, conversation, and laughter) as something that one must restrain in order to "acquire Torah," just as it is later listed with other things (travel, wealth, work, wine, sleep, hot baths, and bloodletting) as "harmful in quantity and beneficial in small measure" for one's health.[78] Sex is not intrinsically moral: it is normal, albeit dangerously distracting for a scholar. Finally, like sex, *derekh erets* in the sense of literal work (3) can be incompatible with the study of Torah, but that does not make it moral or immoral. For example, it seems better to "accept the yoke of Torah [study]" because if one does, one may expect the "yoke of political [life] and the yoke of *derekh erets* [= literal work]" to be miraculously lifted.[79] However, nobody explicitly says that if one fails to prioritize Torah over *derekh erets*, one is transgressing a commandment or otherwise committing a sin.[80] Rather, explicit criticisms, or critical remarks in stories, indicate at most a degree of social pressure within rabbinic circles.[81] At issue, again, are pragmatic rather than moral norms. (Later, and perhaps even among the earliest rabbis, the norm runs in the opposite direction: an "inheritance" offers one the freedom to study Torah.[82]) Death, sex, and labor: these are categories for how things are, "the way of the world." When they bear upon how things *ought* to be, when human embodied reality overlaps with divine and social norms, the discourse remains in a pragmatic register that strives for a prudent hierarchy of norms in particular contexts.

Why, then, is *derekh erets* so often seen as a moral axiom, even as the foundation for all normative order in rabbinic thought? It depends to some extent on which sources one prefers and whether one tries to synthesize them rather than first weighing and distinguishing all (early) senses of the term equally. Kadushin, for instance, assimilates all instances of *derekh erets* to his "concept of the ethical as such."[83] Relying on Seder Eliyahu (a late and altogether peculiar rabbinic work), he defines *derekh erets* as the moral basis for the study and practice of Torah.[84] A subject of rabbinic law does not face a choice between morality and dogged fealty to tradition, Kadushin argues, because both morality and Torah are based on a universal "value-concept" of human nature called *derekh erets*. Kadushin thus uses *derekh erets* to argue against his own reductive version of Kantian morality.[85] For Kadushin, *derekh erets* points to an "organic" rather than rationalistic morality, where Torah norms are grounded not in the absolute but in nature/human nature, thereby avoiding the individual's moral imperative to exercise Kant's "good will" and actively choose conformity to the moral law of Torah. Kant's supposed hierarchy is reversed: Torah is based on morality, which is in turn based on universal natural law (*derekh erets*). For Kadushin, morality, like Torah, is given. And there is no essential gap between Torah, which is unique to Israel, and morality, which applies to everyone. Indeed, these later sources like Seder Eliyahu say that other nations can "have" (i.e., know and practice) *derekh erets* even if they are idolatrous.[86] One can have *derekh erets* even without Torah.

In a similar but less radically humanist and more theologically traditional vein, Novak glosses *derekh erets* as a natural law tradition like the Noahide laws: "The general standards of civilization that preceded the giving of the Torah and are considered the preconditions for the Torah's giving and acceptance."[87] Like Kadushin, he holds that *derekh erets* absorbs the act of accepting a moral law into its own natural givenness and universality. There is no place for Kant's "good will" in freely (i.e., rationally) taking the law on oneself. On the contrary, to the extent that Novak does allow a connection even between positive (rational, human-made) law and *derekh erets*, he naturalizes the former's moral grounding in the latter. Because rabbinic law (oral Torah, tradition) was based not primarily on revelation but on human reason, as Novak holds, the rabbis needed an idea of natural law as "a limit and corrective of positive law made by humans."[88] Like "repairing the world" (*tiqqun ha'olam*), that role was played by *derekh erets*.[89] When early rabbis said, for example, "If there is no *derekh erets*, there is no Torah," and vice versa, a Novakian would gloss them as tempering the moral authority of oral Torah by recalling its bond with natural law.[90]

Because the phrase *derekh erets* literally conjoins the normative ("way") with the natural ("world") and because both Kadushin and Novak seek alternatives to a Kantian morality grounded in the rational will, it makes sense that they appeal to *derekh erets* as the "natural" foundation for both human and Torah norms. Their syntheses of its various senses, however, are supported not by the discourse in early sources but by some later sources filtered through their own modern theologies. Some Amoraic sources contain dicta like "If the Torah had not been given, we would have learned *derekh erets* from the rooster," that is, sexual conduct (2) adhering to social norms (7).[91] This may sound like natural law, yet this dictum is not a definition of *derekh erets*; it may be simply a convenient euphemism. Other Amoraic sources explore aspects of natural law theory *without* the term.[92]

Only in one sense might early rabbinic *derekh erets* bear unambiguously moral force. Even this sense, "good works" (4), never surfaces in a context where it is sharply distinct from literal work (3).[93] However, Flusser and S. Safrai do support a moral interpretation with contextual and comparative evidence. According to their analyses, this moral meaning was the *earliest* rabbinic sense of the term *derekh erets* after the senses of death (1) and sex (2) in its biblical predecessor. For Flusser, "the original and fundamental sense of the term '*derekh erets*' was pure practical morality"; a practical morality that Qumran sectarians, Jewish Christians, and protorabbis envisioned as both universally imperative and independent of the Torah.[94] Flusser argues that this idea originated in the "Two Ways" morality of 1QS, the *Didache,* and other sources, which posits a duality of the "way of life" and " way of death," absolute good and absolute evil, mapping neatly onto a social schism between the elect and the wicked. Such moral dualism, Flusser argues, morphed into the one-"way" model of early rabbis, who advocated adherence to a universal "path" of morality. The "way of life" lost its opposition to the "way of death" and became simply "the way of the world."[95] S. Safrai supports Flusser's conjectures via closer analyses of the term.[96] He agrees that homilies in Avot and some exegetical works reflect a common stock of moral discourse such as the "Two Ways." Safrai also agrees that this discourse developed into the piety (*hasidut*) of Jesus and contemporary Jewish sages and, eventually, into rabbinic *derekh erets*. This mode of piety valued action over study but did not neglect the latter—on the contrary, in some cases, it held stricter legal restrictions, presenting itself as supererogatory ("above and beyond") the law.

In this sense, and only in this sense, we could speak of *derekh erets* as expressing a properly moral norm. Its other senses cover nature and human nature's regularities of conduct and articulate norms for aligning one's conduct with that order, according to criteria and sanctions to be applied and sanctioned within human society. In Kant's terms, they are *pragmatic*. Alternatively, they add nuances or strictures to Torah-law. But only in this sense of pious "good works" (4) may *derekh erets* be an absolute moral norm, whether this means observing norms other than Torah, going above and beyond in Torah-observance, or prioritizing good works over scholarly virtues.[97] Only in this sense does *derekh erets* mean "morality" and not just a pragmatic good.

But what is so good about it? Standard philological approaches to its meaning founder. Other than a vague association with "deeds," a "joyful" way of performing commandments, refraining from theft, or, in later sources, philanthropic "good works" like donating money and fostering peace between people, we cannot tell what makes *derekh erets* in this sense so distinctive—let alone a precondition to receiving the Torah.[98] On the contrary, most of the term's early normative force seems to be concentrated in sense (7), proper conduct, which is pragmatic rather than moral. *Derekh erets*, in that sense (7), clarifies the intent of Scripture; sets paradigms for social and even for divine conduct, instructs would-be sages in manners, and lists the empirical regularities of human behavior. Or, *derekh erets* refers to natural givens of human experience: death, sex, and labor. But its morality is not clearly defined. Between the useful and the natural, it is difficult to define the good that *derekh erets* serves. It is a more practical virtue than Torah-study, yet its social orientation is no different from other normative senses, such as legal "best practice" (5) or "know-how" (7). If anything, *derekh erets* seems like a different—perhaps more sincere or devout—way to do ordinary things. The term's various contextual senses do not reveal how *derekh erets* goes beyond natural and social norms. Nor is the historians' solution—the view that its most common senses (5)–(7) reflect later derivations, or "degradations" of its original, universally moral sense (4)—persuasive, due to vague chronology or circular logic.[99]

Rather than limit the moral dimension of *derekh erets* to a single sense of the term *good deeds* (4), an analogy to Kant prevents conflating this term's confusing semantics with its integrity as a discourse. It bridges what people *are* and *can* be—the pragmatic domain—with what they *should* become, morally speaking. In that respect, *derekh erets* discourse is much like the precritical, anthropological Kant's "pragmatic point of view" (not the critical Kant, against whom Kadushin and Novak tried to redefine this term).

Toward a Solution (By Way of Analogy)

Sharpening the analogy to Kant's "pragmatic point of view" can help clarify how *derekh erets* bridges not only the natural with the social—not only what is *normal* with what we take to be *normative*—but also connects that pragmatic domain with morality. In principle, Kant opposes the pragmatic and the moral, just as he opposes the *Is* of anthropology to the *Ought* of morality. But he also outlines three aspects of "pragmatic normativity," *within* the pragmatic point of view, which contribute to moral development: (1) skill, (2) character, and (3) education.[100] All three terms illuminate how *derekh erets* discourse bridges morality with the pragmatic world of anthropology, as well as the order of nature: a potent triad.

First, as a "doctrine of prudence," the aim of the pragmatic point of view is to teach us to "make proper use of everything," pursuing the telos of our happiness as a species. Prudence is "skill in the choice of means to one's own greatest well-being."[101] This includes morality. If one lacks the skill to absorb morality, then one is preaching rather than teaching about humanity: mere "sermons ... admonitions of which we never tire." If morality does not change one's character, then it is not practical morality but sterile theory. However, if, one can make a prudent use of moral teaching (in the rabbis' case, Torah), it has a transformative effect.

Here lies the second bridge from the anthropological to the moral in *derekh erets*: Kant's twin senses of *character*. Moral character is formed in a different way than our empirical, pragmatic character in the world: by rationally accepting a law of duty (in the rabbis' case, Torah) rather than by "making of oneself" a good citizen of the world. And yet, insofar as the law of duty is only applicable if we know what we are and can be, moral character does require knowledge of empirical character. Anthropology is a propaedeutic to morality. This is what it entails to be "*educated* to the good": via immersion in prudence (a sort of "people skills," also an aspect of *derekh erets*), we can learn to live in a more civilized world. Through the cultivation of prudence, pragmatic anthropology—midway between raw technical skill and lofty pure morality—offers us some practical wisdom, even if we cannot define "the good" a priori or adopt moral imperatives as a rational law of conduct.

By integrating prudence, moral character, and education, *derekh erets* is an applied anthropology no less than Kant's, and in both cases, morality is a key domain to which it is applied. *Derekh erets* investigates human nature and helps an individual to cultivate moral character within the given order of nature and society. At the same time, *derekh erets* teaches prudential normativity that *uses* human nature and social convention as a basis for evaluating one's actions, even as such evaluation remains pragmatic rather than moral in an absolute sense.

As a skill, *derekh erets*, like prudence, offers technical "know-how" that helps one to be a better citizen of the world. Yet it also teaches one how to "make proper use" of morality and to "make of oneself" a better person. If *derekh erets* is not itself character, it is preparation for character. This explains Rabbi Yannai's question to his Torah-unlearned dinner guest: "So much *derekh erets* in you, yet I called you a dog!?"[102] He suddenly sees his guest's good manners (*derekh erets* in the sense of proper social conduct [7]) not as mere politeness but as flutters of a moral pulse. Other strategic ambiguities between two senses of the term (work [3] and "good works" [4]) could be read in a similar light. The adage "*Judge* your words before they come from your mouth / and make your works accountable to *derekh erets*" plays across the gap between the mundane (words; works) and the normative (words *of the law*; *good* works).[103] Again, the presumption is not that an individual is *already* doing something moral when he speaks or talks, or *already* has a moral good in mind. Rather, what one finds in the ordinary social world—its words and works—can *become* a standard of conduct. By means of *derekh erets*, like Kant's prudence, one makes the most skillful use of one's faculties to prepare for character rather than submitting to a "top-down" and purely autonomous moral law. This sort of character is not the result of an imperative or negative maxim any more than it is the result of a divine commandment. It is a projection of the social order onto oneself (and vice versa). Everyday words are remade in the image of law, and deeds are remade in the image of *derekh erets*. In this respect, it is indeed a point of view "on the basis on which the others are formed."

This brings us to the final node of analogy between *derekh erets* discourse and Kant's "pragmatic point of view": education. The pragmatic is not the good, as such. However, it helps one to be *"educated* to the good." The final end of *derekh erets* as a form of moral education is not mere "know-how," "best practices," or "people skills" in social or legal realms (elite etiquette [7], halakhic scruples [5], etc.). Nor is *derekh erets* aimed at a purely descriptive analysis of how people "normally" talk, think, or act (6). Rather, those senses of the term as well as its sense of philanthropic "good works" (4) presume that the social order does reflect pragmatic norms—even if through a glass darkly. Hence a pragmatic point of view is a discourse of prudence: it studies what we are in order to know what we can and—within those limits—should become. As a moral educator, the pragmatic anthropologist—whether philosopher or rabbi—does not define the good and conform to it. Rather, they observe the order of nature and human nature so as to make our world, in a human image, relatively better.

CONCLUSION

This chapter has repositioned Kant at the Talmud/Philosophy intersection or, at least, has revealed the possibility of a very different Kant and a very different sort of intersection. Rather than the father of a transcendental logic that one uses to decipher the back-and-forth of a Talmudic argument, we rediscovered the popular, pragmatic (and profoundly problematic) pedagogue of a budding human science.[104] Correspondingly, rather than the dialectics of halakhah, we have encountered the down-to-earth and didactic discourse of rabbinic *derekh erets*—"the way of the world"—which mediates anthropology with normativity. As these margins of the two canons came into contact, they asked and answered each other's different articulations of a shared fundamental question: *What is the relationship between anthropology and morality?*

I argued that a "pragmatic" point of view and the concept of "prudence," which are Kant's answer to those questions, can be translated into the early rabbinic discourse of *derekh erets*. This conceptual translation, or analogical reconstruction, accounts for connections among the latter term's eight different meanings. Specifically, it strengthens the link between pragmatic and moral aspects of *derekh erets* discourse, a link that has not been explained by analyses of the sources alone. Kant's pragmatic anthropology thus serves as more than a comparandum or "think-piece" with respect to early rabbinic thought. It is a clearer response to the rabbis' own problem: it fills a gap in their system of thought, showing how its internal contradictions could cohere philosophically. At the same time, this approach avoids synthesizing the term's senses or deriving them all from one "master" sense, a procedure that has hampered analyses of *derekh erets* by historians and theologians alike.

To recapitulate the chapter's argument, I began by showing the bridge from anthropology to morality within Kant's "pragmatic point of view." Whereas, in Kant's system, morality is set apart from anthropology, his pragmatic point of view operates as a crucial hinge or mediator between those two areas. It incorporates both a normativity of its own (*prudence*—our skill of "using" people to make ourselves and society better) and a link with morality (as the empirical limit of moral laws and the zone of their practical application). Just as the pragmatic is, so to speak, in the middle of Kant's philosophical system—drawing together technical and moral aspects of our capacities and final ends in the social world—so is prudence the centerpiece of pragmatic inquiry, constantly referring the study of human nature back to the direction and progress of civilization. Although it is not equivalent to morality, prudence can be preparation for, and accessory to, our moral formation in three respects: skill, character, and education. Redefining our skills with things in terms of other humans and teaching us "people skills" in our various social capacities, prudence helps us to remake ourselves in the world. Observing and characterizing patterns of human thought, feeling, and action, it sketches the outlines of that upon which a moral law might act. Educating us as "citizens of the world," it draws us into a practical, sociocentric normativity. Prudence's outward forms of human knowledge and self-knowledge are not a priori laws, but they are valuable nonetheless.

After an interlude on method, I proposed an analogy between the preceding sketch of Kant's "pragmatic point of view" and the classical rabbinic discourse of *derekh erets*; specifically, in terms of how *derekh erets* also mediates between rabbinic anthropology and morality. First, I showed that the most common senses of *derekh erets* are translatable by Kant's "prudence" in terms of how they relate observation and description of nature and society, on one hand, with social norms, on the other. Like Kant's anthropology, the basic orientation of *derekh erets* discourse is pragmatic. It offers situational classifications of what is normal or typical as well as rules of conduct applying to, or modeled on, such situations. Its sources are diverse: inherited oral and Scriptural traditions, both legal and nonlegal, and anecdotes or off-the-cuff generalizations. What draws all of these senses together is their use of human society (and, often, the order of nature) as a norm for one's conduct. Like prudence, *derekh erets* teaches one how to become a social being: it builds *character*, in a nonuniversal sense. The limits of membership in this category are the limits of society, not of morality in general.

Yet to what extent is the normativity of *derekh erets* also moral? Does it have reference to a good, to some universal horizon beyond the social? Where are God and the commandments in this rabbinic version of the "pragmatic point of view," given that Scripture "comes to teach you *derekh erets* from the Torah" and even God's behavior, at times, makes sense within social conventions of *derekh erets*?[105] This is the major quandary. Whereas previous studies have defined this moral dimension of *derekh erets* by privileging one sense of the term, *good works* (4), or by synthesizing its senses into a theology of "natural law" or "the ethical as such," I treated each sense of the term as distinct and coequal yet discursively complementary. By analogy to Kant, I argued that *derekh erets* similarly involves three practical aspects (prudence, character, and education), which structure an agent's moral formation in the pragmatic sphere of society, as a "citizen of the world." These practical aspects define the scope of morality, providing criteria for moral self-evaluation and orientation. To the extent that it emphasizes character development and an education in prudence—that is, the skill of living by immanent norms—*derekh erets* relates anthropology with morality much like Kant's "pragmatic point of view." One does not have to posit *derekh erets* as the foundation of all morality or ascertain those foundations to appreciate its distinctively pragmatic role in bridging observation of norms in the human world—rabbinic anthropology—with the natural order, the normal course of things, and the noumenal brought down to earth. As an education in prudence, *derekh erets* opens a human-centered, pragmatic point of view on morality that is sparse in other rabbinic discourses: not Torah from Sinai but practical teaching for daily life.

I conclude with a reprise of my interlude on method. What I call translation among systems of thought, or "analogical reconstruction," has its utility and its pitfalls. I have surely demonstrated some of both. Philological sifting of terms and their contextual senses can only go so far in grasping an ancient discourse whose social context and wider literary context are full of gaps. We need some way to move from terms to discourse—a whole greater than the sum of its parts, where senses intersect, clash, and complement one another under the pressure of culturally inflected, often opaque problems. Too often, solutions to these problems are forced by imposing an external ("historical") context or monocausal motive ("ideology") onto our sources. Or, within the philological horizon, one tries to marshal more texts, and an invented "tradition" supplies the missing links between them. Analogy is another way. Like translation, analogy is an act of expressing one system in terms of another. Without pretending that two different formulations say the same thing, one can weigh the specific excess, invariance, and incongruity that arise from their juxtaposition. Some relations ("meanings") are added to the original. Others carry over, and still others simply do not fit. In our case, the juxtaposition helped to highlight and fill a gap within the system of *derekh erets* that was clearer in Kant. If "words of Torah are poor in their place and rich in another," [106] all the more so are Talmud and philosophy.

APPENDIX: THE TERM *DEREKH ERETS* IN EARLY RABBINIC SOURCES

The term *derekh erets* (literally, "way of the land" and probably originating from "the way of all the world," *derekh kol ha'arets*, in Gen. 19:31, Josh. 23:14, and 1 Kings 2:2) appears in all branches of classical rabbinic literature: works of both legal and narrative exegesis as well as apodictic and aphoristic ("wisdom") works. It is also preserved in its own set of works with shared contents, likely reflecting oral traditions going back to the

Second Temple period.[107] These works are labeled *derekh erets* according to some Palestinian and Babylonian Amoraim (third-to-fifth century CE) and, much later, by the hands of medieval scribes, who preserved works under that title among what commentators called the "minor," "supplemental," or "external" tractates. These tractates generally take the form of collections of oral traditions according to topic (Converts, Slaves; etc.).[108] Many of those traditions are paralleled in Tannaitic and Amoraic sources, but the relative chronology of these parallels, not to mention the Derekh Erets compilations, has not been fully mapped.

As a term, *derekh erets* is ubiquitous in early rabbinic oral tradition (c. 70–250 CE), which is the focus of this chapter. These early attestations are preserved in late-second to mid-third-century works from Roman Palestine, as well as in later works from Byzantine Palestine and Sasanian Iran, traditions bearing adequate markers (attributions, citation formulas, parallels) to be dated no later than the third century.[109]

These early sources reveal eight contextual meanings. They are, in ascending order of frequency: (1) *natural* death, as opposed to death by the evil eye,[110] or divine punishment;[111] (2) marital sexual intercourse and abstinence, whether voluntary (*perishut derekh erets*) or involuntary;[112] (3) literal work or business;[113] (4) good deeds ("works" in a metaphorical sense, following Safrai);[114] (5) observance of a stringency or precaution with direct legal implications in the local context (what we might call "best practices");[115] (6) accounting for the language of an earlier law as a reflection of real life/how people really talk or classifying something in a biblical story or in real life as "*ab*normal," "*un*natural," or "marvelous" (Josephus: *thaumastos*);[116] (7) lessons in customary/proper conduct, good manners, or "know-how";[117] specifically, how, when, and with how many people to travel on the road;[118] how to be a good host[119] or guest,[120] how to respect the honor of your fellow[121] or your teacher;[122] how to speak properly,[123] how to eat or drink at a banquet;[124] and miscellaneous tips on how to build your banquet-couch[125] or your house;[126] how to look after your health;[127] how to manage your money;[128] when to acquire land, a house, and a wife;[129] how a groom should follow his bride's lead to enter the wedding canopy[130] and during sex.[131] Finally, *derekh erets* designates (8) a body of rabbinic instruction about such matters, although, unfortunately, we can only be sure that it contained in its earliest period a rule for the order in which to put on one's shoes (a matter of dispute, of course).[132]

JAMES ADAM REDFIELD is Assistant Professor in the Department of Theological Studies, Fellow of the Research Institute at Saint Louis University, Visiting Assistant Professor at the University of Chicago Divinity School, and author of *Adventures of Rabbah & Friends: The Talmud's Strange Tales and Their Readers.*

NOTES

1. The epigraph is from "Anthropology Friedländer," in Kant, *Lectures on Anthropology*, 49. Bracketed additions here and throughout are my own [JR]. Compare Kant, *Groundwork*, 23: "The whole of morals, which requires anthropology for its *application* to human beings" (emphasis in original). On the textual history of Kant's anthropology, see Stark, "Historical Notes and Interpretive Questions." I focus on his main publication ("Anthropology from a Pragmatic Point of View" in Kant, *Anthropology, History, and Education*), supplemented by his other writings and transcriptions of his lectures. My thanks to the weekly seminar of the 2019–20 Cornell Society for the Humanities for feedback on this chapter, especially Paul Fleming, Lori Khatchadourian, Ariel Ron, and Samantha Wesner.

2. See Dolgopolski, "Constructed and Denied." Even when the grandson of the Brisker Rav, Joseph B. Soloveitchik, rejected the neo-Kantian Marburg School as a model for reconstructing the philosophy of halakhah, he continued to draw from their dispute with Kant to support his axiom that objectivity is prior to subjectivity. See Soloveitchik, *The Halakhic Mind*, 65–66, 101; Munk, *The Rationale of Halakhic Man*, 14–51. For a more nuanced treatment of his position, see Brafman, "The Objectifying Instrument of Religious Consciousness."

3. For descriptive accounts of the Brisker method of Talmud study, see Solomon, *The Analytic Movement*, 96–239; Blau, *Lomdus: The Conceptual Approach to Torah Learning*.

4. Kühn, "Interpreting Kant Correctly."

5. Here, a landmark is Foucault's 1964 *thèse complémentaire*, which both connected Kant's anthropology to his critical philosophy and set up Foucault's aim, in *Les mots et les choses* (1966), to "anthropologize philosophy." See editors' preface to Foucault, *Anthropologie d'un point de vue pragmatique*, 8. This connection is still central to work on Kant's anthropology. Particularly important for this chapter has been Munzel, *Kant's Conception of Moral Character*.

6. In this chapter, I use *anthropology* for any empirically inflected theory of human nature. I also use the term in the historical sense that it had in a specified context of use. I may alternate between general and historical senses, referring to Kant's "anthropology" (in a general sense) and also to his *"Anthropologie."* I may refer to rabbinic "anthropology" (in the general sense—despite the lack of such a term or science in the rabbis' era). Despite this fluctuation among uses, it should be clear, in context, which sense is meant.

7. Kant, *Groundwork*, 3; Munzel, *Kant's Conception of Moral Character*; Louden, *Kant's Impure Ethics*. Indispensable to any study of Kant's anthropology is Sturm, *Kant und die Wissenschaften vom Menschen*; on the link between anthropology and morality, 502–18.

8. *Klugheitslehre*. On the literature that wrongly treats Kant's notion of "prudence" as instrumental and self-interested, see Graband, *Klugheit bei Kant*, 7–8.

9. Louden, *Kant's Human Being*, 77.

10. Kant defines "popular" as an anthropology that has "reference to examples which can be found by every reader." This has a methodological value: it encourages readers "to make each particular into a theme of its own, so as to place it in the appropriate category" (Kant, *Anthropology, History, and Education*, 233). He seems to have imagined students specializing by descriptive category, according to their tastes. On the pedagogical *Sitz im Leben* of this form, see Brandt, *Kritischer Kommentar*, 89. Kant selected Baumgarten's textbook on empirical psychology as the basis for the first part of his course (*Didaktik*) but used no text for the second part (departing from his own *Observations on the Beautiful and the Sublime* [1764]). On his relationship to Baumgarten, see Wood, "Kant and the Problem of Human Nature," 58n10; Lorini, "The Rules for Knowing the Human Being."

11. James Adam Redfield, "Kant's Racist Anthropology in Context: Ethnographic Archives of the German Enlightenment," (forthcoming in CROMOHS vol. 27 (2024)). On race in the political theology of Israel and the Jews, see Ophir and Rosen-Zvi, *Goy* and Redfield, "Review of *Goy*."

12. Cohen, *Kant and the Human Sciences*, 62–65.

13. What Kant dismisses as a search for "die Quellen der *phaenomenorum*," 1774 ms. of his Geography lectures (in Brandt, *Kritischer Kommentar*, 51).

14. See Diem, "Deutsche Schulanthropologie," 365. See also Tommasi, "Somatology."

15. Kant, *Correspondence*, 141.

16. Zammito, "What a Young Man Needs," 232–35; Brandt, *Kritischer Kommentar*, 56, 68.

17. "Such an anthropology, considered as *knowledge of the world*, which must come after our *schooling*, is actually not yet called *pragmatic* when it contains an extensive knowledge of *things* in the world, for example, animals, plants, and minerals from various lands and climates, but only when it contains knowledge of the human being as a *citizen of the world*. Therefore, even knowledge of the races of human beings as products belonging to the play of nature is not yet counted as pragmatic knowledge of the world, but only as knowledge of the world." Kant, *Anthropology* (1798), 231–32 (emphasis in original). See also Kant, "Anthropology-Mrongovius" (1784–85), in Kant, *Lectures on Anthropology*, 343: "There are two ways to study: in school and in the world. In school one studies scholastic cognitions." And 344: "In scholastic anthropology, I search for the causes of human nature. In pragmatic anthropology, I merely look at the human constitution and attempt to apply it."

18. Kant, *Anthropology, History, and Education*, 231.

19. Ibid.

20. Kant, "Of the Different Races of Human Beings" (1st ed., 1775), in Kant, *Anthropology, History, and Education*, 97.

21. Kant, *Anthropology, History, and Education*, 417.

22. A comprehensive history of the uses and abuses of "applied anthropology" in the modern period is a desideratum, despite important syntheses such as Asad, *Anthropology and the Colonial Encounter*; Gusterson, "Anthropology and Militarism." Regardless, what Kant means by "use" is certainly quite different.

23. Kant, *Anthropology, History, and Education*, 418.

24. Compare Kant, "Lectures on Pedagogy" in Kant, *Anthropology, History, and Education*, 444: the *civilizing* form of cultivation requires, inter alia, "prudence": the ability to "use all human beings for one's own final purposes." Again, the reference to *final* end (see his use of *letzter Zweck*) means that cultivation has a social end, not a selfish one.

25. Kant, *Correspondence*, 141. See Kant, "Anthropology-Mrongovius," 345, and further references in Kain, "Prudential Reason."

26. Summarizing Kant, *Anthropology, History, and Education*, 417–20.

27. "Anthropology Friedländer," 49. Similarly, in the life span of an individual, "middle age [...] is the age of prudence, where one can rightly estimate the worth of things," as one is no longer misled by passion and not yet too old to *use* one's judgment. "Anthropology Friedländer," 167 (see Kant, *Anthropology, History, and Education*, 308).

28. For a strong reading of this analogy, see Pozzo, "Kant on the Five Intellectual Virtues," 178–80. That said, the proximal origins of Kant's term "pragmatic" lie less in Aristotle than in Polybius: much as ethnography and historiography coevolved from Herodotus on, so did "pragmatic anthropology" emerge from a debate on "pragmatic historiography" in Enlightenment Germany. See Sturm, *Kant und die Wissenschaften vom Menschen*, 311–12.

29. Kant in Pozzo, "Kant on the Five Intellectual Virtues," 179 (my emphasis) n26.

30. Kant, *Anthropology, History, and Education*, 316 (my emphasis).

31. Kant lectured to men, and "human" (*Mensch*) or impersonal locutions (*man*; *sich*) are often gendered male, as they are here. Additionally, he excludes women from whole anthropological categories (e.g., Kant, "Anthropology-Mrongovius," 410: "Wisdom is the ultimate purpose [...] women do not have it." The same goes for his concept of "character": see Brandt, *Kritischer Kommentar*, 293). However, I view the androcentrism of Kant's anthropology as less absolute than do some of his interpreters and translators, which is not to deny the misogynistic elements in his thought. He hopes that his observations of human character will be appreciated "even [!] by ladies at their dressing-table" (Kant, "*Menschenkunde*-Petersburg" [1781–82?], in *Lectures on Anthropology*, 291). Furthermore, when analyzing relationships between the sexes, he pays far more attention to women and, in many ways, sees women as more significant in society. A female subject of his anthropology should be kept in view, even if she is not the normative subject. On her paradoxical role as "the alien other of the *Anthropology par excellence*," see Clark, "Kant's Aliens," 266–72.

32. Kant's textbook definition of pragmatic (*Anthropology, History, and Education*, 231 [my emphasis]). The pragmatic and educational (as opposed to the technical preservation or moral governance of our species) similarly align at Kant, *Anthropology, History, and Education*, 417.

33. Compare Kant, "Lectures on Pedagogy," in *Anthropology, History and Education*, 473: "Practical education includes 1) skill, 2) worldly prudence and 3) morality." Here the "pragmatic" and "practical education" are synonymous. As Brandt notes (*Kritischer Kommentar*, 119), according to this threefold division elsewhere in Kant's writings, Kant could not say "*and should* make of himself" as he does in the textbook. Kain, "Prudential Reason," 238, also notes this important internal contradiction of the system but does not analyze it.

34. See Kain, "Prudential Reason"; Madrid, "Prudence and the Rules for Guiding Life"; Graband, *Klugheit bei Kant*, 72–79.

35. "In fact, one of the most significant developments in Kant's conception of prudence over the course of the anthropology lectures is an increasing emphasis on the significance of the human social context." Kain, "Prudential Reason," 246.

36. Summarizing Kant, "*Menschenkunde*-Petersburg," 291.

37. Kant, "Anthropology-Busolt" (1788–89?), in *Lectures on Anthropology*, 521.

38. See Kant, *Anthropology, History, and Education*, 338: "the pragmatic point of view," in terms of a human individual's happiness, is "the well-being that he intends to secure through skill and prudence."

39. Kant, "Anthropology-Mrongovius," 344.

40. Kant, *Anthropology, History, and Education*, 232 (emphasis in original).

41. Ibid., 233. For a clear discussion of these obstacles, see Louden, *Kant's Human Being*, 70–72. For the genealogy of "fieldwork" in different national traditions of anthropology, see Debaene, *Far Afield*, 35–44.

42. Kant, *Anthropology, History, and Education*, 384.

43. Ibid., 389–90.

44. Ibid., 391–92: specifically, such maxims are *not to* (a) lie, (b) dissemble, (c) break promises, (d) have bad friends, (e) listen to gossip. The pietistic tone rings loud and clear.

45. See the definition of pragmatic as what a human being "can or should make of himself," nn. 32–33.

46. Kant, *Anthropology, History, and Education*, 392.

47. The former is Munzel's translation; see her *Kant's Conception of Moral Character*, xvi and 23–70, on "conduct of thought."

48. As Zammito notes ("What a Young Man Needs," 237–40), this structure varied a great deal over the lecture course.

49. The margin of Kant's ms. reads under this heading: "In what can one recognize the particularity [*Eigentümlichkeit*] of each human being?" This is a better description of *Charakteristik* than the printed subtitle, "On the Way of Cognizing the Interior of the Human Being from the Exterior," which may not be his own; see Brandt, *Kritischer Kommentar*, 125.

50. See Munzel, *Kant's Conception of Moral Character*, 26–27.

51. Ibid., 53.

52. Kant, *Anthropology, History, and Education*, 384. See Mensch, "Caught Between Character and Race."

53. Ibid., 385, 394. On physiognomy, race, and difference in Kant, see nn. 11, 13, and 14 above.

54. Kant, *Anthropology, History, and Education*, 394. See also p. 399: the habitual facial expressions of religious groups may become "hardened" into the characteristic expression of an entire society, but it does not follow that they are true characters of individuals. Nobody can rationally explain how to distinguish natural variations from morality in this case.

55. Kant, *Anthropology, History, and Education*, 408.

56. Ibid., 420 (emphasis in original).

57. Ibid., 420–21 and 425–29, defines these obstacles and political forms.

58. Kant, *Anthropology, History, and Education*, 423. The actual example may not belong at this location: Brandt, *Kritischer Kommentar*, 496.

59. Kant, *Anthropology, History, and Education*, 390 (emphasis in original).

60. Kant, "Anthropology Friedländer," 49. See Sturm, *Kant und die Wissenschaften vom Menschen*, 293.

61. Like Kant's pragmatic anthropology (see n. 31), *derekh erets* discourse does acknowledge the possibility of a female audience, but this is not its normative audience and sometimes actively marginalized. Some of its contents are gender-neutral—a woman might also want to know, for instance, to light a candle before dusk on the Sabbath, a *derekh erets* "best practice" rule. Sometimes, gender-neutral language (*adam*, "human,"

not *ish*, "man") even seems deliberate. But much of the discourse is addressed exclusively to male sages or to men who take their advice seriously. Even if we include sources outside our period, in works compiled near the end of late antiquity, the only one that asks if a woman "has *derekh erets*" (a *daughter* of a sage, at that) answers that it depends on whether her *husband* is learned (Yes) or unlearned (No). *Derekh erets* is not a consistently misogynistic discourse—yes, it is declared "normal" (*derekh erets*) for a man to forsake his wife for a prettier one, but several *derekh erets* rules are aimed to safeguard a wife's conjugal rights. The discourse, however, has an androcentric, patriarchal profile, resembling some other strains of rabbinic wisdom literature.

62. The research in this section is drawn from Redfield, "The Sages and the World," 141–206; the appendix is adapted from 157–60 ad loc. The context, however, and therefore most of the content, differ.

63. Kant, "Anthropology Friedländer," 49.

64. Items in parentheses (1–8) refer to the eight senses of the term *derekh erets* as documented in the appendix. I designate a more verbatim parallel source with =, and a less verbatim parallel source (or a very similar source) with ≈.

65. m. Qiddushin 1:10 (ed. Albeck III:317) = Avot of Rabbi Natan B 32:23 (ed. Becker, 370). The term settled world could refer to society, or it could refer, not to this world, but to the next (hence, exclusion from *future* society of a more radical kind, as in the infamous catalog at m. Sanhedrin 10:1: "All Israel has a portion in the world to come. [...] And the following have no portion"). Compare Hebrews 2:5, where οἰκουμένη ("the inhabited world") means "the world to come" (עולם הבא). Similarly, at Massekhet Kallah 3 (ed. Higger, 126), to "have דרך ארץ" is equated with "having a portion in עולם הבא." Contrast Avot of Rabbi Natan A 28:20 (ed. Becker, 218–19): "Anyone who makes דרך ארץ primary in this world (עולם הזה) and words of Torah secondary is made secondary in this world." The next parable does not say such a person *will* be primary in the "world to come," it simply stresses the need for a middle way between Torah and *derekh eretz*. For דרך ארץ reflecting rabbinic knowledge of the term οἰκουμένη, see Fischel, "Greek and Latin Languages," 58.

66. b. Qiddushin 41a. The "b." refers to the Babylonian Talmud in the standard edition of reference (Vilna).

67. b. Berakhot 22a, attributed to R. Yehudah (bar Ilai). Similarly, one *may* discuss laws of the bathhouse there, but only those laws, later preserved in the Derekh Erets corpus (*Pereq Hanihas* 3, ed. Higger, *Massekhtot Kallah*, 295–305).

68. On these cases, see Novick, *What Is Good, and What God Demands*, 68–79; Rosen-Zvi, "Structure and Reflectivity in Tannaitic Legal Homilies," 287–88. On "Scripture" (*ha-katuv*) as a dynamic hypostasis of the interpretive process and its distinction from the figure of "the Torah," see Yadin, *Scripture as Logos*, 23–33.

69. Sifra §Aharei Mot 7:2, attributed to Rabbi (ed. Weiss 84c; here, cited from ms. Vatican ebr. 66 via https://maagarim.hebrew-academy.org.il) = b. Hullin 84a, *baraita*. In this chapter, the Bible is cited in the translation/versification of the King James Version.

70. It is possible that the term is used here in this less common, nonsocial sense due to an association with the local literary context, which involves the physical earth. A similar case is t. Shevi'it 4:2 (and, see further, Lieberman, *Tosefta Kifeshutah: Shevi'it*, 527–28), where "*derekh erets*" labels a halakhic precaution ("best practice," we might say) but does so in an agricultural context, rendering it ambiguously metaphorical.

71. Mekhilta §Vayassa VII (ed. Lauterbach, 129) ≈ Mekhilta of Rabbi Shimeon bar Yohai 17:3 (ed. Epstein and Melammed, 117).

72. On this norm ("line of justice," *shurat ha-din*) in the Babylonian Talmud, see Barer, "Law, Ethics, and Hermeneutics." On the earlier sources, and ours in particular, see Novick, "Naming Normativity," at 397. Novick sees *derekh erets* and *shurat ha-din* as contextual synonyms that "interchange" in this passage (400). I see the latter as defined in terms of the former.

73. Sifre Deuteronomy §34 (ed. Finkelstein, 62) = Midrash Tannaim (ed. Hoffmann, I:27).

74. For example, Mekhilta §Kaspa II (ed. Lauterbach, II:465–66 [my emphasis]); see Harris, *How Do We Know This?*, 33–43.

75. Unless "the settled world" is a synonym for "the world to come," which has some philological basis; see n.65. Despite this possible exception, the point is that violations of *derekh erets* are not consistently sanctioned, unlike violations of moral norms (a.k.a. "sins"). Hence it seems to be of a very different normative order from morality. This vagueness of sanctions for violating *derekh erets*, in contrast to law, has been virtually ignored by theologians who see *derekh erets* as equivalent to morality and is a significant problem for that approach, such as a Novakian "natural law" reading of *derekh erets*.

76. y. Bikkurim 2:1, 64d (ed. Academy of the Hebrew Language [AHL], 354:47) = Treatise Semahot 3:9 (ed. Higger, 114). In this chapter, I cite the Palestinian Talmud ("y.") according to halakhah and Venice pagination, following by column and line in the *Talmud Yerushalmi* published by the AHL.

77. Amoraim were reluctant to condemn Lot's daughters, commenting: "They thought that the world had been entirely destroyed as in the generation of the flood" (Gen. Rabbah 41:8 [ed. Theodor and Albeck, 537]). Rashi (commenting on Gen. 19:31) ventriloquizes Hillel: "*If not now, when?* Perhaps he will die or become infertile." Compare Didymus Caecus, *Scr. Eccl., In Genesim* (cited from the *Thesaurus Linguae Graecae*): "it was not done out of passion but for the sake of survival (καὶ ὅτι οὐκ ἐμπαθῶς τοῦτο πεποιήκασιν, ἀλλὰ ζώπυρον ὑπολιποῦσαι)." Chrysostom sermonizes: "Let no one ever presume to condemn the just man or his daughters. After all, how could it be other than a mark of extreme folly and stupidity on our part, laden as we are with such countless burdens of sin, to condemn those whom Sacred Scripture discharges of all sin and for whom it rather even supplies such a remarkable defense." (*Homilies on Genesis*, §44, 465–66). Scribal dots over this verse are read as a justification in *The Zohar* (ed. Matt, II:160n340).

78. Avot (Qinyan Torah, an independent and later unit), 6:5, in Mishnah (ed. Albeck, IV:384); b. Gittin 70a.

79. Avot 3:5. As Flusser noted, the three "yokes" parallel the Stoic division of theoretical, political, and practical lives. Compare Epicurus's aphorism in Seneca, *Epistles*, I:40–41): "If you would enjoy real freedom, you must be the slave of philosophy."

80. On the larger issue of the tension between the demands of work and study, see Baer, "Talmud Torah vederekh erets"; Urbach, *The Sages*, 602–19 and references at 963n81; Boyarin, *Carnal Israel*, 134–66; Boyarin, "Internal Opposition in Talmudic Literature."

81. Avot of Rabbi Natan A 28:20, see n. 65. See also b. Berakhot 35b. Avot of Rabbi Natan A 1:5–6 (ed. Becker, 6–7): "It is not right to forsake the words of the Living God and get swept away by *derekh erets*."

82. Ecclesiastes Rabbah 7:11, 1 (*Midrash Rabbah* ed. Jadler, XII:267) interprets the aphorism "Well-joined is Torah with *derekh erets*" in sense (3), literal work, by citing it as evidence for Solomon's claim that "Wisdom is good with an inheritance" (Eccles. 7:11). In the original context, Avot 2:2 (ed. Albeck, IV:357), *derekh erets* may just as easily mean proper conduct (5) or "good works" (4). Avot 3:17 (ed. Albeck, IV:367): "Rabbi Elazar ben

Azaryah says: 'If there is no Torah, there is no *derekh erets*; if there is no *derekh erets*, there is no Torah.'" He then lists two other pairs of spiritual virtues that are interdependent (wisdom/fear [of God]; discernment/knowledge) and concludes: "If there is no flour, there is no Torah; if there is no Torah, there is no flour." This context invites two glosses of *derekh erets*: it could be like *flour*, in the sense of earning a living, literal work (3), or it could be related to those other spiritual virtues, in the sense of pragmatic "know-how" (7).

83. Kadushin, *Organic Thinking*, 113–67; *Worship and Ethics*, 39–62; *Conceptual Approach to the Mekhilta*, 56–57, 85–86, 109–10, 203–4; *Conceptual Commentary on Midrash Leviticus Rabbah*, 63–64. In *Worship and Ethics*, 46–54, Kadushin is the most precise about the term's distribution and internal tensions, but he still absorbs the rabbis' uses of the term into his own concept of *derekh erets*.

84. See Lehmhaus, "'Derekh Eretz im Tora.'"

85. Following Jaffee, "Halakhic Personhood," 97.

86. Kadushin, *Organic Thinking*, 120.

87. Novak, *The Image of the Non-Jew in Judaism*, 149. Presumably, he is alluding to passages like Leviticus Rabbah 9:3 (ed. Margulies, I:179; = Leviticus Rabbah 35:6); (ed. Margulies, IV:823–24), where it is said that "*derekh erets* preceded the Torah" as it was given to the generations between Adam and Moses and that its role was "to keep the way [*derekh*] of the Tree of Life [i.e. Torah]" (Gen. 3:24). I read that source differently (Redfield, "Sages and the World," 172–84), but, in any case, it is Amoraic, not from the early discourse.

88. Novak, "Judaism and Natural Law," 130.

89. As another discussion of this term indicates (Novak, *The Image of the Non-Jew*, 14n24), he relies less on ancient sources for *derekh erets* than on an important modern synthesis of the concept, by S. R. Hirsch, founder of the "Torah with *derekh erets*" school of Orthodoxy. Novak's conflation between *derekh erets* and *tiqqun ha'olam* is not well supported by early rabbinic sources. In certain cases, *tiqqun ha'olam* does function as a "limit and corrective to positive law" (e.g., m. Gittin 4:7: a man who vowed to divorce his wife is *not* allowed to retract by rabbinic law, but in one case, the sages permitted it "for the sake of repairing the world"). In contrast, *derekh erets* is a separate body of rules (app., items 7, 8), a legal precaution or stringency (5), or an inner-legal mode of interpreting legal wording (6). It is not used to "correct or limit" the scope of positive law (oral Torah) but flexibly adapted to it in many ways.

90. m. Avot 2:2 (ed. Albeck, IV:357) ≈ Avot of Rabbi Natan B 32:21–22 (ed. Becker, 366).

91. b. Eruvin 100b, attributed to R. Yohanan (d. 279 CE).

92. See, for example, b. Hullin 57b, which explores whether or not the animal kingdom is ruled by a king and thematizes the tension between using the written Torah, on one hand, and observation, on the other, to determine the order of nature.

93. This debate goes back to medieval commentators; see Kadushin, *Worship and Ethics*, 248 n. 71.

94. Flusser, "Ezohi derekh yesharah sheyavor lo ha-'adam?" 175.

95. See van de Sandt and Flusser, *The Didache*, 179 and *passim*. Brock, "The Two Ways and the Palestinian *Targum*," 139–52, shows that the Two Ways discourse in Targumim is characterized by synthesizing and expanding verses that mention the choice of a moral "way" (Jer. 21:8, Deut. 30:15–19, Gen. 3:4), although it is less dualistic than 1QS.

96. Safrai, "Muvano shel ha-munaḥ 'derekh erets'"; "Teaching of Pietists in Mishnaic Literature," especially 27–28 (rev. version, "*Mišnat ḥasidim b'sifrut ha-tannaim*," in Safrai,

In Times of Temple and Mishnah, II:501–17); "Ḥasidim v'anshe ma'aseh." See also Büchler, *Types of Jewish-Palestinian Piety*.

97. For observing norms other than Torah, see Avot 2:2 (ed. Albeck, IV:357) (≈ Avot of Rabbi Natan B 32:21–22 [ed. Becker, 366]), "Well-joined is Torah to *derekh erets*, for striving in both makes sin forgotten." Even here, the meaning could be literal work (3) as opposed to "good works" (4). For going above and beyond in Torah-observance, see, for example, Leviticus Rabbah 34:8 (ed. Margulies, 792): "The Torah taught you *derekh erets*, that when a man performs a commandment, he should perform it with a joyful heart." For prioritizing good works over scholarly virtues, see Avot 3:17 (ed. Albeck, IV:367–68) = Avot of Rabbi Natan A 22:5–8 (ed. Becker, 192–93) = Avot of Rabbi Natan B 34:13–16 (ed. Becker, 368).

98. For refraining from theft, see Deuteronomy Rabbah §Shofetim (ed. Lieberman, 96): "See what *derekh erets* is in her, that she shirks [literally "flees from"] theft." For good works like donating money, see Kallah 21 (ed. Higger, 159). For making peace between people, see Leviticus Rabbah 9:3 (ed. Margulies, 178).

99. Contra Flusser ("Ezohi derekh yesharah," 169–70), I see no evidence that Avot 2:2 is later than Avot 3:17, whereas 3:5 is later than both; neither do I see that "the original sense of *derekh erets* is preserved" in Seder Eliyahu (see n. 84). This speculative chronology is based on Flusser's assumption that the earliest and broadest sense of the term *good works* (4) gradually narrowed to literal work (3) and other senses. The circular justification for his chronology is his vision of a primordial Jewish-Christian universalism that later splintered into "hollow *halakhic* norms" and "pure ivory-tower scholarship" in the hands of the rabbinic guild (van de Sandt and Flusser, *The Didache*, 173).

100. See nn. 32–33.

101. Kant, *Groundwork*, 26–27.

102. Leviticus Rabbah 9:3 (ed. Margulies, 178). Redfield, "Sages and the World," 175, and n. 87.

103. Derekh Erets Zutta (ed. Sperber, 27 [my emphasis]).

104. See n. 11.

105. For example, Mekhilta of Rabbi Shimeon bar Yohai §Shemot 3:8 (ed. Epstein-Melammed, 2; best text according to the version of R. Avraham Halahmi): "He made His word accord with *derekh erets*, that the nations of the world would not say"; for example, Derekh Erets Rabbah (Pirke Ben Azzai) (ed. Higger, 181–82): "A man shall not take leave of his fellow or his teacher without asking his permission. And everyone should learn *derekh erets* from the Omnipresent." On the latter, see Ehrlich, "Asking Leave," 13, and "Verbal and Non-Verbal Rituals," 13.

106. y. Rosh Hashanah 3:5, 58d (ed. AHL, 675:32).

107. See Kahana, *Sifre on Numbers*, III:653–54, 667–68, 684–85; *The Two Mekhiltot*, 298–99, especially 298–99n46; Paz, "From Scribes to Scholars," 59–56; "Re-Scripturizing Traditions," 285–86.

108. Lerner, "The External Tractates," 379–89. Medieval sources refer to *derekh erets* literature in various ways, for example, "the way of the disciples of the sages" (Rashi, b. Berakhot 22a, s.v. הלכות דרך ארץ). A maximalist description of this literature and its parallels is Higger, *Massektot Ze'irot*, 7–69. For a more complete list of mss., see van Loopik, *The Ways of the Sages*, 12–19. For an analysis of the families of mss. and recensions, see Higger, *Treatises Derek Erez*, 19–24. (On Higger's method and its problems, see Briata, "Derek Ereṣ Rabbah e Derek Ereṣ Zuṭa," 1–20). On the sections and indirect witnesses

to these tractates, see Sperber, *Derech Eretz Zutta*, 71–74, 77–79, and Sperber, *A Commentary on Derech Ereẓ Zuṭa*. For a case for a relatively early, and coherent, redaction of a Derekh Erets tractate, see Krauss, "Le traité talmudique déréch éréç (suite et fin)," *Revue des études juives* 37 no. 73 (1898): 45–64, at 50–64. On the sources and witnesses of this nominal tractate, see Krauss, "Le traité talmudique dérech éréç," *Revue des études juives* 36 no. 71 (1898): 27–46; 205–21; 214–18. Provocative cultural analyses of the Derek Erets tractates include Briata, "Dereḵ Ereṣ Rabbah," 21–46; Sperber, "Rabbinic Manuals of Conduct," 9–26; Schofer, *Confronting Vulnerability*, 57–63.

109. I culled this selection of "early" (Roman Palestinian) *derekh erets* discourse in four stages: (1) Cataloging roughly ninety-four literary units including the term in all rabbinic works possibly redacted by the end of the Amoraic era (including, at this initial stage, the Babylonian Talmud); (2) Removing all units in post-Tannaitic-redacted works that *did not* display at least one of the following: a formula introducing a *baraita*, an attribution to a Tannaitic sage, or a Tannaitic parallel; (3) Identifying parallels among the remaining sources as well as with both recensions of Avot of Rabbi Natan and Tanhuma-Yelammedenu sources; (4) Correlating possibly later sources (cited in square brackets) that offer useful comparanda for determining the sense of *derekh erets* in the corresponding Tannaitic sources. This procedure left a corpus of sixty-one unique sources (more may be preserved in post-Amoraic midrashic works and the Seder Eliyahu literature, but these are under-studied, their content seems to have been elastic, and most viable candidates lack attributions). NB: I did *not* remove sources attributed to seven first-generation Amoraim in Amoraic works, as these sources may overlap with the redactional period of Tannaitic works. The line between Tannaim and first-generation Amoraim (including sages whom I did not remove, Rav and R. Yohanan) was debated from the start (see Kimelman, "Rabbi Yohanan of Tiberias," 154–56 at 173n163). Further, even if all instances based on attributions and citation formulas were removed, each of my eight contextual meanings would still be attested in at least one Tannaitic work; except for (1), which is already in the Tanakh and Targumim. This method thus yields solid evidence for my object, that is, the early semantic range of this term and basic contours of early *derekh erets* discourse. Of course, the sense of *derekh erets* in a given context may not be clear or singular. My gloss is based on a study of the context, direct parallels (=), indirect parallels (≈), and cited comparanda [in brackets]. I allow for interplay between several senses of the term in each context.

110. b. Bava Metziʻa 107b, attributed to Rav.

111. y. Bikkurim 2:1, 64d (ed. AHL, 354:47) = Semahot 3:9 (ed. Higger, 114). Compare b. Moʻed Qatan 28a (*baraita*), מיתת כל אדם. Compare b. Sotah 47a (*baraita*), which refers to "the illness of which Elisha died" and y. Sanhedrin 10:2, 29b (ed. AHL, 1325:9), which refers to Elisha's "illness according to the way of the world" (although the latter seems to mean an ordinary illness, rather than a natural death; as we say, "the *common* cold").

112. y. Ketubbot 5:7, 30b (ed. AHL, 984:25–30; = Mekhilta §Neziqin III, ed. Lauterbach, II:374); Midrash Tannaim 26:7 (ed. Hoffmann, II:173) ≈ b. Yoma 74b, *baraita* cited as דבי רבי ישמעאל תנא ≈ Safrai and Safrai, *Haggadah of the Sages*, §16, 196–297); Genesis Rabbah 85:2, attributed to R. Yehoshua ben Qarha (ed. Theodor-Albeck, 1031–32; = Genesis Rabbah 18:6, ed. Theodor-Albeck, 168–69). Compare y. Shabbat 9:7, 12b (ed AHL, 421:32), cited under תמן אמרין, a formula often introducing Babylonian traditions; here, a prescription for a sex-depressant. At b. Shabbat 90b, Abbaye, the Babylonian Amora, prescribes a similar remedy for one who wants to acquire wisdom (!) Compare Abbaye's

remedy for impotence, b. Gittin 70a, where, again, *derekh erets* means "sex-drive." It also refers to sex at b. Gittin 70a (≈ §Qinyan Torah, Avot 6:5, ed. Albeck, IV:384) as well as Ecclesiastes Rabbah 9:9,1 (*Midrash Rabbah* ed. Jadler, XII:327), לא נהג בה דרך ארץ: "he did not consummate the marriage").

113. M. Avot 3:5, attributed to R. Nehunya ben Haqanah; Sifre Deuteronomy §42, attributed to R. Yishmael (ed. Finkelstein, 90) = Midrash Tannaim 11:14 (ed. Hoffmann, I:35) = b. Berakhot 35b, *baraita* cited under תנו רבנן—interpreted *ad loc.* as literal work. Compare Genesis Rabbah 19:3 (ed. Theodor-Albeck, 171–72); Avot of Rabbi Natan 28:20, attributed to R. Yehudah bar Ilai (ed. Becker, 218–19 = b. Berakhot 35b); Avot of Rabbi Natan A 1:5 (ed. Becker, 6–7); Avot of Rabbi Natan B 32:1 (ed. Becker, 365; = m. Avot 3:17); m. Avot 2:2 = Ecclesiastes Rabbah 7:11,1 (*Midrash Rabbah* ed. Jadler, XII:267). Both Avot 2:2 and 3:17 place the term in a redactional setting where the contextual meaning is ambiguous: either literal work (3) or "good works" (4). However, both cited parallels to those sources more clearly interpret the term as literal "work," weakening the case that (4) was the original sense.

114. There is no source where the specific pietistic sense for which Safrai argued is unambiguously distinct from the general, nonpietistic sense of "proper conduct," etiquette, know-how, and so on, or a body of teaching about those matters (meanings [7] and [8], respectively). Bearing that caveat in mind, the best candidates for Safrai's thesis are m. Qiddushin 1:10; t. Qiddushin 1:17; m. Avot 2:2 (≈ Avot of Rabbi Natan B 32:21–22, ed. Becker, 366); m. Avot 3:17 (≈ Avot of Rabbi Natan A 22:5–8, ed. Becker, 192–93; ≈ Avot of Rabbi Natan B 34:13–16, ed. Becker, 368); b. Berakhot 32b (*baraita* cited under תנו רבנן); Leviticus Rabbah 9:3 (ed. Margulies, I:179; = Leviticus Rabbah 35:6, attributed to R. Eliezer [ed. Margulies, IV:823–24]). Compare Kallah 21, ed. Higger, 159; Derekh Eretz Zuta 3:1 (ed. Sperber, 27); Avot of Rabbi Natan A 8:8 (ed. Becker, 100–1; = m. Avot 1:6); Avot of Rabbi Natan A 28:2, attributed to R. Natan (ed. Becker, 214–15).

115. T. Shevi'it 4:2 (ed. Lieberman, 527–28); Sifra §Aharei Mot 11, attributed to Rabbi (ed. Weiss 84c; = b. Hullin 84a, *baraita* cited under תנו רבנן); Sifre Dceuteronomy §75 (ed. Finkelstein, 140 ≈ Midrash Tannaim 12:20); (ed. Hoffmann I:52–53 ≈ t. Arakhin 4:26, attributed to R. Eliezer ben Azarya); (ed. Zuckermandel, 548 ≈ Tanhuma-Yelammedenu to Numbers 11:23, attributed to Rabbi [Judah], in Mann and Sonne, *The Bible*, II:78, compare b. Betzah 25a, attributed to Rami b. Abba; and b. Yoma 75b); Sifre Deuteronomy §306 (ed. Finkelstein, 342 = b. Berakhot 45a = b. Berakhot 53b = b. Yoma 37a, compare y. Berakhot 1:1, 2c [ed. AHL, 2:33], attributed to Rav Huna); Mekhilta §Beshallah I (ed. Lauterbach, I:126); Genesis Rabbah 7:5, attributed to Rabbi (Judah) (ed. Theodor-Albeck, 54); Pesiqta of Rav Kahana 10:7, attributed to R. Hoshaya, ed. Mandelbaum, I:169; = Tanhuma §Re'eh 15 (ed. *Midrash Tanḥuma ha-mefo'ar*, II:528); Deuteronomy Rabbah §Shofetim 2, attributed to Rav (ed. Lieberman, 96; see n. 109 ≈ b. Eruvin 100b, attributed to R. Yohanan). Compare Genesis Rabbah 20:12, attributed to R. Levi (ed. Theodor-Albeck, 196).

116. Exodus Rabbah 1:26 (ed. Shinan, 81–82 ≈ Josephus *Ant.* 2.230); Mekhilta §Vayassa VII (ed. Lauterbach, I:251 ≈ Mekhilta of Rabbi Shimeon bar Yohai 17:3); (ed. Epstein-Melammed, 117); Mekhilta of Rabbi Shimeon bar Yohai 19:4 (ed. Epstein-Melammed, 138); Sifra §Behuqotai (ed. Weiss, 111a); Sifre Deuteronomy §34 (ed. Finkelstein, 62 = Midrash Tannaim, ed. Hoffmann, I:27); Sifre Deuteronomy §215, attributed to Rabbi Ishmael (ed. Finkelstein, 248 = Midrash Tannaim [ed. Hoffmann, I:128]); y. Eruvin 6:5, 23c (ed AHL, 480:21, attributed to R. Yehudah [bar Ilai]); y. Sanhedrin 7:11, 25d (ed. AHL, 1306:6 = b. Sanhedrin 67a, *baraita* cited under תנו רבנן); Genesis Rabbah 6:3, attributed to

R. Yose bar Ilai (ed. Theodor-Albeck, 42 ≈ Pesiqta of Rav Kahana 3:14, ed. Mandelbaum, 103). Compare Song of Songs Rabbah 1:1,10, attributed to R. Yonatan (ed. *Midrash Rabbah Ha-mevo'ar*, I:38); y. Berakhot 1:1, 2c (ed. AHL, 2:33), attributed to Rav Huna; y. Ketubbot 5:6, 50b (ed. AHL, 984:38–39); y. Gittin 6:5, 48a (ed. ARN, 1082:8–9), but meaning differs in the parallel = y. Pe'ah 3:7, 17d (ed. AHL, 93:46–47); Genesis Rabbah 20:18 (ed. Theodor-Albeck, 194 ≈ Pesiqta of Rav Kahana 19:5 attributed to R. Abbahu, ed. Mandelbaum, I:308); Genesis Rabbah 32:7, attributed to R. Levi (ed. Theodor-Albeck, 294); Leviticus Rabbah 32:2, attributed to R. Levi (ed. Margulies, IV:737); Pesiqta of Rav Kahana 11:8 (ed. Mandelbaum, I:184 = Exodus Rabbah 20:11); (ed. *Midrash Rabbah Ha-mevo'ar*, 516–17 = Tanhuma); (ed. Buber, II:58 ≈ Mekhilta §Vayassa III, attributed to Rabban Shimeon ben Gamliel); (ed. Lauterbach, II:111), but Mekhilta has מעשה בראשית instead of דרך ארץ, just as Exodus Rabbah 1:27 (ed. Shinan, 84) has כדרך (כל) העולם instead of דרך ארץ at Exodus Rabbah 1:26); Ecclesiastes Rabbah 5:12 (*Midrash Rabbah* ed. Jadler XII, 209); Avot of Rabbi Natan B 32:2–3 (ed. Becker, 365; see m. Avot 3:5; see Avot of Rabbi Natan A 20:2–8, ed. Becker, 184–85; see b. Niddah 69b, *baraita* cited under תנו רבנן).

117. This broad sense of the term covers roughly twenty-eight sources, slightly under half of the total corpus.

118. Mekhilta §*Pisha* VIII, attributed to R. Yose Ha-galili (ed. Lauterbach, I:36); Mekhilta §*Pisha* XI (ed. Lauterbach, I:60); Leviticus Rabbah 26:7 (ed. Margulies, III: 599–600; ≈ Avot 3:4; ≈ Genesis Rabbah 55:8, attributed to R. Abbahu (ed. Theodor-Albeck, 594) ≈ Tanhuma, ed. *Midrash Tanḥuma ha-mefo'ar*, II:163, attributed to a second-generation Palestinian Amora).

119. Midrash Tannaim 23:5 (ed. Hoffmann, II:145; = Song of Songs Rabbah 2:5,3, attributed to R. Eliezer); (ed. *Midrash Rabbah Ha-mevo'ar*, I:271). Compare Avot of Rabbi Natan A 20:5–6, ed. Becker, 184–85; Derekh Eretz Rabbah 2:2 (ed. Higger, 176–77).

120. b. Bava Metzi'a 87a, attributed to R. Yose; Genesis Rabbah 70:14, attributed to R. Yose (ed. Theodor-Albeck, 813, see variant attributions [compare y. Pe'ah 3:7, 17d (93:46–47)]).

121. Mekhilta §*Amalek* I (ed. Lauterbach II:257; = Tanhuma §Beshallah 26, ed. *Midrash Tanḥuma ha-mefo'ar*, I:423 ≈ Avot 4:12); Derekh Eretz Rabbah. 3:2, דרך ארץ של חכם (ed. Higger, 186).

122. b. Shabbat 114a, attributed to תנא דבי רבי ישמעאל (see n. 112); Derekh Eretz Rabbah 3:1 (ed. Higger, 181–82). Compare Derekh Eretz Rabbah 7:3, ed. Higger, 234.

123. Mekhilta §Bahodesh II:2 (ed. Lauterbach, II:299 ≈ Mekhilta of Rabbi Shimeon bar Yohai §*Yitro* 19:8 [ed. Epstein-Melammed, 140]); Mekhilta of Rabbi Shimeon bar Yohai §Shemot 3:8 (ed. Epstein-Melammed, 2); Mekhilta of Rabbi Shimeon bar Yohai §Shemot 6:2 (ed. Epstein-Melamed, 4); Sifre Numbers §102 (ed. Kahana, I:253–44); Derekh Eretz Rabbah 3:2, ed. Higger, 182–83; Sifre Numbers §105 (ed. Kahana, I:261–62 [compare b. Yoma 4b, attributed to R. Eliezer]). In Mekhilta of Rabbi Shimeon bar Yohai §Shemot 3:8, *derekh erets* is an antonym of "improper" (לא כדין). An early intimacy of דרך ארץ with דין also appears at Mekhilta §Vayassa VII (ed. Lauterbach, I:251); Mekhilta §Neziqin III (ed. Lauterbach, II:374). Similarly, in Tanhuma §Vayyiqra 1, ms. Cambridge Add. 1212 (Maagarim database—see n. 69) reads אינו דרך ארץ where other witnesses read אינו דין.

124. b. Betzah 25b, *baraita* cited under תנו רבנן (= b. Pesahim 86b, *baraita* cited under תנו רבנן ≈ Derekh Eretz Rabbah 4:5); (ed. Higger, 211–12 [compare Derek Eretz Rabbah 5:1]); (ed. Higger, 214–15); Derekh Eretz Rabbah 5:2 (ed. Higger, 215–17). Compare the quotation attributed to ben Sira, b. Sanhedrin 100b.

125. Genesis Rabbah 31:11, attributed to R. Yitshaq (ed. Theodor-Albeck, 285). Compare Genesis Rabbah 31:10, ed. Theodor-Albeck, 282.

126. Song of Songs Rabbah 1:17, 2, attributed to R. Yohanan (ed. *Midrash Rabbah Ha-mevo'ar*, I:228).

127. Mekhilta §Neziqin VI (ed. Lauterbach, II:393).

128. Genesis Rabbah 76:3, attributed to R. Hiyya Rabba (ed. Theodor-Albeck, 899). Compare Genesis Rabbah 20:12, attributed to R. Levi (ed. Theodor-Albeck, 196), see n. 129 for similar sources. Compare b. Sanhedrin 39b, attributed to R. Eliezer.

129. t. Sotah 7:20 (ed. Lieberman, III:199) (ms. Erfurt) = b. Sotah 44a, *baraita* cited under תנו רבנן. Compare Genesis Rabbah 60:16 (ed. Theodor-Albeck, 656–57) and a Tanhuma fragment in Mann and Sonne, *The Bible as Read and Preached*, II:169].

130. Pesiqta of Rav Kahana 1:1, attributed to R. Hanina (ed. Mandelbaum, I:1).

131. b. Eruvin 100b, attributed to R. Yohanan; see Ruth Rabbah 2:16, attributed to R. Yohanan (ed. *Midrash Rabbah Ha-mevo'ar*, 82).

132. This body of teachings is called *derek ha'arets*, y. Shabbat 6:2, 8a (ed. AHL, 397:3, *baraita* cited under כהדא דתניא בדרך הארץ ≈ Derekh Eretz Rabbah 8:1, ed. Higger, 298–99). Compare other *derekh erets* rules about left and right: y. Shabbat 9:7, 12b (ed. AHL, 421:32); Derekh Eretz Rabbah 3:2 (ed. Higger, 186); and further sources at Ehrlich, *The Non-Verbal Language of Prayer*, 302. This corpus is also called "laws of *derekh erets*": b. Berakhot 22a, attributed to R. Yehudah (bar Ilai). *Derekh erets* or *derekh ha'arets* may already be a body of teaching in m. Qiddushin 1:10; t. Qiddushin 1:17; t. Shevi'it 4:1; Mekhilta §Pisha XI (ed. Lauterbach, I:60). Important, but possibly later, sources about its contents include b. Niddah 70b–71a (where *derekh erets* teaching at b. Niddah 69b, in a *baraita* cited under תנו רבנן, is *explicated* by teachings that have early parallels: ≈ m. Avot 2:5 (ולא כל המרבה סחורה מחכים) ≈ ben Sira 38:26, חסר עסק הוא יתחכם (ed. Segal, 251). The key terms underscored reflect Greek πολυπράγμων). Another Babylonian exposition of "*derekh erets*" (Ar.: *orah ar'a*) derives from this teaching by interpreting one of Ben Sira's sayings "in an extended sense" (מדרשא), b. Sanhedrin 100b. A final crucial source for early Amoraic crystallization of some sort of *derekh erets* corpus is Pesiqta of Rav Kahana 11:8 (see n. 116), where a (forced) rabbinic interpretation of this phrase's only exact attestation in the Bible (Exod. 13:17), which has no shared meaning with biblical *derekh kol ha'arets* or rabbinic *derekh erets*, is attached to a list of "*derekh erets*" rules, in sense (7): how a sage should serve his master (compare Genesis Rabbah 32:7, attributed to R. Yose bar Ilai [ed. Theodor-Albeck, 42; Kadushin, *Worship and Ethics*, 248n69]). Compare Mekhilta §Beshallah I (ed. Lauterbach, I:116) to the same verse, responding to the question of *why* God made Israel take the long road to the Promised Land. "God said, 'If I let Israel enter the Land now, everyone will immediately take possession of his field or his vineyard and they will neglect the Torah.'" In that version, it is possible that biblical "*derekh erets*" (Exod. 13:17) is also being glossed as (3), "work"—specifically, agriculture, which figured very early in the labor-versus-Torah-study debate (on which, see nn. 70 and 79).

5

Systematicity and Normative Closure in Lithuanian Talmudism

YONATAN Y. BRAFMAN

INTRODUCTION

The phrase *halakhic system* has become commonplace in communal and scholarly discourse about Jewish law. A Google Ngram search, for instance, reveals that usage of the term, at least in English, increased dramatically in the 1970s and 1980s.[1] This rise may be explained by the influence of Joseph Soloveitchik's thought and writings, specifically *Halakhic Man*. The book's protagonist, who is meant to represent the sensibility of the Talmud scholar, is compared to the modern mathematician and natural scientist, for whom "to know means to construct an ideal, lawful, unified system."[2] There is thus a recent tendency to view Jewish law as constituting a "system" that seems to have its roots in the tradition of Lithuanian Talmudism of which Soloveitchik was the scion. Yet there has been no similar tendency in Jewish thought or law to investigate what it means for something to be a "system," let alone a "halakhic system," or what the consequences of conceiving halakhah as a system might be.

In this chapter, I begin this work through a process of conceptual analysis, historical genealogy, and textual study. I first reflect on the concept of a "system" and recent theoretical discussions of the concept of a "legal system."[3] This enables an understanding of both the virtues and vices of legal systematicity. Then I turn to a short genealogy of legal systematicity to locate its emergence in the thought of G. W. Leibniz and to track some of such systematicity's troubling consequences in both secular and Jewish law. I next shift my attention to the focal point of this chapter: assessing the implications of "halakhic systematicity" through a comparative analysis of the patterns of justification in two classic texts by major figures in the tradition of Lithuanian Talmudism: Ḥayyim Soloveitchik—Joseph Soloveitchik's grandfather—and Shimon Shkop. I suggest that although Soloveitchik's thought may encourage fears that concern with legal systematicity leads to ignoring other considerations—arguments and claims—that are correspondingly construed as extralegal, Shkop's thought provides evidence that such normative closure is not inevitable.

CONCEPTUAL ANALYSIS: SYSTEM AND CLOSURE

I provisionally define a *system* as a set of interrelated elements thought of as a unity. This definition expresses four aspects of what it is to be a system. First, a system must have parts; it cannot be an unarticulated whole. Second, these parts must be organized; they cannot be a jumble. Third, such organization is possible through the relations among the parts. And fourth, this entails that there must be a boundary or limit between the system and its environment. For a system to emerge, there must be certain relations that the parts share that they do not share with anything else.

This general definition of a system is informed by but not identical to recent work in systems theory. According to Niklas Luhmann, "Society is a functionally differentiated social system."[4] It consists of subsystems like the economy, state, and law, which are distinguished by their function. Such "functional subsystems," he writes, "are always self-referential systems.... They constitute their components by the arrangement of their components and this 'autopoietic' closure is their unity."[5] While these subsystems interact with one another as part of a larger social system, they are also relatively closed to one another; that is, they each operate according to their own internal "logic" to fulfill their specific function. It is because of this internal logic that a subsystem is better able to fulfill its function. In the case of law, Luhmann claims that this is conflict resolution. For example, while economic acts like the exchange of goods have legal effects, they must first be recognized by law and translated into its language as "transference of property ownership" in order to resolve any disputes about them. Each system has its own environment, which it constitutes, and only interacts with those parts of its surroundings that it recognizes and then only on its own terms.[6] Thus, even while law possesses what Luhmann calls *cognitive* openness, it is characterized by *normative* closure.

By normative closure, I mean the tendency of a system to disregard considerations—arguments and claims—that are not posed in its terms or that it does not consider relevant to its function. The normative closure of a legal system, then, would be the disregard of normative considerations that are not rendered in legal terms or not understood to be legally relevant. Normative closure is what accounts for the not-infrequent disconnection between what is legal and what is morally right or politically expedient.

The relation between legal systematicity and normative closure can be further examined in the thought of legal theorists, including proponents of both legal formalism and legal positivism. While positivism and formalism are often conflated, they are distinct. Stated heuristically, positivism is primarily concerned with the source of law, whereas formalism focuses on legal interpretation. The basic claim of positivism is that a norm is a law by virtue of having been validly enacted by the institutions and through the processes recognized in a society for establishing law. Formalism, by contrast, concerns the relations among laws and how laws are interpreted; it posits that there are rational connections among laws and that laws should be interpreted in view of their underlying rationality. Because positivism and formalism differ in their focuses, there can be a tension between them. For positivism, a norm is a law solely because it has been validly enacted, whereas for formalism, a norm might be a law because it is logically entailed by other laws, or it might not be a law because it logically conflicts with other laws. In other words, for positivism, a set of norms might be deeply incoherent but would still be part of the same legal system because they were all validly enacted by the same institutions and through the same processes. For formalism, however, norms must share much more to be part of the same legal system.

Systematicity has been uniquely valued by legal formalists. Ernest Weinrib claims that "law is intelligible as an internally coherent phenomenon," which possesses an "immanent moral rationality."[7] The content of law is not reducible to political decisions; rather, it is self-generated as a result of the rational connections among laws. Specifically, Weinrib articulates a coherentist account of legal justification: each law or legal institution derives its justification from the system as a whole, while the system derives its justification from the relations among its parts. Legal systems must have rational coherence, and the justification of specific laws must make that coherence manifest. He writes, "Justification, therefore, cannot properly be truncated. It must be allowed to expand completely into the space it naturally fills."[8] This means that norms that are entailed by existing laws must also be recognized as law. It also means that existing laws and legal institutions must be revised to become more coherent. For example, Weinrib rejects economic approaches to tort liability, in which questions of negligence are dismissed in favor of efficient cost-sharing, because focusing solely on economic efficiency is incompatible with the underlying logic of civil law. The goal of this effort of entailment and revision is to make the law fully coherent. Such an ideal legal system would possess the virtue of integrity, which, Weinrib claims, grants it normative force. It is because a legal system coheres that it possesses normativity.

If the virtue of systematicity is made clear by formalists, its potential vice—normative closure—is revealed by positivists. Though positivism is concerned with all laws being traceable back to a source, it is less concerned than formalism with conceptual relations among the laws. As previously indicated, their only shared relation could, in theory, be their common origin. Still, the relation between systematicity and normative closure in positivism is made clear by a prominent supporter of positivism—Hans Kelsen. In his *Introduction to the Problems of Legal Theory*, he describes the positivist focus on the source of the law: "A plurality of norms form a unity, a system, an order, if the validity of the norms can be traced back to a single norm as the ultimate basis of validity."[9] And because law is a system, he claims, "all legal problems are confronted and can be solved as systematic problems."[10] Specifically, legal problems are not resolved by moral principles or political decisions but by laws.

The practical effects, both positive and negative, of normative closure are that the resources for a judge's and other legal subjects' decision-making are limited. Joseph Raz, a more recent positivist theorist, makes this clear in his *Practical Reason and Norms*: "Normative systems . . .

include both norms guiding individuals and norms setting up institutions for solving disputes from the application of such norms. . . . [Such a system] is an exclusionary system. Its norms exclude the application of reasons, standards, and norms which do not belong to the system and are not recognized by it."[11] Again, moral principles or political decisions, for example, so long as they have not been incorporated into the legal system in some way, must be excluded for there to be a system at all. This exclusion, however, is not simply due to a fixation on order or an aesthetic obsession with system. It is necessary so that a normative system like law can guide action. According to Raz, the purpose of norms is to offer protected reasons for action.[12] A protected reason for action combines both a reason to do the action and a reason not to act on reasons against doing the action. This is how norms differ from advice; it is how they command actions. However, this purpose is defeated if the individuals subject to the norm consistently reflect on what other reasons they might have either to do or not to do the action. Moreover, at a higher level, a normative system and its institutions become superfluous if any and all considerations are relevant for settling disputes about its norms. Practical-reason accounts of law like Raz's fill in the details of Luhmann's system theory of law. Law can resolve conflicts by offering norms and authorities to settle them, but they can only do that if they restrict the types of arguments and claims that can be offered. The price of the type of action guidance offered by law and of the conflict resolution provided by legal systems is thus normative closure—the restriction of considerations.

Legal systematicity thus has several virtues. From the perspective of systems theory, it constitutes a subsystem whose function is to resolve conflicts within society. Legal positivism explains how it performs this function by guiding action through norms and authorities. Legal formalism emphasizes how integrity and even normativity emerge through ever-expanding coherence. However, all of this is at the cost of normative closure—the separation of law from morality and politics.

HISTORICAL GENEALOGY: SECULAR AND JEWISH LAW

The two-faced character of legal systematicity is illustrated by its historical genealogy in secular law. In *The Gift of Science: Leibniz and the Modern*

Legal Tradition, Roger Berkowitz argues that Leibniz enacted a revolution in legal theory by insisting that jurisprudence be a science.[13] In his *New Essays on Human Understanding*, Leibniz wrote, "One of the chief ways of making jurisprudence more manageable, and of surveying its vast ocean, as though in a geographical chart, is by tracing a large number of particular decisions back to more general principles."[14] However, this project of scientific jurisprudence was motivated by more than pedagogical efficiency. It followed from Leibniz's commitment to the principle of sufficient reason, which, in Yitzhak Melamed's and Martin Lin's terms, "stipulates that everything must have a reason, cause, or ground."[15] As Leibniz says, it is the principle "by virtue of which we consider that we can find no true or existent fact, no true assertion, without there being a sufficient reason why it is thus and not otherwise."[16] Applied to jurisprudence, each decision or law would find its reason in legal principles, which, in turn, would be unified in some higher order. Leibniz aimed to construct a *Systema Iuris*, which would be a science of law as system. With such a system in hand, Leibniz writes that "he who knows [the] universal concepts can divide into classes the abundance of innumerable [laws], so that nothing can escape him."[17]

Leibniz maintained that the most universal concept of law was *caritas sapientis* (charity of the wise). This concept provided the higher-order unity for legal principles, and so law and justice were connected. However, his successors severed this connection. Berkowitz writes, "The result of Leibniz's scientific understanding of law is that law is subordinated to its reasons and justification. . . . As law retreats behind reasons and grounds, it loses its natural connection to any ideas of truth and justice except those that are given as its justification."[18] Such jurisprudence leads to an exclusive focus on systematicity and thus closure to any claims or arguments construed as external. According to Berkowitz, it eventuated in the legal theory of Rudolf von Jhering, in which the pursuit of political ends in accordance with the form of legality substitutes for substantive justice. Jhering's theory is concerned with legal systematicity; however, a legal system can serve whatever inputs it receives from duly elected political actors.[19]

The thesis that the development of the science of law as system results in a preoccupation with mere legality precisely because of its commitment to reason and justification seems counterintuitive. Yet it appears to correspond to developments in Jewish law. Rachel Adler, in *Engendering Judaism*, labels contemporary halakhic discourse as "methodaltrous" because its methods have become "a kind of false god."[20] That is, "questions that do not conform to the system's method and categories are simply reclassified as non-data and dumped out."[21] In her trailblazing article "Towards a Gender Critical Approach to the Philosophy of Jewish Law (Halakhah)," Ronit Irshai describes a tactic in contemporary halakhic discourse about gender that she terms "formalistic reductionism." She writes, "Whenever one identifies an effort to uncover the morally problematic value system implicit in a halakhic ruling with respect to women, the conservative counterattack goes something like this, 'You misunderstand entirely; it's an entirely formalistic matter, and questions of values, if one is concerned about them, are situated totally elsewhere.'"[22] For example, according to the Talmud (b. Megillah 23a), women may have been eligible to read from the Torah in the synagogue were it not for concerns about the honor of the congregation (*kavod hatsibbur*). It seems that calling a woman to read from the Torah might imply that none of the men were capable of doing so, which would dishonor the congregation. Jewish feminists have therefore criticized the Orthodox practice of excluding women from reading the Torah in the synagogue as based on misogynistic assumptions about how a woman's ability would cast aspersions on men's ability. Traditionalist commentators have argued in response that this is a misunderstanding of the Talmud. *Kavod hatsibbur* does not in any ordinary sense mean the honor of the congregation, and so women being excluded from reading the Torah in the synagogue would not dishonor the congregation—that would be to conflate halakhic with moral categories. *Kavod hatsibbur* is instead a technical term within the halakhic system that is defined only in terms of its circumstances and consequences of application within that system. No one should therefore take offense because of it.[23]

Formalistic reductionism thus seems to rely on a conception of halakhah as system. The concern has become the internal relations among halakhic concepts and specifically the overall coherence of the halakhic system as opposed to correspondence to standards of truth or justice that are now construed as "external." As its name suggests, formalistic reductionism tends to emerge within formalism, but it can also plague positivism. According to legal positivism, the action-guiding benefits of law rely on the exclusion of considerations that are rendered nonlegal. Questions about the truth of halakhic categories or justice of halakhic rulings are sidelined. Systematicity again results in normative closure. If this is so, it is important to establish whether this development was as inevitable as Berkowitz's historical genealogy or contemporary halakhic discourse concerning gender suggests. Perhaps there are ways to maintain the virtues of legal systematicity without the vice of normative closure.

TEXTUAL STUDY: SYSTEMATICITY IN LITHUANIAN TALMUDISM

To explore this possibility, it is useful to return to early expressions of the drive for halakhic systematicity in Lithuanian Talmudism. Lithuanian Talmudism is a genus of Jewish learning that is popularly known by its most distinguished species—the *Brisker Derekh*, often described as the "analytical movement" or "conceptual approach" to Talmud study.[24] Founded by Ḥayyim Soloveitchik (1853–1918) and named for the town of Brest, Belarus, in which he was the rabbi, this approach focuses on the development of abstract categories in order to justify halakhic rulings and understand disputes among halakhic authorities. It therefore does not explain such features in view of textual disagreements or social and political context.

The *Brisker Derekh* has deep roots in the thought of Eliyahu of Vilna (1720–97) and his student Ḥayyim of Volozhin (1749–1821). Eliyahu of Vilna's notes on the *Shulḥan Arukh* draw the reader's attention away from the settled ruling and back to the source texts of rabbinic literature.[25] Ḥayyim of Volozhin's masterwork *Nefesh haḥayyim* leverages Kabbalistic discussions of creation and revelation in order to motivate concentrated study of the Talmud.[26] This vision took on an institutional form in the seminary he established, the Etz Ḥayyim Yeshiva in Volozhin, which emphasized learning for its own sake as distinct from any concern with practical application. This was matched by the educational framework, which removed students from sustained interaction with ordinary Jewish life.[27] Following in the footsteps of his father, Yosef Dov Soloveitchik (1820–92), Ḥayyim Soloveitchik studied and taught at the Etz Ḥayyim Yeshiva before becoming the rabbi of Brest. Shimon Shkop (1860–1939) studied with Soloveitchik while he taught in Volozhin. Shkop went on to lead seminaries in Telsiai and Grodno. He, too, founded an approach to Talmud study, which is identified with this first seminary as the *Telz Derekh*, or "approach." The influence of Soloveitchik's thought is evident in Shkop's method; however, as I show, there are crucial differences regarding the connection between legal systematicity and normative closure. To illustrate this, I compare representative texts by Soloveitchik and Shkop. But first, a caveat: My aim is not to present comprehensive accounts of their thought or methods of halakhic analysis. I rather take these classic texts simply as two examples to test the notion that systematicity leads to closure.

ḤAYYIM SOLOVEITCHIK: CATEGORIZATION AND CLOSURE

The first text is Soloveitchik's famous analysis of Moses Maimonides's *Mishneh Torah*, "Laws of Leavened and Unleavened Bread" 1:3, in which Maimonides (1135–1204) discusses the circumstances under which one is lashed for possessing leavened bread (*hamets*) on Passover.[28] Some background: In Exodus chapters 12–13, three references are made to not possessing leavened bread on Passover. Exodus 12:15 states, "Seven days you shall eat unleavened bread; on the very first day you shall remove (*tashbitu*) leaven from your house." Exodus 12:19 states, "No leaven shall be found (*lo yimmatse*) in your house for seven days." Exodus 13:7 states, "No leavened bread shall be found (*lo yera'eh*) with you." While the last two verses are understood to be one prohibition against owning leavened bread (*bal yera'eh u-val yimmatse*), Soloveitchik's investigation concerns that prohibition's relation to the prescription to remove the leavened bread (*tashbitu*) and, by extension, the nature of that commandment.

Soloveitchik's investigation proceeds in four steps. First, he notes a contradiction between the *Mishneh Torah* and the Talmud regarding the punishment for owning leavened bread on Passover. He then takes a seeming detour from this subject to adjudicate a debate between Jacob ben Asher (1270–c. 1340), author of the *Arba'ah Turim*, and Akiva Eiger (1761–1837) concerning the status of any remainder from the disposal of the *hamets*. Yet this detour enables him to create categories that will be useful for resolving the contradiction. Third, he develops these categories further before, fourth, applying them to resolve the contradiction.

1. The Contradiction. Maimonides states that one is lashed for violating the prohibition of owning leavened bread on Passover if one actively purchases it on the festival day. Soloveitchik notes, however, that this conflicts with a statement in the Talmud (b. Pesaḥim 95a), which asserts that the prohibition of owning leaved bread on Passover is a prohibition that is transformed into the prescription (*lav hanitak la'aseh*) of the removal of the leavened bread. That is, if one violates the prohibition of owning leavened bread, one is then commanded to remove it. There should thus be no lashing for violating the prohibition because, in general, one is not punished for violating such prohibitions (see b. Makkot 15a). How can Maimonides seemingly agree with the Talmud about the nature of the prohibition of owning leavened bread yet simultaneously rule that one is lashed for violating it?

2. The Detour. Having revealed this contradiction, Soloveitchik turns to a related but seemingly distinct matter: the proper method of fulfilling the prescription to dispose of the leavened bread. This topic is debated in the Mishnah with Rabbi Judah holding that it must be disposed of by being burned and the Rabbis maintaining that it may be disposed of in any manner, such as burial (m. Pesaḥim 2:1). Joseph ben Asher interprets this debate as concerning how to categorize leavened bread on Passover. He then draws different conclusions from the various categorizations, namely, whether whatever remains from the method of disposal is permitted or prohibited for use (*Arba'ah Turim,* Oraḥ Ḥayyim, §445). The two general categories are prohibited objects that must be burned, and prohibited objects that may be buried. Rabbi Judah places leavened bread in the category of objects that must be burned, while the Rabbis place leavened bread in the category of objects that may be buried. Correspondingly, leavened bread inherits the consequences of these categories. Since the remains of objects that must be burned—that is, their ashes—are permitted for use, Rabbi Judah contends that the ashes of burned leavened bread are similarly permitted for use. In contrast, since the remains of objects that may be buried are forbidden for use, the Rabbis hold that the remains of leavened bread are likewise forbidden for use.

Eiger, however, prevents Jacob ben Asher's application of these general categories to the debate between Rabbi Judah and the Rabbis and thus blocks the drawing of differential consequences.[29] To do this, he cites Tosafot's commentary on the Talmud, which suggests that, in general, the remains of objects that must be burned are permitted for use because there is a commandment to burn the object and, once that commandment is fulfilled, the object is permitted. In contrast, the remains of objects that may be buried are forbidden because there is no commandment to bury them; they are only buried to prevent accidental use of the object.[30] However, Eiger argues, Rabbi Judah and the Rabbis both agree that there is a prescription to dispose of the leavened bread—that is not in dispute. They only disagree on the means of disposal. Therefore, they should agree that any remains from the leavened bread are permitted once the commandment of disposing of it is fulfilled.

3. The Construction. Here Soloveitchik intervenes in the debate between Jacob ben Asher and Eiger. He puts the different consequences drawn by Jacob ben Asher for each position on firmer ground by developing alternative categories. Taking into account Eiger's point that both Rabbi Judah and the Rabbis recognize that there is a commandment to remove the leavened bread, there is a distinction between their views on the nature of this commandment that leads to their different positions on the means to dispose of the leavened bread and the status of any remains from it. The alternative categories are the opposition of thing (*heftza*) and person (*gavra*), which can also be described as the difference between an obligation in rem and an obligation in personam. On the in rem view, the object x must have some action a done to it by some person. On the in personam view, person p must perform action a on some object. Soloveitchik further argues that these categories have implications for the status of the object after the obligation has been fulfilled. Whereas an object that has had its obligation in rem performed is thereafter permitted for use, an object that has had an obligation in personam performed on or through it is not then permitted. These alternative categories and their consequences are then applied to the debate between Rabbi Judah and the Rabbis. Because Rabbi Judah holds that the leavened bread must be burned, he clearly believes that the commandment is an obligation in

rem. This leavened bread must be burned by some person. Consequently, once it is burned, Rabbi Judah must hold that its remains are permitted. In contrast, because the Rabbis hold that the leavened bread may be disposed of in any manner, they clearly maintain that the commandment is an obligation in personam. This person must dispose of leavened bread. Consequently, even after the leavened bread is disposed of, its remains are still forbidden.

4. The Resolution. Having resolved the debate between Jacob ben Asher and Eiger, Soloveitchik uses the alternative categories he has constructed (the commandment as an obligation in rem or as an obligation in personam) to further categorize the prescription to dispose of the leavened bread. He moves from that distinction, which concerns the locus of the commandment (in the object versus in the person), to the type of commandment and its relation to the prohibition of owning leavened bread on Passover. In Rabbi Judah's view, again, the disposal of leavened bread is an obligation in rem, and the leavened bread must be disposed of by burning, and its remains are permitted. But, Soloveitchik argues, this means that he must also hold that the commandment to dispose of the leavened bread is a prohibition transformed into a prescription (*lav hanitak la'aseh*). If the prohibition of owning leavened bread is violated, then this prescription of disposal is incurred. Consequently, according to this position, there are no lashes for violating the prohibition. In contrast, according to the Rabbis, the disposal of the leavened bread is an obligation in personam, and the leavened bread may be removed by any means, and its remains are forbidden. But, Soloveitchik argues, this means that they must hold that the disposal of the leavened bread is a prescription to refrain (*issur aseh*) from an action, namely, the action of owning leavened bread. Active violation of the prescription by purchasing leavened bread thus does incur lashing.

Soloveitchik has thus provided two competing categorizations of the prescription to dispose of the leavened bread. These categorizations focus on the type of commandment it is and its relation to the prohibition of owning leavened bread on Passover. It is either a prohibition transformed into a prescription or a prescription to refrain. Soloveitchik also shows how these different categorizations result in other categorizations, such as between an obligation in rem or an obligation in personam, explains known differential consequences, like whether the leavened bread must be burned or whether it may be disposed of by any means, and entails others, such as whether the remains are permitted or forbidden and whether one is lashed for owning leavened bread on Passover.

This analysis also resolves the contradiction between Maimonides and the Talmud, for Soloveitchik assigns to them different categorizations. The Talmud follows Rabbi Judah, who holds that the commandment to remove leavened bread is a prohibition transformed into a prescription, and so there are no lashings for owning leavened bread on Passover. Maimonides, however, follows the Rabbis, who hold that the prescription to remove leaved bread is a prescription to refrain, and so there are lashings for owning it when the prescription is actively violated by buying such bread on Passover. This is supported by his ruling, like the Rabbis, that the leavened bread can be disposed of in any manner ("Laws of Leavened and Unleavened Bread," 3:11).

Soloveitchik's argument can be outlined as follows: A textual difficulty, the contradiction between Maimonides and the Talmud, initiates Soloveitchik's investigation, and its resolution marks its conclusion. In light of this resolution, he adopts existing categorizations, develops them, and creates new ones. He sets up relations between these categorizations, accounts for known differences through them, and draws consequences from them. When he is finished, there are higher-order categorizations that result in further categorizations and conclusions. Moreover, these categorizations are used to resolve the initial difficulty.

There are three important points to consider. First, such categorization represents a high degree of systematization. Instead of a confusion of norms and their details, there is integrity. However, the systematization is somewhat truncated. Instead of merely a contradiction between Maimonides and the Talmud or two different rulings, there are two entirely different ways of categorizing, understanding, and applying a single commandment. Moreover, no reason is given for the different categorizations of Rabbi Judah and the Rabbis/Maimonides. Of course, this means that these categorizations cannot be evaluated, and a theoretical and practical decision cannot be made between them. There simply remains two different ways of categorizing the commandment. There is thus a certain unrationalized givenness retained by the categorizations. This givenness is also apparent in the connection of the categorizations to their consequences. It is not apparent why it is specifically prohibitions transformed into prescriptions that preclude lashings or why only the fulfillment of an obligation in rem results in the permissibility of the object.

One could certainly offer reasons for these categorizations and consequences, but Soloveitchik does not do so. It is possible that if one asked such questions—for example, why the prescription to dispose of leavened bread is either a prohibition transformed into a prescription or, alternatively, a prescription to refrain, or why only the former precludes lashings, or why only the fulfillment of an obligation in rem results in the permissibility of the object—one would have transgressed the boundaries of the halakhic system. There may be debate about the basic categories of the system or how they connect to practical rulings; however, the categories themselves are simply given. When they have been made manifest, one could say, quoting Ludwig Wittgenstein, "I have reached bedrock and my spade is turned."[31] Systematization has reached its limit.

SHIMON SHKOP: FROM JEWISH LAW TO LAW AS SUCH

The second text is from Shkop's *Ḥiddushim* on Bava Qamma #1.[32] Shkop's thought has been analyzed by Avi Sagi and, more recently and extensively, by Shai Wozner. Sagi and Wozner have debated the relation between halakhah and natural law in Shkop's thought: whether, in addition to revealed divine law, Shkop recognizes reason as an independent source of normativity. I do not directly intervene in this debate, but, by focusing on systematicity, I hope to bypass it initially but ultimately shed new light on it.

Shkop makes systematization the primary goal of his analysis of the Talmud. He begins with a rabbinic statement that manifests a drive to systematicity. The Mishnah in Bava Qamma 1:1 states: "There are four primary categories of damages: the goring ox, the pit, the *mav'eh*," which is either a grazing ox or a person, "and fire." It even provides a more abstract conceptualization of these categories by describing their shared features: "They each damage, and one is obligated to supervise them." Seeming to take his cue from the Mishnah, Shkop develops an overarching account of the reason for liability (*sibah hamiḥaiyevet*) for torts that applies to all of these categories. In the first step of his five-step investigation, he offers an preliminary analysis of the Mishnah and uses cases from elsewhere to problematize it. Second, he offers an initial proposal for the reason for liability and rejects it. Third, he offers an alternative proposal. After supporting it, he, fourth, further refines it. Fifth, he provides a summary statement of his account.

1. Analysis and Problematization. As indicated, the Mishnah provides four categories of damages (goring ox, pit, *mav'eh*, and fire) and their common denominators (they each cause damage, and one is obligated to supervise them). Added to these categories is damage directly done by one's body, for example, when someone throws a vase to the ground and shatters it. Shkop complicates matters by showing how this first common denominator is not all that common. In each case, the damage is caused in different ways. Sometimes, the damage is done by one's body, other times by one's property, and still other damage results indirectly from one's actions. Yet each type of damage shares the fact that one is obligated to supervise them. Shkop thus raises the implicit question: Since in each category the damage is caused in different ways, what unites them? Further, setting aside the category of damage done by one's body, there seem to be cases in which one is liable for damage yet the object that caused the damage is not one's property, nor did one's actions indirectly cause the damage. For example, a trustee is liable for damage caused by an object in his care, and a thief is liable for damage caused by an object he stole, even when the damage does not seem to result from their actions.

2. Initial Proposal. An indication for a proposal is provided by Tosafot (see b. Bava Qamma 56a s.v. *peshita*), which seems to suggest that the duty of supervision precedes and entails some form of ownership in the context of damages. Instead of focusing on the first common denominator mentioned by the Mishnah (that they each cause damage), one should thus focus on the second (the obligation of supervision). Shkop's initial proposal is correspondingly that negligent supervision—the breach of this obligation—is the reason for liability. The obligation of supervision, in turn, can be established through diverse relations with the object. The object could be one's property, or it could be established in other ways, such as in the case of the pit. Digging a new pit or opening an existing one directly establishes the duty to supervise. What is key, though, is that the

reason for liability is negligent supervision. The underlying rationale for this proposal seems to be to assimilate all the categories of damages to those caused indirectly by one's actions. One did not supervise the object and thus indirectly caused the damage that it directly caused.

But Shkop offers a counterexample to reject this proposal. He argues that, according to it, one would be forever liable for the damage caused by a runaway ox. For once one was negligent in its supervision—for instance, by leaving the barn door open—one would always be liable for its actions, even if one was no longer its owner by the time it caused the damage. It is established in the Talmud, however, that this is not the case. Once one is no longer considered the owner of the ox, one is no longer liable for its damages (b. Bava Qamma 13b).

3. Alternative Proposal. Shkop then offers an alternative proposal: ownership, of some form, is the reason for liability, and negligent supervision only serves as an enabling condition for this reason. The underlying rationale for this proposal seems to be that a parallel is thereby established between damages caused by one's body and by one's property. Returning to the original three categories of damages (caused by one's body, by one's property, and indirectly by one's actions), the latter category (represented by the pit and fire) now seems like an outlier. Such damage is not caused by one's body, nor does it seem to be caused by one's property because there is no obvious sense in which one owns fire or a pit dug in the public domain. Yet Shkop argues that one does indeed have a form of ownership over the fire and the pit. In support of this claim, he writes, "He prepared the damager and thereby is considered its owner. [For] just as ... the laws of the Torah and the laws of the nations agree (*muskam al pi dine hatorah vedine ha'amim*) that anyone who creates something new is the owner of it for any benefit, so too the Torah considers anyone who prepares an impediment its owner—the owner of the pit or the fire—and [the Torah] made the owner ... liable for damages."[33] Shkop develops a parallel between the type of ownership one has over something beneficial one invents and over something harmful that one produces. In the process, he emphasizes the similarity between Jewish and non-Jewish law on this point. Both assign ownership of an object to individuals based on their having created it. While Shkop does not ground his argument on this similarity, it is remarkable

that he thinks that this commonality between Jewish and non-Jewish law concerning ownership speaks in favor of it.

4. Refinement. Shkop then offers some further arguments, which I will not elaborate. In short, he argues for ownership and against negligent supervision as the reason for liability. Still, Shkop refines his proposal by incorporating negligent supervision into it as, what Jonathan Dancy has called, an enabling condition.[34] An enabling condition itself does not serve as a reason, but it allows something else to serve as a reason. Without the enabling condition, the reason could not be the type of reason it is. In this case, negligent supervision is not the reason for liability, but it allows ownership to serve as that reason. Further stressing the parallelism between damages caused by one's property and by one's body, Shkop shows how this understanding of negligent supervision makes sense of seemingly problematic cases of the latter as well.

Shkop also refines his proposal by describing the types of ownership that can serve as the reason for liability. De jure ownership is not necessary. De facto control of the object is sufficient, so long as it endures until the time of the damage. One can thus also be liable for the damage caused by an object one has been entrusted to supervise or that one has stolen, even when the damage does not indirectly result from one's actions, because one has de facto control of the object. Of course, these were the initially problematic cases, but now they have been reconciled into a general account of tort liability

5. Summary Statement. Shkop concludes with a statement of this general account: the Torah's reason for making one liable for damage is that the damage was caused by either one's property or one's body. Negligence serves as an enabling condition for the application of this reason: one's prior intentions and will must result in the actions of one's body or property.

Shkop's argument can be outlined as follows: His aim from the beginning to the end of his analysis is to provide a general account of tort liability. His initial question is based on the Mishnah's incipient categorization and common denominator, which he tests through problematic cases. And he explicitly offers a more comprehensive categorization. He examines his initial proposal using established laws. Then he provides an alternative proposal, supports it, and refines it. This refinement incorporates the earlier proposal as well as cases that it seemed to handle more effectively. The result is a general account of an area of law that brings unity to it. Moreover, when Shkop reaches this level of systematization of Jewish law, analogies between it and non-Jewish law begin to emerge. The reason that is manifest is that of law as such.

JEWISH LEGAL CATEGORIES AND PHILOSOPHY

When Soloveitchik and Shkop analyses are compared, there is an increased concern with systematization as well as resultant systematization in Shkop's thought. While categorization emerges from Soloveitchik's attempt to reconcile Maimonides with the Talmud, Shkop's main goal is to provide a comprehensive explanation of tort liability in Jewish law. He is concerned not simply with the category of such liability but also with the *reason* for it. Additionally, Soloveitchik reconciles Maimonides with the Talmud by showing how each has conflicting categorizations, while Shkop shows the single, proper way of comprehending liability. If an authority—Tosafot, in this case—does not agree with this understanding, so much the worse for the authority. Further, whereas Soloveitchik leaves certain connections and consequences among his categories unrationalized, Shkop tries to reveal the rationality common to law—both Jewish and non-Jewish—as such. Shkop sees it as evidence supporting his general account of tort liability that this account creates a similarity between Jewish and non-Jewish conceptions of ownership. It is difficult to imagine Soloveitchik making a similar comment, even in passing.

This point is crucial to answering the question about systematization and closure. There is increased systematization from Soloveitchik to Shkop: less is left unrationalized, and a more general account of Jewish law is pursued and provided. Yet it is Shkop who is interested in the similarities between Jewish norms and other norms. The reason that is revealed, again, is not just that of Jewish law but of law as such. This interest is expressed, however, not by directly considering the claim of non-Jewish or purportedly universal norms on Jewish law; this would disrupt the systematization of Jewish law. It is rather expressed by considering the deep points of intersection of Jewish law and non-Jewish law that emerge as a halakhic system is elaborated. Law as such is constructed by reflecting on a particular law—halakhah.

This perspective offers a different view of the debate between Sagi and Wozner about how to categorize Shkop's thought. Sagi claims that Shkop is the rare explicit proponent of natural law in the Jewish tradition.[35] Wozner challenges this claim by showing that Shkop's way of thinking has positivistic features.[36] Specifically, Wozner rightly contends that Shkop does not claim that all halakhic laws derive their normativity from reason or have universal application. Indeed, Wozner shows the importance of the distinction between *ḥiyyuvei mammon*, which define legal statuses, and *ḥovot hitnahegut*, which prescribe actions. While independent reason might define legal statuses—for example, whether some individual or another owns an object—only revealed law prescribes action; in this case, an individual must transfer possession of the object to another. This is a crucial distinction. However, Shkop's interest in the systematization of Jewish law and its deep points of intersection with non-Jewish law may provide a better position from which to assess his connection to natural law thinking than the theoretical issues of law's normativity and universality. For the view that natural law consists of abstract and tradition-independent reason and prescribes universally applicable norms is not the only available position, nor is it the most plausible one.

Adopting the perspective of systematicity and closure reveals affinities between Shkop's thought and David Novak's conception of natural law out of the source of the Jewish tradition. Novak describes the Noahide laws as "an attempt to constitute a universal sphere on one's own cultural horizon without attempting the impossible task of constituting a universal whole to totally contain one's own cultural matrix and all others as well.... The sphere of the universal is constituted as a consequence of the constitution of a comparative dimension."[37] Similarly, Shkop may deny that reason is the source of normativity for all Jewish laws or that Jewish law is universal in application. The sources of normativity of Jewish law may be diverse, with a corresponding diversity of application. Some norms may stem from a particular relationship with the divine and so would only apply to Jews. Other norms may circumscribe necessary conditions of human life and so would apply more universally. Importantly, though, these classes of norms are not differentiated a priori but rather are constructed a posteriori. Only by reflecting on halakhic norms and attempting to render them consistent and coherent can one determine what is particularly Jewish and what is universally human. In addition to the Noahide laws, Novak explains how such "universalization from within" occurs in the imposition of rabbinic enactments (*taqqanot*) and decrees (*gezeirot*) as well as the philosophical project of attributing reasons to the commandments (*ta'amei hamitzvot*).[38] Shkop would add that providing reasons (*sibbot*) is also necessary for halakhic analysis, and so, here too the underlying rationality evident in law as such is revealed.

Shkop's approach could serve as a model for the pursuit of systematicity without normative closure. System theorists and positivists are correct that for law to effectively achieve its function and guide action, it must limit the considerations that are relevant for judges and other legal subjects. Otherwise, every argument or claim may be offered, and legal norms would make no practical difference in the deliberations of those subject to them.[39] But this, as Raz notes, requires law to be an exclusionary system. Formalists are also right that a particular virtue—integrity—can only arise through explicating the internal connections among legal norms and categories while revising them when necessary to increase coherence. Attempting to incorporate every moral claim or political preference, directly and separately, would result in an incoherent confusion of norms. Fortunately, there is another way to avoid normative closure—through further systematization. While the systematization of law may result in normative closure in the short term and perhaps even in the midterm, this occurs only when it is not yet systematic enough. By ascending from particular norms to legal categories and onward to the structure of law as such, the initial closure that emerges from systematization ultimately allows for normative openness.

This will not solve all legal problems, nor will it ensure specific moral or political outcomes. For example, in the context of American law, the prohibition of abortion can be defended by an appeal to natural law just as it can be justified according to an originalist interpretation of the Constitution. More to the point, in the context of halakhah, opposition to women's participation in Jewish ritual life can be expressed on textual grounds or for theological reasons. What this approach does prevent is what Irshai has called formalistic reductionism and what I—observing how it emerges in part from necessary features of law—have called normative closure. Both formalistic reductionism and normative closure can be used to cut off debate and rule certain objections out of bounds—what Charles Sanders Peirce calls "blocking the path of inquiry."[40] This approach suggests that engagement with halakhic texts and concepts can lead to considering the types of universal questions—like the categories of law as such—that are thought to be the domain of open-ended inquiry, what we might rightly describe as philosophy. When studied in this way, Talmud becomes philosophical.

A comparison of Shkop's approach to methods in contemporary Anglo-American philosophy—in philosophy of law and beyond—also suggests that Philosophy becomes talmudic. Instead of abstract reflection on the nature of human agency, responsibility, or ownership, one begins with the practices of a community and prevalent ways of describing them and then tries to rationally reconstruct them. While this process begins within a particular community—whether the ordinary language of twentieth-century Britons or the interpretations of classical and medieval rabbinic texts—the goal is to reveal concepts and norms that transcend them. When closure is avoided, there is little difference between the conceptual analysis that takes place in the philosophy seminar and the dialectics of the talmudic shiur.

YONATAN Y. BRAFMAN is Assistant Professor of Modern Judaism in the Religion Department and Program in Judaic Studies at Tufts University. He is the editor, with Leora Batnitzky, of *Jewish Legal Theories: Writings on State, Religion, and Morality* and author of *Critique of Halakhic Reason: Divine Commandments and Social Normativity*.

NOTES

1. Google Ngram search "halakhic system" and "halachic system." Thanks to the members of the Princeton Seminar in Jewish Thought, the Jewish Studies Virtual Workshop, and the Herbert D. Katz Center for Advanced Judaic Studies Fellows' Seminar for insightful feedback and comments on earlier drafts of this chapter.

2. Soloveitchik, *Halakhic Man*, 18–19.

3. Two notable exceptions include Moses, *System and Revelation*; and Pollack, *Franz Rosenzweig*. However, they do not discuss law in general or halakhah in particular.

4. Luhmann, "The Self-Reproduction of Law," 112.

5. Ibid.

6. Thanks to Alexander Weisberg for convincing me to clarify this point.

7. Weinrib, "Legal Formalism."

8. Ibid., 972.
9. Kelsen, *Introduction to the Problems*, 56.
10. Ibid., 53.
11. Raz, *Practical Reason and Norms*, 145.
12. Raz, *The Authority of Law*, 18.
13. Berkowitz, *The Gift of Science*.
14. Leibniz, *New Essays on Human Understanding*, 371.
15. Melamed and Lin, "Principle of Sufficient Reason."
16. Ariew and Watkins, *Readings in Modern Philosophy*, 288; cited in Melamed and Lin, "Principle of Sufficient Reason" from the original source.
17. Leibniz, *Philosophische Schriften*, 6:2791; cited in Berkowitz, *The Gift of Science*, 55.
18. Berkowitz, *The Gift of Science*, 51–52.
19. Systematicity from Leibniz onward has also been expertly discussed in Franks, *All or Nothing*. However, Franks's concern is specifically with its role in resolving questions about skepticism in German Idealism.
20. Adler, *Engendering Judaism*, 28.
21. Ibid.
22. Irshai, "Toward a Gender Critical Approach," 70–71.
23. Ibid., 73–75.
24. See Solomon, *The Analytic Movement*; Blau, *Lomdus*; Saiman, "Legal Theology"; and *Halakhah*, 195–212.
25. Stern, *The Genius*, 115–42.
26. Ḥayyim of Volozhin, *Nefesh Haḥayyim*.
27. On the Etz Ḥayyim Yeshiva, see Stampfer, *Lithuanian Yeshivas*, 15–251.
28. Soloveitchik, *Ḥiddushei Rebbenu Ḥayyim Ha-Levi*, 42–43; See Batnitzky and Brafman, *Jewish Legal Theories*, 69–73 for translation and further discussion of this text.
29. Soloveitchik states Eiger's view and argument without offering a citation.
30. It seems that Eiger's sources are b. Pesaḥim 21b s.v. *bahade deqa saref leh lithani minneh* and b. Temurah 33b s.v. *hanisrafin afran muttar*.
31. Wittgenstein, *Philosophical Investigations*, para. 217.
32. Shkop, *Ḥiddushei Rebbe Shimon Yehudah Ha-Kohen*, III:5–7; see Batnitzky and Brafman, *Jewish Legal Theories*, 74–76 for translation and further discussion of this text.
33. Shkop, *Ḥiddushei Rebbe Shimon Yehudah Ha-Kohen*, 5.
34. Dancy, *Ethics without Principles*, 38–52.
35. Sagi, "Ha-Mitzvah Ha-Datit."
36. Wozner, *Ḥashiva Mishpatit Be-Yeshivot Lita*, 220–84.
37. Novak, *Natural Law in Judaism*, 141.
38. See Novak, "Natural Law and Judaism."
39. See Himma, "Inclusive Legal Positivism," for a discussion of the practical difference objection to non-positivist legal theories.
40. Peirce, *Collected Papers*, I:135.

6

The Talmudic Concept *Hamar Gamal* (Donkey Driver–Camel Driver)

A Legal and Literary-Somatic Analysis of Talmudic Imagery

LYNN KAYE

INTRODUCTION

Examining the Talmud's images that appear in legal passages can bring Talmudic literature, which incorporates many different kinds of reasoning and thinking practices, into productive collision with areas of philosophy that question how one might deal with concepts that are not fully determined, or that intentionally signify in such a way as to leave room for future engagement without resolution. This collision allows for the construction of Talmudic thought that can engage philosophical questions without forcing Talmud to fit into philosophical categories, nor does it limit inquiry to the Talmudic authors' own interests. The process of finding Talmudic thought in its images starts with reading the text while cognizant of its historical context, visualizing the images offered by figurative language or images from case law, and then allowing those images to suggest their range of meanings without reducing them to a single message.[1] It can be more productive to think in images because they contain more than a single definition: they do not definitively delineate the boundaries of an idea but rather invite association and multivalent interpretation. Furthermore, images are not purely cognitive; they can communicate somatically as well, and this point is not often described in literary-analytic Talmudic studies. The case study of this chapter is the rhetorical operator *hamar gamal* (someone trying to lead both a donkey and a camel at once), and it signifies its legal meaning both intellectually and somatically. By somatically, I mean that hamar gamal evokes sensations in the human body through its specific imagery and deployment in a legal context about limiting physical movement. This chapter analyzes the hamar gamal through a multidisciplinary analysis of the hamar gamal incorporating historical contextualization, literary analysis, legal significance, and kinesthetic theory from performance studies. It demonstrates that Talmudic legal imagery demands a nonreductive definition of thought and reasoning, one that can signify in many different ways concurrently and that also offers challenging modes of thinking to philosophers interested in language, modes of communication, and the relationship between thought and expression.

HISTORICAL BACKGROUND AND SCHOLARLY CONTEXT

Hamar gamal is a Tannaitic phrase adopted by the Amoraim in both Palestine and Babylonia. Most scholars understand the figure hamar gamal as an image or a metaphor that describes an unfortunate legal status related to an *eruv tehumin* (*pl. eruvei tehumin*), which creates a temporary home for a person at a distance of two thousand cubits from their residence, enabling the person to walk farther than would ordinarily be allowed on the Sabbath. Sometimes, a situation can arise in which, due to unclear speech or action or because of events beyond a person's control, the eruv is possibly in effect and possibly not in effect. This results in the situation of hamar gamal, which describes being subject to two contradictory legal realities at once. In the first reality, the eruv is in effect, and the person's home for the Sabbath is at the eruv. In the second, the eruv is not in effect and the person's home for the Sabbath is their primary residence. Rather than attempt to decide which of these possibilities is correct, hamar gamal describes, leaves unresolved, and legally accommodates two competing realities—to the detriment of the person who must observe the laws pertaining to both. Without knowing why the Tannaim chose this image, it is nevertheless notable how particularly well suited it is to describing the effects of indeterminate *eruvei tehumin* on people. And though hamar gamal is a relatively rare image within Tannaitic, Amoraic, and post-Amoraic language, it is worth studying because it exemplifies the way images capture conceptual complexity differently from rabbinic argumentation.

Hamar gamal is an image that resists conceptual resolution. Talmudic images like this one can productively unsettle conceptual inquiry by being elusive and yielding final judgments that are not entirely definitive because of their invitation to interpretation. Figurative speech in Talmudic texts, like in poetry and fiction, demands a reading strategy that respects an image's indirect and irreducible significance.

This chapter builds on two areas of conceptual Talmudic scholarship that do not consistently engage with one another, even as each analyzes the conceptual implications of figurative language of the Talmud. One body of research is the interdisciplinary field of Talmudic legal conceptualization, research of which is conducted in a variety of ways, including by means of intellectual history, text criticism as well as through the philosophy of language. Scholars such as Leib Moscovitz, Jeffrey L. Rubenstein, and Shana Strauch Schick are each scholars of Talmud who employ aspects of intellectual history and text-critical methods, while Ariel Furstenberg engaged philosophy of language, as well as knowledge of Talmud, to trace the development of concepts and their relationship to thought. Their research differs from one another in method and emphasis, but all address the manner in which concepts develop in rabbinic texts over time.[2] Conceptual growth is charted in legal passages: the style of law (case-based or conceptual), naming a concept where it had been implicit before, or applying a concept to a new case. Sometimes conceptual change is signaled by the use of figurative language or parables to convey a concept. Alternatively, an image may be applied to a new case, changing, or expanding the significance of the image.[3]

The other area of research that studies figurative language in normative Talmudic texts is literary-critical Talmudic scholarship. It incorporates not only theories of interpretation from literary studies, including approaches to metaphor, but also more broadly feminist and gender theories, narratology, and prosody or poetics, all of which aid in interpreting figurative language. Scholars including Charlotte Fonrobert, Jeffrey L. Rubenstein, Suzanne Last Stone, and many writing in Hebrew, such as Ofra Meir, have advanced the current understanding of the Talmud's legal texts as requiring literary analytical tools for comprehensive understanding.[4] This chapter knits together the field of Talmudic legal conceptualization and the literary study of rabbinic figurative language. It adds a somatic interpretation drawn from dance studies, incorporating the insights of dance historian and movement analyst, Hannah Kosstrin, and an interest in the reception of Talmudic imagery in the modern period.[5]

THE LEGAL SENSE OF HAMAR GAMAL: SUGGESTING MEANING THROUGH FEELING

Hamar gamal suggests the idea of being limited by the strictures of two competing realities with a visceral sense of physical pressure. This conveys the law's limitation on travel in a physical way, not just a conceptual one. Hamar gamal is an image that, when visualized by the audience, appeals to what they know in their bodies (kinesthetic knowledge). It therefore has more potential significance than a prosaic description. Dance studies scholar Tomie Hahn describes how a student learns movement through "kinesthetic empathy, an empathy rooted in the body that draws on kinesthesia, the sense that comprehends the body's weight, spatial orientation, and movement of muscles, tendons and joints. Kinesthetic empathy is mediated via visual and tactile modes of transmission."[6]

According to Hahn, the student observes a teacher's movement and learns it through empathetic feelings in her body. Picturing an image from a text is also a form of visual engagement that creates a bodily empathy and enables comprehension of the text in the feeling of physical force.[7] The concept of taking in the significance of a textual image through the body also aligns with Kimmerer LaMothe's description of religion as dance. She describes "a defiantly dialectical relation between reason and experience [which] produces meaning of different kinds, both conceptual and kinesthetic."[8] The image of a hamar gamal does not stop its signifying at the intellect but reaches toward the body to suggest the "bind" the legal subjects are in as they occupy a legal reality in which two contradictory possibilities operate. This operator could have potentially fruitful and enriching connections with social and political philosophy engaged with normative discourse, the ways language can bind and limit people, and related studies of the philosophy of language.[9]

Visualization and empathetic imagination are also modes that feminist archaeologist Janet Spector uses to shift her discipline from being "objective, object-oriented and objectifying."[10] While kinesthetic empathy is not primary in Spector's "reverse archaeology," she describes her affiliation with what Nobel prize winner Toni Morrison called "the feelings that accompany the picture."[11] Like the Talmudic use of hamar gamal, Spector's archaeological method uses visual images to incorporate, whether through bodily sensation or other feelings, a broader range of sources of meaning than just intellectual meaning.

> I eventually developed more precise pictures of the array of sites the Dakota used over the course of a year by analyzing women's and men's activity patterns as described in written sources. I supplemented those images with information from nineteenth-century illustrations of Dakota communities. Then, in a kind of reverse archaeology, I imagined the same places as they might appear shortly after people had left them and intentionally or inadvertently abandoned items that might enter the archaeological record as imperishable remnants of their daily lives. Finally, I compared what we actually found at Little Rapids with what would be found at these idealized types of sites.[12]

When analyzing Talmudic images like hamar gamal, body feelings and emotional feelings could be important sources of knowledge for interpretation. Those feelings are accessible through the visualization of the images portrayed in the written texts. Talmudic images offer different ways to conceptualize law from those in the analysis of rabbinic legal argumentation. Images and the potential feelings they evoke can ground Talmudic thought in material objects, emotions, and the body.

HAMAR GAMAL IN MODERN TEXTS

Hamar gamal is a relatively rare expression in rabbinic literature. It occurs twice in the Mishnah as well as twice in the Tosefta.[13] It appears in three places in the Palestinian Talmud and in two different contexts in the Babylonian Talmud.[14] As far as I know, it does not appear in midrashim or minor tractates. Despite the small number of occurrences of hamar gamal in classical rabbinic literature, the phrase lived on and expanded after the Talmuds in responsa and even in early modern Hebrew literature, which reflects the potency of the image. It also sparks curiosity about the fact that in classical rabbinic literature, this image with so much potential to express the difficulty of legal indeterminacy was applied narrowly to Sabbath boundaries.

In modern Hebrew and halakhic literature, the term hamar gamal has been used to express contradictory forces pulling a person or subject in opposite directions. This creates a picture of dysfunction and intense traction in two directions that results in no forward movement. Mendele Mokher Seforim (the pen-name of S. Y. Abramovitsh), a major early figure in nineteenth-century Hebrew and Yiddish literature, introduced hamar gamal in quite a few of his Hebrew writings. Abramovitsh invoked this image as a physical expression of conflict, such as a conversation swirling out of control as more people participated, pulling it in different directions, or two internal voices struggling inside a narrator's head, "pulling me in this direction and that" so that "I do not know whither I can escape from them," or a description of disparate groups of people, "one pulls here and one pulls there," while the winner of such a pointless struggle is "the one with the biggest fists" riding a hamar gamal.[15] These conflicts do not turn inward but instead face outward, pulling against each other with neither benefit nor escape for those involved.[16]

Hamar gamal expanded in medieval and modern halakhic literature as well. It became an expression of an intolerable legal predicament in which a legal action undermines itself, sometimes because of the performance of a foolish action. In a number of modern responsa by Sephardic and Ashkenazic rabbis, hamar gamal helped writers express a legally contradictory situation in which two conflicting legal statuses undermined the requirements of one another. For instance, the eighteenth-century responsum *Shevut Ya'akov* by Rabbi Ya'akov Reischer, later quoted in the contemporary responsa *Yabia Omer* and *Lehorot Natan*, deliberated about whether an *onen*—a mourner who is relieved of obligations to pray except on the Sabbath—should say the evening prayer that concludes the Sabbath. Rabbi Reischer writes of hamar gamal: "[An onen] is like he is riding on two horses, since he is initially required to pray because it is Shabbat and onen status does not pertain to him, but afterwards when he prays and divides Sabbath from the weekday, he is forbidden to pray because of being onen; behold this is hamar gamal."[17]

In other words, by virtue of the person fulfilling an obligation to pray, it becomes forbidden for him to pray. The legal range of hamar gamal in modern halakhic literature extends well beyond its origin in Talmudic discussions of Sabbath boundaries. The phrase expresses a variety of conflicts including two substances that are applied to a circumcision wound that work against each other, a foolish stringency in divorce law, a studious shopkeeper criticized by a rabbi for getting himself into a hamar gamal position in which he "dishonors torah" and has to pay taxes—which is portrayed as a doubly negative outcome.[18] These examples provide a glimpse into the life of hamar gamal after the Talmud, a reminder of the importance of Talmudic images in the development of Judaism and Jewish cultures.

THE COLLISION OF TALMUD AND PHILOSOPHICAL THEORIES OF SIGNIFICATION

Images can provoke a multifaceted set of responses—emotional, somatic, and intellectual—which may be less rigidly structured than propositions with truth-values when the latter are organized into a dialectical argument. Rather than beginning with a stated problem, interrogating possibilities, and delving into the limitations and advantages of these possibilities, an image engages senses, whether visual or visceral, and unfolds possibilities in less structured ways. By a differently structured or less-structured way, I mean that images may prompt analogical connections, as well as somatic or emotional responses, which can link ideas in contradictory ways or offer two different, simultaneous, and even contradictory meanings held in suspension. Here it is possible to suggest an interaction between Talmudic conceptual images and the fields of philosophy of language, semiotics, and semantic theory. The Talmudic hamar gamal image could enter into dialogue with these fields, offering a different set of tests for how words make meaning relative to their contexts. The hamar gamal image and its unusual ways of signifying in its Talmudic context also contribute to reevaluating Kant's notion of an image.

Attending to the images of thought in Talmudic texts exposes their thinking practices without making the mistake of describing or evaluating

Talmudic texts by their success in answering questions they are not asking. Sergey Dolgopolski, in his 2009 book, *What Is Talmud: The Art of Disagreement*, argued for the need to "return Talmud to the Talmud" by considering the intellectual art of Talmud, which he situates in relation to "the major intellectual projects and traditions of the West: philosophy, rhetoric, sophistry and, more specifically, the philosophical arts of logic, grammar, and rhetoric."[19] Talmudic images include the concrete examples, analogies, and proofs from which analysis sharpens into concepts or with which a rabbinic thinker will convey his insight. These include biblical quotations, where the operative imagery is not created by a rabbi but is rather selected and recontextualized. Imagery includes folk sayings or original analogies that convey a legal difficulty. Some images or references may be original to a speaker, whereas others were shared broadly across the culture in late antique Mesopotamia or Palestine. Some may recur, while others leave few echoes.[20] In that spirit, Talmudic texts might enhance different traditions of philosophical thought through collision. Studying images in Talmud allows for the discovery of new material for comparisons and dialogue between Talmud and various fields of philosophy concerned with signification, coercion, paradox, multiplicity of meanings, and ambiguity.

THE CONCEPTUAL DEVELOPMENT OF HAMAR GAMAL INTO A TALMUDIC EXPRESSION OF INDETERMINACY

The Semantic Field

Images of donkeys and camels and their human companions form part of a larger group of images in rabbinic texts that consider legal problems involving priority or conflicts, by imagining bodies moving in relation to one another.[21] These images aid rabbinic legal conceptualization. Hamar gamal likely developed from two words for human professions in a longer list, into an image that signifies abstract content through visual and somatic suggestion. This development adds weight to the argument that Talmudic thought and the interaction between Talmud and philosophy deepen in reference to Talmudic images.

Donkey and camel caravans facilitated trade in the late ancient Near East.[22] The familiarity with these caravans likely enabled the images to become ready sources for conceptualization. For example, b. Sanhedrin 32b considers the different legal standards for evidence. The Babylonian Talmud's description of two camel drivers trying to safely navigate a narrow mountain pass conveys the importance of compromise in financial disputes.[23] "Similarly, two camels that were climbing the ascent of Beth Horon and they meet each other. If they both climb, they will both fall off. If they climb one after the other, then they can both climb up" (b. Sanhedrin 32b).[24]

Richard Hidary's commentary on this passage notes that Beth Horon was a city about eleven miles from Jerusalem "with a steep narrow Roman road between the upper and lower settlements."[25] According to Josephus, in 66 CE, that road was the site of a Jewish ambush on retreating Roman troops. Using its steep incline and lack of alternative routes, Judeans blocked Roman soldiers and forced them over the edge.[26] The Babylonian Talmud sketches an image of camels and their human partners traversing a precarious path and choosing to pass in succession rather than trying to force the caravan onto the path at the same time. By allowing one party to go first, both are saved from falling. Similarly, compromise in a financial dispute allows both parties to gain something, even if neither party gains everything they wanted. The loss is shared between both parties and neither experiences a total loss. The image of camels and humans moving past one another across a narrow area helps the Talmud depict competing financial claims and hope for compromise.

The Tannaitic Evidence of Conceptual Content

According to Catherine Hezser, in the Mishnah, the phrase *hamar vegamal* ("donkey driver and camel driver") refers to two individuals who, due to the nature of their professions, are considered by rabbis to be suspect in their commitment to rabbinic laws.[27] The donkey driver is described in disparaging terms later in rabbinic literature, for example, in tractate Sanhedrin in the Palestinian Talmud, where Rabbi Yohanan criticizes Hizkiyah for asking a "donkey driver's question."[28] In the Babylonian

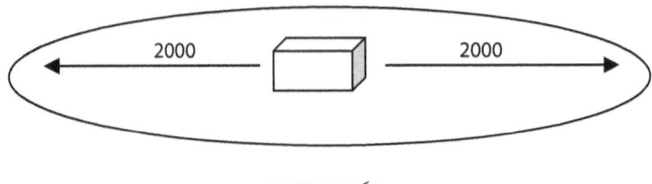

FIGURE 6.1.

Image by author and Sofia Xenia Economou.

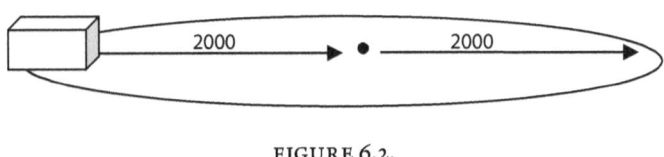

FIGURE 6.2.

Image by author and Sofia Xenia Economou.

Talmud, however, the image hamar gamal comes to mean more than two professions. The conceptual development of the phrase "donkey driver and camel driver" (hamar vegamal) begins in Mishnah Eruvin 3:4. In that mishnah, hamar vegamal represents a legal position, one of a pair of rulings given by rabbis in response to a questionable eruv.[29] The legal background to the case is that rabbinic law allows a Jew to travel up to two thousand cubits in any direction from their residence on the Sabbath (see fig. 6.1 and fig. 6.2).

If a person needs to travel more than that distance, an eruv can be established at a distance of two thousand cubits in a certain direction from that person's home (in the form of food, represented in fig. 6.2 as a black dot). The location of the eruv then becomes the person's legal residence for the Sabbath, allowing them to travel a further two thousand cubits in the same direction as the eruv.

In m. Eruvin 3:4, something happens to the eruv so that it is no longer accessible, edible, or permitted to be eaten, which means it does not function as it was intended.

> If [the food for the *eruv*] rolled outside of the boundary or a rock fell on it, or if it burned or if it was consecrated for priestly use and became impure, if this happened while it was still Friday during the day, this is not a valid

eruv. If it happened once it was dark (on Sabbath eve), behold this is a valid *eruv*. If it is unknown (*safeq*) [whether it happened while it was day or once it was night], Rabbi Meir and Rabbi Yehudah say, "Behold this is a donkey driver and a camel driver (hamar vegamal)." Rabbi Yose and Rabbi Shimon say, "It is valid."[30]

The decisive time for an eruv to become a person's legal residence for the Sabbath is Friday at twilight. Hence, the Mishnah reasons, as long as the eruv was not ruined until after dark on Friday, the person's change of legal residence took effect. Whatever happened to that food afterward is of no consequence. However, if the eruv food was ruined before it had a chance to take effect at twilight, the eruv is invalid. The interesting, in-between case occurs when it is unknown or "in doubt" (*safeq*) when the eruv was ruined. "If it is in doubt [whether it happened while it was day or once it was night], Rabbi Meir and Rabbi Yehudah say, 'Behold this is a donkey driver and a camel driver.' Rabbi Yose and Rabbi Shimon say, 'It is valid.'"

Hezser understands Rabbi Meir and Rabbi Yehudah's comment "Behold this is a donkey driver and a camel driver" as a typical thing to happen to careless people. But according to that interpretation, "a donkey driver and a camel driver" does not directly address the validity of the eruv. A better explanation seems to be that, hamar vegamal (and hamar gamal)[31] expresses an in-between legal state, one that is apparently at odds with the eruv being valid and also with the eruv being invalid.[32] Perhaps Hezser means to explain why "behold this is hamar gamal" is chosen as a metaphor for conflicting legal situations. In my opinion, Albeck and Goldberg are right to believe that hamar gamal is understood as a metaphor with conceptual content from the Tannaitic period.[33]

The Talmudic Evidence of Conceptual Development

There is only a little development in the conceptual content of this image from the Tannaitic period through the Talmuds, mainly because the connection between the donkey and camel drivers, and the legal position represented by hamar gamal, are not explained until the medieval period. There are three ways that hamar gamal develops as a concept in the Talmuds. First, Amoraic and post-Amoraic statements clearly use hamar gamal as a legal position or concept. Therefore, even if there was some ambiguity in the Tannaitic period, the concept is recognized in the Talmuds. Second, a passage in the Palestinian Talmud (Eruvin 3:5, 21b) compares Rabbi Meir's idea of hamar gamal to Rabbi Yehudah's idea of hamar gamal.[34] While in m. Eruvin 3:4, "behold this is hamar gamal" is attributed to Rabbi Meir and Rabbi Yehudah together, the Palestinian Talmud separates the Tannaim and interprets them as meaning different things by hamar gamal in light of the rabbis' rulings in other matters. Comparing different Tannaitic meanings of hamar gamal constitutes a serious conceptual engagement with the position, if not the meaning, of the image and therefore is a development beyond the Tannaitic sources. Third, b. Eruvin 49b extends hamar gamal to a mishnaic case that the Mishnah itself does not describe as hamar gamal. In summary, hamar gamal develops modestly as a concept in transmission to the Talmuds. The meaning of the image is understood and applied, but only after the close of the Babylonian Talmud do medieval Jewish interpreters, Rashi and Rabbenu Hananel, explain why hamar gamal means what it appears to mean: being subject to legal stringencies of two contradictory possible realities: an in-between legal state at odds with the eruv being valid, and also with the eruv being invalid.

Precisely how one should imagine this donkey driver and camel driver is not explicit. Later interpreters such as Rashi explain the image of hamar gamal as a single person trying to guide two different animals, coaxing one from behind and leading one from the front, never able to focus attention on either direction for long enough to lead effectively.[35] One of two mutually contradictory legal events took place, but it is unknown which of the two actually happened.[36] If it is unknown whether or not an eruv took effect, the person's legal residence for the Sabbath may be their house or the location of their eruv. The person is hamar gamal: stringently subject to both locations as Sabbath residences. This person can only travel within the two thousand cubits that are in both the diameter surrounding the house and the diameter surrounding the eruv (see fig. 6.3).[37]

The person's ineffective establishment of an eruv reduces their Sabbath travel rather than extending it. The indeterminacy of hamar gamal is more precise than the Mishnah's phrase *safeq*, "in doubt." Doubt could mean a state of indecision that will eventually be resolved once there is

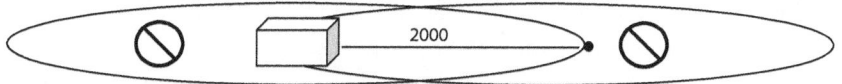

FIGURE 6.3.

Image by author and Sofia Xenia Economou.

FIGURE 6.4.

Image by author.

enough information. In this case, semantic laxity allows two conflicting legal systems to act on the person, of which each could be the case and each could have purchase on legal reality at that moment.[38]

Babylonian Talmud Eruvin 49b, as previously mentioned, extends the semantic and conceptual reach of the image, hamar gamal, by applying it to a location; specifically, at the base of a tree. Here, too, the image hamar gamal describes a situation where an individual is legally limited in their movement. The Talmud analyzes m. Eruvin 4:7.

In that law, a person wants to establish an eruv to continue traveling to their destination on the Sabbath. This person uses their sight, walking, and words, as opposed to food, to establish a Sabbath residence. The individual identifies aloud the particular location of their eruv on Friday before Sabbath begins. The eruv is two thousand cubits from their current position, and the ultimate destination is a further two thousand cubits beyond the eruv. Therefore, establishing the location of the eruv as a legal residence would allow the individual to walk the four thousand cubits to the final destination on the Sabbath.

> One who was travelling on a journey, and it was getting dark, and he recognized a tree or a wall, if he said, "my Sabbath camp will be below it" he has not said anything.
>
> If he said, "my Sabbath camp is at its base," he can walk from the position of his feet to its base, and from its base to his home, two thousand cubits, with the result that he walks 4000 cubits after it gets dark. (m. Eruvin 4:7; see fig. 6.4.)

This mishnah raises questions for its Amoraic and later interpreters (b. Eruvin 49b) because its two cases seem almost identical. Why is saying "my camp will be below it" ineffective but specifying "at its base" creates an eruv? The intention in both cases is the same, but the semantic laxity in one statement creates a legal problem. Most interpreters decide that the first statement ("below" the tree) is insufficiently specific, potentially including too much territory. "What does 'he has not said anything' mean? Rav said, 'He did not achieve anything at all [in establishing a settled residence for the Sabbath], so he cannot even travel to the base of the tree.' Shemuel said, 'It means "he did not say anything regarding getting to his home, but he is allowed to walk to beneath the tree."'"

Rav suggests that the traveler has no fixed abode for the Sabbath, so they may not travel even two thousand cubits toward home on the Sabbath.[39] Shemuel is a little more lenient. The Talmudic editors use the term hamar gamal, though it does not appear in this mishnah, to specify the travel limitations even with respect to Shemuel's relatively lenient view. "And below the tree is made hamar gamal: If he comes to measure (how

FIGURE 6.5.

Image by author.

far he can walk) from the north, (the law) measures for him from the south, if he comes to measure (how far he can walk) from the south, (the law) measures for him from the north" (b. Eruvin 49b).

Since "below the tree" was not specific, the traveler's walking distance is measured to his disadvantage. If he wants to walk north, the two thousand cubits are measured starting at the south side of the tree, pulling him south (see fig. 6.5). If he wishes to travel south, his distance is measured starting at the north side of the tree, pulling him north and limiting how far he can travel south (see fig. 6.6).

VISUALIZING AND FEELING A HAMAR GAMAL

The hamar gamal embodies the Babylonian Talmud's definition of being subject to two stringent legal predicaments.[40] It is an image of physical tension expressing conceptual dissonance and emphasizing its seriousness

FIGURE 6.6.

Image by author.

through a suggestion of physical discomfort. It is difficult to know how exactly the Talmudic authors imagined the hamar gamal. The sketch in figure 6.7 depicts someone trying to lead both a donkey and a camel as Rashi and other Talmudic interpreters understood those activities.

According to Talmudic rules governing methods to acquire animals, the orientation of the hamar gamal's body is uncomfortable. His chest is opened out toward the reader because he is trying to get the camel to move along with him. If he were to square his shoulders to face in the same direction as the donkey, he would have a comfortable position from which to encourage the donkey forward, but his arm holding the reins of the camel would be pulling out directly behind him. In this position, he could perhaps move a step at a time, turning one way and then the other to encourage the two animals forward, but his attention and body orientation are not optimal for communicating with both animals at the same time. The hamar gamal is unable to face a single direction and

FIGURE 6.7.

Image by Tamara Kaminsky.

move forward. He is like a legal subject governed by two legal realities simultaneously.

Another way to visualize the hamar gamal is as a single person who is trying to be in two places at once, but who cannot be. Chanoch Albeck suggests a "middle path," conceptually, and here in the illustrations I suggest imagining the physical manifestations of those options suggested by the images.[41]

In figure 6.8, the donkey driver is behind his donkey, and the camel driver is ahead of his camel. The sense of the physical pressure of being pulled in two directions comes from the driver desiring to stand in between the animals at the position of the question mark, or perhaps moving towards that position. One is unable to be both behind the donkey and ahead of the camel, but one might imagine themselves moving sideways, pulling against the weight of the forward direction of the animals, as the human tries to position themselves both from behind and ahead of

FIGURE 6.8.

Image by Tamara Kaminsky.

two animals. The animals do not understand the instructions and cannot move in harmony with the person, or each other. The experience is halting, and a physical bind. This contrasts with the ordinary connotations of the image of donkey or camel driver: that of profitable movement towards a destination.

Finally, Rabbenu Hananel offers a third possibility. The hamar gamal is a single figure who has reversed his orientation toward the two animals such that he is behind the camel and ahead of the donkey. In this position, his attempts to move the animals are met with resistance—the animals are not accustomed to receiving direction in this way, and progress is not possible.[42]

However one visualizes hamar gamal, two legal potentialities exist and pull or push the subject into a position where it is impossible to move. Crucially, in Talmudic uses of hamar gamal, the pull is legal and material; the force exerted by two competing legal realities is concretized in the limitations on the traveler. These limitations hold one back from their destination, pulling back from north or south like a leash. In the earlier passages (b. Eruvin 49b, figs. 6.6 and 6.7, as well as b. Eruvin 35b, fig. 6.3), the legal subject is also held back from walking as far as desired by opposing possible legal realities, one in which their legal residence is the eruv, and the other in which their legal residence is the home. Because the law treats one's legal residence as whatever would give the person less room to walk, the two conflicting and overlapping legal realities tether the person to their disadvantage.

As previously described, later rabbinic writing uses hamar gamal to convey two possibilities in tension with one another, in a wide variety of legal applications. In the Babylonian Talmud, however, hamar gamal is limited to cases of restricted travel due to eruvin (pl. of eruv). In both Talmuds, the hamar gamal remains closely associated with eruvin, and it is not until the post-Talmudic period that the image moves beyond the rules of eruvin.[43] The limitation of the figure to this legal context emphasizes just how well-suited hamar gamal is to describe the force of rules preventing a person from walking from one area to another. The hamar gamal suggests feelings of conflicting forces on a body, concretizing somatically the outcome of two coexisting possibilities. The person's attempt to alter their legal home changed them from a person using the law to their advantage by establishing reality through legal means, into a person suffering under the law, as two operative legal possibilities pull them like reins. A camel driver–donkey driver tries to exert force, but their attempt to direct the animals results in being subject to the animals' weight and direction. When the Talmud suggests the image hamar gamal, it is more than a figure for undetermined legal facts due to sloppy designation or unwise action. It expresses the coexistence of competing legal realities visually and somatically.[44]

CONCLUSION

The methodology I suggest begins with studying a text with knowledge of its historical context, tracing conceptual development of a Talmudic image, picturing an image in a legal expression and allowing the image's ways of signifying (intellectual, somatic, emotional) to expand beyond a simple correlation of one image to one message. This methodology indicates that imagery, particularly imagery that can signify somatically through practices akin to "kinesthetic empathy," can mean more than declarative sentences.

In her novel *Always Coming Home* (1985), Ursula K. Le Guin gives substance to how an image might signify within a culture through many different ways, including visually and aurally. The novel's narrator says that "the heyiya-if, two spirals centered on the same (empty) space was the material or visual representation of the idea of heyiya." The narrator goes on to call this "heyiya-if" a "visual form of an idea," "an inexhaustible metaphor" that was a "gesture in dance," an element in architecture, musical instruments, movement in dramatic staging, and "a subject of meditation."[45] Le Guin's narrator creates an image that is meaningful beyond a single idea and a solely visual-conceptual connection. As Hannah Kosstrin noted to me, Le Guin is arguing for "a kinesthetic way of thinking," and for valuing knowledge that is not logocentric.[46] The same is true for my interpretation of hamar gamal. Hamar gamal is an expression of indeterminacy, related to Talmudic "doubt." But it is not a general, blank idea of doubt; it is specific and rooted to its legal context, which concerns restriction of movement on the Sabbath. Therefore, hamar gamal expresses how legal doubt can produce a situation of almost physical discomfort. Through visualization and kinesthetic engagement, the rabbinic authors warn against actions that could create this difficult legal predicament by helping their audience imagine themselves feeling physically uncomfortable.

Le Guin expresses how narratives, like metaphors and other images, cannot be reduced to a message. She argues that readers of such material should try to allow the various meanings to permeate their understanding instead of looking for a clean and direct "message." I contend that the same argument can be made regarding conceptual images like hamar gamal in the Talmud. They, too, demand an analytical approach that respects an image's enriching indirectness and the many ways it might signify in addition to the intellectual. Le Guin writes, "As a fiction writer, I don't speak message. I speak story. Sure, my story means something, but if you want to know what it means, you have to ask the question in terms appropriate to storytelling.... Any reduction of that language into intellectual messages is radically, destructively incomplete."[47]

Hamar gamal situations show that Talmudic imagery has significance even if the Talmud's discussion cannot determine a truth value for a statement or establish facts decisively about a case.[48] The capaciousness of an image allows the Talmud to emphasize the difficulty of being subject to two competing legal possibilities rather than gloss over it as a situation whose full facts are unknown or in "doubt." A definitive declarative statement could not have conveyed this meaning as fully. The hamar gamal as a possibility operator does more than convey what might or might not be the case. It expresses the feeling of opposing forces on a body and magnifies the tension of being subject to the stringencies of two competing legal realities.

Analyzing this kind of imagery is a necessary complement to studying rabbinic modes of argumentation, in order to trace rabbinic conceptualization. The images rabbis generate or adopt are crucial to studying the methods of signification, definitions of ambiguity, and the ability to hold contradictory possibilities in abeyance. Potential meanings in images, such as legal force, may be suggested sensorily, through weight in the body, and, in the case of hamar gamal, an image may bolster the presence of indeterminacy in a legal position, by virtue of expressing it through an image, which is itself irreducible to a simple "message."

Talmudic images and modes of signification can engage philosophical, as well as literary theoretical discourses, without requiring the Talmud to share the same concerns as philosophers. This approach takes neither a purely external nor a purely internal position toward Talmudic thinking. It is not "thinking about" rabbinic thought from the outside, nor is it "thinking within" the limits of Talmudic imaginative boundaries.[49] Studying rabbinic images is another way into Talmudic thought, allowing the theoretical and Talmudic corpora to maintain their divergent concerns and methods, without limiting the reader to either of them.

LYNN KAYE is Associate Professor of Rabbinic Literature and Thought at Brandeis University and author of *Time in the Babylonian Talmud: Natural and Imagined Times in Jewish Law and Narrative* and, with ed. with Sarit Kattan Gribetz, *Time: A Multidisciplinary Introduction*.

NOTES

* I wish to thank Sergey Dolgopolski for inviting me to reflect on this topic and for his help and suggestions as I developed the ideas. I am grateful to Leigh Bloch, Alexander Kaye, Hannah Kosstrin, Ila Nagar, and Alex Weisberg for commenting on drafts and to Dana Hollander for sharing her valuable thoughts in conversation. I wish to thank Aharon Amit and Arnon Atzmon of the Talmud and Oral Law Department at Bar-Ilan University for inviting me to present a paper at the 2019 conference, "Generations: Evolution and Transmission of the Rabbinic Text" and to thank those who responded to that presentation. I am also grateful to Judaica librarian Jim Rosenbloom for his research assistance. This chapter owes a debt to the affinity group "Thinking with Rabbinic Texts" organized by Dana Hollander, Chaya Halberstam, and others. Thank-you as well to the copy editor at Indiana University Press for their work on this chapter.

1. This is a central idea in literary studies. In Talmudic scholarship, Barry Wimpfheimer articulated this when he wrote that narratives in the Talmud should not be reduced to a single message, even though the Babylonian Talmud's editorial layer sometimes does precisely that, "flattening the story into a singular moral or didactic legal message." Wimpfheimer, *Narrating the Law*, 164.

2. Moscovitz, *Talmudic Reasoning*; Furstenberg, *Languages of Talmudic Discourse*. Furstenberg's book, as well as his articles on lost property in early rabbinic law, explain the way that concepts form in rabbinic texts in light of scholarship in the philosophy of language. Shana Strauch Schick takes an intellectual historical approach, situating conceptual development in its Sasanian historical context in *Intention in Jewish Law*. Jeffrey L. Rubenstein contributed to the study of rabbinic conceptualization as well as to the study of rabbinic culture and literature. See "On Some Abstract Concepts in Rabbinic Literature," and idem, "Explanation of Tannaitic Sources by Abstract Concepts."

3. For a longer history of Talmudic logic and rhetoric, those interested may consult earlier scholarship, for example, Jacobs, *Studies in Talmudic Logic* as well as his *Talmudic Argument*; and Friedman, "Pereq Ha-Isha Rabba in the Babylonian Talmud." Of relevance for philosophers and scholars of Jewish thought and philosophy is the significant scholarship in comparative logic, including Abraham, Gabbay, and Schild, *Studies in Talmudic Logic*. This recent work adds subject-specific depth and new methodology to previous scholarship on Talmudic logic and reason, including Kraemer, *Mind of the Talmud*; Sion, *Judaic Logic*; Fisch, *Rational Rabbis*; and Maccoby, *Philosophy of the Talmud*. Another approach with both earlier and more recent examples are comparative studies of Greco-Roman structures and rhetoric in Talmudic argumentation, such as Brodsky, "From Disagreement to Talmudic Discourse"; Hidary, "Classical Rhetorical Arrangement," and note Hidary's references to previous scholarship on pp. 33–36 as well as Hidary's *Rabbis and Classical Rhetoric*. In *Controversy and Dialogue in the Halakhic Sources*, Ben-Menahem, Hecht, and Wosner also examine the dialogical means of reasoning and argumentation in a comparative legal framework.

4. Wimpfheimer, *Narrating the Law* and Belser, *Power, Ethics, and Ecology* each focus on the role of aggadah in Talmudic legal reasoning, as does the work of Jeffrey Rubenstein on the interpretation of Talmudic narratives in their halakhic contexts, such as *Talmudic Stories*. For further engagements of law and narrative see Suzanne Last Stone, "Rabbinic Legal Magic," Aryeh Cohen, *Rereading Talmud*, and Ofra Meir, *Poetics of Rabbinic Stories*. Ochs and Levene, *Textual Reasonings* addressed thinking in relation to texts in a similar direction to that taken here. The scholarship of Charlotte Fonrobert, "Regulating the Human Body," idem, *Menstrual Purity*, and Labovitz, *Marriage and Metaphor*, analyze rabbinic metaphor; this chapter continues that work and adds a somatic perspective.

5. Kosstrin, "Kinesthetic Seeing," 26–28.

6. Hahn, *Sensational Knowledge*, 83–84. See also Bakan, *Music of Death and New Creation*, 281–91; Sklar, *Dancing with the Virgin*; and Smyth, "Kinesthetic Communication in Dance."

7. I am indebted to Hannah Kosstrin for introducing me to dance studies and kinesthetic knowledge in her work, for example, Kosstrin, *Honest Bodies*.

8. LaMothe, *Between Dancing and Writing*, 60, quoted in Schaefer, *Religious Affects*, 190. See also Schaefer, *Religious Affects*, 181 for an affective description of religion as something that creates ties between bodies and their environment and causes bodies to move: "moves bodies by creating affective ligatures between bodies and their worlds."

9. Such as the work of Samia Hesni, "How to Disrupt a Social Script" and "Normative Generics and Social Kind Terms."

10. Spector, *What This Awl Means*, 3. Dry writing, furthermore, led to feelings of boredom with the subjects of the scholarship—an ethical problem for Spector, as was the issue of academics, "archaeologists and anthropologists [that] exploit Indian sites and materials to build their own careers." Spector, *What This Awl Means*, p. 13, citing McNickle, "American Indians Who Never Were," and Medicine, Ortiz, and McNickle, "The Anthropologist," in Spector, *What This Awl Means*, 1–3. I think it is worth considering this as a problem for scholarship of rabbinics as well.

11. Morrison, "Site of Memory," 112, quoted in Spector, *What This Awl Means*, 79.

12. Ibid. This sympathetic use of imagination allowed Spector to advance specific archaeological knowledge about the different types of sites that existed. Previous observers and archaeologists "labeled any Indian community, settlement or site, a 'village,' regardless of the community's size, composition of function," while Spector describes a more specific set of Dakota encampments to life through a dialogue among imagining lived life, written and visual sources, and tangible remains.

13. m. Eruvin 3:4 and 4:10 and t. Eruvin 4:2 and 6:10.

14. y. Qiddushin 3:3 (64a) by Rabbi Yose, y. Eruvin 3:4 (21a), which is a Mishnah excerpt, and y. Terumot 3:1 (14b) by Rabbi Yonah. b. Eruvin 35a and 49b: the first is a quotation from the Mishnah, while in 49b, it appears twice by Rav Sheshet and the anonymous editors.

15. Abramovitsh, *Lo nachat be-ya'akov*, 39; and *Bimei ha-ra'ash*, 48; I think Abramovitsh is describing a forceful figure riding atop the struggle, which he has described as hamar gamal, donkey driver–camel driver, and he uses "riding atop" to tie into the meaning of this figure. Abramovitz, *Mah anu?*, 472.

16. Moshe Leib Lilienblum, a Hebrew, Yiddish, and Russian writer and maskil, used hamar gamal to express how loving couples needed to be matched in their ideas and intellects for them to succeed. In his autobiography, he wrote that they should not be "like hamar gamal, so one pulls this way and one pulls that way, rather both of them should aim to one place." *Hata'ot Ne'urim*, II:109. *Hamar gamal* was also the title of a short-lived Hebrew humorous newspaper published in 1908–9, according to Malachi, *Mineged Tir'eh*, 194.

17. Rabbi Ovadia Yosef, *Yabia Omer*, vol. 6, Yoreh De'ah 33 (Jerusalem, 1956–1993), and Rabbi Nosson Gestetner, *Lehorot Natan*, vol. 5:16 (Bnei Brak, 1986). Each one quotes eighteenth-century Rabbi Yaakov ben Yosef Reischer in his responsum *Shevut Yaakov*, vol. 1, no. 8 (Lemberg, 1861). Interestingly, the responsum uses another Amoraic image that deserves its own study: "riding two horses." In its Talmudic context (b. Ketubot 55b, b. Bava Batra 152a), it means something different from the way Reischer appears to be using it. As Michael Sokoloff translates: "he gave his claim double force." Sokoloff, *A Dictionary of Jewish Babylonian Aramaic*, 1083.

18. Twentieth-century Rabbi Chaim Eliezer Shapiro, *Minchat Elazar: Selections* 15 (Jerusalem, 1996); sixteenth-century Rabbi Shemuel de Medina of Salonika, *Shut Meharashdam* Even Ha'ezer 31 (Lemberg, 1862); seventeenth-century Egyptian Rabbi Mordechai

Halevy *Darchei Noam* (Venice, 1697). Cited by twentieth-century Rabbi Benzion Uzziel, Sephardic Chief Rabbi of Palestine, then Israel, in *Mishpetei Uzziel*, vol. 2, Yoreh De'ah 40 (Jerusalem, 1995–2000), and Rabbi Yosef Shalom Eliashiv in his commentary on Talmud Berakhot, *Shiurei Maran*, Berakhot 27b, 300. See also the exegetical comment by Rabbi Shmuel Eidels of seventeenth-century Poland (Maharsha) on Berakhot 61a (Vilna: Romm, 1886–1897, all accessed digitally via the Responsa Project Database).

Maharsha notes that if the first woman and man were, as one midrash has it, created as a single figure back-to-back, it must be that one side led and the other followed, or else they would be like hamar gamal. He uses this to explain why, in general, men should walk in front of women.

19. Dolgopolski, *What Is Talmud?*, 1.

20. It is not my goal to compile a comprehensive lexicon of rabbinic thought imagery, though assembling lexicons specific to Amoraic generation and locale might be possible in light of scholarship charting the intellectual history of rabbinic Babylonia, for example, Elman, "A Tale of Two Cities"; Cohen, *Legal Methodology*; Schick, "Negligence and Strict Liability," "Reading Aristotle in Mahoza?" and *Intention in Talmudic Law*.

21. Rabbinic texts consider the temporal sequence of activities by imagining human bodies running or walking and passing one another in Kaye, *Time in the Babylonian Talmud*, 33–38.

22. Hezser, *Jewish Travel in Antiquity*, discusses donkeys and donkey drivers as well as camel caravans on pp. 130–60. See also Aberbach, *Labor, Crafts and Commerce*, 220–24; and Safrai, *Economy of Roman Palestine*, 234–37, 264–68, 289–91.

23. Building on an image of boats passing one another on a river (cited in t. Bava Qamma 2:10).

24. Translation by Hidary, "A Proposal for a New Translation and Commentary," 10.

25. See ibid., 13n58–59.

26. Ibid.

27. Hezser, *Jewish Travel in Antiquity*, 140, writes, "According to a statement attributed to Rabbi Meir in m. Er. 4:10 'Everyone who was able to make an eruv and did not make one behold this is an ass driver [or] a camel driver.' And according to m. Dem. 4:7 ass drivers are not always considered trustworthy in regard to tithing. The suspicions regarding ass drivers and camel drivers may have been based on the fact that they worked outside of the spheres of local supervision." Hezser's interpretation of "Behold this is a donkey diver and a camel driver" aligns with the comment "anyone who could make an *eruv* and did not, behold this is a donkey driver and a camel driver" in m. Eruvin 4:10, but even in that case, the label *hamar vegamal* could also mean what I argue it means in m. Eruvin 3:4. Both Goldberg and Albeck interpret hamar vegamal in m. Eruvin 3:4 as a legal position or, in Albeck's case, "a parable." Goldberg, *The Mishnah Treatise Eruvin*, 129; and Albeck and Yalon, *Shishah Sidre Mishnah*, 92–93.

28. y. Sanhedrin 6:1 (23b). It could mean a donkey's question, but both Jastrow and Sokoloff translate it as a question of a "donkey driver." Jastrow, *A Dictionary of the Targumim*, 480; Sokoloff, *A Dictionary of Jewish Palestinian Aramaic*, 530.

29. I translate "donkey driver and a camel driver" not "donkey driver or a camel driver," as Hezser did in her discussion of m. Eruvin 4:10 because in this case, the force of this image is due to the presence of two figures, not in them as alternatives. For scholarship on eruvin (pl. of eruv), see Fonrobert, "Neighborhood as Ritual Space"; "Gender Politics in the Rabbinic Neighborhood"; "The Political Symbolism of the Eruv"; Fonrobert,

"From Separatism to Urbanism"; Klein, "Squaring the City" and "Torah in Triclinia"; Cousineau, "Rabbinic Urbanism in London"; Weissman, *Sefer Yetsi'ot ha-Shabat*; Ades, *Sefer 'Eruv ke-hilkhato*; Mintz, *Halakhah in America*.

30. Translation of ms. Kaufmann in Goldberg, *The Mishnah Treatise Eruvin*, 77.

31. The phrase hamar vegamal joined with the conjunction *ve* ("and") appears in the Kaufmann manuscript, but as Goldberg notes in his critical edition, the conjunction is omitted by many other manuscripts of the Mishnah (including Parma), Goldberg, *The Mishnah Treatise Eruvin*, 77. Goldberg also notes that ms. Kaufmann tends to add and omit *vav* conjunctions, and, in fact, m. Eruvin 3:4 is an example of how ms. Kaufmann adds *vav* conjunctions between words in an expression describing a single matter. Goldberg, *The Mishnah Treatise Eruvin*, 41 in the Hebrew numbering. Therefore, I do not think it advisable to claim that the shift from ms. Kaufmann's term hamar vegamal (using *and*) to the consistent Babylonian Talmud term hamar gamal (without *and*) signifies a shift toward concretizing the phrase as a legal abstraction. In the Tosefta (Eruvin 4:2 and 6:10 in Lieberman's edition numbering), hamar gamal appears without the conjunction *vav* in rules that in Mishnaic parallels, in ms. Kaufmann, have the conjunction. In the Babylonian Talmud, hamar gamal appears without the conjunction in every textual witness to Eruvin 35a and 49b. The only Babylonian Talmud passage that has hamar vegamal (with *and*) is ms. Vatican 110–11 of Qiddushin 82a, in which the professions appear in a list of undesirable professions a Jewish man should not teach his son. There, the two professions of donkey driver and camel driver are linked with a conjunction, and several other professions in the same list are also paired with a conjunction. The Palestinian Talmud uses hamar gamal and hamar vegamal (the phrase with and without the conjunction) when referring to the image as a Tannaitic legal position. For example, the Venice ed. Qiddushin 4:9 (66b) and Qiddushin 3:3 (64a) reads hamar gamal, but Venice Eruvin 3:4 (21a) reads hamar vegamal. In all of those cases, the phrase refers to a legal position, in other words, a concept rather than two professions. In summary, the Babylonian Talmud always reads hamar gamal without a conjunction, in all available witnesses, while the Palestinian Talmud may or may not use a conjunction in Amoraic discourses and still refers to the image as a concept.

32. Goldberg interprets hamar gamal in the Mishnah as a legal situation as well, "he cannot walk from the place of his *eruv* 2000 cubits, perhaps his *eruv* was not established for him. And likewise he is not like those of his town, since perhaps his *eruv* was established for him." Goldberg, *The Mishnah Treatise Eruvin*, 78.

33. Both Albeck and Goldberg understand "*harei zeh hamar vegamal*" as a legal position, which Albeck calls a "parable," and I share this view. This is also the sense in t. Eruvin 4:2 (Lieberman) t. Eruvin 6:10 (Lieberman). Further evidence can be found in two instances in the Palestinian Talmud and the Babylonian Talmud, in which the phrase changes from "behold this is hamar gamal" to "*na'aseh hamar gamal*," or "becomes hamar gamal." If someone or something can "become" hamar gamal, this indicates that hamar gamal is certainly a legal predicament and a concept. y. Terumot 3:1 (14b); b. Eruvin 49b, in all extant versions.

34. Lieberman, *Hayerushalmi Kifshuto*, I:268–69 discusses this passage.

35. Rashi, b. Eruvin 35a, s.v. hamar gamal. Following Rashi, Frank, *A Practical Talmud Dictionary*, 108, writes "One individual who is simultaneously serving as both a donkey-driver and a camel-driver. Since a donkey is driven from behind, while a camel is led from the front it is difficult to drive both animals simultaneously. Hence this expression is used

to describe a person who is confronted by a paradoxical halakhic situation." I have not determined whether being a donkey driver and camel driver is part of a broader cultural context in the rabbinic period, and I continue to seek parallels in Roman Palestine or earlier Hebrew texts. In b. Bava Metziʻa 8b–9a, one acquires a camel with different actions than one does a donkey: a camel is pulled from the front, while a donkey is driven forward from behind. In both cases, the owner has to cause the animal to move, but they are moved in ways conventional to them. That same passage describes two people attempting to both drive a donkey and lead a camel, not one person alone. B. Ketubbot 62b observes that the occupations of camel driver and donkey driver are different enough that a man who is a donkey driver cannot become a camel driver without his wife's permission because the travel patterns and home time are different. In other words, these professions are not interchangeable, whether at the specific level expressed by a "donkey driver and camel driver" who is pulled in two different directions, or at a more general level of travel and lifestyle.

36. This degree of indeterminacy is circumscribed: the eruv was either fit or unfit. Other options, such as *A* could have happened, *B* could have happened, or neither *A* nor *B* could have happened, are not entertained. Goldberg comments about this mishnah that the simple reading should be that even with a hamar gamal situation, the person can still travel the two thousand cubits from home to the eruv. The Palestinian Talmud (21a) cites disagreement among Amoraim about whether the person can even travel back home in this case. Goldberg, *The Mishnah Treatise Eruvin*, 78.

37. There is a dispute about whether an eruv is a circle or square of two thousand cubits about a person's residence; see Kaye, *Time in the Babylonian Talmud*, 114n11. I am using a circle here for simplicity.

38. I thank Sergey Dolgopolski for this formulation.

39. Rabbenu Hananel b. Eruvin 49b. According to Rav, when the traveler tried to designate "below the tree" as his residence, he lost his current position as a stable residence. But since he never actually acquired that new residence, he does not even have two thousand cubits diameter from his current position, just the four cubits around him. He is in a worse position than if he had said nothing and made his current location his Sabbath residence.

40. y. Eruvin 3:4 (22a) takes hamar vegamal as a legal predicament as well.

41. "This is a parable: One who leads the donkey walks after him and urges him with a stick to run fast, and one who leads a camel walks in front of him and pulls him forward, and behold he is forced to walk in the middle path, not like a donkey driver and not like one who leads a camel. Such is one in whose eruv appears a doubt." Albeck, *Shishah Sidre Mishnah*, 92–93.

42. Rabbenu Hananel on Eruvin 35a–b, s.v. hamar gamal.

43. While hamar gamal appears in a discussion of betrothal and *terumot* (priestly portions), in both passages, the term is closely tied to cases of eruvin. y. Qiddushin 3:3 (64a), in Guggenheimer, *The Jerusalem Talmud: Nashim*, 284, debates whether the key legal issue in a contingent betrothal is the proper formulation of the contingency or whether it is "doubt." The Talmud brings the eruv case of Rabbi Meir and Rabbi Yehudah "behold this is hamar gamal" (omitting the conjunction in the Mishnah's version of their statement) as an example of "doubt." While the passage is interested in problematic legal declarations beyond eruvin, its use of the image hamar gamal remains tied to eruvin. y. Terumot 3:1 (14b) in Guggenheimer, *The Jerusalem Talmud: Terumot and Ma'aserot*, 97, presents

another case of "doubt" when a bitter melon might be either terumah or not terumah (priestly portion), depending on whether it is considered food or not. As an example, if the terumah was used to make an eruv, would it make its owner hamar gamal, limiting movement? There is no difference in this phrase in the Venice edition, ms. Leiden, or ms. Vatican of the Palestinian Talmud.

44. In personal communication during the editing of this chapter, Sergey Dolgopolski suggested that hamar gamal is like a Kantian schema for unwise action and forces of coeventuality. As a philosophical echo, a schema could be especially resonant because the image of donkey driver and camel driver reaches beyond a relationship between image and concept to the sensation of forces on a body and the plurality of possibilities rooted in the single expression. "Schemata are needed by Kant in order to overcome two apparent gaps: an ontological gap between abstract universals and concrete particulars on the one hand, and a cognitive gap between concepts and intuitions on the other hand ... schemata can mediate between the one side (abstract universals, empirical concepts, pure concepts) and the other side (concrete particulars, empirical intuitions, objects of experience) precisely because they are at once figural-formal and *also* intrinsically sensory." Hanna, "Kant's Theory of Judgment."

45. Le Guin, *Always Coming Home*, 45.
46. Personal communication.
47. Le Guin, "A Message about Messages."
48. For further work on indeterminacy in Talmudic thinking, see Schiffman, "Ha-safeq be-halakhah u-ve-mishpat"; Ben-Menahem, "Is there Always One"; Koppel, "Probabilistic Foundations"; Halberstam, *Law and Truth*; Hidary, *Dispute for the Sake of Heaven*; Halbertal, "The Limits of Prayer"; Halbertal, *Birth of Doubt*; and Kaye, *Time in the Babylonian Talmud*, 110–39.
49. Thanks to Sergey Dolgopolski for the language for these options.

The Language of Plants and Human-World Entanglement in Midrash and Walter Benjamin's Philosophy of Language

ALEXANDER WEISBERG

INTRODUCTION

This chapter explores several Amoraic rabbinic exegetical traditions based on Genesis 2:5, found in Genesis Rabbah 13, that offer ontological descriptions of the interdependence and entanglement of the Creation and nonhuman communication and agency.[1] To better understand these traditions, I read them together with Walter Benjamin's early philosophy of language, which he explicates through readings of Genesis 2 in his essay "On the Language of Man, and Language as Such."[2] I highlight the ways Benjamin's philosophical reading of Genesis and his attendant theological anthropology are similar to and different from the rabbis' readings and anthropology, and through this comparison, I indicate junctures and disjunctures between rabbinic and philosophical thought. The rabbinic traditions present human prayer as a creative performative act and understand the world as an entanglement of human and nonhuman agency. Benjamin helps reveal this rabbinic depiction through his explanation in "On Language as Such and on the Language of Man," stating that the possibility of thought through language becomes a possibility only because of humanity's deep material interconnection with the nonhuman world. However, the rabbinic traditions, as opposed to Benjamin, avoid the widely prevalent subject/object divide, which is a hallmark of the Western philosophical tradition. In Benjamin's essay, there is a clear-cut distinction between human subject and nonhuman object, even as all of the Creation has linguistic capability.[3] For Benjamin, human speech transcends nonhuman language because of humanity's ability to raise the Creation toward God through prayer. Nonetheless, Benjamin's narrative of human/nonhuman difference helps us to understand the ontological vision of human/nonhuman difference in Genesis Rabbah. Thus I argue that these rabbinic texts support an alternative discourse about humans and nonhumans that differs in significant ways from the modern dominant philosophical discourse, which, in Aaron Gross's words, is "correlated with a series of hierarchical dichotomies that not only privilege the human over the animal but also mind over body, transcendence over immanence, spirituality over materiality, spirit over letter, faith over law, modern over primitive, West over East, Christian over Jew, and so on."[4] In this rabbinic ontology, the shared linguistic capacity of various entities of the Creation shapes, forms, and shifts the Creation in a multitude of ways. In this respect, Genesis Rabbah provides us with a depiction of the human and nonhuman as entangled in both materiality and language as well as in the capriciousness of rain and sustenance.

This chapter explores how Genesis Rabbah 13, along with parallels found in b. Hullin 60b and a Genizah fragment of an unidentified midrash, understand Genesis 2:5 as depicting the prayer of the first human as the act that brings forth the vegetation of the world. Genesis 2:5 reads:

וְכֹל ׀ שִׂיחַ הַשָּׂדֶה טֶרֶם יִהְיֶה בָאָרֶץ וְכָל־עֵשֶׂב הַשָּׂדֶה טֶרֶם יִצְמָח כִּי לֹא הִמְטִיר יְהֹוָה אֱלֹהִים עַל־הָאָרֶץ וְאָדָם אַיִן לַעֲבֹד אֶת־הָאֲדָמָה

> When no shrub of the field was yet on earth and no grasses of the field had yet sprouted, because the Lord God had not sent rain upon the Earth and there was no man to work the land.

These rabbinic traditions, analyzed in the following pages, read both parts of the second half of the text "the Lord God had not sent rain upon the Earth and there was no man to work the land" as the reason for there being no vegetation on Earth.[5] According to this reading, humanity and its prayers were a necessary component in the formation of the Land and its vegetation. These traditions present human prayer as a creative performative act and understand the world as an entanglement of human and nonhuman agency. I elucidate the ontological elements of these traditions not only through reading them with Benjamin's early philosophy of language but also through Donovan Schaefer's description of affective economies.⁶

In reading Genesis Rabbah together with b. Hullin 60b and the Genizah fragment, I demonstrate that there is no clear-cut separation between the physical and the spiritual in these related midrashic traditions and that the relationship between humans and the nonhuman—while hierarchical in some respects—does not follow the same logic of ontological distinctions that Gross discusses in the dominant Western philosophical tradition. Rather, these texts display an entanglement of nonhuman and human agency and subjecthood that does not take the subject/object divide as its ground, as well as a shared process of worldmaking involving humans, Land, vegetation, language, rain, and the divine. This is similar to Donna Haraway's notion of the "material-semiotic net," in which materiality and language are mutually constitutive.⁷

GENESIS RABBAH 13, B. HULLIN 60B, AND PERFORMATIVE READING

Genesis Rabbah, a late fourth-century Palestinian exegetical midrashic collection, opens its thirteenth chapter with an argument between two rabbis on how to understand Genesis 2:5 in the context of Genesis 2:9:

> [וכל שיח השדה] הכא את אמר וכל שיח השדה ולהלן את אמר ויצמח י"י אלהים וגו' (בראשית ב ט) אתמהא, אמר ר' חנינא להלן לגן עדן וכן לישובו של עולם, תני ר' חייא אילו ואילו לא צימיחו עד שירדו עליהן גשמים.⁸

> [It is written in Genesis 2:5, "when no shrub of the field (was yet on earth and no grasses of the field had yet sprouted)."] Here you say, "no shrub of the field [and no grasses of the field]" and further on [in Genesis 2:9] you say, "And from the ground the Lord God caused to grow [every tree that was pleasing to the sight and good for food, with the tree of life in the middle of the garden, and the tree of knowledge of good and bad.]" This does not make sense! R. Ḥanina says, [the verse] later on [refers] to the Garden of Eden [Genesis 2:9], whereas this [verse, Genesis 2:5 refers] to the inhabited world. R. Ḥiyya taught, both here and here nothing grew until rain descended upon them.⁹

In this section, two verses seem to contradict one another, but it is difficult to understand the exact contradiction between the verses. Harry Freedman and Jacob Neusner have suggested that the problem is related to the order of Creation, predicated on the two different creation stories in Genesis 1 and 2.[10] The first verse in the midrash, Genesis 2:5, does not accord with the creation story of Genesis 1, where plants are created before humanity, but the second verse, Genesis 2:9, does correspond with the story in Genesis 1. This suggestion, however, ignores the context of Genesis 2:9. In Genesis 2:9, God causes the trees to grow in the Garden of Eden only after humanity has been created (verses 2:5–8). Therefore, this explanation of the conflict between the two verses cannot stand, and both verses contradict the order of creation described in Genesis 1.[11] Theodor and Albeck have similarly noted that both verses contradict the order of creation in Genesis 1.[12] The argument between R. Ḥanina and R. Ḥiyya hinges on different interpretations of Genesis 2:9 and whether humanity's first prayer was involved in the creation of the vegetation in the Garden of Eden, as it was in the creation of the vegetation in the rest of the inhabited world. While this reading is not explicitly stated in Genesis Rabbah, it is made clear by looking at this tradition along with other parallel traditions found in b. Ḥullin 60b and in an unidentified midrashic Genizah fragment, with the context of their oral transmission and performance in mind.

B. Ḥullin 60b reads:

רב אסי רמי, כתיב: ותוצא הארץ דשא בתלת בשבתא, וכתיב, וכל שיח השדה טרם יהיה בארץ במעלי שבתא! מלמד שיצאו דשאים ועמדו על פתח קרקע, עד שבא אדם הראשון ובקש עליהם רחמים, וירדו גשמים וצמחו; ללמדך: שהקב"ה מתאוה לתפלתן של צדיקים. רב נחמן בר פפא הויא ליה ההיא גינתא, שדי ביה ביזרני ולא צמח, בעא רחמי - אתא מיטרא וצמח, אמר: היינו דרב אסי.[13]

Rav Assi pointed out a contradiction [between verses]. One verse [in Genesis 1:12] says, "And the earth brought forth grass," referring to the third day, whereas another verse [in Genesis 2:5] when speaking of the sixth day says, "No shrub of the field was yet on the earth." This teaches us that the plants started to sprout but stopped just as they were about to break through the soil, until *Adam* came and prayed for rain for them; and when rain fell, they sprouted forth. This teaches you that the Holy One, Blessed Be He, longs for the prayers of the righteous. Rav Naḥman bar Papa had a garden and he sowed in it seeds but they did not grow. He prayed; rain came, and they began to grow. That, he exclaimed, is what Rav Assi had taught!

The Genizah tradition in a synoptic table with the Babylonian Talmud tradition can be found in table 7.1.[14]

According to these two parallel traditions of Genesis Rabbah 13:1, when Genesis 2:5 says that *there was no man to work the ground*, this means that there was no human to pray for the Land. The vegetation of the Land needed rain that would only come because of the prayers of the first human, which God desired. This understanding is predicated on an earlier exegetical oral tradition, a performance of which can be found in the third-century Tannaitic midrashic collection Sifre Deuteronomy, in which the Hebrew word for *work* (*avodah*) is understood as the work of the heart, which is prayer.[15] All three of the Amoraic traditions rely on the understanding of avodah as prayer, and this prayer was a required part of the plan of Creation to bring rain. Thus the best translation of Genesis 2:5 for all of the traditions discussed is "And when no shrub of the field was yet on the Land and no grasses of the field had yet sprouted, for the Lord God had not caused rain to come down on the Land *because* there was no human to *pray* for the Land." This understanding of the verse is fairly explicit in the Babylonian Talmud and the Genizah traditions; however, it is not clear that this exegetical understanding underlies Genesis Rabbah 13:1. Nonetheless, when we look at these traditions together through oral-performative methodology, we can better use the Babylonian Talmud and Genizah to understand Genesis Rabbah 13:1.[16]

An oral-performative reading of rabbinic literature assumes oral composition, performance, and transmission of traditions. Rather than assuming the existence of an authoritative and earlier version of any given tradition, this reading suggests that there is a transcript of possible performances that circulated orally. Of any given transcript, what may be currently available are individual performances that have been translated into the media of manuscript. Any given performance may alter the order of a script and combine it with other oral traditions. According to Martin Jaffee, "The oralist textual scholar is in a sense engaged in an effort to 'restage' the oral-performative milieu of the textual tradition by comparing various written testimonies to the shaping of the texts and enabling the contemporary reader of the finished texts to 'rehear' them in their multiple versions.... We should not imagine ourselves to be retrieving any authoritative original version of a text or tradition;

Table 7.1 The First Prayer and the Creation of Vegetation

b. Ḥul. 60b	b. Ḥul. 60b	Genizah Fragment ed. Mann 53:5	Genizah Fragment ed. Mann 53:5
הר ראה פרץ בארץ אשר אמר לכן אחנבה, אמהבה ראה פרץ בכל הן את האדמה ברא יום חיה לא יאנש!	Rav Assi pointed out a contradiction [between verses]. One verse [in Gen. 1:12] says, "And the earth brought forth grass," referring to the third day, whereas another verse [in Gen. 2:5] when speaking of the sixth day says, "No shrub of the field was yet on the earth."	[It is written in Gen. 2:5], "No shrub of the field was yet on Earth." But has it not already been said [in Gen. 1:12], "And the Earth brought forth grass." And what [does the continuation of Gen. 2:5] mean, "no grasses of the field had yet sprouted."	הן שיח כל הרי היה סעב שיח בארץ (סע, ב', א'), הן נאמר אומר אדמה הארץ ברא (סע, ג', י"ב), הן ה'א הנה הרי ברא הארץ סעב כל הרי היה.
מלמד שהיה דשאים ועמדו על פתח קרקע	This teaches us that the plants started to sprout but stopped just as they were about to break through the soil,	R. Ḥananya bar Papa said that they stood on edge of the soil.	הקרקע פתח על עמדו אבה בר ה' רהנא
		And did not come out to the light of the world until rain fell.	גשמים ירדו עד עולמו אורו ויצאו לא [ה]שוף
עד שבא אדם ובקש עליהם רחמים, ופירה גשמים, וצמחו	until Adam came and prayed for them; and when rain fell, they sprouted forth.	And even its form was not created until rain fell upon it.	גשמים... [ת] אלא תתקים תולדותיה ועד... ידו על
ללמדך ה"ב הקב"ה מתאוה לתפלתן של צדיקים	This teaches you that the Holy One, Blessed Be He, longs for the prayers of the righteous.	[To teach you that rain] only falls because of prayer.	הלבה, [תפלה דבר אלא] יורדין אינן ידי על

(Continued)

Table 7.1 The First Prayer and the Creation of Vegetation (*Continued*)

b. Ḥul. 60b	b. Ḥul. 60b	Genizah Fragment ed. Mann 53:5	Genizah Fragment ed. Mann 53:5
רב נחמן בר פפא הוה ליה ההוא גינתא, שדי ביה ביזרני ולא צמח - בעא רחמי אתא מיטרא וצמח. אמר: היינו דרב אסי.	Rav Naḥman bar Papa had a garden and he sowed in it seeds but they did not grow. He prayed; rain came, and they began to grow. That, he exclaimed, is what Rav Assi had taught!	And the world only continues to exist because of prayer and rain. Rav Assi said, you should know that this is also why the sages fixed the blessing of rain in the blessing for the resurrection of the dead. That through rain, The Holy One, Blessed Be He, will raise the dead in the future as it says [in Isa. 26:19], "Oh, let Your dead revive! Let corpses arise! [Awake and shout for joy, You who dwell in the dust!—For Your dew is like the dew on fresh growth; You make the land of the shades come to life.]"	ואין העולם מתקיים אלא על ידי תפילה ומטר, א' ר' אסי תדע לך [הוא עצמו] שקבעו חכמ׳ ברכת המטר בתחיית המתים מפני שהמטר חיותא דעלמא ובמטר עתיד הב״ה להחיות מתים מן התלבל שנ' יחיו מתיך, אבלה תקומון הקיצו ורננו וגו' (יש' כ"ו, י"ט)

[1] The Venice and Soncino printings have this same reading. The three printings are almost identical, with no significant variants. Manuscript Munich reads תכן.

[2] This reading of Genesis 2:5 is also shared with another tradition found in Pesiqta Rabbati §27: היה יורד מטר מבראשית ועד עכשיו לא היה העולם יכול לעמוד אלא עד אדם (ה' ב' בראשית) וגו' יצא.

rather ... we may at best offer a ... representation or reconstruction ... [of] the living tradition."[17]

In this context, the rabbis are viewed less as authors of texts and more as creative performers of traditions that existed within an oral-cultural milieu of late antique Jewish culture. The benefit of such a perspective toward rabbinic traditions is that it allows the underlying cultural and conceptual basis of related parallel traditions to come forward. Methodologically, parallel traditions can be presented side by side to enable a better understanding of the shared conceptual concerns involved in the various traditions. Small changes between parallel traditions are understood as alternative performances, and unity between traditions is sought even in the case of larger linguistic changes, provided that the traditions share unified conceptual concerns.[18] In this way, the traditions from the Babylonian Talmud, the Genizah, and Genesis Rabbah can be seen as alternative performances of the same oral transcript and, through this view, make sense of the underlying argument and midrashic exegesis of Genesis Rabbah 13:1.

While the redaction of the Babylonian Talmud is a complicated issue, it likely occurred at least several centuries later than the redaction of Genesis Rabbah and in Babylonia, under the rule of either the Abbasid Caliphate or the Sasanian Persians.[19] If we were adhering to a source-critical methodology, we would be limited in the usage of this Babylonian Talmud tradition in understanding Genesis Rabbah 13:1. However, the oral-performative approach opens a different relationship to tradition, in which we can view the tradition in the Babylonian Talmud as one possible performance of a script that is older and more pervasive than the Babylonian Talmud itself, which relies on the connection between avodah as prayer and rain. The Genizah tradition's linguistic and exegetical similarities lend support to this analysis.[20] Below is a presentation of the Genizah fragment in a synopsis with the significant witnesses of b. Ḥullin 60b.

While these traditions are similar, there are differences (both minuses and plusses; the latter are indicated by underlined text in tables 7.2 and 7.3). The Genizah tradition is attributed to an early Palestinian Amora rather than a Babylonian Amora, as in the Babylonian Talmud tradition. While all of the Babylonian Talmud versions ascribe some of the traditions to Rav Assi, a first-generation Babylonian Amora, he is noticeably

Table 7.2 Synopsis of b. Hullin 60b & Genizah Fragment

הגניזה מכתב יד לונדון 5558	דפוס ד-ונציה 122	דפוס ד-ונציה 123	על כתב יד וטיקן 120 [כתב יד] "ותיקה מיד המאוחרת היא זו"
אמר רב אסי רמי רבי יוחנן: כתיב "ויעש אלהים את שני המאורות הגדולים" וכתיב "את המאור הגדול ואת המאור הקטן"!	אמר רב אסי רמי [כ]תיב "ויעש אלהים את שני המאורות הגדולים" וכתיב "את המאור הגדול ואת המאור הקטן"	אמר ר' אסי רמי רבי יוחנן כתיב "ויעש אלהים את שני המאורות הגדולים" וכתיב "את המאור הגדול ואת המאור הקטן" (ב"ר, ו, א, פס' ד, ה).	אלהים. (ה, ג, ה) וכתיב ה (מאור) וכתיב - המאורות אלא זו "[ה מאור] "ויעש מאורת הגדול את הגדול
אמרה ירח לפני הקב"ה: רבש"ע אפשר לשני מלכים שישתמשו בכתר אחד	אמרה ירח לפני הב"ה רבש"ע אפשר לשני מלכים שישתמשו בכתר אחד	אמרה לבנה לפני הקב"ה רבון העולמים, אפשר לשני מלכים שישתמשו בכתר אחד	
אמר לה לכי ומעטי את עצמך	א"ל לכי ומעטי את עצמך	א"ל לכי ומעטי את עצמך.	
אמרה לפניו רבש"ע הואיל ואמרתי לפניך דבר הגון אמעיט את עצמי?	אמרה לפניו רבש"ע הואיל ואמרתי לפניך דבר הגון אמעיט את עצמי.	אמרה לפניו רבונו של עולם הואיל ואמרתי דבר הגון לפניך אמעיט עצמי	עד ות פמר לה [א] הדרי וכי...
			על אלא דידך (דף ו, ע"ב)
א"ל לך ומשול ביום ובלילה	א"ל לכי ומשול ביום ובלילה	א"ל לך 4 כפרה ומשול ביום ובלילה	[רבא: בג) [רבאל מאל בגלל...]
אמרה ליה מאי רבותיה דשרגא בטיהרא מאי אהני	אמרה לו [מא]י רבותיה מאי אהני שרגא בטיהרא	אמרה ליה מאי רבותא דשרגא בטיהרא מאי אהניא	
א"ל זיל ליקרו צדיקי בשמיך יעקב הקטן שמואל הקטן דוד הקטן	א"ל זיל לקרו בשמיך צדיקייא יעקב הקטן שמואל הקטן דוד הקטן	א"ל זיל ליקרו ישראל על שמך 3 אפס קטן יעקב קטן שמואל הקטן דוד הקטן.	

[1] The Venice and Soncino prints have this same reading. The three prints are almost identical with no significant variants. Manuscript Munich reads כמר.
[2] Venice and Soncino prints and manuscript Munich have this same reading.
[3] Manuscript Vatican 120–21 also shares this reading.
[4] This is the only manuscript that has this reading.

Table 7.3 Translated Synopsis of b. Hullin 60b & Genizah Fragment

b. Hul. 60b (Vilna)	b. Hul. (ms. Vatican 122)	b. Hul. (ms. Vatican 123)	Genizah Fragment ed. Mann 53:5
Rav Assi pointed out a contradiction [between verses]. One verse [in Gen. 1:12] says, "And the earth brought forth grass," referring to the third day, whereas another verse [in Gen. 2:5] when speaking of the sixth day says, "No shrub of the field was yet on the earth."	[R]av [A]ssi pointed out a contradiction [between verses]. One verse [in Gen. 1:12] says, "And the earth brought forth grass," referring to the third day, whereas another verse [Gen. 2:5] says, "No shrub of the field was yet on the earth": on the eve of the seventh day!	Rav [A]ssi pointed out a contradiction [between verses]. One verse [in Gen. 1:12] says, "And the earth brought forth grass," referring to the third day, whereas another verse [Gen. 2:5] says, "No shrub of the field was yet on the earth": on the evening [of] the seventh day!	[It is written in Gen. 2:5], "No shrub of the field was yet on Earth." But has it not already been said [in Gen. 1:12], "And the Earth brought forth grass," And what [does the continuation of Gen. 2:5] mean, "no grasses of the field had yet sprouted"?
This teaches us that the plants started to sprout but stopped just as they were about to break through the soil,	This teaches that the plants started to sprout but stopped just as they were about to break through the soil,	This teaches that the plants started to sprout but stopped just as they were about to break through the soil,	R. Hananya bar Papa said that they stood at the edge of the soil.
until *Adam* came and prayed for rain for them; and when rain fell, they sprouted forth.	but they did not sprout forth until *Adam* prayed for them; then rain fell and they sprouted forth, as it is said, *But a stream would rise from the earth, and water [the whole face of the ground; Gen. 2:6, NRSV]*.	but they did not sprout forth until *Adam* prayed for them, then they sprouted forth.	And did not come out to the light of the world until rain fell. And even its form was not created until rain fell upon it.

(*Continued*)

Table 7.3 Translated Synopsis of b. Hullin 60b & Genizah Fragment (Continued)

b. Hul. 60b (Vilna)	b. Hul. (ms. Vatican 122)	b. Hul. (ms. Vatican 123)	Genizah Fragment ed. Mann 53:5
This teaches you that the Holy One, Blessed Be He, longs for the prayers of the righteous.	This teaches that the Holy One, Blessed Be He, longs for the prayers of the righteous.	R. Hananya bar Papa said,[1] "This is to teach you that the Holy One, Blessed Be He, longs for the prayers of the [wicked][2] righteous."	[To teach you that rain] only falls because of prayer. And the world only continues to exist because of prayer and rain.
Rav Naḥman bar Papa had a garden and he sowed in it seeds but they did not grow. He prayed; rain came, and they began to grow. That, he exclaimed, is what Rav Assi had taught!	R. Hananya bar Papa had a garden and he sowed in it seeds but they did not grow in the light. He prayed; they began to grow. "That," he exclaimed, " is what Rav Assi had taught! As he said: 'From that [resolution of the contradiction between the verses above, we learn further] that the Holy One, Blessed Be He, longs for the prayers of the righteous.'"	R. Hananya bar Papa had a garden where he sowed seeds but they did not grow [added in ms: into the light.] He prayed; they began to grow. "That," he exclaimed, "is what Rav Assi had taught! And it supports [the position of] Hananya bar Papi [sic],[3] who said: 'From that [resolution of the contradiction between the verses above, we learn further] that the Holy One, Blessed Be He, longs for the prayers of the righteous.'"	Rav Assi said, you should know that this is also why the sages fixed the blessing of rain in the blessing for the resurrection of the dead. That through rain, The Holy One, Blessed Be He, will raise the dead in the future as it says [in Isa. 26:19]: "Oh, let Your dead revive! Let corpses arise! [Awake and shout for joy, You who dwell in the dust!—For Your dew is like the dew on fresh growth; You make the land of the shades come to life.]"

[1] This is the only manuscript that has this reading.
[2] This error is corrected within the manuscript.
[3] This is the only manuscript that has this reading.

absent from the Genizah tradition. Rabbi Ḥananya bar Papa, a third-generation Palestinian Amora, to whom the Genizah fragment is attributed, however, is found in some of the Babylonian Talmud traditions. This may indicate an earlier dating of the Genizah performance, as some of the Babylonian Talmud versions may have been influenced by the Genizah tradition. However, shifting focus to an oral-performative approach reveals that an oral tradition might have circulated independently of all of the available manuscript performances and that this tradition served as the underlying conceptual frame and transcript for all three of these traditions.[21] Through comparing the three available traditions, it can be proposed that the underlying conceptual transcript for the shared exegesis among the three Amoraic traditions of Genesis 2:5 is that humanity's prayer was necessary for the creation of the vegetation of the Land. This conceptual link relies on the understanding of avodah as prayer, first attested in Sifre Deuteronomy. While this exegesis and understanding of avodah as prayer is certainly more explicit in the Babylonian Talmud and the Genizah performances, it is implied in Genesis Rabbah as well. This is the case because it makes sense of the argument between R. Ḥanina and R. Ḥiyya. Without this exegetical understanding of Genesis 2:5 and the underlying conceptual frame attested to in Sifre Deuteronomy, their argument is still unclear.

By reading Genesis Rabbah 13:1 with the understanding that it relies on this shared exegetical transcript, it is clear that the argument between R. Ḥanina and R. Ḥiyya is over the role of humanity in bringing forth the vegetation of the Land. According to Rabbi Ḥiyya, who reconciles Genesis 2:5 and 2:9 by saying that "in both the inhabited world and the Garden of Eden nothing grew until rain descended upon them," humanity's prayer was necessary in both locations in order for the vegetation to grow. According to his reading, Genesis 2:9 is ambiguous because it excludes the prayer of humanity as the reason God caused rain to descend. R. Ḥiyya relies on the order of the verses in Genesis 2, understanding that Genesis 2:9 follows the creation of humanity, and the explicit statement in Genesis 2:5 that there was not yet rain, vegetation, or humanity on Earth. However, R. Ḥanina, who says that "Genesis 2:9 refers to the Garden of Eden, whereas Genesis 2:5 refers to the inhabited world," explains that humanity's prayer caused the vegetation to grow in the inhabited world, while God alone caused the vegetation to grow in the Garden of Eden. He interprets Genesis 2:9 in isolation from the rest of the chapter. Without re-creating the underlying conceptual transcript that humanity's prayer was necessary for the creation of the vegetation and its reliance on the understanding of "work" as prayer, first attested to in Sifre Deuteronomy, this Amoraic argument is much too terse to make sense of.

It is easy to see why Freedman and Neusner suggested that the argument in Genesis Rabbah 13:1 hinged on the order of Creation. They were correct to identify the Babylonian Talmud tradition as related, but they read b. Ḥullin 60b into Genesis Rabbah 13 rather than comparing the two traditions through a contiguous reading that maintains their integrity. The scriptural problem in b. Ḥullin 60b does rest on two different temporalities of Creation and is reconciled by suggesting that the vegetation waited under the surface until the first rain fell. However, this is not an issue in the Genesis Rabbah tradition. By attending to the underlying exegetical tradition shared among b. Ḥullin 60b, the Genizah fragment, and Genesis Rabbah, we can understand Genesis Rabbah 13:1 without removing the differences among the various traditions and, in the process, identify both the shared and different ontological dimensions of these traditions.

Thus we can see that the same conceptual idea that humanity needed to pray for rain for the vegetation to grow underlies all three of the Amoraic traditions. However, each of these traditions deploys this concept differently. To reconcile the two different creation stories found in Genesis 1 and 2, the Genizah and Babylonian Talmud performances add that the vegetation was sitting just below the surface, waiting for *Adam* to pray for rain and that God set up the Creation in this way because he desired the prayers of humanity.[22] Genesis Rabbah, which is concerned with a different contradiction in verses, specifies which part of Creation humanity helped create. The Genizah fragment also adds an interesting dimension of ontological entanglement to these traditions by explaining that the vegetation did not yet have a fixed form until the first prayer was said and rain fell on it. According to this tradition, the performance of prayer and human desire give form to the vegetation of the Creation.

GENESIS RABBAH 13:2–3, WALTER BENJAMIN, AND THE LANGUAGE OF THE WORLD

Genesis Rabbah 13:2–3 reads:

2. *וכל שיח השדה* כל האילנות כאילו מסיחין אלו עם אלו, כל האילנות כאילו מסיחין עם הבריות, כל האילנות להצוותן שלבריריות נבראו, מעשה באחד שבצר את כרמו ולן בתוכו ונשבה הרוח ופגעתו, וכל שיחתן שלבריריות אינן אלא על הארץ, עבדת ארעא לא עבדת אתמהא, וכל תפילתן שלבריריות אינן אלא על הארץ, מרי תעבד ארעא מרי תצלח ארעא, כל תפילתן שלישראל אינן אלא על בית המקדש, מרי תבני בית מקדשא, ואימתי תבנה בית המקדש.

3. כי לא המטיר י"י אלהים על הארץ מזכיר שם מלא על עולם מלא, כך הוא מזכיר שם מלא בירידת גשמים, אמר ר' שמעון בן יוחי ג' דברים שקולים זה בזה ואילו הן ארץ ואדם ומטר, אמר ר' לוי בר חייתה ושלשתם מן שלשה אותיות ללמדך שאם אין ארץ אין מטר ואם אין מטר אין ארץ ואם אין שניהם אין אדם.

2. [It is written in Genesis 2:5,] "No shrub of the field." [This means that] all the trees were as if conversing with each other; all the trees were as if conversing with humanity; all the trees were created for humanity's companionship. [For example,] A man was once picking grapes in his vineyard and slept in it, and the wind blew and affected him. All the conversation of humanity is only about the Land: Has the earth produced, or has the earth not produced? And all of humanity's prayers are only about the Land: May my Lord make the Land produce. May the Lord make the Land succeed. All the prayers of Israel [, however,] are only about the Temple, "May my Lord build the Temple. When will it be until you build the Temple?"

3. [It is written in Genesis 2:5,] "For the Lord God had not caused it to rain upon the earth." The full Name [of God] is employed in connection with a full world; it is similarly employed in connection with the fall of rain. Rabbi Shimon ben Yoḥai said: Three things are equal in importance, and what are these: Land, *Adam*, and rain. R. Levi bar Ḥiyyata says, and the three of them are each made of three letters to teach you that if there is no Land, there is no rain, and if there is no rain, there is no Land, and if the two of them are not, then there is no *Adam*.

This section opens by stating that "all the trees were as if conversing with each other; all the trees were as if conversing with humanity; all the trees were created for humanity's companionship." While scholars, including Theodor and Albeck, have not read this tradition ontologically, I understand Genesis Rabbah's reading of Genesis 2:5's wording as an ontological statement about the metaphysics of plants and communication.[23] Not only does this way of reading this tradition fit with the larger concerns of Genesis Rabbah 13—which will be further explored throughout this chapter—it also makes sense of the implicit exegesis of this tradition. According to this tradition, when the Hebrew Bible says *siah*, it is actually speaking about trees (האילנות) and thus could have chosen various other words for *tree*. In the understanding of Genesis Rabbah, this word choice is significant and reveals something about trees and their capacity for communication. Based on the meaning of the Hebrew word for *shrub* used in Genesis 2:5, *siaḥ*, which means both "conversation" and "shrub," the midrash suggests that plants somehow communicate with one another and with humanity. However, the midrash signals that the communication of plants is not exactly like that of humanity by using the word כאילו. It is "as if" the vegetation of the world speaks among itself and communicates to humanity, but it is not exactly a conversation between two people. The precise meaning of what the midrash interprets as plant communication and what it means by "as if" in this scenario, however, is not clear. Walter Benjamin's theory of language makes sense of this problem in Genesis Rabbah 13:2, aligning with this rabbinic tradition and drawing out its ontological assumptions. In the process, suppositions about differences and similarities between rabbinic and later philosophical thought can be made.

Walter Benjamin explains in his early essay "On the Language of Man, and Language as Such" that, on one hand, the nonhuman world partakes in language, but, on the other hand, it relies on humanity for its full enunciation.[24] Benjamin suggests that the nonhuman world both has language and does not have language. This means that animals, plants, and nonanimate things all have a communicative ability, but their communicative capacities do not allow them to fully communicate themselves in their communication—part of themselves and their interior essence evades communication. Humans are the opposite: they have the capacity to fully communicate themselves, and the nonhuman world, through human language. Benjamin writes, "All communication of the contents of the soul is language. . . . The existence of language, however, is coextensive not only with all the areas of the expression of the human soul in which language is always in one sense or another inherent, but with absolutely everything. There is no event or thing in either animate or inanimate nature that does not in some way partake of language, for it is in the nature of each one to communicate the contents of its soul."[25]

Nonhuman entities have language, but it is a language that cannot fully express the completeness of their inner being. Benjamin's claim that all entities in the world have a soul can be understood in the same way that many indigenous people attribute interiority or soul to nonhumans.[26] Elements of Benjamin's philosophy in this chapter are rooted in the ontology of the Hebrew Bible, as he quotes Genesis 2 throughout, even as his explanations and theories are not intended to be faithful to the biblical text. This is why I believe that Benjamin's philosophical discussion can be used to shed light on Genesis Rabbah 13 and its ontological characteristics. However, Benjamin differs from Genesis Rabbah in his drawing of an ontological divide between human and nonhuman communication. While his theory helps to shed light onto Genesis Rabbah 13:2, Genesis Rabbah 13, as we shall see, avoids any sort of firm divide between human and nonhuman communication in its attribution of greater-than-human communicative capacities to nonhumans such as rain.

Benjamin continues by explaining that even for humans, "within all linguistic formation a conflict is waged between what is expressed and expressible and what is inexpressible and unexpressed."[27] It is not that humans communicate their full selves through language at all times but rather that they have the capacity to do so. Benjamin goes on to say that language itself is the conflict between what is expressed and what is not expressed, nonetheless explaining that "name as the heritage of human language therefore vouches for the fact that language as such is the soul being of man; and only for this reason is the soul being of man, alone among all soul entities, communicable without residue."[28] Thus while all beings have a soul, or interiority, only humans are able to communicate their whole soul through language, even if the highest expression of language is not always reached. For Benjamin, this is what makes human language distinct from the language of the nonhuman world. The difference between humans and nonhumans is in degrees, not in absolute ability.

Benjamin argues later that the nonhuman world is only fully expressed through human language. This is why the whole world is in constant communication with humans. Benjamin explains: "All nature, insofar as it communicates itself, communicates itself in language, and so finally in man.... God's creation is completed when things receive their names from man, from whom in name language alone speaks."[29] According to Benjamin, the world gains completion through the language of humanity, which bestows meaning to the nonhuman world, but for this to happen, the nonhuman world must be in communication with humanity. In this respect, Benjamin describes a nonhuman world full of soul and linguistic potential. He summarizes "On the Language of Man, and Language as Such":

> The language of an entity is the medium in which its soul is communicated. The uninterrupted flow of this communication runs through the whole of nature, from the lowest forms of existence to man and from man to God. Man communicates himself to God through name, which he gives to nature and (in proper names) to his own kind; and to nature he gives names according to the communication that he receives from her, for the whole of nature, too, is imbued with a nameless, unspoken language, the residue of the creative word of God, which is preserved in man as the cognizing name.[30]

Benjamin's world is one alive with life and communication.[31] For him, the whole of the Creation is alive with agency and potential for communication because of "the residue of the creative word of God." Thus the difference between the human and the nonhuman, and among various nonhuman entities, is not which entity has interiority or a soul but rather how much of any given entity's interiority or soul is able to be communicated. Regardless of the level of consciousness of a being, each communicates a spiritual content. As Benjamin says, "we cannot imagine a total absence of language in anything."[32] While humanity stands in the middle of the cosmos as the conduit between the physical world and God, this does not mean that the nonhuman world does not have its own existence or potency outside and separate from humanity. For humanity to be able to communicate the nonhuman to God, through naming or prayer, the nonhuman must be able to communicate with humanity. Even though humanity is an integral part of the world, it remains entangled with the linguistic communication and needs of the nonhuman.

From this explanation, the term *as if* in Genesis Rabbah 13:2 can be interpreted similarly to Benjamin's suggestion about the language of the nonhuman world. It is only *as if* the nonhuman world has language. It does have the ability to communicate, but it does not have the language of prayer like *Adam* and the rest of humanity, which have the capacity for a fuller degree of communication. We should read Genesis Rabbah 13:2 as directly in communication with 13:1, in which humanity's capacity for prayer is so potent that it participates in the very creation of the vegetation of the Land. Genesis Rabbah 13:1 establishes the foundation for this tradition by ontologically defining the highest capacity of language in the Creation as *Adam's* prayer, which literally created the vegetation of the Creation. It is in relation to this powerful creative capacity of human language that it is only *as if* trees communicate. Even though Benjamin points to a different capacity of humanity, the power to name, rather than what we find in the rabbinic traditions, which point to humanity's prayer, in both cases, humanity is needed to communicate the nonhuman world to God. Furthermore, in these traditions, like in Benjamin's ontology, humanity does not communicate with God in isolation from the nonhuman world. The difference between human and nonhuman communication for Genesis Rabbah is also in degrees, not in absolute ability. For humanity to be able to pray for the needs of the nonhuman world, the nonhuman world must be able to communicate with humanity. Thus Genesis Rabbah 13 presents an ontology in which nonhuman communication is assumed.

Genesis Rabbah differs from Benjamin, however, by being concerned not with whether plants or humans can communicate their interiority through language but rather with what level of material creative potential is inherent in the linguistic capacities of each entity. Thus a picture of an entangled ontology emerges in these various traditions as *Adam's* first prayer is directly tied to a lack in the Creation. The Babylonian Talmud and the Genizah fragment tell us that this is precisely what God desired in the way he formed the Creation. This reading of Genesis Rabbah 13:2 assumes the reading previously suggested for 13:1, that the first prayer of humanity was instrumental in the completion of the creation of the Land. For the rabbis, the nonhuman world was incomplete without humanity and was waiting for the first human to listen to its cacophony of sounds, to make sense of what it was lacking, and to pray for it. Genesis Rabbah 13:2 follows Genesis Rabbah 13:1 with an implicit ontological question and answer: If the nonhuman world could not communicate with humanity, how could the first human know what to pray for? To answer this question, Genesis Rabbah 13:2 explains that "all the trees were 'as if' conversing with humanity; and all the trees were created for humanity's companionship." Genesis Rabbah 13:2 thus explains that the first human knew what to pray for because the nonhuman world was communicating its needs, but only in a way that can be deemed *as if* in relation to the power of humanity's language, which has the power to create and give definition to the Creation.[33]

AN ENTANGLED RABBINIC AFFECTIVE ECONOMY

These rabbinic traditions provide performative textual materials that can be read as an ecology of affect, like the one Donavan Schaefer outlines in his book *Religious Affects: Animality, Evolution, and Power*: "Affect suggests the complexity, clunkiness, inefficiency, and heterogeneity of bodies themselves; rather than a compact metaphysical circuit, affects are jagged, uneven, and fluid; rather than a linear system, affect points us in the direction of analyses of laterality; rather than a predictable hierarchy assembled under the sovereign sign of *logos*, affects coalesce to form regimes of accidents. . . . Affect is better understood as sketching bodies that are much more complex, much fuzzier, and all around less predictable than determinist or adaptationist models can accommodate."[34]

In Schaefer's terms, these rabbinic midrashic performances present a world that is made up of material and affectual entanglements. According to b. Ḥullin 60b, there would not be a vegetal world if it were not for affect—God desired the prayers of humanity and structured Creation in such a way that humanity would have to pray for rain to ensure life-sustaining vegetation on the planet.[35] This prayer is a work of the heart, as understood through the tradition from Sifre Deuteronomy, and an affective stance that sets in motion the life process of the Creation.[36] In the conceptual ontology of this tradition, the nonhuman world, far from being a separate and efficient domain of functional and linear interlocking pieces, begins from a divine desire that turns the affects of the human heart. The Genizah tradition similarly depicts the ontological makeup of the Creation as filled with gaps, such as the vegetation lacking form. These gaps can only be filled by the affective economy among God, Land, rain, and *Adam*. For the vegetation of the Land did not have a form until *Adam* prayed for it. According to the Genizah fragment, this was not because it was waiting under the ground fully formed but rather that its form was co-created by *Adam* and God in *Adam's* prayer. The fragment explicitly states that "even its form was not created until rain fell upon it." The form that the vegetation of the Creation would take was interactively determined through humanity's prayer and the rain that it brought. The very fabric of the Creation, according to this Genizah fragment, is potentiality and entanglement.[37]

Genesis Rabbah 13:2 adds the rest of the nonhuman Creation into this affective economy by showing how humanity's prayers are predicated on the communicative ability of trees and the rest of the vegetal world. Genesis Rabbah 13:2 also suggests a genealogy of desire, showing how the later prayers of humanity for the Land and its productivity are rooted in the prayer of the first human and his awareness of the lack of the Creation and its need for rain.[38] This tradition makes clear, however, that the particular role of humanity to pray to God on behalf of the Creation does not preclude nonhumans from partaking in language or communication and is in fact predicated on this ability of the nonhuman world. Speech is never isolated from the Creation but rather participates in the affective economy of life.

While humanity may have a greater degree of agency in these rabbinic traditions, the nonhuman world has value and agency as well. Benjamin and Schaefer explain that it was through meeting the rest of Creation, in understanding the speech of the nonhuman world and what it needed, that humanity first prayed. The story in Genesis Rabbah 13:2, "a man was once picking grapes in his vineyard and slept in it, and the wind blew and affected him," in context, functions to show that the nonhuman world has agency and can impact humanity. Genesis Rabbah 13:3 builds on this theme: "Rabbi Shimon ben Yoḥai said: Three things are equal in importance, and what are these: Land, *Adam*, and rain. R. Levi bar Ḥiyyata says ... if there is no Land, there is no rain, and if there is no rain, there is no Land, and if the two of them are not, then there is no *Adam*." Land, rain, and *Adam* are of equal importance because they rely on one another for their existence. We have already seen how there is no rain without humanity's prayers and no vegetation on the Land without rain. Genesis Rabbah

13:3 adds that, just as the nonhuman world is created through its interaction and entanglement with humanity, humanity is also constituted by the nonhuman. This tradition presents an entangled reality where the existence of each of these entities depends on the existence of the others. The Land and rain are dependent on each other for their existence, and in accordance with the Genizah fragment, they also provide each other with definition. While the end of this statement could be understood as simply implying that humanity relies on the Land and rain for food, in the context of the rest of the chapter of Genesis Rabbah 13, it has a much deeper significance. If humanity gives definition and delineation to the Creation through the enunciation of prayer, then this same act of delineation also shapes what humanity is and will become. Genesis Rabbah 13:3 presents us with a world that is constituted not only through humanity but also with a humanity that is constituted by the nonhuman world. Through the first prayer, the Land, rain, and humanity were all given definition and completed in tandem, remaining entangled even in their definition.

While the Babylonian Talmud only presents God's desire for the prayers of humanity, Genesis Rabbah describes a more expansive view of creation in which God is given full enunciation in the Creation only when the entangled dependence of everything is presented and delineated. This is why Genesis Rabbah 13:3 connects God's full name to rain when it states: "The full Name [of God] is employed in connection with a full world; it is similarly employed in connection with the fall of rain." This fullness is signified in the biblical text by the use of the two names for God, which is His full name. Reading Schaefer's affect theory and Benjamin's theory of language, we can understand that in this iteration of a rabbinic ontology, the world is full because of the entanglement of needs and existence of all of the Creation. The first rain of Creation found in Genesis 2:5 is the act that embodies the worldly entanglement between language and Creation most for the rabbis. For in the biblical text, the first human is created from the admixture of Land and water, both of the elements that he is charged to pray for in the rabbinic traditions. Humanity is formed from these elements of the lacking universe, and perhaps it is because of this material entanglement that the first human knows what is lacking in the entities from which he is made.[39] Genesis Rabbah, in its explication of an entangled and mutually constitutive universe, presents a metaphysics that, unlike Benjamin, does not rely on the subject/object divide for its ground. While human prayer may have a greater level of affect and intensity than some forms of nonhuman communication, this does not set humans as subject and nonhumans as object because nonhumans also have agency and the ability to affect humanity. In our rabbinic traditions, nonhumans do not exist only for the sake of humanity or humanity for the sake of their redemption, as is found in Benjamin's essay. This metaphysical supposition is further elucidated in the continuation of Genesis Rabbah 13.

GENESIS RABBAH 13:4–5: THE AGENCY OF THE RAIN

The continuation of Genesis Rabbah 13 in 13:4–5 sets the devotional genealogy of the Creation within a tripart flow of materiality, energy, and care among humanity, rain, and Land:

4. אמר ר' הושעיה קשה היא גבורת גשמים ששקולה כנגד כל מעשה בראשית מה טע' עושה גדולות עד אין חקר (איוב ה ט) במה בנותי מטר על פני ארץ ושולח מים על פני חוצות (איוב ה י), ר' אחא מייתי לה מן הכא עושה ארץ בכוחו וגו' (ירמיה י יב) לקול תתו המון מים בשמים וגו' (ירמיהו י יג) ואין קול אלא גשמים היך מה דאת אמר תהום אל תהום קורא לקול צנוריך (תהלים מב ח)

5. ר' יצחק [אמר] מרצה בקורבנות רצית י"י ארצך (תהלים פה ב), ר' סימון אמר מכנסת את הגליות שבתה שבות יעקב (תהלים פ"ה ב), ר' יוחנן אמר אוספת העברה אספת כל עברתך (תהלים פ"ה ד), ר' תנחום בר חנילאי אמר מכפרת על החטאים שנ' נשאת עון עמך וגו' (תהלים פ"ה ג)

4. R. Hoshaya says, "Strong is the power of rain, that it is measured against all of the work of Creation."

What is the reason? [It is written in Job 5:9:] "Who performs great deeds which cannot be fathomed, wondrous things without number." And what are these? [It is written in Job 5:10]: "He gives rain on the Land and sends water on the field." R. Aḥa brings it from here [where it is written in Jeremiah 10:12]: "He made the earth by His might, [established the world by His wisdom, and by His understanding stretched out the skies]," and [from Jeremiah 10:13]: "At the call of His giving a multitude of waters in the heavens"

And there is no meaning for "call" other than rain. And from where do you say this? [It is written in Psalms 42:8]: "deep calls to deep in the call of your channels [all Your breakers and billows have swept over me.]"

5. R. Yitshaq [says], "[Rain], like sacrifices, appeases the Land, [as it is written in Psalms 85:2]: "It, Oh Lord, has appeased your Land." R. Shimon says, "[Rain] gathers in the exiles, [as it is written in the end of the same verse]: It has returned the exiles of Yaakov." R. Yohanan says, "[Rain] contains divine wrath, [as it is written in Psalms 85:4]: "It contains all Your anger, [it turns you away from Your rage.]" R. Tanhum bar Hanilai says, "[Rain] atones for sins as it is written [in Psalms 85:3]: "It forgives Your people's iniquity, [it pardons all their sins; Selah.]"

Genesis Rabbah continues describing the language and agency of the nonhuman by looking at the powers and language of rain. Through biblical verses from Jeremiah and Psalms, rain is depicted as a form of divine communication, and, at the same time, the various bodies of water of Creation are shown to express themselves linguistically. They are both divine portents and agents in themselves that speak and act on the Creation. In these traditions, the deep calls to the deep, and the call of the rain is an actual language that resounds throughout the Creation. In this depiction of the rain, which is both a material entity and a linguistic phenomenon, there is no clear-cut distinction between the semiotic and the material. Materiality is entangled in language, and vice-versa. We can see in this tradition an example of Benjamin's description of the nonhuman as expressing itself in language through itself, and an example of Haraway's semiotic-material net in which the semiotic and the material are tied up in one another in the processes of worldmaking and becoming. This tradition differs from Benjamin, however, in the capacity for rain's communication to directly impact humanity and the history of the Creation through its agency.

Genesis Rabbah 13:5 continues to portray rain as an active agent in the affective economy of the Creation, extending beyond communication and bringing redemption and expiation from sin. The rabbis read the beginning of Psalm 85 as an ode of the rain directed to God, and the rain as the subject of the deeds listed in Psalms 85:2–4, not God, which is how it is typically understood and translated.[40] The rabbis in this tradition are extolling the agency of the rain and the greatness of its effects on the Creation. In this respect, Genesis Rabbah 13:4–5 is a performance of human prayer: the Psalmist hears the call of the rain and communicates it to God by praising its various deeds. Genesis Rabbah also understands rain as an agent and actant that has an impact on both the terrestrial and the divine realm, appeasing the Land and driving away divine wrath. It forgives human sin and is implicated in the ingathering of the exiles. Acts that were typically associated with God are attributed to the rain and its capacities. This is a prime example of a rabbinic ontology that gives agency to the nonhuman world. Furthermore, in this description, we can see how humanity, Land, vegetation, and rain are entangled in one another, bound up in a material-spiritual-discursive reality. Far from there being a separation between the physical and the spiritual, there is only enmeshment and entanglement among all the actors involved. For the rabbis, it is not only humanity that can bring redemption to a silent world, even though it was humanity's first prayer that gave the Creation its final delineation. Rather, the nonhuman world acts without humans and can even bring redemption to humanity. In this entanglement, the rabbis move beyond Benjamin in positing a more robust, more entangled, and more balanced vision of creation in which nonhuman communication and agency have the potential to exceed those of humanity.

GENESIS RABBAH 13:8: A COVENANT WITH THE LAND

Genesis Rabbah continues its depiction of nonhuman agency and the decentering of the human in 13:8 to explain that while the Creation was completed by humanity's prayer in the Primeval History of Genesis 1–11, sometime after that, the ontology of Creation shifted so that the Land and vegetation would no longer depend on humanity:

> המטיר י"י על הארץ אפילו אדם אין, ברית כרותה לארץ שנ' להמטיר על ארץ לא איש מדבר לא אדם בו (איוב לח כו).

> [It is written in Genesis 2:5], "The Lord God caused it to rain upon the Land,"—Even if there is no human [for] a covenant was made with the Land, as it says [in Job 38:26], "To rain down on uninhabited land, On the wilderness where no man is."

Genesis Rabbah reads a verse from Job in conjunction with Genesis 2:5 to mean that God made a later covenant with the Land stipulating that God will bring rain to the Land even if there is no human to pray for it. This exegetical tradition establishes agency and subjecthood of the Land.[41] Genesis Rabbah 13:8 presents the Land as an actor that has its own covenant with God, which stipulates that He will bring rain even if there is no humanity. In the flow of the chapter of Genesis Rabbah, this tradition explains that even though humanity was instrumental in the creation of the original vegetation and the completion of the Land, the relationship among God, Land, and rain that was set in motion by that first prayer will continue with or without humanity because of a later covenant that God made with the Land, recorded in the book of Job. So even though in Genesis Rabbah 13 we initially see an affective economy that relies on the emotions of the human heart, this economy is later changed to encompass a world that no longer relies on humanity for its existence. In fact, Genesis Rabbah 13:8 marks a shift in this chapter of Genesis Rabbah from the affective origins of the Creation that relies on humanity to an understanding of the Creation that continues with or without humanity.

Thus, according to Genesis Rabbah 13:8 in a postbiblical world, even without humanity, God's affectual ecosystem continues functioning. In this picture, humanity is decentered, and God stands in the center of this future affective economy of which humanity is just one part. The ontology of the first half of Genesis Rabbah 13, correlated with the Garden of Eden, is a world in which the proper functioning of the Creation depends on humanity. According to this reading of Genesis Rabbah 13, it is only later in the unfolding of biblical history that the metaphysics of the Creation shifted and resulted in a Creation in which the Land would have a covenant with God separate from humanity. In this respect as well, Genesis Rabbah differs from Benjamin's metaphysics, which affords humanity an essential role that the universe could not exist without. While humanity is also given a central and important role in Genesis Rabbah, humanity is also decentered not only by affording great powers to the communicative ability of rain but also through describing a covenant that God has with the Land independent of humanity.

ALEXANDER WEISBERG is an independent scholar, rabbi, and environmental philosopher. He has previously published articles in the *Journal of Ancient Judaism* and *Jewish Studies Quarterly*, and he has edited a special journal issue, *New Approaches to Jewish Environmental Ethics*, in *Worldviews: Global Religions, Culture, and Ecology*.

NOTES

1. By entanglement, I refer to the notion that entities in the world rely on other entities for their existence and being. See Hodder, "The Entanglements of Humans and Things."
2. I focus especially on Benjamin, "On the Language of Man."
3. As discussed by Rodolphe Gasché ("Saturnine Vision," 79), this chapter envisions an "Adamic naming language": language is expressed by a person's act of naming each thing as it calls out to them in its singularity. Language is thus both in the world and in things. Yet humanity retains a distinct, necessary role in its "communication," an anthropocentric premise. See Section 3. It has been argued that Benjamin's theory of language goes beyond Kant's subject/object distinction, developing Kant's idea of "intensity" to reimagine a pure and "transcendental" Language existing only in translation (Hamacher, "Intensive Languages"). This seems to go beyond the non/human ontological boundary, yet I am not convinced that, even in Benjamin's later theory of language, he avoids anthropocentricism. He contrasts "life of works of art" with "life of the animal species," again defining human consciousness as what can "recognize" the gap between the two (Benjamin, "The Task of the Translator," 71). Here, we can still see the early essay's Adamic structure of naming.
4. Gross, *The Question of the Animal and Religion*, 13.
5. For modern treatments of this verse with similar exegetical outcomes, see my discussions in Weisberg, "Before There Was Nature," 102–18; see Swenson, "Care and Keeping East of Eden"; Jørstad, "The Ground That Opened Its Mouth."
6. Schaefer, *Religious Affects*.
7. Haraway, "Situated Knowledges," 585, 588.
8. All text from Genesis Rabbah in this chapter is according to Theodor and Albeck, *Midrash Bereshit Rabba*.
9. All translations are my own.
10. Freedman, *Midrash Rabbah*, I:99–100; Neusner, *Genesis Rabbah*, 135.
11. Neusner and Freedman arrive at this suggestion only by reading b. Hullin 60b into this tradition. The difference in approach between their reading and an oral-performative reading that seeks the shared underlying transcript without erasing difference will be made evident through my reading.
12. Theodor and Albeck, *Midrash Bereshit Rabba*, I:113–44.
13. Reading according to the Vilna Babylonian Talmud. See the following presentation of the various mss. The Vilna reflects the same manuscript tradition as ms. Munich as well as the original Soncino and Venice printings.
14. Mann, *The Bible as Read and Preached*, 53.
15. Sifre Deuteronomy Parsha Eqev §Piska 41:8, text and translation according to ed. Jaffee:

> "And to serve Him" (Deut. 11:13)—this refers to prayer (*tefillah*). You claim this refers to prayer! Perhaps it simply refers to the sacrificial service? The Teaching states: "With all your heart and with all your soul" (Deut. 11:13)—Now, is there a sacrificial service in the heart? What, then, does the Teaching mean by "And to serve Him?" (Deut.

11:13). This refers to prayer. And so David says: "Let my prayer be equivalent to incense before You, And my uplifted hands like a sweet offering" (Ps. 141:2). And He says [of Daniel]: "And he knelt upon his knees three times a day and prayed" (Dan. 6:11). And He continues: "O, Daniel, servant of the Living God! Is the God whom you constantly serve able to save you from the lions?" (Dan. 6:21). Now was there a sacrificial rite in Babylonia? What, then, does the Teaching mean by "And to serve Him?" (Deut. 11:13). This refers to prayer! And just as the work of the Altar is called service, so, too, prayer is called service.

16. I show how these traditions are linguistically and conceptually related in the following passages. These traditions can be considered alternative performances of the same underlying transcript.

17. Jaffee, "What Difference Does the 'Orality,'" 18.

18. See Alexander, *Transmitting Mishnah*, 1–34. For more on orality studies and rabbinic literature, see Rosen-Zvi, "Orality, Narrative, Rhetoric." See also Simon-Shoshan, *Stories of the Law*, 97–111 for a comparison between the textualist and performative approaches to rabbinic literature.

19. For different recent treatments of this issue, see Halivni, *The Formation of the Babylonian Talmud*; Vidas, *Tradition and the Formation of the Talmud*; Brody, *The Geonim of Babylonia*; and Secunda, *The Iranian Talmud*.

20. The Genizah fragment is Palestinian in origin but contains the same basic exegetical understanding as the Babylonian Talmud of Genesis 2:5; namely, the reason there was no vegetation on Earth was because the first human had not yet been created to pray for rain.

21. The Genizah fragment, in tandem with the various Babylonian Talmud versions, supports an oral-performative analytic as a way to understand what is at stake conceptually in all of these traditions because of the similar concerns and Amoriam across the traditions.

22. See later in this chapter for more on the significance of God's desire for *Adam's* prayer.

23. Theodor and Albeck, *Midrash Bereshit Rabba*, I:114 do not understand Genesis Rabbah in this way. Instead, they understand Genesis Rabbah 13:2 as simply speaking about the sound of trees when wind blows through them.

24. Benjamin, "On the Language of Man."

25. Ibid., 62. Translation slightly altered.

26. Benjamin's ontology of nonhuman interiority and soul is similar to Phillipe Descola's Analogist dispositif in Descola, *Par-delà Nature et Culture*, in which everything has interiority and exteriority, but everything is also different from everything else. Various indigenous groups hold this type of ontology. Out of Descola's four-fold ontological map, only the modern Naturalist dispositif does not have the capacity to afford nonhumans interiority like that of humans.

27. Benjamin, "On the Language of Man," 66.

28. Ibid., 65.

29. Ibid.

30. Ibid., 74.

31. It has been suggested that Benjamin's early ideas should be correlated not only with the Hebrew Bible but also with the ideas of Jakob Boehme for whom everything in the world, including inert objects, has a divinely bestowed life force or soul. Boehme, like

Benjamin, affords agency and interiority to all nonhumans. See Hanssen, "Language and Mimesis."

32. Benjamin, "On the Language of Man," 62. Translation slightly altered.

33. While such is the task of the first human, Genesis Rabbah 13:2 portrays Jews as having an additional capacity for their prayer. While the rest of humanity is always concerned with praying for the Land and rain, Genesis Rabbah 13:2 explains that "all the prayers of Israel are only about the Temple, 'May my Lord build the Temple. When will it be until You build the Temple?'" In praying for the Temple rather than sustenance and the productivity of the Land, they are also praying for the elevation of all of these elements to God and for their redemption. For the Temple lies at the heart of a unified and functioning world in other midrashic traditions in Genesis Rabbah and elsewhere in rabbinic literature. For example, Genesis Rabbah 1:2 portrays the destruction of the Temple as the unhinging and split of the whole world, while its rebuilding is akin to the reunification of the Creation. We also find in Genesis Rabbah 56:2 that the Temple is associated with one of the last stages of the redemption and elevation of the world, directly before the resurrection of the dead.

34. Schaefer, *Religious Affects*, 149.

35. In this description of affect, I closely follow Schaefer and the phenomological line of affect, which sees emotion and affect as coinciding. This differs from the Deleuzian school of affect. For more on the two branches of affect theory, see Schaefer, *Religious Affects*, 23–27.

36. Genesis Rabbah 13:7 also reinterprets avodah to mean service of the divine.

37. Even Benjamin, who suggests that the nature of the nonhuman is to be nontransparent in communication, leaves room for this understanding. Rather than reading this nontransparency of the soul of things as an epistemological lack, this nontransparency could be reread as an ontological lack—in the sense that things are not fully delineated until they are brought into definition through the naming language of humanity, much in the same way that *Adam's* prayer gives form to the biosphere in the rabbinic traditions.

38. The rest of humanity fulfills an important role in communicating what is and what has happened and its upkeep by praying for the Land to continue to produce. In the same way, the Creation can continue to function, and Israel speaks an even higher need to God through the Creation: the rebuilding of the Temple and the redemption of existence.

39. This picture of the entanglement of the Creation is conceptually rooted in the biblical presentation of Genesis 1–4.

40. For example, according to JPS translation, Psalm 85:2–4 reads: "O Lord, You will favor Your land, restore Jacob's fortune; You will forgive Your people's iniquity, pardon all their sins; You will withdraw all Your anger, turn away from Your rage, Selah."

41. See my discussion of Land as agent and subject in Leviticus 25:2 in Weisberg, "Before There Was Nature," 168–71, 418–28.

8

Between Philosophy and Rhetoric
The Mishnah Yoma as a Case Study

SOPHIA AVANTS

Philosophy, as Plato develops the term throughout numerous dialogues, is a way of living and thinking: a person's actions should be the result of thinking correctly. This sort of thinking, Socrates proposes in *Phaedrus*, is the result of knowing the truth.[1] As Charles Young interprets Plato in the *Crito*, persuasion is the presentation of proofs that a person's reasons are right.[2] In contrast, Aristotle, in *The Art of Rhetoric*, develops a theory of argument "where certainty and conclusive truth are not to be had."[3] As opposed to working toward an ideal through a presented dialogue, Aristotle differentiates types of audience engagement, whether they are meant to judge past events, deliberate on courses of action, or merely listen and be persuaded (epideictic). He calls the logical proof of a proposition ἐνθύμημα, *enthymeme*, which is defined as a συλλογισμός. Classical philosopher Myles Burnyeat cautions that this term should not be translated as *syllogism*, as that word undergoes a transformation from ancient Greek to Stoic philosophy. Burnyeat offers "considerations for the audience to think about," leaning on the etymology of *enthymeme*, ἐν θυμός, in thought, to access Aristotle's meaning.[4] Consideration allows for arguments that may not be logically sufficient, but they allow the hearer to give or withhold assent.[5] But Burnyeat finds that Cicero (106–43 BCE) and Quintilian (ca. 35–100 CE) shift the meaning of *enthymeme* to be *incomplete syllogism*—likening the openness of *consideration* to a formal three-part logic exercise that is missing its middle part, its proof.

This means that if one were to state a certain position that was contrary to the fact presented, the conclusion is foregone. Burnyeat notes the ironic twist that Stoic rhetoricians created arguments not to engage thinking but rather to demonstrate a conclusion.[6]

Alongside Quintilian were small groups of Jewish teachers who discussed a variety of topics in Roman Palestine. These teachers, or rabbis, set themselves apart from other groups and outsiders, the *am ha'arets*, in how they practiced purity and established and maintained sacred space. Collations of many of their traditions were recorded by Rabbi Yehudah Hanasi at the end of the second century and the beginning of the third as the Mishnah. This six-tractate collection contains narratives, debates, and rulings on various matters. The expression of differing viewpoints, unlike Platonic works such as the *Crito*, are not lengthy expositions but rather are short, reported statements of rabbis' varying opinions. These rabbis are depicted as not interacting with each other and were often historically distant from each other. Further, a conclusion or resolution of the difference is not explicit, although traditions in which rabbis' opinions were accepted as authoritative developed within the movement. The inclusion of these contrasting opinions, and even the lack of a resolution, resonates with Aristotle's proposals for rhetorical purpose, especially considering past cases. Richard Hidary and others have placed rabbis within their broader cultural setting, especially as witnesses of and participants in civic and social institutions. Even if members of rabbinic associations were never formally trained in the Greek or Roman classroom, they absorbed the techniques of the Second Sophistic.[7]

Many questions arise after noting the location of rabbis within this context. First, can we understand the disputes recorded in rabbinic texts within the context of Israelite and Second Temple Jewish writings? Second, are there echoes within that tradition of philosophical and rhetorical elements that clarify the Mishnaic process of thinking? In the following paragraphs, I look at one small disagreement between R. Eliezer and R. Akiva in the section on the Day of Atonement, Mishnah Yoma. This dispute is interesting in that it stems from conflicting reports in the biblical corpus and with a tradition of differences in Second Temple sources. However, more than just the record of the conflicting opinions of two rabbis in Yoma, one opinion would shift the entire order of the day's sacrifice so that the editor's choice of the placement of the dispute created a third party of engagement. For this reason, this particular mishnah stands in its own unique place between a philosophy that reaches for the ideals of God's word and the location of the holy and a rhetoric that recognizes a certain autonomy of positions, including an editor who acts as a participant within the debate. If we focus on *and*—that space between truth and persuasion—this Mishnah situates itself as a presenter of views, available for engagement.

The Mishnaic dispute that concerns us here does not "teach logic," as some have observed of Talmudic discussions.[8] The Babylonian Talmud presents extended points and counterpoints not included in the surface of Mishnah Yoma. It is only through the deep structure of intertextual references that a historiography emerges in this mishnah. This places Yoma (and perhaps Mishnah more broadly) in a unique position, namely, the Talmudic texts of this volume. As a stand-alone text and not the point of demarcation for later Talmudic discussions, the editor can be viewed as an engaged player, not just a shaper of traditions. This moves beyond dialectic and Sophistic interpretations of Aristotle because the contrasting position has its own traditions and proofs.

The dispute in question is between Rabbi Akiva and Rabbi Eliezer over the burnt or עוֹלָה offering. In general, Yoma follows Leviticus 16's depiction of the High Priest's actions on Yom Kippur. However, while seeming to agree with the biblical account, the compiler of this mishnah adds a number of challenges to it.[9] The dispute between the two rabbis presents a dialectical moment where the account of Yom Kippur in Leviticus seems to conflict with the account in Numbers, but it is resolved because the placement of their exchange favors one of the disputants. However, as Mikhail Bakhtin points out in a landmark essay on Dostoevsky, the inclusion of this dispute reveals a character who stands up against the editor so that the presumed audience also finds that they have standing.[10] Authority is shifted to an interpretive, dialogical process, placing the text in contradistinction to Stoicism.[11]

Mishnah Yoma draws on other biblical texts to fill in Leviticus's procedural gaps, and the dispute between R. Akiva and R. Eliezer highlights the difficulty (קושיא) provided by the sacrificial description of the עולה in Numbers 29. Leviticus distinguishes between the purification, or חטאת

offering, and the עולה, Numbers includes the חטאת הכפורים within a set of rituals comprising the עולה. This not only implies a conflicting number of animals but also indicates a different time of day. However, the positions of R. Akiva and R. Eliezer both have a deep structure of proof-texts that act as premises for their propositions. These unspoken texts, well known and implied in the position, are the considerations, or *enthymemes*, in the Aristotelian sense. The editor is well aware of these points and proofs, as he provides his stance via his structuring of the Mishnah. The following will present this dispute, its place in Yoma—important as a time marker for the עולה, and then the background texts of Leviticus and Numbers. A second component, as it adds a discourse layer that takes place before the early (Tannaitic) rabbis, is the Temple Scroll. This Second Temple text aligns with the Numbers account but also includes elements of Leviticus. It is interesting to note the different theological perspectives of its author(s), especially in light of Yoma's stance. A further comparison is made on the level of discourse by way of the Tosefta on this topic, which amplifies Tannaitic voices. It was probably composed a bit later than the Mishnah: it complicates the stated opinions in Yoma but proves, by doing so, that this is not a closed dialectic but a community process, open to further considerations.

THE עולה OFFERING

The dispute between R. Akiva and R. Eliezer occurs at Mishnah Yoma 7.3:[12]

ג ואם בבגדי בוץ קרא קידש ידיו ורגליו ופשט ירד וטבל עלה ונסתפג הביאו לו בגדי זהב ולבש קידש ידיו ורגליו יצא ועשה את אילו את איל העם שבעת כבשים תמימים דברי ר אליעזר ר עקיבא אמ' עם התמיד של שחר היו קריבים אבל פר העולה ושעיר הנעשה בחוץ היו קריבים עם התמיד של בין הערבים.

> 3. And if he reads in linen clothing, he sanctifies his hands and his feet and undresses, goes down and immerses, goes up and dries himself. They brought him gold clothing and he washes, sanctifying his hands and feet. He went out and sacrificed his ram and the people's ram, the seven unblemished male sheep: the words of R. Eliezer. R. Akiva said: they used to be sacrificed with the daily morning offering but the burnt offering ox and the male goat, done outside, was sacrificed with the daily afternoon offering.

This debate can be found within a broad outline of the High Priest's activities:

Table 8.1 High Priest's Activities for the עולה Offering

Yoma	
3.3	Immerse (טבל) 5x
	Sanctifies (קידש) hands and feet 10x
3.4	Immerses, dresses, washes hands and feet
3.4	עולת תמיד
3.5	Incense offered between blood and limb offering
3.6	Sanctifies hands and feet. Undresses. Immerses. Dresses. Washes hands and feet.
3.8	Confession on ox (first time)
4.1	Draws lots for goats
4.2	Confession on ox (second time)
4.3	Ox slaughtered in courtyard
5.1	Blood collected in basin, stirred
	Coal and incense from courtyard altar brought behind curtain of Holy of Holies
5.3	Filled chamber with smoke
	Short prayer in outer chamber
	Collects bowl of blood and brings to Holy of Holies
	Blood sprinkled on altar
5.4	Goat slaughtered
	Blood collected
	Blood sprinkled on H of H altar
5.5	Combined ox and goat blood applied to the Altar Before the Lord
	Leftover blood poured on the western base of outer altar
	Leftover blood from outer altar poured out onto southern base
	Leftover blood mixed and drained into the Kidron Valley
6.2	Confession on Azazel goat
	Priests and people kneel and prostrate
6.7	Ox and goat burned on outer altar
7.3	עולה dispute
7.4	Goes home for feast

The Mishnah's narrative of Yom Kippur can be compared with Leviticus 16:

Table 8.2 The Mishnah's Narrative of Yom Kippur

16:3		Bull for חטאת Ram for עולה	Aaron's offering for himself and his household, neither offered yet
16:5		2 male goats חטאת 1 ram עולה	Offerings for the people of Israel (בני ישראל), neither offered yet
16:7		2 male goats	Aaron lets stands before LORD
16:8		2 male goats	Lots determine goats' destinations
16:9		1 male goat for חטאת 1 male goat for release	Designated for LORD Designated for Azazel
16:11		Slaughter of bull חטאת	[Blood,] coals, incense brought to altar behind the curtain
			Blood sprinkled on east side of cover and sprinkled 7x in front of cover
16:15		Sacrifice of goat חטאת	Blood brought and sprinkled in same way
16:16		Blood of Bull & Goat	"altar before LORD": blood on each horn of altar, and 7x on altar
16:20		2nd goat to wilderness	
16:24		Ram עולה Ram עולה	Aaron's ram offered People's ram offered
16:25		Fat from חטאת animals	Turned into smoke
16:27		Hide, flesh, and dung of חטאת	Taken outside and consumed in fire

R. Eliezer's claim situates the עולה after the combined bull and goat blood is applied to the altar in the same order as Leviticus. As a logical statement, it follows Leviticus 16, which has the truth value of reported divine speech. R. Akiva, however, also presents a statement that has truth value, but it is from a different biblical text. This text, found in Numbers 29, draws on other biblical texts as well. Numbers, as a Second Temple composition, may also have a relationship with remembered practices, a point discussed shortly. Following syllogistic structures, passages from Exodus are understood as the proofs that make the Numbers 29 account true. Thus R. Akiva can hold that the seven male sheep are sacrificed with the daily or תמיד offering (a sacrifice not mentioned in Leviticus 16's account) because these animals are mentioned in Numbers 29:8–11, which also stipulates what should be done on the tenth day of the seventh month:

והקרבתם עולה ליהוה ריח ניחוח פר בן בוקר אחד איל אחד כבשים בני שנה שבעה 8
תמימים יהיו לכם 9 ומנחתם סלת בלולה בשמן שלשה עשרונים לפר שני עשרונים לאיל
האחד 10 עשרון עשרון לכבש האחד לשבעת הכבשים 11 שעיר עזים אחד חטאת מלבד
חטאת הכפרים ועולת התמיד ומנחתה ונסכיהם

8. And your burnt offerings for YHWH will be a pleasing odor: one bull of the herd, one ram, seven yearling unblemished sheep for you. 9. And their meal offering [is] choice flour with oil: three tenths for the bull, two tenths for the one ram. 10. One tenth for each of the seven lambs. 11. One goat is a חטאת offering in addition to the חטאת הכפרים and the daily עולה, with its meal and libation offerings.

While Leviticus stipulates only two rams for the עולה, Numbers 29 increases the animals and provides grain and oil supplements. A חטאת (Exod. 29:36) and חטאת הכפרים offering (Exod. 30:10), plus the עולת תמיד (Exod. 29:38–42 and Num. 28:3–8) expands the definition of an עולה for this day even more. While Exodus 30:10 does not specify the animals for the חטאת הכפורים, Baruch Levine sees a clear reference in Exodus to Leviticus 16, which calls for a double sin offering of a bull and goat. He thus defines the atoning purification as a complex set of rituals at the incense altar, the Holy of Holies, and the Courtyard.[13]

Ritual theorists break down descriptions such as the preceding ones to grasp a certain internal logic that would make a member of a group recognize proper procedures or be able to innovate proper new ones. Naphtali Meshel posits that sacrifices, as rule-based systems, are "generative, rigorous, amenable to concise formulation, partially unconsciously internalized, and have some relation to meaning."[14] He locates generativity in "the interface of the 'agent,' 'object,' and 'target' components."[15] While not identical to languages, rituals can be mapped for their syntactical structures. Meshel suggests that texts that report the same sacrifice differently reveal meaning points for the respective authors.

Numbers 28 can thus be contrasted with Leviticus 16. Numbers 29:8 identifies a task for the עולה—it produces "a pleasing odor"—while the following lines (9–11) indicate that this is a complex that includes an עולה of a bull, ram, and seven sheep; the חטאת הכפרים of a goat and bull; and the עולת התמיד, which is the sacrifice of a lamb that takes place in the morning and the evening. The author does not indicate whether the עולה (of the bull, ram, and sheep) and the חטאת הכפורים are done with the morning or evening lamb. By incorporating the חטאת into the עולה, how can a sacrifice that is made to obtain blood to apply to the altar (the חטאת) be included in a "whole burnt" complex? Meshel resolves this by suggesting that the חטאת blood was applied but that the remaining animal carcass was burned in the manner of an עולה.[16]

The differences between Leviticus and Numbers are at the heart of the dispute between R. Eliezer and R. Akiva. Leviticus 16, with far fewer animals mentioned, places the עולה of two rams after the bull and goat blood application, the חטאת הכפורים. It does not mention a daily offering, either in the morning or in the evening, so it, too, is ambiguous in this regard. Leviticus 16 seems to regard the חטאת as distinct from the עולה.

Israel Knohl has proposed that the Yom Kippur segment of Numbers 29 consists of several strata. Verse 11 notes that the חטאת הכפרים and the goat are in addition (מלבד) to the עולה מלבד חטאת הכפרים ועולת התמיד ומנחתה ונסכיהם. Knohl says this indicates an editorial hand from the Holiness School, dating to either the exile or later.[17] Jan A. Wagenaar offers a different perspective on how the Numbers calendars were composed, noting that Exodus 29:38–42 and Numbers 28:3–8 both stipulate two burnt offerings per day, whereas Ezekiel 46:13–15 and 2 Kings 16:5 only prescribe one עולה.[18] Using Wagenaar's thesis that the increase marks the difference between preexilic and exilic or postexilic, it is noteworthy that Leviticus 16 only mentions one burnt offering, the two rams, without supplements. Wagenaar also characterizes the Leviticus 23 calendar as a 'principle' on which other lists are based.[19] Baruch Levine goes further in proposing that "Ex 29:38–42 lines were introduced to provide a basis for Num 28:3–8."[20] He reads both these sections as designed to enhance late-afternoon or evening rituals and as evidence that the עולה was developing in prominence.[21] He and Wagenaar agree that Numbers 28 and 29 were written later than Leviticus 23, positioning them in the postexilic period.²² Levine's theory that the sacrifices occur later in the day, however, would mean that the חטאת would not be done until after the blood was needed for the altar applications. The Temple Scroll, analyzed as follows, seems to "solve" the problem by positioning the עולה in the morning.

Milgrom dates Leviticus 23 as exilic, while also claiming that its composition was to preserve the (preexilic) cultic calendars.²³ His opinion on the calendric portion of Numbers seems to be a minority position. He supports his position by observing that the specifics of the offerings are not mentioned, indicating that the audience already knew the details because they are spelled out in Numbers 28. But as Christophe Nihan argues, while Leviticus 23's delineation of three pilgrimage festivals is similar to other Torah calendars, Leviticus 23 differs in that it conflates those traditions with the one reported in Ezekiel 45:18–25. The latter divides the year into two, celebrating festivals in the first and seventh months.²⁴

The text-critical scholarship supports a change from preexilic sequencing of the עולה (after many other rituals, so probably occurring in the afternoon) to a postexilic sequence where additional offerings are stipulated. Levine counters that the Numbers rite would occur late in the day, marking a shift from Ezekiel 46:13–15 and 2 Kings 16:5, where the עולה is a morning offering. If Numbers 29 were written during the Second Temple, it was done so with knowledge of actual Temple practices. Ezekiel, however, was a text based on memory, perhaps idealized. It is hard to say how much of Leviticus 16 expresses observed or idealized representations. The significant point to consider, however, is that the practical text exhibits modifications of the "language" of what constitutes a "pleasing odor."

The rabbis' knowledge of these texts was not so stratified. But their knowledge of Tanakh and oral memories of Temple operations was consistent with the Greek ἐν θυμός, which can be further translated as "spirit," "feeling," or "passion." Aristotle's full definition of *enthymeme* in *Prior Analytics* also clarifies how a reference to the עולה can point to the deeper structure: Ἐνθύμημα μὲν οὖν ἐστὶ συλλογισμὸς ἐξ εἰκότων ἢ σημείων (an *enthymeme* is a "syllogism" from probabilities and signs. *APr.* 70a11). In the Temple Scroll, the sign, עולה, can have multiple significations.

THE עולה IN THE TEMPLE SCROLL

Three versions of this scroll were found in Qumran Cave 11. The best, 11Q19 (11QTa), can be dated to the first century CE and has sixty-seven columns. The earliest edition of the scroll, or possibly a source of the scroll, 4QRT, can be dated to 150 BCE. The current consensus is that it originated outside of Qumran, however, the community that created it is still a topic of debate.[25]

The Temple Scroll presents itself as divine direct speech and provides a detailed account of the Temple's construction, furnishings, and sacrifices. This authoritative account would seem to be the work of priestly circles, but it describes theologies that counter the priestly narrative. As we will see, certain of these views correspond to those found in rabbinic debates.

Many commentators have noticed that Deuteronomic views underlie the composition of the Temple Scroll.[26] Michael Wise, in his form and redaction critical study of the scroll, lists 179 citations from Deuteronomy 12–23, with several from Deuteronomy 15, 16, and 28. Almost all of the citations occur in columns 55 and 59–66.[27] While the cited chapters from Deuteronomy are mostly halakhic, some material, such as Deuteronomy 19–20, prescribes how the new nation should be formed and the extended functions of the Levitical priesthood, such as Deuteronomy 18. Wise and others have labeled these the "Deuteronomic paraphrase."

Distinct from the Deuteronomic material, Wise identifies the calendar section, which includes Yom Kippur columns 25:10 to 27:10 as a redactional layer. He posits a proto–Temple Scroll that was modeled on Leviticus 23, which he calls "Deuteronomized," but this was replaced with details found in Numbers 28–29.[28] Indeed, the redactor's systemization of scattered biblical laws is a hallmark of the whole scroll and has been noted by many.[29] The Yom Kippur columns thus comprise Leviticus 16, 23:26–32 and Numbers 29:7–11, but while these are from the Priestly source, Aharon Shemesh notes that the scroll redactor rejects the Priestly theology of holiness.[30]

Shemesh points to the concluding lines of the Festival section (29:2–10), which characterizes "the house" where the sacrifices just delineated will be performed as the place where "I will cause my name to dwell."[31] The "name" or שם dwelling in the house is a mark of Deuteronomic literature, distinct from כבוד, commonly translated as "Presence," but more properly "body," dwelling within the tabernacle or משכן.³² The Priestly source develops a concern for how this Presence is maintained in the face of airborne transgressions that accumulate within the Temple. The Deuteronomists, in contrast, locate God's body in the heavens. If the Temple Scroll uses sacrificial accounts developed from a theology of tension between transgression and Presence but also proposes that "only" the Name dwells in the Ark, then there are questions about how this document represents a particular Second Temple discourse.

In some ways, competing ideologies open a text to interpretation, but because this text positions itself as direct divine speech, it also closes discussion. It opens thought by heightening readers' engagement. The redactor seemingly inserts Priestly material to rethink the order of sacrifices and their components. Once his audience is engaged with reported divine speech, he uses it as a proof for the theology of the Name. This type of proof resembles the syllogism of the Stoic philosophers. There, as Burnyeat reads arguments from incompatibility, by positing a contrary situation—A. The Name is in the House, God is in the House (the Priestly sources), B. The Name is in the House, therefore C. God is not in the House—the truth of the conclusion is known from the beginning.³³ The premises, the sacrifices are not an argument for Presence but rather show that they were directed to the Name all along.

Within the presentation of the Priestly material, however, the Temple Scroll privileges the עולה. As mentioned previously, three parts of the Temple Scroll were discovered at Qumran, one of which was extensive (11Q19). This scroll is missing sections, and scholars working with it have used the other scrolls and made assumptions that partially cited lines from Leviticus and Numbers can be used to reconstruct gaps in the scrolls. Column 25, line 10 begins the section on Yom Kippur. It follows a description of the festival for the first day of the seventh month where the עולת תמיד is listed (25.7). Lawrence Schiffman concludes that the עולה for Yom Kippur follows the same pattern, after the תמיד.³⁴ There are no gaps from the beginning of the Yom Kippur section to the end of the column. It provides us with its account of the עולה.³⁵

ובעשרה בחודש הזה יום כפורים הוא ותענו בו את נפשותיכמה כי כול הנפש אשר לוא
תתענה בעצם היום הזה ונכרתה מעמיה והקרבתמה בו עולה ליהוה פר אחד איל אחד

כבשים בני שנה שביה (תמימים)³⁶ שעיר עזים אחד לחטאת לבד מחטאת החפורים
ומנחתמה ונסכמה כמשפטמה לפר לאיל ולכבשים ולשעיר ולחטאת הכפורים תקריבו אלים
שנים לעולה אחד יקריב הכוהן הגדול עליו בית אביהו

> 10 And on the tenth of this month 11 is Yom Kippur. And you shall afflict yourselves on it because every person who does not 12 afflict themselves on this day will be cut off from his nation. And you shall offer on it a burnt offering 13 to YHWH—one bull, one ram, seven (unblemished) yearling lambs. 14 One male goat—for expiation. Additionally, the purification offering of expiation, and the meal and drink offering, 15 according to its law, for the ox, ram, goat, and for the purification offering of expiation, 16 two rams, one for the High Priest and one for his father's house.³⁷

These lines are a collection of עולה citations from Numbers 29:8–11 and Leviticus 16:3 and 5. The section ends at the bottom of column 25, and the next column is blank for a number of lines. Based on the words that are visible, it can be understood that what follows the preceding quoted passage is a description of the חטאת, using language from Leviticus 16:11–14.³⁸ The first two reconstructed lines, following Schiffman, command a bull and two goats for expiation. One goat is the Azazel goat, and the other goat is paired with the bull. As noted, Levine understands this pair to be the חטאת הכפורים. The Temple Scroll adds the two rams to the goat/bull pair (but separately), and, as before, the חטאת הכפורים is part of the complex set that achieves the task of producing a "pleasing odor." This aroma is produced in the place where the Name dwells.

Cana Werman makes a different argument for placing the עולה at the beginning of the day. She notes that the second mention of the עולה animals, in column 27.3–4, reads אחר יעשה את הפר ואת ה[א]יל ואת ה[כבשים כמש] [ע]ולה לבני ישראל פטמה על מזבח העולה ונרצתה ה but is a combination of the aforementioned Numbers and Ezekiel 43:18.³⁹ Ezekiel reports that when the Sanctuary altar was constructed, it was to be purged via חטאת and עולה sacrifices for a week (Ezek. 43:25). On the eighth day onward, burnt and well-being offerings would be accepted (רצי) by Adonai, meaning that the Temple Scroll author added this to indicate that the עולה is necessarily first, to sanctify the altar.⁴⁰

There was the previous question of how the blood manipulations of the חטאת could fit with an עולה. The Temple Scroll answers this in column 26.1–8. The goat and bull's fat, along with its meal and libation offerings, is to be burned on the עולה altar. The חטאת, by itself, would not have meal and libation subordinate offerings, so it is interesting that the text goes further than Numbers 29 in its incorporation of the bull and goat into the עולה category. Schiffman determines that what is seen in the Yom Kippur ritual is true for the other Temple Scroll festivals: the author of this section has worked to extend the עולה into various new festivals. Milgrom posits that the עולה is the more ancient ritual, but it was "usurped" by the sacrifices devised to purge the tabernacle of contaminations.[41] This fits with Leviticus 16, where the חטאת is the principal ritual. The evidence of the Temple Scroll, then, provides evidence of a shift in worldview. Interestingly, it accomplishes this shift within a rhetorical structure current during the Second Sophistic.

THE MISHNAIC DISPUTE

The author of the Temple Scroll uses his audience's knowledge to establish the authority of his position. If the scroll dates to about 150 BCE, then it was composed at the dawn of the Hasmonean age. Mishnah Yoma, however, was composed in the third century CE, after the destruction of the Temple. The repetition of the sacrificial procedures thus carried the authority of divine rules "God said to Moses" while also being rites that could only be imagined. This did not detract from their significance; instead, they were the vehicle through which new ways of atonement were thought.

The dispute between R. Akiva and R. Eliezer, while engaging in the ambiguities between Leviticus and Numbers, has more to do with the composer's positioning of the debate—in the place where Leviticus would put the עולה—and the position of R. Akiva, which would upend the carefully constructed order of the Mishnah's depiction of the rites. Far from claiming that his text is "from Sinai," the Mishnaic composer retains a human debate that challenges his composition.

Referring back to the tables at the beginning of this chapter, it can be seen that the Mishnah follows Leviticus 16. The asterisk signals R. Yehudah's disagreement: he says that goat and ox blood were alternately sprinkled. This contradicts the Levitical account. The Mishnah adds the morning תמיד (the afternoon offering is noted in m. Yoma 7.4). If the dispute between R. Eliezer and R. Akiva had not been inserted, the only עולה would be the two rams, offered at the same point as the Leviticus account positions it. Thus there would have been a clear distinction between חטאת and עולה rituals, unlike Numbers 29, where the חטאת הכפורים is part of the עולה sequence. If we follow Levine, who claims the חטאת הכפורים is described in Leviticus 16:12–19, then Yoma's narrative of blood application is also a חטאת הכפורים and differs only in that, instead of an expiation of the Tent of Meeting (Lev. 16:16), the Mishnah has the leftover blood poured on the base of the outer altar, ultimately to run into the Kidron Valley. This seems to agree with Exodus 33:7, which places the Tent outside of the camp.

The problem raised by the dispute mirrors the ambiguity of Numbers 29. R. Eliezar supplements Leviticus's rams with Numbers's seven lambs. It can be assumed that it is afternoon, based on the Mishnah's description of the day's events. But it is R. Akiva who completes the Numbers's command by including the ox and male goat. Numbers is unclear about whether the עולה animals are added to the morning or evening תמיד lamb. R. Akiva seems to split the difference by saying that "they" (the two rams and seven lambs) were brought in the morning, as well as the ox. He then moves the Numbers's חטאת goat—presumably an additional one, since the Yoma account already paired its חטאת goat with the bull—to the evening rites but physically separates the חטאת from the תמיד. In Yoma, R. Akiva seems presciently to concur with Schiffman and Werman that these עולה animals were done in the morning. His account could be close to the Temple Scroll in this matter, except that he retains the distinction between חטאת and עולה. Put in relation to the narrative as constructed, his tradition overturns the order that the Mishnah has established.

The Tosefta is another text within the field of Tannaitic discourse. Tosefta Kippurim 3.19 reports that both rabbis couple the ox and goat, implying a חטאת הכפורים. While Akiva placed the ox and goat in the afternoon עולת תמיד in the Mishnah version, the Tosefta version relates that Eliezer understands the ox and goat to be offered during the morning עולת תמיד. The Tosefta thus has Eliezer increasing the goat/ox pairs. The Tosefta's account of R. Eliezer uses the word נעשה, "prepared," not קריבין, "sacrificed," raising the question of whether his morning goats are the same goats that will later be designated as "for YHWH" and "for Azazel."[42] Here is the Tosefta:[43]

> ר' ליעזר או' כך סדר הקרבנות היו הקריבין פר העולה ושעיר הנעשה בחוץ היו קריבין עם תמיד של שצר ואחר כך פר ושעיר הנעשה בפנים ואחר כך אילו ואיל העם ואחר כך שבעת כבשים תמימים

> R. Eliezer says, this is the order of sacrifice: an ox for burnt offering, and a goat which is done/prepared outside, are sacrificed with the daily morning offering. After that, an ox and goat are done/prepared inside [the Temple], and after that, his ram and the ram of the people, and after that, seven unblemished sheep.

The Tosefta goes on to report R. Akiva's opinion:

> ר' עקיבא או' פר העולה ושבית כבשים תמימים היו קריבין עם תמיד של שחר. שנאמר: מלבד עולת הבקר אשר לעולת התמיד ואחר כך פר ושעיר הנעשה בפנים ואחר כך שעיר הנעשה בחוץ. שנאמר: מלבד חטאת הכפורים ועולב התהיד ומנחתה ונסכיהם ואחר כך אילו ואיל העם.

> R. Akiva says: an ox for a burnt offering and seven unblemished sheep were sacrificed with the daily morning offering. As it says: "in addition to the morning burnt offering which was for the daily burnt offering" (Num. 28:23). After that an ox and a goat were prepared inside, and after that a goat was prepared outside. As it says: "besides the purification offering of expiation and the burnt offering of the daily and meal and their drink offerings" (Num. 29:11), after that his ram and the people's ram.

A third opinion is added by Kippurim, who does not specify which animals are meant:

> ר' יהודה או' בשם ר' ליעזר: אחד קרב עם תמיד של שחר וששה קריבין עם תמיד של בין הערבים

> R. Yehuda says in the name of R. Eliezer: one is offered with the daily morning sacrifice and six offered with the daily evening sacrifice.

Except for the quote from Numbers 29:11, none of these opinions mention the supplementary offerings, what the Temple Scroll referred to as the law or rule. It is unclear in the Tannaitic texts whether jugations are trace elements understood at the mention of an עולה animal or whether this is being deliberately deemphasized. Still, these rabbinic traditions stand in sharp contrast to other texts, particularly the Aramaic Levi Document, for whose author the sacrificial accompaniments seem paramount.

Ritual theorist Seth Kunin proposes that ritemes, the ritual equivalent of phonemes, act as signals when they emphasize or deemphasize.[44] We have seen, for instance, how in the Temple Scroll, the fat of the חטאת

offering was added to the regular עולה pairings. More broadly, Numbers incorporated the חטאת into the sequence for the עולה, while Leviticus maintains a distinction. The rabbis turn their attention from the offerings' manipulation to the offerings' sequencing. This shift reveals that sequencing conveys a certain significance in their grasp of the ritual. Although we do not know what that is, Akiva's position upends the Mishnah's account.

Rabbi Akiva's assertion, across the Mishnah and Tosefta, that eight lambs should be sacrificed in the morning, holds a particular meaning. In commenting on the Temple Scroll, Werman points to Ezra 43 as requiring sacrifices for sanctifying the altar. Akiva's Tosefta statement aligns most closely with this by requiring both the ox and the lambs in the morning. In this regard, his thinking is closer to Priestly traditions. At the same time, his statement that the rams should be sacrificed in the morning contradicts Leviticus, and by upholding a separation between the חטאת and עולה, as Yoma does more generally, he rejects the Second Temple trend toward an emphasis on the עולה. Mishnah Yoma, while keeping the Levitical tradition, challenges itself by also including Akiva's position. By placing the challenge at the juncture where Leviticus 16 locates the עולה, the Yoma adds narrativity to its account.

Of the texts reviewed, the Temple Scroll is the most innovative in privileging of the עולה. It positions itself as Sinaitic revelation and says that its innovation is actually the halakhah that was given at Sinai. By claiming a divine origin, this discourse tries to silence any response from those who hear it. The author of Mishnah Yoma constructs a narrative sequence that actively elicits response, demonstrated by the fact that it includes views contrary to its sequencing, such as R. Akiva's. R. Eliezer, whose view on the time of the עולה follows the presentation of the Levitical order that the Mishnaic narrative presents is given a voice that challenges not the timing but the animals. In Eliezer's view, at least some of the Numbers 29 animals should be added to the rams. Authority is relocated from Sinai to dialectic—a dialectic that openly challenges its own presentation. But it is through this challenge that "dialectic" turns into "dialogism": each voice—Akiva, Eliezer, the compiler—presents an independent interpretation of the sources.

Bakhtin suggests that the mark of dialogism is in "the intensification of someone else's thought" so that a "relationship to that other consciousness" is established.[45] The compiler, working after the generation of Rabbis Akiva and Eliezer, seems to take on such a relationship of consciousness, but the Tosefta, with its development of the positions, shows that the material remains in the community as an issue to consider. Since Kippurim is not written in the narrative style of Yoma, its compiler does not undertake the same role of participant. We see through the Tosefta that there was not a resolution, as a classic Platonic dialogue would strive to accomplish, but a relocation of thought from characters to community.

One could argue against this reading by suggesting that the arranger of the text is expressing his personal view by way of his composition, without adding an explicitly anonymous voice. To borrow terms from recent debates in Classics scholarship, might it be possible to claim that R. Eliezer is the "mouthpiece" of this Mishnah? Debra Nails, in an article on the representation of Socrates in Platonic dialogues, argues that Socrates's positions are distinct from Plato's—for the express purpose of providing "exemplary philosophical discussions."[46] She points to their display of dialectical reasoning while concluding that the complexity of the arguments opens the text "for critique."[47] Daniel Boyarin cites Nails in his presentation of the Platonic dialectic. He notes the paradox of the presentation of the opposing opinion as a deeply dialogical move. The decision to present the rabbinic dispute allows for a consideration of the עולה's discourse history, and the dispute, positioned at the point that Leviticus assigns it, provides a paradox. But since R. Eliezer's opinion only partially fits the Priestly account, the inclusion of his voice eliminates him as a "mouthpiece"; it moves the dispute to the space between philosophy and rhetoric. Eliezer, Akiva, and the inclusion of Eliezer and Akiva—contrary to the order Rabbi Yehudah Hanasi decides to present—undermine the progression toward an ideal for the Day of Atonement. *And* the work is not crafted to persuade. The disputants present their positions within a logic that resembles Aristotle's theory of argument, but even the editor makes an independent case. Instead, the Tosefta reveals that these positions are not meant to persuade us but rather to serve as points for us to consider. The Tannaitic project is an open one, within the bounds of its community.

Chaya Halberstam provides another view of Tannaitic discourse. She identifies the rabbinic uncertainty evidenced in debates as a hallmark of

Tannaitic literature. The ambiguities noted previously between Numbers and Leviticus as a cause for the dispute between Akiva and Eliezer certainly fit her paradigm. Reading along with David Weiss Halivni and Moshe Halbertal, she observes the tension between heavenly truth and practical truth.[48] The difficulties between biblical texts, each of which claims to represent divine decree, can possibly be read against practices (lost in the destruction of the Second Temple) that privileged the עולה. Halberstam's cases differ in structure from Yoma in that the dispute comes in a narrative of a now fictional world, while her disputants bring real-world situations to the ideal world of law. Yoma, therefore, provides a different view of rabbinic thought, where the text is structured to engage its readers.

The compiler makes a number of moves that call into doubt whether the tractate is an argument for a point of view. If the reader would be satisfied that the debate appears at the point it does, and R. Akiva's position is not placed at the point where he would assign the עולה, that satisfaction should be short-lived. The compiler gives R. Akiva the last word, a statement that plays on the Hebrew מקוה as both "hope" and "immersion pool" and arguably upends Levitical cosmology, for the deity is not "in heaven" or "in the Tabernacle" but within the practice of purity. Indeed, Yoma as a whole provides multiple differences, seemingly shaking the assumptions of the Levitical tradition by adding immersions, composing the words to a petitionary prayer—and multiplying its recitation.

The original ambiguity of Numbers—as well as its difference from Leviticus—opens the door to inference. The question remains as to how wide this door was opened for the intended audience: The Temple is gone, but is this debate about animals a proxy for a consideration of Israel's relationship with the Deity? The inclusion of R. Akiva's final statement about מקוה opens the door wider. The reception history instantiates "the Mishnah" as much as it instantiates "the Talmud," but the challenge is to recall how these layers of text argue points of theology through ritual—where Presence is located, the purification that results from fire, the need to consider how to resolve the effects of transgressions. For us, the dispute is a reminder that we are not reading a story, a mere narrative of the High Priest on Yom Kippur but instead witnessing a cultural engagement with the past to shape a future. The composition puts us on a path where neither the other versions of rhetoric nor the dominant versions of philosophy had tread before.

SOPHIA AVANTS is Visiting Scholar at Duke University and Associate Fellow at the Albright Institute in Jerusalem. She has previously published on the notion of forgiveness in rabbinic thought. She received her PhD from Claremont in 2021 on *Mishnah Yoma: Narrative as Cultural Thought*.

NOTES

1. Nightingale traces the development of Plato's idea of philosophy, positioning his dialectic within Athenian culture. Young dissects Plato's reasoning in the dilemma presented in the *Crito*. Young captures the issue as twofold: (1) thinking that one is correct and (2) that the reasons for thinking that one is correct are also correct. A summary of Socrates's position can be found at 277b8f. Nightingale, *Genres in Dialogue*; Young, "Plato's *Crito*," 79; Plato, Phaedrus. 277.B [Fowler].

2. Young, "Plato's *Crito*," 87.

3. Burnyeat, "Enthymeme," 7.

4. Ibid., 12. For Aristotle's initial presentations of *enthymeme*, see *Rhet.* 1.1 1354a7: "*Enthymemes* are the body of proof" and *A.Pr.* II.27 70a11: "*Enthymeme* is a syllogism/'consideration' from probabilities or signs."

5. For a detailed presentation of the relevant passages, see Burnyeat, "Enthymeme," 35–36, especially note 91.

6. Burnyeat, "Enthymeme," 44.

7. See especially the introduction and notes 18–32, where he documents schools and identities in Roman Palestine. Hidary, *Rabbis and Classical Rhetoric*, 2–8.

8. Gibbs and Ochs, "Gold and Silver," 101.

9. Two prominent examples are the increase in the number of immersions required of the High Priest and the report of the High Priest's words of confession, which are said three times to Leviticus's once. While creating a detailed narrative of the High Priest's journey through the Temple, it omits what seems primary in Leviticus, that the חטאת blood atones. There is also the intriguing juxtaposition of the reading of Aharei Mot at the time of the Azazel goat's trip, as if suggesting that the reading could hold an equivalent value.

10. Bakhtin, *Problems of Dostoevsky's Poetics*, 6; "Discourse in the Novel," 349.

11. Daniel Boyarin makes a similar observation regarding the Babylonian Talmud. While his is a broad discussion, centered on writings from Sasanian Persia, this chapter considers an earlier, Palestinian example. I owe *The Fat Rabbis* inspiration for insight and further reading. Boyarin, *Socrates*, 141.

12. All of the following excerpts from Mishnah Yoma are transcribed from the Kaufman manuscript. However, what I have identified as 7.3, following Albeck, the Kaufman scribes assign to 7.2 and 7.3. I have used Albeck's 7.3, in accordance with most scholars. The translation of this and other texts are my own, unless otherwise noted.

13. Levine, *Numbers 21–36*, 388–89.

14. Meshel, *The "Grammar" of Sacrifice*, 207.
15. Ibid., 163.
16. Meshel, "Toward a Grammar of Sacrifice," 549, 552; *The "Grammar" of Sacrifice*, 119.
17. Knohl, "The Priestly Torah Versus the Holiness School," 89.
18. Wagenaar, *Origin and Transformation*, 150.
19. The single quote marks are his, although he does not attribute the term. Wagenaar, *Origin and Transformation*.
20. Levine, *Numbers 21–36*, 398.
21. Ibid., 400.
22. Ibid., 47.
23. Milgrom, *Leviticus 23–27*, 2055.
24. Nihan, "Israel's Festival Calendars," 213.
25. The two other cave 11 scrolls are 11Q20 (11QT^b) and 11Q21 (11QT^c). Himmelfarb documents the dating debate in note 31 to page 93. She cites the date of the fragment 4Q524 as evidence that a presectarian composition existed. See also Himmelfarb, *A Kingdom of Priests*, 93; Vroom, *The Authority of the Law*, 101–4.
26. Schwartz carefully separates the sources of Deuteronomy from the scroll now part of the Torah. The sources were written in conjunction with the administration of King Josiah and are Deuteronomic. The scroll is Deuteronomistic: it was written after 586. The scroll (D) was used by scribes to form a history (DtrH) that is in the books of the Former Prophets. Schwartz, "The Pentateuchal Sources and the Former Prophets," 784.
27. Wise, *A Critical Study of the Temple Scroll*, 239–41.
28. Besides Wise, Marvin Sweeney, in a private conversation (March 3, 2021), notes that the Temple Scroll typically puts Deuteronomy into conversation with other texts from the Torah to produce new and innovative readings of the Torah and the conceptualization of its contents. Wise, *A Critical Study of the Temple Scroll*, 132.
29. Vroom provides a review of some of this scholarship. Vroom, *The Authority of the Law*, 105–7.
30. Shemesh, "Holiness according to the Temple Scroll," 374.
31. Ibid.
32. Sommer argues against "presence" because its depictions are concrete. He notes Exodus 33:18–23, where the כבוד has a face, hand, and back. Sommer, *The Bodies of God*, 60.
33. Burnyeat, "Enthymeme," 43.
34. This is an interesting point. The Temple Scroll's excerpt from Numbers 29 does not include the daily עולה, yet, earlier in the chapter, we saw that since this sacrifice occurred in the morning and afternoon, the text was unclear about whether the preceding offerings were with the morning or afternoon lamb. Schiffman seems to propose that the Temple Scroll offers a solution to the problem. Schiffman, *The Courtyards of the House of the Lord*, 359.
35. Qimron, *The Temple Scroll*, 39.
36. Qimron adds this as most probable since it corresponds with the Masoretic text.
37. This translation follows Schiffman. He graciously replied to clarifying questions. Schiffman and Gross, *The Temple Scroll*, 76–77.
38. See, for instance, Schiffman and Gross, *The Temple Scroll*, 78–81 and Vroom, *The Authority of the Law*, 112 for detailed reviews of both the scrolls.
39. "After he does the ox, ram, and sheep as prescribed, on the burnt offering altar and the burnt offering is accepted for the children of Israel."

40. Werman, "Appointed Times," 103.

41. Milgrom, *Leviticus 1–16*, 176.

42. Saul Lieberman, editing the Tosefta, seems to confirm a translation of נעשה as "prepare" because he suggests that the priest is laying his hands on the goats in blessing. Lieberman, *Tosefta*, II:248, n. 89. Lieberman also calls them "מוספים לתמיד" since they are the purification component of the daily offering. Lieberman discusses the rams in his commentary on the Tosefta, תוספתא כפשוטה. He says that the "ram for the people" is the one ram listed in Numbers 29:8, a claim that implies that Numbers 29 lies beneath the Leviticus text. Lieberman cites Sifra Aharei Mot, parsha ב, where Rabbi Yehudah Hanasi states that R. Eliezer has added the ram from Numbers to the ram in Leviticus. This tradition is also cited in b. Yoma 70b. Lieberman, *Tosefta Kifeshutah*, IV:803.

43. The citations are from Lieberman. The translation is my own. Lieberman, *Tosefta*.

44. Kunin, *We Think What We Eat*.

45. Bakhtin, *Problems of Dostoevsky's Poetics*, 69.

46. See Nails's article, but many of the essays in the book also argue for the philosophical merits of the debates in the corpus. Nails, "Mouthpiece Schmouthpiece," 25.

47. Nails, "Mouthpiece Schmouthpiece."

48. Halberstam, *Law and Truth*, 6.

Postscript
Ein talmudisches Etwas über die philosophische Literatur: A Talmudic Observation on Philosophy[1]

KARMA BEN-JOHANAN

> Yet, the moment the Talmud becomes generally known to the non-Jewish population, Judea's rule is irretrievably lost; therefore, every German family should possess a copy of the Talmud just as it possesses the Gospel. Therefore, may every good German take pains to spread the Talmud all around.[2]

Who mediates between talmud and philosophy? Where do the authors of this book stand, as mediators, between these two words, between these two worlds of meaning? How do they embody the *and*? Though the *ands* provided by the authors vary significantly, the project points to a new philosophical-talmudic conversation—complex, polyphonic, not predetermined—a conversation that seems to have become possible only recently. Today's *and* is seemingly nothing like the previous *ands* that accompanied rabbinic literature and rabbinic learning throughout their history in Western thought. Something in the power relationship between talmud and philosophy has changed, destabilizing the relationship and inviting new investigations.

In this postscript, I briefly revisit previous reincarnations of the *and*, which connects but also separates talmud and philosophy through their bittersweet encounters in the history of the West and, more specifically, the history of Western Christianity. In this history, the mediators play a central role.

THE CRISIS OF DISCOVERY

The moment when the Christian West "discovered" the Talmud was a moment of crisis in European Jewish history.[3] At this time, the Otherness of Judaism—or of Jews—began to be seen as intolerable, in contrast to the relative tolerance Jews enjoyed in the early Middle Ages. This transition to intolerance, which emerged from a multitude of changes within European medieval society, was accompanied by a Christian change of perception of Jews from (tolerable) "Old Testament Jews" and (intolerable) "Talmudic Jews."

The adherence of Jews to the Hebrew Scriptures was acceptable in early medieval Europe and even played a role in the Christian history of salvation. The blind and stubborn Jewish attachment to the "literal" meaning of the Old Testament (OT) was erroneous, of course, but it testified to Christian truth. According to the influential Augustinian perception, the steadfast observance of Jews to the OT Law was a faithful witness to the fact that Christians neither forged their scriptures nor invented them.[4] This endowed Christianity with the gravity of an ancient religion and a continuity and fulfillment of old prophecies. This testimony also had a political component: the Jewish people's miserable diasporic existence and especially their scattering among Christendom were fulfillment of OT prophecies that proved that their own interpretation of the OT prophecies was false; their worldly failure was evidence that the prophecies were not fulfilled in the way Jews have read them, while the Christian interpretation was triumphant.[5]

The identification of Jews with the OT was ambivalent. Without the mediation of the Christological reading, a reading that was strongly juxtaposed—at least since the Patristic writings of the second century—with the Jewish reading, the OT was a collection of brutal, abhorrent stories not unlike the Homeric epics, without philosophical mediation.[6] It was the Christian interpretation that redeemed the OT from its apparent brutality.[7] The Jewish interpretation—which was traditionally perceived as "literal" by Christian thinkers, was therefore obsolete, but it was also an enduring and powerful symbol of the past, even a persistence of the past within the present of Christianity. In other words, Jews were there to point to the past for the Christian future, to the progress of the emergence from darkness into light, the carnal to the spiritual, the conditional to the eternal, and the particular to the universal. The Otherness of Jews was therefore tolerable as a witness, a remnant, and a phase in a teleological program. It was an Otherness that had to be Christologized and spiritualized in order to become (and remain) meaningful. On their own, the Hebrew Scriptures were repulsing and outdated. But mitigated through a Christian hermeneutic, their true significance was revealed. Christianity provided the hermeneutic framework that made the Jewish tradition and, by extension, Jews tolerable. In this sense, it was this ambivalence, sometimes called "supersessionism," that enabled the persistence of Jewish life in medieval Christendom.[8]

The discovery of the Talmud in the twelfth and thirteenth centuries subverted the foundations of the supersessionism of the two testaments. One of the reasons for the crisis in Jewish-Christian relations at that time was the Christian realization that Jews carried their Otherness in a different direction than the route paved to it within Christendom and the Christian imagination. The Talmud was perceived as a Jewish rebellion against the Augustinian model, which provided the intellectual framework for the toleration of Jews as witnesses to the truthfulness of Christianity. It was a change, but not progress since progress was only possible in the direction leading from the OT to the New Testament, not from the OT to another textual corpus and another hermeneutical system. So Jews could no longer faithfully represent the past, but they were not oriented to the future either. Their place in history became indeterminate, and their role in the history of salvation was also diminishing. This gives another meaning to the status of the Talmud as a "diasporic" corpus, as a diaspora of sacred Christian time. The moment of the Talmud's discovery was also the moment when the toleration of Jews—or, at least, of so many of them—was no longer readily justified in Christian terms.[9]

The preoccupation of Christian intellectuals with postbiblical Judaism first occurred with a growing sophistication in Christian learning. Those scholars (most prominently Peter the Venerable and Peter Alfonsi, a Jewish convert) who carried out the turn to philosophy in the twelfth century were also the first to acknowledge and study Talmudic texts. The critical and intellectual faculties at work in philosophy were also involved in facilitating the Christian interest in postbiblical Judaism, which those

Christian scholars saw as profoundly irrational and full of contradictions, errors, and absurdities. By the thirteenth century, however, the accusations against the Talmud had diversified. If, in the twelfth century, Christians considered irrationality to be the problem with the Talmud, in the thirteenth century, the Talmud was seen as an outright heresy, a Jewish deviation from the OT, and a replacement of the Law of the Torah with another.[10] Thus the rationalization of Christianity and the centralization of Western Christendom coincided with a sharp decrease in the tolerance toward Jews.[11] Imaginary Jews, or 'Jews of the past,' were better accepted in the Christian society than actual, present ones who centered their lives on the Talmud. Talmud was therefore discovered as the opposite of Christian reasoning and teleology.

The medieval mediators who drew Christian attention to the Talmud were often converts from Judaism. It was the *and* of thirteenth-century Christians like Nicholas Donin and Pablo Christiani that formed the Christian gaze on the Talmud as heretical and anti-Christian, provoking the famous public polemics on the Talmud that culminated in its burning[12] and its banning or confiscation, and in the long tradition of the Talmud's Christian censorship. Talmudic subjectivity was thus perceived as anti-Christian, Christian subjectivity—as anti-Talmudic. The tradition that saw these two intellectual horizons as incommensurable, further evolved by Protestant thinkers from Luther on, persisted into the twentieth century.[13]

INCLUSION AND AMBIVALENCE

Yet the Talmud was not only burned, despised, and confiscated. Rabbinic literature was not only unbearable beyond toleration. Christian scholars (and convert Pablo Christiani is credited for that trajectory as well) soon found ways to incorporate the Talmud into Western subjectivity, applying the guarded ambivalence toward the OT to rabbinic literature as well. The Talmud was perceived not only as a demonic text but also as containing proofs and hints to the Christian truth and as useful for the Christian understanding of the New Testament. It was also a tool in the hands of missionaries, who labored to understand the rabbinic corpus in its original languages in order to lead Jews to Christianity by means of their own literature.[14] The Christian learning of postbiblical Jewish literature increased, and, with the emergence of early modern print shops in Europe, rabbinic literature was printed for both Jewish and Christian consumption. Print facilitated the flourishing of Christian learning of Jewish texts, which was an essential component in the evolution of the humanist sciences of philology, religion, and ethnology, to name only a few.[15]

However, not unlike in the case of the Hebrew bible, the affirmation and legitimacy of the Talmud necessitated a mediation and adaptation of the texts to Christian sensitivities. This was largely the work of printers, editors, and censors, who had to ensure that the transmission of the Talmud would not transgress the limits of Christian good taste. In other words, the fascination of the West with the Talmud has both threatened the Talmud and given it a place within Western civilization. Christian censorship, often accompanied by authoritative ecclesiastical approvals of the printing of censored editions, has partially assisted in turning the Talmud into a sympathetic Other, exotic, unthreatening, and unoffensive to Christian sensibilities. Clear distinctions between gentiles of the Talmud and Christians of the time, and the omission of the few ascetic Talmudic slanders against Jesus and Mary had formed the foundation of the legitimation of the Talmud as well as its integration into Christian learning. Moreover, as Raz-Krakotzkin has shown, these revisions were not done by Jews only to appease the Christian authorities; they were internalized into Jewish culture and seen by Jews as reflective of their own values and attitudes toward European culture. The joint labor of Jews and Christians in the production and printing of the Talmud created new synergies and a common cultural and ethical worldview shared by both communities. This commonality also informed Jewish learning and was an essential part of the construction of Jewish studies.[16]

Here, too, the mediators had a central role.[17] Those mediators usually came in the role of censors, and the censors were, once again, often converts to Christianity who were personally acquainted with both worlds of meaning. Both the Christian censor (whether a convert or not) and his Jewish counterparts were required to reflectively read the Talmud through a Christian lens. Both sides were leaning on a close acquaintance with rabbinic literature on the one hand and, on the other hand, on a critical distance from which they could look into rabbinic texts from outside their faith community, interpreting them differently from their traditional reading in a way that corresponded to the sensibilities of the Christian—and the enlightened—milieu.[18]

In other words, the Talmud was included in the Western milieu (by both Jews and Christians) as an object of thought, not as a way of reasoning. The price of that new *and*, which came to represent the compatibility of rabbinic Judaism with modernity, necessitated the creation of a differentiation between—to use Lapidot's terminology—talmud and Talmud, that is, between talmud as a way of thought and Talmud as an object of thought, the object of Western subjectivity.[19]

This differentiation was epitomized in Leopold Zunz's "Etwas über die rabbinische Litteratur"—the first work by a Jewish scholar that applied historicist methods to rabbinic literature. Zunz's work was deliberately intended to legitimize the rabbinic tradition by measuring it according to the standards of Enlighted German reasoning and, in particular, contemporaneous Protestant theology.[20] Zunz's move, and the evolving discipline of *Wissenschaft des Judentums*, enabled an overcoming of Jewish Otherness and particularity by looking at them from the point of view of Western sameness, yet still regarding Otherness as useful and important in the self-establishment of this sameness. Needless to say, this move was supersessionist in its own right.

CONVERTING PHILOSOPHY TO TALMUD

Following Carlo Ginzburg, Raz-Krakotzkin has depicted Jewish historians of Judaism as still standing—perhaps with Zunz—behind the ear of the early modern censor, fossilizing the Talmud as an object of thought, as a remnant of the past that no longer makes any normative, existential, or cognitive demands. But is this still the case today, at least for the *and* of this current anthology? Do we also want to say something, an *Etwas*, *über die rabbinische Litteratur*, as the spiritual descendants of Jewish converts to legitimize the Jewish tradition as a partner in the "sameness" of the West? Or is the current task of mediation no longer to legitimize the Talmud by converting it to Western thought but rather the obverse—to legitimize philosophy by converting it to talmud? Could there be a conversation between the two that does not surrender the one tradition to the logic of the other?

The flexible *and* that Dolgopolski chose as the organizing principle of the book leaves the horizon of the relationship between talmud and philosophy entirely open. Yet what enables the reexamination of the talmud and philosophy relationship—and perhaps not only an examination but an actual renewal as well—is that philosophy has acquired in the last decades an eagerness to examine its cultural conditions of possibility, to no longer assume its neutrality and universality, and to relativize its very foundations. Contemporary philosophy is, to a great extent, a critique of philosophy, and this critique necessitates an ability to look at philosophy from the outside, to confront philosophy with another kind of reasoning and another tradition of thought. Contemporary philosophy is attempting, in a sense, a self-Othering in order to transcend its tedious Western sameness and reencounter its cognitive Others in new analogies and synergies. Philosophy seeks to turn itself from philosophy to Philosophy, to turn philosophical subjectivity against the Western philosophical tradition as an object of thought. In the overall project of the current anthology, there is an underlying exploration of the ways talmudic thought can assist philosophy in reflecting on itself and understanding and perhaps transcending its boundaries. Reexamining the *and* may help philosophy to further shake its traditional binary divisions between self and other, between universal and particular, between the rational and the irrational, between West and East, between the past and the future, and so forth. It is therefore *useful* for philosophy to think with and about talmud.

According to this logic, the authors play a complex role. On one hand, they are still standing "behind the ear of the censor," extracting from the Talmud what can be useful for their intellectual tradition. Yet, on the other hand, it is not the legitimization of the Talmud they are seeking but that of philosophy; if anyone requires conversion, it is no longer the Talmud that has to be philosophized, Christianized, and systematized but the obverse: philosophy has to become more talmudic to liberate it from its rigidity when unmediated by the non-Western, nonlinear reasoning of the talmud—the Jewish diasporic tradition. It is the tradition of Western thought that seems to have lost its hold on the ground, at least ethically, because of its encompassing efforts to submit all of its Others to its logic, a system whose greatest embodiment was, of course, the obliteration of Jewish Otherness in the Holocaust (or the *shoah*, as the converted term has it). The current *and* strives to appropriate the Talmud no longer only as an object of thought but as a paradigm shift. It is philosophy's time to prove its compatibility with modernity by demonstrating its openness to Otherness, indeed, its becoming Otherness. Philosophy strives to turn itself into the wandering Jew, into Ahasver in order to find a new foothold.

Yet as newcomers, as converts from philosophy to talmud embarking on it from within the break of the Western universal, we are bound to imprint the philosophical past onto our talmudic future. What would a supersession of a supersessionist tradition with a stubbornly unsupersessionist way of thinking look like? In this anthology, both traditions question themselves in light of their respective other, looking for new *ands* that will be intelligible without teleology.

KARMA BEN-JOHANAN is Senior Lecturer in the Department of Comparative Religion at the Hebrew University of Jerusalem, and author of *Jacob's Younger Brother: Christian-Jewish Relations after Vatican II*.

NOTES

1. As will be shown in this chapter, the title of this postscript indicates a reversal in Leopold Zunz's approach to rabbinic literature in Zunz's essay "Etwas über die rabbinische Litteratur." See Zunz, "Remarks on Rabbinic Literature."

2. An excerpt from the "Talmud-Auszug," disseminated in Berlin in May 1892. Quoted in Wiese, *Challenging Colonial Discourse*, 110.

3. Funkenstein, *Perceptions of Jewish History*, 172–200; Cohen, *Friars and the Jews*, 51–76.

4. Augustine, *De civitate Dei*, xviii: 46.

5. Cohen, *Friars and the Jews*, 14–15; Fredriksen, *Augustine and the Jews*, 226, 286.

6. Buffiere, *Les Mythes de Homere*.

7. Martyr, *Dialogue with Trypho*. For example, chapters 29, 34, 67. See also Nirenberg, *Anti-Judaism*, 87–134.

8. See here the controversy between Fredriksen and Cohen over the positive significance of the Augustinian doctrine of the witness to medieval Jewish life: Cohen, "Review Article," 77–78.

9. Cohen, *Friars and the Jews*, 76.

10. See ibid., 322. Cohen's discussion of Gregory IX's decrees against the Talmud.

11. In this postscript, I follow Jeremy Cohen's argumentation in *Living Letters of the Law*, which relates the discovery of the Talmud by Christians and its perception as heretical, with the decrease in Christian tolerance toward Jews in the High Middle Ages.

12. For a completion of Cohen's narrative, see Chazan, *Daggers of the Faith*.

13. Though one among many, the most famous Protestant attack on the Talmud is the *Entdecktes Judenthum* by Andreas Eisenmenger (1711). On the Protestant discourse on the Talmud in Wilhelmine Germany, see Wiese, *Challenging Colonial Discourse*, 109–22.

14. Cohen, *Living Letters of the Law*, 334–42. See the various contributions in Coudert and Shoulson, *Hebraica Veritas?*; Dunkelgrün, "The Christian Study of Judaism," 316–48; Raz-Krakotzkin, *The Censor, the Editor, and the Text*, chapter 4; Abulafia, *Christian-Jewish Relations 1000–1300*, 210–12; Burnett, *From Christian Hebraism to Jewish Studies*; Wiese, *Challenging Colonial Discourse*, 109–58; Golling and von der Osten-Sacken, *Herman L. Strack*.

15. On the inappropriateness of the word *Hebraism* for this, see Dunkelgrün, "The Christian Study of Judaism," 345; see also Grafton and Weinberg, *I Have Always Loved the Holy Tongue*, 290.

16. Raz-Krakotzkin, *The Censor, the Editor, and the Text*, 198–200. See also Miller, "Rabbi Samson Raphael Hirsch."

17. On the complex and ambivalent role of converts in Jewish-Christian relations, as "bridge builders" on the one hand and as inciters against Jews and Judaism on the other, see Stuczynski, "Converso Paulinism and Residual Jewishness"; Yisraeli, "Constructing and Undermining Converso Jewishness"; Carlebach, *Divided Souls*.

18. See the extensive study of van Boxel, *Jewish Books in Christian Hands*.

19. This distinction is close to Sergey Dolgopolski's differentiation between The Talmud and, simply, Talmud. See Dolgopolski, *What Is Talmud*.

20. Wiese, *Challenging Colonial Discourse*, 79–81.

BIBLIOGRAPHY

Aberbach, Moshe. *Labor, Crafts and Commerce in Ancient Israel*. Jerusalem: Magnes Press, 1994.
Abraham, Michael, Dov Gabbay, and Uri Schild, eds. *Studies in Talmudic Logic*. 14 vols. London: College Publications, 2010–2017.
Abramovitsh, Shalom Yankev (Mendele Mokher Seformim). *Bimei ha'ra'ash*. 1894. https://maagarim.hebrew-academy.org.il/.
———. *Lo nahat be-ya'akov*. 1892. https://maagarim.hebrew-academy.org.il/.
———. *Mah anu?* 1875. https://maagarim.hebrew-academy.org.il/.
Abulafia, Anna Sapir. *Christian-Jewish Relations 1000–1300: Jews in the Service of Medieval Christendom*. Harlow, UK: Pearson, 2011.
Ades, Avraham Hayim. *Sefer 'Eruv ke-hilkhato: kolel: dine reshiyot shabat, hafekhat reshuyot li-reshut ha-yahid, tsurat petah, 'eruv hatserot*. Jerusalem: Avraham Hayim ben Daniyel 'Ades, 2005.
Adler, Rachel. *Engendering Judaism: An Inclusive Theology and Ethics*. Boston: Beacon, 1999.
Albeck, Chanoch, and J. Theodor, eds. *Bereschit Rabba*. 3 vols. Berlin: Akademie Verlag, 1912–1929.
Albeck, Chanoch, and Henoch Yalon ed. and vocalization. *Shishah Sidre Mishnah*. Jerusalem: Mosad Bialik, 1952.
Alexander, Elizabeth Shanks. *Transmitting Mishnah: The Shaping Influence of Oral Tradition*. Cambridge: Cambridge University Press, 2006.
Ariew, Roger, and Eric Watkins, eds. *Readings in Modern Philosophy: Volume I: Descartes, Spinoza, Leibniz and Associated Texts*. Indianapolis: Hackett, 2000.
Asad, Talal, ed. *Anthropology and the Colonial Encounter*. London: Ithaca Press, 1973.
Assmann, Jan. "The Mosaic Distinction: Israel Egypt and the Invention of Paganism." *Representations* 56 (1996): 48–67.
Badiou, Alain. "Discussion Argumentée avec Ivan Segré." *Lignes* 30, no. 3 (2009): 201–6.
———. *Polemics*. Translated by Steve Corcoran. London: Verso, 2006.
Baer, Yitshaq. "Talmud Torah vederekh erets." *Bar-Ilan Annual* 2 (1964): 134–62.
Bakan, Michael. *Music of Death and New Creation: Experiences in the World of Balinese Gamelan Beleganjur*. Chicago: University of Chicago Press, 1999.
Bakhtin, Mikhail. *The Dialogic Imagination: Four Essays*. Edited by Michael Holquist. Translated by Caryl Emerson and Michael Holquist. Austin: University of Texas Press, 2008.
———. *Problems of Dostoevsky's Poetics*. Translated by Caryl Emerson. Minneapolis: University of Minnesota Press, 1984.

Barer, Deborah. "Law, Ethics, and Hermeneutics: A Literary Approach to *Lifnim Mi-shurat Ha-din*." *Journal of Textual Reasoning* 10, no. 1 (2018): 1–14.
Bar Ilan Responsa Project. *Responsa Project Database*. Ramat Gan: Bar-Ilan University, 2007.
Batnitzky, Leora, and Yonatan Y. Brafman, eds. *Jewish Legal Theories: Writings on State, Religion, and Morality*. Waltham, MA: Brandeis University Press, 2018.
Becker, Hans-Jürgen, and Christoph Berner. *Avot de-Rabbi Natan: Synoptische Edition beider Versionen*. Tübingen, Germany: Mohr Siebeck, 2006.
Belser, Julia Watts. *Power, Ethics, and Ecology in Jewish Late Antiquity: Rabbinic Responses to Drought and Disaster*. Cambridge: Cambridge University Press, 2015.
Benjamin, Walter. "On the Language of Man, and Language as Such." In *Walter Benjamin: Selected Writings*, edited by Howard Eiland and Michael Jennings, 1:62–74. 4 vols. Cambridge, MA: Harvard University Press, 2004–2006.
———. "The Task of the Translator." In *Illuminations*, translated by Harry Zohn, 69–82. New York: Schocken, 2007.
Ben-Menahem, Hanina. "Is There Always One Uniquely Correct Answer to a Legal Question in the Talmud?" *Jewish Law Annual* 13 (1987): 164–78.
Ben-Menahem, Hanina, N. S. Hecht, and S. Wosner. *Controversy and Dialogue in the Halakhic Sources*. Boston: Boston University School of Law, 1991.
Benveniste, Émile, and Elizabeth Palmer. "Religion and Superstition." In *Dictionary of Indo-European Concepts and Society*, translated by Elizabeth Palmer, 526–37. Chicago: Hau Books, 2016.
Berkovits, Eliezer. *Not in Heaven: The Nature and Function of Jewish Law*. New York: KTAV, 1983.
Berkowitz, Roger. *The Gift of Science: Leibniz and the Modern Legal Tradition*. New York: Fordham University Press, 2010.
Biale, David. *Gershom Scholem: Kabbalah and Counter-History*. Cambridge, MA: Harvard University Press, 1982.
———. *Not in the Heavens: Tradition of Jewish Secular Thought*. Princeton, NJ: Princeton University Press, 2011.
Bielik-Robson, Agata. *The Saving Lie: Harold Bloom and Deconstruction*. Evanston, IL: Northwestern University Press, 2011.
Blau, Yosef, ed. *Lomdus: The Conceptual Approach to Jewish Learning*. Jersey City, NJ: KTAV, 2006.
Bloom, Harold. *The Anxiety of Influence: A Theory of Poetry*. New Haven, CT: Yale University Press, 1997.
Blumenberg, Hans. *The Legitimacy of the Modern Age*. Translated by Robert M. Wallace. Cambridge, MA: MIT Press, 1985.
Boyarin, Daniel. *Carnal Israel: Reading Sex in Talmudic Culture*. Berkeley: University of California Press, 1993.
———. "Internal Opposition in Talmudic Literature: The Case of the Married Monk." *Representations* 36 (1991): 87–113.
———. *Intertextuality and the Reading of Midrash*. Bloomington: Indiana University Press, 1994.
———. *Socrates and the Fat Rabbis*. Chicago: University of Chicago Press, 2009.
———. *Sparks of the Logos: Essays in Rabbinic Hermeneutics*. Leiden: Brill, 2003.
———. *A Traveling Homeland: The Babylonian Talmud as Diaspora*. Philadelphia: University of Pennsylvania Press, 2015.

Brafman, Yonatan Y. "'The Objectifying Instrument of Religious Consciousness': Halakhic Norms as Expression and Discipline in Soloveitchik's Thought." *Diné Israel* 32 (2018): 1–38.
Brandt, Reinhard. *Kritischer Kommentar zu Kants Anthropologie in pragmatischer Hinsicht (1798)*. Hamburg, Germany: Meiner, 1999.
Briata, Ilaria. "Derek Ereṣ Rabbah e Derek Ereṣ Zuṭa: Due trattati deuterotalmudici su come si sta al mondo." PhD diss., Ca'Foscari, Venice, 2015.
Brock, Sebastian. "The Two Ways and the Palestinian *Targum*." In *A Tribute To Geza Vermes*, edited by Philip R. Davies and Richard T. White, 139–52. Sheffield, UK: Sheffield Academic Press, 2009.
Brodsky, David. "From Disagreement to Talmudic Discourse: Progymnasmata and the Evolution of a Rabbinic Genre." In *Rabbinic Traditions between Palestine and Babylonia*, edited by T. Ilan and R. Nikolsky, 173–231. Leiden: Brill, 2014.
Brody, Robert. *The Geonim of Babylonia and the Shaping of Medieval Jewish Culture*. New Haven, CT: Yale University Press, 2013.
Büchler, Adolph. *Types of Jewish-Palestinian Piety from 70 B.C.E. to 70 C.E.: The Ancient Pious Men*. New York: KTAV, 1968.
Buffière, Felix. *Les Mythes de Homère et la pensée grecque*. Paris: Les Belles Lettres, 1973.
Burnett, Stephen. *From Christian Hebraism to Jewish Studies: Johannes Buxtorf (1564–1629) and Hebrew Learning in the Seventeenth Century*. Leiden: Brill, 1996.
Burnyeat, Myles. "Enthymeme: Aristotle on the Logic of Persuasion." In *Aristotle's Rhetoric: Philosophical Essays*, edited by David Furley and Alexander Nehamas, 3–56. Princeton, NJ: Princeton University Press, 1994.
Carlebach, Elisheva. *Divided Souls: Converts from Judaism in Germany, 1500–1750*. New Haven, CT: Yale University Press, 2001.
Chazan, Robert. *Daggers of Faith: Thirteenth-Century Christian Missionizing and Jewish Response*. Berkeley: University of California Press, 1989.
Chrysostom, John. *The Fathers of the Church: St. John Chrysostom, Homilies on Genesis 18–45*. Translated by Robert C. Hill. Washington, DC: Catholic University of America Press, 1990.
Clark, David. "Kant's Aliens: The 'Anthropology' and Its Others." *CR: The New Centennial Review* 1, no. 2 (2001): 201–89.
Cohen, Alix. *Kant and the Human Sciences: Biology, Anthropology, and History*. London: Palgrave, 2018.
Cohen, Aryeh. *Rereading Talmud: Gender, Law and the Poetics of Sugyot*. Atlanta: Scholars' Press, 1998.
Cohen, Barak S. *The Legal Methodology of Late Nehardean Sages in Sasanian Babylonia*. Leiden: Brill, 2011.
Cohen, Hermann. *Reason and Hope: Selections from the Jewish Writings of Hermann Cohen*. Translated by Eva Jospe. New York: W. W. Norton, 1971.
Cohen, Jeremy. *The Friars and the Jews: The Evolution of Medieval Anti-Judaism*. Ithaca, NY: Cornell University Press, 1982.
———. *Living Letters of the Law: Ideas of the Jew in Medieval Christianity*. Berkeley: University of California Press, 1999.
———. "Review Article: Revisiting Augustine's Doctrine of Jewish Witness." *Journal of Religion* 89, no. 4 (2009): 564–78.
Coudert, Allison P., and Jeffrey S. Shoulson, eds. *Hebraica Veritas? Christian Hebraists and the Study of Judaism in Early Modern Europe*. Philadelphia: University of Pennsylvania Press, 2004.

Cousineau, Jennifer. "Rabbinic Urbanism in London: Rituals and the Material Culture of the Sabbath." *Jewish Social Studies* 11, no. 3 (2005): 36–57.
Dancy, Jonathan. *Ethics without Principles*. Oxford: Oxford University Press, 2004.
Debaene, Vincent. *Far Afield: French Anthropology between Science and Literature*. Chicago: University of Chicago Press, 2014.
Derrida, Jacques. *Acts of Religion*. Edited by Gil Anidjar. New York: Routledge, 2002.
———. *Dissemination*. Translated by Barbara Johnson. Chicago: University of Chicago Press, 1981.
———. *Specters of Marx: The State of Debt, the Work of Mourning, and the New International*. Translated by Peggy Kamuf. London: Routledge, 1994.
Derrida, Jacques, and Avital Ronell. "The Law of Genre." *Critical Inquiry* 7, no. 1 (1980): 55–81.
Descartes, René. *Meditations on the First Philosophy*. Translated by Michael Moriarty. Oxford: Oxford University Press, 2008.
———. *Philosophical Writings of Descartes*. Translated by John Cottingham, Robert Stoothoff, and Dugald Murdoch. 2 vols. Cambridge: Cambridge University Press, 1985.
Descola, Philippe. *Par-delà nature et culture*. Paris: Éditions Gallimard, 2005.
Detienne, Marcel, Pierre Vidal-Naquet, and Janet Lloyd. *The Masters of Truth in Archaic Greece*. New York: Zone Books, 1996.
Diem, Gudrun. "Deutsche Schulanthropologie." In *De Homine: Der Mensch im Spiegel seines Gedankens*, edited by M. Landmann, 357–419. Freiburg, Germany: Alber, 1962.
Dolgopolski, Sergey. "Constructed and Denied: 'The Talmud' from the Brisker Rav to the Mishneh Torah." In *Encountering the Medieval in Modern Jewish Thought*, edited by James A. Diamond and Aaron W. Hughes, 177–200. Leiden: Brill, 2012.
———. "How Else Can One Think Earth?: The Talmuds and Pre-Socratics." In *Heidegger and Jewish Thought: Difficult Others*, edited by E. Lapidot and M. Brumlik, 221–44. London: Rowman & Littlefield, 2017.
———. *Other Others: The Political after the Talmud*. New York: Fordham University Press, 2018.
———. *What Is Talmud?: The Art of Disagreement*. New York: Fordham University Press, 2009.
Dunkelgrün, Theodor. "The Christian Study of Judaism in Early Modern Europe." In *The Cambridge History of Judaism*, vol. 7, edited by Jonathan Karp and Adam Sutcliffe, 316–48. Cambridge: Cambridge University Press, 2017.
Ehrlich, Uri. "Asking Leave (*netilat reshut*) and Granting of Leave (*haftara*), A Chapter in the Laws of *Derekh Erets*." [In Hebrew.] In *Shefa Tal: Studies in Jewish Thought and Culture Presented to Bracha Sack*, edited by Howard Theodore Kreisel and Boaz Huss, 13–26. Beer Sheva, Israel: Ben-Gurion University Press, 2004.
———. *The Non-Verbal Language of Prayer*. [In Hebrew.] Jerusalem: Magnes Press, 2003.
———. "Verbal and Non-Verbal Rituals of Leave-Taking in Rabbinic Culture: Phenomenology and Significance." *Jewish Studies Quarterly* 8, no. 1 (2001): 1–26.
Elman, Yaakov. "A Tale of Two Cities: Mahoza and Pumbedita as Representing Two Halakhic Cultures." In *Torah Le-Shamma: Essays in Jewish Studies in Honor of Professor Shamma Friedman*, edited by David Golinkin, 3–38. Jerusalem: Schechter Institute, 2007.
Epstein, Y. N., and E. Z. Melammed. *Mekhilta deRabbi Shimeon bar Yoḥai*. Jerusalem: Mekitse Nirdamim, 1954.
Fagenblat, Michael. *A Covenant of Creatures: Levinas' Philosophy of Judaism*. Stanford, CA: Stanford University Press, 2010.

Finkelstein, Louis. *Sifre on Deuteronomy*. [In Hebrew.] New York: Jewish Theological Seminary, 1993.
Fisch, Menachem. *Rational Rabbis: Science and Talmudic Culture*. Bloomington: Indiana University Press, 1997.
Fischel, Henry A. "Greek and Latin Languages, Rabbinical Knowledge of." In *Encyclopedia Judaica*, vol. 8, edited by Fred Skolnik, 56–59. Jerusalem: Keter, 2007.
Flusser, David. "Ezohi derekh yesharah sheyavor lo ha-'adam?" *Tarbiz* 60, no. 2 (1991): 163–78.
Fonrobert, Charlotte. "From Separatism to Urbanism: The Dead Sea Scrolls and the Origins of the Rabbinic Eruv." *Dead Sea Discoveries* 11, no. 1 (2004): 43–71.
———. "Gender Politics in the Rabbinic Neighborhood: Tractate Eruvin." In *Introduction to the Feminist Talmud Commentary—Seder Moed*, edited by Tal Ilan, Tamara Or, Dorothea M. Salzer, Christiane Steuer, and Irina Wanderey, 43–60. Tübingen, Germany: Mohr Siebeck, 2007.
———. *Menstrual Purity: Rabbinic and Christian Reconstructions of Biblical Gender*. Stanford, CA: Stanford University Press, 2000.
———. "Neighborhood as Ritual Space: The Case of the Rabbinic Eruv." *Archiv für Religionsgeschichte* 10 (2008): 239–58.
———. "The Political Symbolism of the Eruv." *Jewish Social Studies* 5, no. 3 (2005): 9–35.
———. "Regulating the Human Body: Rabbinic Legal Discourse and the Making of Jewish Gender." In *The Cambridge Companion to the Talmud and Rabbinic Literature*, edited by C. Fonrobert and M. Jaffee, 270–94. Cambridge: Cambridge University Press, 2007.
Foucault, Michel. *Anthropologie d'un point de vue pragmatique précédé de l'Introduction à l'Anthropologie*. Edited by D. Defert, Fr. Ewald, and F. Gros. Paris: Vrin, 2008.
Frank, David. "Arguing with God, Talmudic Discourse, and the Jewish Countermodel: Implications for the Study of Argumentation." *Argumentation and Advocacy* 41, no. 2 (2004): 71–86.
Frank, Yitzhak. *A Practical Talmud Dictionary*. Jerusalem: Maggid Press, 1991.
Franks, Paul W. *All or Nothing: Systematicity, Transcendental Arguments, and Skepticism in German Idealism*. Cambridge, MA: Harvard University Press, 2005.
Fredriksen, Paula. *Augustine and the Jews: A Christian Defense of Jews and Judaism*. New Haven, CT: Yale University Press, 2010.
Freedman, Harry, ed. *Midrash Rabbah*. 10 vols. New York: Soncino Press, 1983.
Friedman, Shamma. "Pereq Ha-Isha Rabba in the Babylonian Talmud: A Critical Study of Yevamot X with a Methodological Introduction." [In Hebrew.] In *Texts and Studies, Analecta Judaica*, vol. 1, edited by Hayyim Zalman Dimitrovsky, 275–441. New York: Jewish Theological Seminary of America, 1977.
Frye, Charles. "Carl Schmitt's Concept of the Political." *Journal of Politics* 28, no. 4 (1966): 818–30.
Funkenstein, Amos. *Perceptions of Jewish History*. Berkeley: University of California Press, 1993.
Furstenberg, Ariel. *The Languages of Talmudic Discourse: A Philosophical Study of the Evolution of Amoraic Halakha*. [In Hebrew.] Jerusalem: Magnes Press, 2017.
Furstenberg, Yair. "The Rabbinic View of Idolatry and the Roman Political Conception of Divinity." *Journal of Religion* 90, no. 3 (2001): 335–66.
Gasché, Rodolphe. "Saturnine Vision and the Question of Difference: Reflections on Walter Benjamin's Theory of Language." *Studies in 20th Century Literature* 11, no. 1 (1986): 69–90.

Gibbs, Robert. "Disagree, for God's Sake! Jewish Philosophy, Truth and the Future of Dialogue." Address presented at the Celebration for the New Polonsky-Coexist Lectureship in Jewish Studies, Faculty of Divinity, Cambridge, UK, February 24, 2011. https://www.interfaith.cam.ac.uk/resources/lecturespapersandspeeches/disagreeforgodssake.

Gibbs, Robert, and Peter Ochs. "Gold and Silver: Philosophical Talmud." In *Textual Reasonings: Jewish Philosophy and Text Study at the End of the Twentieth Century*, edited by Peter Ochs and Nancy Levene, 90–102. Grand Rapids, MI: Eerdmans, 2002.

Ginzburg, Carlo. "Just One Witness: The Extermination of the Jews and the Principle of Reality." In *Threads and Traces: True, False, Fictive*, translated by Anne Tedeschi and John Tedeschi, 165–79. Berkeley: University of California Press, 2012.

Goldberg, Abraham. *The Mishnah Treatise Eruvin: Critically Edited and Provided with Introduction, Commentary and Notes*. [In Hebrew.] Jerusalem: Magnes Press, 1986.

Golling, Ralf, and Peter von der Osten-Sacken. *Herman L. Strack und das Institutum Judaicum in Berlin*. Berlin: Institut Kirche und Judentum, 1996.

Graband, Claudia. *Klugheit bei Kant*. Berlin: de Gruyter, 2015.

Grafton, Anthony, and Joanna Weinberg. *"I Have Always Loved the Holy Tongue": Isaac Casaubon, the Jews, and a Forgotten Chapter in Renaissance Scholarship*. Cambridge, MA: Harvard University Press, 2011.

Granel, Gérard. *Traditionis Traditio*. Paris: Gallimard, 1972.

Gross, Aaron S. *The Question of the Animal and Religion: Theoretical Stakes, Practical Implications*. New York: Columbia University Press, 2014.

Gross, Raphael. *Carl Schmitt und die Juden: Eine deutsche Rechtslehre*. Frankfurt: Suhrkamp Taschenbuch, 2000.

Guggenheimer, Heinrich W., trans. *The Jerusalem Talmud*. 17 vols. New York: de Gruyter, 2000–2020.

Gusterson, Hugh. "Anthropology and Militarism." *Annual Review of Anthropology* 36 (2007): 155–75.

Gvaryahu, Amit. "A New Reading of the Three Dialogues in Mishnah *Avodah Zarah*." *Jewish Studies Quarterly* 19, no. 3 (2012): 207–29.

Hahn, Tomie. *Sensational Knowledge: Embodying Culture through Japanese Dance*. Middletown, CT: Wesleyan University Press, 2007.

Halberstam, Chaya. *Law and Truth in Biblical and Rabbinic Literature*. Bloomington: Indiana University Press, 2010.

Halbertal, Moshe. *The Birth of Doubt: Confronting Uncertainty in Early Rabbinic Literature*. Providence, RI: Brown University Press, 2020.

———. "Coexisting with the Enemy: Jews and Pagans in the Mishnah." In *Tolerance and Intolerance in Early Judaism and Christianity*, edited by Graham N. Stanton and Guy S. Stroumsa, 159–72. Cambridge: Cambridge University Press, 1998.

———. "The Limits of Prayer." *Jewish Review of Books* 2 (2010). https://jewishreviewofbooks.com/articles/250/the-limits-of-prayer/.

Halivni, David Weiss. *The Formation of the Babylonian Talmud*. Translated by Jeffrey Rubenstein. New York: Oxford University Press, 2013.

Hamacher, Werner. "Intensive Languages." *MLN* 127, no. 3 (2012): 485–541.

Handelman, Susan. *Slayers of Moses: The Emergence of the Rabbinic Interpretation in Modern Literary Theory*. Albany: SUNY Press, 1983.

Hanna, Robert. "Kant's Theory of Judgment." In *Stanford Encyclopedia of Philosophy* (Winter 2017 Edition), edited by Edward N. Zalta. https://plato.stanford.edu/archives/win2017/entries/kant-judgment/.

Hanssen, Beatrice. "Language and Mimesis in Walter Benjamin's Work." In *The Cambridge Companion to Walter Benjamin*, edited by D. S. Ferris, 54–72. Cambridge: Cambridge University Press, 2004.
Haraway, Donna J. "Situated Knowledges: The Science Question in Feminism and the Privilege of Partial Perspective." *Feminist Studies* 14, no. 3 (1988): 575–99.
Harris, Jay M. *How Do We Know This? Midrash and the Fragmentation of Modern Judaism*. Albany: SUNY Press, 1996.
Hayes, Christine. *Between the Babylonian and Palestinian Talmuds: Accounting for Halakhic Differences in Selected Sugyot from Tractate Avodah Zarah*. New York: Oxford University Press, 1997.
Hayyim of Volozhin. *Nefesh Hahayyim*. Bnei Brak, Israel: Mekhon le-'Arichat Sefarim, 1989.
Hertz, Joseph Herman. *Pirke Avot*. Springfield, NJ: Behrman House, 1986.
Hesni, Samia. "How to Disrupt a Social Script." *Journal of the American Philosophical Association* 10 (2024): 24–45. https://doi.org/10.1017/apa.2023.10.
———. "Normative Generics and Social Kind Terms." *Inquiry: An Interdisciplinary Journal of Philosophy* (February 3, 2022). https://doi.org/10.1080/0020174X.2022.2032323.
Hezser, Catherine. *Jewish Travel in Antiquity*. Tübingen, Germany: Mohr Siebeck, 2011.
Hidary, Richard. "Classical Rhetorical Arrangement and Reasoning in the Talmud: The Case of Yerushalmi Berakhot 1:1." *AJS Review* 43, no. 1 (2010): 33–64.
———. *Dispute for the Sake of Heaven: Legal Pluralism in the Talmud*. Providence, RI: Brown Judaic Studies, 2010.
———. "A Proposal for a New Translation and Commentary of the Mishnah, Yerushalmi and Bavli: The First Sugya of Sanhedrin Chapter 4, 'From Judicial Discretion to Redemption.'" Unpublished manuscript.
———. *Rabbis and Classical Rhetoric: Sophistic Education and Oratory in the Talmud and Midrash*. Cambridge: Cambridge University Press, 2017.
Higger, Michael. *Massekhtot Kallah*. New York: JTS, 1936.
———. *Masektot Ze'irot*. Jerusalem: Maqor, 1969.
———. *Treatise Semaḥot and Treatise Semaḥot of R. Ḥiyya and Sefer Ḥibbut ha-Ḳeber and Additions to the Seven Minor Treatises and to Treatise Soferim II*. [In Hebrew.] New York: JTS, 1931.
———. *The Treatises Derek Erez: Masseket Derek Erez, Pirke Ben Azzai, Tosefta Derek Erez*. [In Hebrew.] New York: Debe Rabanan, 1935.
Himma, Kenneth Einar. "Inclusive Legal Positivism." In *The Oxford Handbook of Jurisprudence and Philosophy of Law*, edited by Jules Coleman and Scott Shapiro, 125–65. Oxford: Oxford University Press, 2004.
Himmelfarb, Martha. *A Kingdom of Priests: Ancestry and Merit in Ancient Judaism*. Philadelphia: University of Pennsylvania Press, 2006.
Hodder, Ian. "The Entanglements of Humans and Things: A Long-Term View." *New Literary History* 45, no. 1 (2014): 19–36.
Hoffman, David. *Midrasch Tannaïm (Midrasch Tannaïm Zum Deuteronomium)*. 2 vols. Berlin: H. Itzkowski-M. Poppelauer, 1908.
Irshai, Ronit. "Toward a Gender Critical Approach to the Philosophy of Jewish Law (Halakhah)." *Journal of Feminist Studies in Religion* 26, no. 2 (2010): 55–77.
Jacobs, Louis. *Studies in Talmudic Logic and Methodology*. London: Vallentine Mitchell, 1961.
———. *The Talmudic Argument: A Study in Talmudic Reasoning and Methodology*. New York: Cambridge University Press, 1984.
Jadler, Isak Wolf, ed. *Sefer Midrash Rabbah*. Bene Berak: Tiferet Tsiyon, 1963.

Jaffee, Martin S. "Halakhic Personhood: The Existential Hermeneutic of *Worship and Ethics*." In *Understanding the Rabbinic Mind: Essays on the Hermeneutic of Max Kadushin*, edited by Peter Ochs, 95–112. Atlanta: Scholars' Press, 1990.

———. "What Difference Does the 'Orality' of Rabbinic Writing Make for the Interpretation of Rabbinic Writings?" In *How Should Rabbinic Literature Be Read in the Modern World?*, edited by Matthew Krauss, 11–34. Piscataway, NJ: Gorgia Press, 2006.

Jastrow, Marcus. *A Dictionary of the Targumim, the Talmud Babli and Yerushalmi, and the Midrashic Literature: With an Index of Scriptural Quotations*. New York: Judaica Press, 1992.

Jonas, Hans. *Gnosis und spätantiker Geist I: Die mythologische Gnosis*. Göttingen, Germany: Vandenhoeck & Ruprecht, 1934.

———. *Gnosis und spätantiker Geist II: Von der Mythologie zur mystischen Philosophie*. Göttingen, Germany: Vandenhoeck & Ruprecht, 1954.

Jørstad, Mari. "The Ground That Opened Its Mouth: The Ground's Response to Human Violence in Genesis 4." *Journal of Biblical Literature* 135, no. 4 (2016): 705–15.

Kadushin, Max. *A Conceptual Approach to the Mekhilta*. New York: JTS, 1969.

———. *A Conceptual Commentary on Midrash Leviticus Rabbah*. Atlanta: Scholars' Press, 1987.

———. *Organic Thinking: A Study in Rabbinic Thought*. New York: Bloch, 1976.

———. *Worship and Ethics: A Study in Rabbinic Judaism*. Evanston, IL: Northwestern University Press, 1964.

Kahana, Menahem I. *Sifre on Numbers: An Annotated Edition*. [In Hebrew.] 4 vols. Jerusalem: Magnes Press, 2011.

———. *The Two Mekhiltot on the Amalek Portion: The Originality of the Version of the Mekhilta d'Rabbi Ishma'el with Respect to the Mekhilta of Rabbi Shim'on ben Yohay*. [In Hebrew.] Jerusalem: Magnes Press, 1999.

Kain, Patrick. "Prudential Reason in Kant's Anthropology." In *Essays on Kant's Anthropology*, edited by Brian Jacobs and Patrick Kain, 230–65. Cambridge: Cambridge University Press, 2003.

Kant, Immanuel. *Anthropology, History, and Education*. Translated by Robert B. Louden. Cambridge: Cambridge University Press, 2007.

———. *Correspondence*. Edited and translated by Arnulf Zweig. Cambridge: Cambridge University Press, 1999.

———. *Die Religion innerhalb der Grenzen der bloßen Vernunft*. Hamburg, Germany: Meiner, 2003.

———. *Groundwork of the Metaphysics of Morals*. Edited and translated by Mary Gregor. Cambridge: Cambridge University Press, 1997.

———. *Lectures on Anthropology*. Edited by Allen W. Wood and Robert B. Louden. Cambridge: Cambridge University Press, 2012.

Kaye, Lynn. *Time in the Babylonian Talmud: Natural and Imagined Times in Jewish Law and Narrative*. Cambridge: Cambridge University Press, 2018.

Kelsen, Hans. *Introduction to the Problems of Legal Theory*. Translated by Bonnie Litschewski Paulson and Stanley L. Paulson. 1934. Reprint, Oxford: Clarendon, 2002.

Kimelman, R. Reuven. "Rabbi Yohanan of Tiberias: Aspects of the Social and Religious History of Third Century Palestine." PhD diss., Yale University, 1977.

Klein, Gil P. "Squaring the City: Between Roman and Rabbinic Urban Geometry." In *Phenomenologies of the City: Studies in the History and Philosophy of Architecture*, edited by Henrietta Steiner and Maximilian Sternberg, 33–48. Manchester: Ashgate, 2015.

———. "Torah in Triclinia: The Rabbinic Banquet and the Significance of Architecture." *Jewish Quarterly Review* 102, no. 3 (2012): 325–70.

Knohl, Israel. "The Priestly Torah Versus the Holiness School: Sabbath and the Festivals." *Hebrew Union College Annual* 58 (1987): 89.

Koppel, Moshe. "Probabilistic Foundations of Rabbinic Methods for Resolving Uncertainty." *Studia Humana* 6, no. 2 (2017): 116–25.

Kosstrin, Hannah. *Honest Bodies: The Revolutionary Dances of Anna Sokolow*. New York: Oxford University Press, 2017.

———. "Kinesthetic Seeing: A Model for Practice-in-Research." In *Futures of Dance Studies*, edited by Susan Manning, Janice Ross, and Rebecca Schneider, 19–35. Madison: University of Wisconsin Press, 2020.

Kraemer, David. *The Mind of the Talmud: An Intellectual History of the Bavli*. New York: Oxford University Press, 1990.

Krauss, Samuel. "Le traité talmudique déréch éréç." *Revue des Etudes Juives* 36 (1898): 27–46.

———. "Le traité talmudique déréch éréç (suite et fin)." *Revue des Etudes Juives* 37 (1898): 45–64.

Kripke, Saul A. *Naming and Necessity*. Cambridge, MA: Harvard University Press, 1972.

Kühn, Manfred. "Interpreting Kant Correctly: On the Kant of the Neo-Kantians." In *Neo-Kantianism in Contemporary Philosophy*, edited by Rudolf A. Makkreel and Sebastian Luft, 113–31. Bloomington: Indiana University Press, 2010.

Kunin, Seth Daniel. *We Think What We Eat: Neo-Structuralist Analysis of Israelite Food Rules and Other Cultural and Textual Practices*. New York: T & T Clark International, 2004.

Labovitz, Gail. *Marriage and Metaphor: Constructions of Gender in Rabbinic Literature*. London: Lexington Books, 2009.

Lacan, Jacques. *On Feminine Sexuality: The Limits of Love and Knowledge*. Edited by Jacques-Allain Miller, translated by Bruce Fink. New York: W. W. Norton, 1998.

LaMothe, Kimerer L. *Between Dancing and Writing: The Practice of Religious Studies*. New York: Fordham University Press, 2004.

Lapidot, Elad. "Deterritorialized Immigrant: The Talmudic Ger and Exilic Yisrael." *Jewish Culture and History* 20 (2019): 23–42.

———. "Gnosis und Spätantiker Geist II: Hans Jonas' The Lost Book." In *Hans Jonas-Handbook*, edited by Michael Bongardt, Holger Burckhart, John-Stewart Gordon, and Jürgen Nielsen-Sikora, 88–95. Stuttgart, Germany: J. B. Metzler, 2021.

———. *Jews Out of the Question: A Critique of Anti-Anti-Semitism*. Albany, NY: SUNY Press, 2020.

———. "Heidegger's Tshuva?" *Heidegger Studies* 32 (2016): 33–52.

———. "On the Translation of Philosophy and תרגום התורה [targum ha-tora] in German." In *Sprache, Erkenntnis und Bedeutung. Deutsch in der jüdischen Wissenskultur*, edited by Arndt Engelhardt and Susanne Zepp, 19–36. Leipzig: Leipziger Universitätsverlag, 2015.

———. "Jew, Uses of the Word." In *Alain Badiou Dictionary*, edited by Steve Corcoran, 162–69. Edinburgh: Edinburgh University Press, 2015.

———. "Prisoner-of-War: Critique of International Humanitarian Law." [In Hebrew.] In *Prisoners of War*, edited by Merav Mack, 151–81. Jerusalem: Van Leer Jerusalem Institute/Zalman Shazar Center, 2014.

Lauterbach, Jacob C. *Mekhilta De-Rabbi Ishmael*. 2 vols. New York: JTS, 2004.

Le Guin, Ursula K. *Always Coming Home*. Berkeley: University of California Press, 1985.

———. "A Message about Messages." *CBC Magazine*, November 28, 2005. https://www.ursulakleguin.com/message-about-messages.

Lehmhaus, Lennart. "'Derekh Eretz im Tora'—Seder Elijahu Zuta als Universale, religiöse Ethik für rabbinische und nicht-rabbinische Juden." PhD diss., Martin-Luther-Universität Halle-Wittenberg, 2013.

Leibniz, G. W. *New Essays on Human Understanding*. Edited by Karl Ameriks and Desmond M. Clarke. Translated by Peter Remnant and Jonathan Bennett. Cambridge: Cambridge University Press, 1996.

———. *Philosophische Schriften*. Vol. 6. Edited by Leibniz-Forschungsstelle der Universitaet. Berlin: Akademie-Verlag, 1999.

Lerner, M. B. "The External Tractates." In *The Literature of the Sages, Part One: Oral Torah, Halakha, Mishna, Tosefta, Talmud, External Tractates*, edited by S. Safrai and Peter J. Tomson, 367–403. Minneapolis: Fortress, 1987.

Levinas, Emmanuel. *Difficult Freedom: Essays on Judaism*. Translated by Seán Hand. Baltimore: Johns Hopkins University Press, 1990.

Levine, Baruch A. *Numbers 21–36: A New Translation with Introduction and Commentary*. New Haven, CT: Yale University Press, 2009.

Lieberman, Saul. *Hayerushalmi Kifeshuto*. Jerusalem: Drom, 1935.

———. *Midrash Devarim Rabbah: Edited for the Time from the Oxford Ms. No. 147 with an Introduction and Notes*. [In Hebrew.] Jerusalem: Wahrmann, 1964.

———. *Tosefta*. [In Hebrew.] 4 vols. New York: JTS, 1955–2001.

———. *Tosefta Kifeshutah: A Comprehensive Commentary on the Tosefta*. [In Hebrew.] 10 vols. New York: JTS, 1955–2001.

Lilienblum, Moshe Leib. *Hata'ot Ne'urim*. 1876. https://maagarim.hebrew-academy.org.il/.

Lorini, Gualtiero. "The Rules for Knowing the Human Being: Baumgarten's Presence in Kant's Anthropology." In *Knowledge, Morals and Practice in Kant's Anthropology*, edited by Gualtiero Lorini and Robert B. Louden, 62–80. New York: Palgrave, 2018.

Louden, Robert B. *Kant's Human Being: Essays on His Theory of Human Nature*. Oxford: Oxford University Press, 2007.

———. *Kant's Impure Ethics: From Rational Beings to Human Beings*. New York: Oxford University Press, 2000.

Luhmann, Niklas. "The Self-Reproduction of Law and Its Limits." In *Dilemmas of Law in the Welfare State*, edited by Gunther Teubner, 111–27. New York: de Gruyter, 1986.

Maccoby, Hyam. *The Philosophy of the Talmud*. London: Routledge Curzon, 2002.

Madrid, Nuria Sánchez. "Prudence and the Rules for Guiding Life: The Development of Pragmatic Normativity in Kant's Lectures on Anthropology." In *Kant's Lectures/Kants Vorlesungen*, edited by von Bernd Dörflinger, Claudio La Rocca, Robert Louden, and Ubirajara Rancan de Azevedo Marques, 163–76. Berlin: de Gruyter, 2015.

Malachi, Eliezer Raphael. *Mineged Tir'eh: Asufa mi-ma'amarei A. R. Malachi be-inyanei erets yisrael*. Edited by Elhanan Reiner and Haggai Ben-Shammai. Jerusalem: Yad Ben-Zvi, 2001.

Mandelbaum, Bernard, ed. *Pesiqta deRav Kahana*. [In Hebrew.] 2 vols. New York: JPS, 1987.

Mann, Jacob. *The Bible as Read and Preached in the Old Synagogue: A Study in the Cycles of the Readings from Torah and Prophets, as Well as from Psalms, and in the Structure of the Midrashic Homilies*. New York: KTAV, 1971.

Mann, Jacob, and Isaiah Sonne. *The Bible as Read and Preached in the Old Synagogue*. Cincinnati: Mann-Sonne, 1940.

Margulies, Mordecai. *Midrash Wayyikra Rabba: A Critical Edition Based on Manuscripts and Geniza Fragments with Variants and Notes*. [In Hebrew.] 5 vols. Jerusalem: Academy for Jewish Research, 1956.

Martyr, Justin. *Dialogue with Trypho, a Jew.* Translated by Marcus Dods and George Reith. Buffalo, NY: Christian Literature, 1885.

Matt, Daniel C., ed. and trans. *The Zohar.* 12 vols. Stanford, CA: Stanford University Press, 2003–2017.

McNickle, D'Arcy. "American Indians Who Never Were." In *The American Indian Reader: Anthropology,* edited by Jeanette Henry, 29–36. San Francisco: Indian Historical Press, 1972.

Medicine, Bea, Alfonso Ortiz, and D'Arcy McNickle. "The Anthropologist: The Man and His Discipline." In *The American Indian Reader: Anthropology,* edited by Jeanette Henry, 1–3. San Francisco: Indian Historical Press, 1972.

Meir, Ofra. *Poetics of Rabbinic Stories.* [In Hebrew.]. Tel-Aviv-Yafo: Sifriat Po'alim, 1993.

Melamed, Yitzhak Y., and Martin Lin. "Principle of Sufficient Reason." In *Stanford Encyclopedia of Philosophy* (Spring 2018 Edition), edited by Edward N. Zalta. https://plato.stanford.edu/archives/spr2018/entries/sufficient-reason/.

Mensch, Jennifer. "Caught Between Character and Race: 'Temperament' in Kant's Lectures on Anthropology." *Australian Feminist Law Journal* 43, no. 1 (2007): 124–44.

Meshel, Naphtali S. *The "Grammar" of Sacrifice: A Generativist Study of the Israelite Sacrificial System in the Priestly Writings, with a "Grammar" of [Sigma].* New York: Oxford University Press, 2014.

———. "Toward a Grammar of Sacrifice: Hierarchic Patterns in the Israelite Sacrificial System." *Journal of Biblical Literature* 132, no. 3 (2013): 549.

Midrash Rabbah Ha-mevo'ar. 17 vols. Jerusalem: Machon ha-Midrash ha-mevoa'ar, 1983–1999.

Midrash Tanḥuma ha-mefo'ar. 2 vols. Jerusalem: Tiferet ha-Sefer, 1993.

Miles, Jack. *God: A Biography.* New York: Knopf, 1995.

Milgrom, Jacob. *Leviticus 1–16.* Vol. 3. *The Anchor Bible.* New York: Doubleday, 1991.

———. *Leviticus 23–27.* New Haven, CT: Yale University Press, 2010.

Miller, Moshe. "Rabbi Samson Raphael Hirsch and Nineteenth Century German Orthodoxy on Judaism's Attitude toward Non-Jews." PhD diss., Yeshiva University, 2014.

Mintz, Adam. *Halakhah in America: The History of City Eruvin, 1894–1962.* PhD diss., New York University, 2011.

Moretti, Franco. *Distant Reading.* Konstanz, Germany: Konstanz University Press, 2016.

Morrison, Toni. "The Site of Memory." In *Inventing the Truth: The Art and Craft of Memoir,* edited by William Zinsser, 183–200. Boston: Houghton Mifflin, 1987.

Moscovitz, Leib. *Talmudic Reasoning: From Casuistics to Conceptualization.* Tübingen, Germany: Mohr Siebeck, 2002.

Moses, Stephane. *System and Revelation: The Philosophy of Franz Rosenzweig.* Detroit: Wayne State University Press, 1992.

Munk, Reinier. *The Rationale of Halakhic Man: Joseph B. Soloveitchik's Conception of Jewish Thought.* Amsterdam: Gieben, 1966.

Munzel, G. Felicitas. *Kant's Conception of Moral Character: The "Critical" Link of Morality, Anthropology, and Reflective Judgment.* Chicago: University of Chicago Press, 1999.

Nails, Debra. "Mouthpiece Schmouthpiece." In *Who Speaks for Plato? Studies in Platonic Anonymity,* edited by Gerald Press, 15–26. Lanham, MD: Rowman and Littlefield, 2000.

Naiweld, Ron. "The Organization of Religious Signs and the Imperial Mind of Some Early Rabbis." *Images Re-vues* n.s. 6 (2018). https://journals.openedition.org/imagesrevues/4378.

———. "The Rabbinic Model of Sovereignty in Biblical and Imperial Contexts." In *Legal Engagement: The Reception of Roman Law and Tribunals by Jews and Other Inhabitants of the Empire,* edited by Katell Berthelot, Natalie Dohrmann, and Capucine Nemo-Pekelman, 409–28. Rome: Publications de l'École française de Rome, 2021.

Nancy, Jean-Luc. *A Finite Thinking*. Edited by Simon Sparks. Stanford, CA: Stanford University Press, 2003.
Neusner, Jacob. *Genesis Rabbah: The Judaic Commentary to the Book of Genesis*. Atlanta: Scholars' Press, 1985.
Neusner, Jacob, and Bruce Chilton. *The Intellectual Foundations of Christian and Jewish Discourse: The Philosophy of Religious Argument*. London: Routledge, 1997.
Nightingale, Andrea Wilson. *Genres in Dialogue: Plato and the Construct of Philosophy*. Cambridge: Cambridge University Press, 1995.
Nihan, Christophe. "Israel's Festival Calendars in Leviticus 23, Numbers 28–29 and the Formation of 'Priestly' Literature." In *The Book of Leviticus and Numbers*, edited by Thomas Römer, 177–231. Leuven: Uitgeverij Peeters, 2008.
Nirenberg, David. *Anti-Judaism: The Western Tradition*. New York: W. W. Norton, 2014.
Novak, David. *The Image of the Non-Jew in Judaism: The Idea of Noahide Law*. Liverpool: Liverpool University Press, 2011.
———. "Judaism and Natural Law." *American Journal of Jurisprudence* 43 no. 1 (1998): 117–34.
———. "Natural Law and Judaism." In *Natural Law: A Jewish, Christian, & Islamic Trialogue*. Oxford: Oxford University Press, 2014.
———. *Natural Law in Judaism*. Cambridge: Cambridge University Press, 1998.
Novick, Tzvi. "Naming Normativity: The Early History of the Terms ŠÛRAT HA-DÎN and LIFNÎM MIŠ-ŠÛRAT HA-DÎN." *Journal of Semitic Studies* 60, no. 2 (2010): 391–406.
———. *What Is Good, and What God Demands: Normative Structures in Tannaitic Literature*. Leiden: Brill, 2010.
Ochs, Peter, and Nancy Levene. *Textual Reasonings: Jewish Philosophy and Text Study at the End of the Twentieth Century*. Grand Rapids, MI: Eerdmans, 2003.
Ophir, Adi, and Ishay Rosen-Zvi. *Goy: Israel's Multiple Others and the Birth of the Gentile*. Oxford: Oxford University Press, 2018.
Paz, Yakir. "From Scribes to Scholars: Rabbinic Biblical Exegesis in Light of the Homeric Commentaries." [In Hebrew.] PhD diss., Hebrew University, 2014.
———. "Re-Scripturizing Traditions: Designating Dependence in Rabbinic Halakhic Midrashim and Homeric Scholarship." In *Homer and the Bible in the Eyes of Ancient Interpreters*, edited by Maren R. Niehoff, 269–98. Leiden: Brill, 2012.
Peirce, Charles S. *Collected Papers of Charles Sanders Peirce*. Cambridge, MA: Harvard University Press, 1931.
Plato. *Plato, with an English Translation. Euthyphro, Apology, Crito, Phaedo, Phaedrus*. Translated by Harold North Fowler. Vol. 1. LCL. London: William Heinemann, 1914.
Pollack, Benjamin. *Franz Rosenzweig and the Systematic Task of Philosophy*. Cambridge: Cambridge University Press, 2009.
Pozzo, Riccardo. "Kant on the Five Intellectual Virtues." In *The Impact of Aristotelianism on Modern Philosophy*, edited by Riccardo Pozzo, 173–92. Washington, DC: Catholic University of America Press, 2002.
Qimron, Elisha. *The Temple Scroll: A Critical Edition with Extensive Reconstructions*. Beer Sheva, Israel: Ben Gurion University of the Negev Press, 1996.
Raz, Joseph. *The Authority of Law: Essays on Law and Morality*. Oxford: Oxford University Press, 1979.
———. *Practical Reason and Norms*. Oxford: Oxford University Press, 1999.
Raz-Krakotzkin, Amnon. *The Censor, the Editor, and the Text: The Catholic Church and the Shaping of the Jewish Canon in the Sixteenth Century*. Translated by Jackie Feldman. Philadelphia: University of Pennsylvania Press, 2007.

———. *Toda'at Mishnah, Toda'at Mikra: Tzfat ve-Hatarbut Hatziyonit*. Jerusalem: Van Leer Publishing and Hakibutz Hameuhad, 2022.
Redfield, James Adam. "Review of *Goy: Israel's Multiple Others and the Birth of the Gentile*." *Reading Religion*. https://readingreligion.org/9780198744900/goy/.
———. "The Sages and the World: Categorizing Culture in Early Rabbinic Law." PhD diss., Stanford University, 2017.
Rosen-Zvi, Ishay. "Orality, Narrative, Rhetoric: New Directions in Mishnah Research." *AJS Review* 32, no. 2 (2008): 235–49.
———. "Structure and Reflectivity in Tannaitic Legal Homilies, Or: How to Read Midrashic Terminology." *Prooftexts* 34 (2014): 271–301.
Rosenzweig, Franz. *Star of Redemption*. Translated by Barbara Galli. Madison: University of Wisconsin Press, 2005.
Rubenstein, Jeffrey L. "The Explanation of Tannaitic Sources by Abstract Concepts." In *Neti'ot Le-David: Jubilee Volume for David Weiss Halivni*, edited by Yaakov Elman, Ephraim Bezalel Halivni, and Zvi Arie Steinfeld, 275–304. Jerusalem: Orhot, 2004.
———. "On Some Abstract Concepts in Rabbinic Literature." *Jewish Studies Quarterly* 4 (1997): 33–73.
———. *Talmudic Stories: Narrative Art, Composition, and Culture*. Baltimore: Johns Hopkins University Press, 1999.
Safrai, Shmuel. "Ḥasidim ve'anshe ma'aseh." *Zion* 50, no. 1 (1985): 133–54.
———. *In Times of Temple and Mishnah: Studies in Jewish History*. [In Hebrew.] Jerusalem: Magnes Press, 1994.
———. "Muvano shel ha-munaḥ 'derekh erets.'" *Tarbiz* 60, no. 2 (1991): 147–62.
———. "Teaching of Pietists in Mishnaic Literature." *Journal of Jewish Studies* 16 (1965): 15–33.
Safrai, S., and Z. Safrai, eds. *Haggadah of the Sages*. Jerusalem: Carta, 2009.
Safrai, Zeev. *The Economy of Roman Palestine*. London: Routledge, 1994.
Sagi, Abraham (Avi). "Ha-Mitzvah Ha-Datit ve-Ha-Ma'arekhet Ha-Mishpatit: Perek Be-Haguto Ha-Hilkhatit Shel Ha-Rav Shimon Shkop." *Da'at* 35 (1995): 99–114.
Saiman, Chaim N. *Halakhah: The Rabbinic Idea of Law*. Princeton, NJ: Princeton University Press, 2018.
———. "Legal Theology: The Turn to Conceptualism in Nineteenth Century Jewish Law." *Journal of Law and Religion* 21, no. 1 (2006): 39–100.
Schaefer, Donovan O. *Religious Affects: Animality, Evolution, and Power*. Durham, NC: Duke University Press, 2015.
Schäfer, Peter. *Jesus in the Talmud*. Princeton, NJ: Princeton University Press, 2009.
Schick, Shana Strauch. *Intention in Jewish Law: Between Thought and Deed*. Boston: Brill, 2021.
———. "Negligence and Strict Liability in the Babylonian and Palestinian Talmuds: Two Competing Systems of Tort Law in the Rulings of Early Amoraim." *Dine Israel* 29 (2013): 139–76.
———. "Reading Aristotle in Mahoza? Actions and Intentions in Rava's Jurisprudence." *Jewish Law Association Studies* 25 (2014): 262–91.
Schiffman, Lawrence H. *The Courtyards of the House of the Lord*. Leiden: Brill, 2008.
Schiffman, Lawrence H., and Andrew Gross. *The Temple Scroll: 11Q19, 11Q21, 11Q22, 4Q524, 5Q21 with 4Q365a*. Vol. 1. Dead Sea Scrolls Editions. Leiden: Brill, 2021.
Schiffman, Pinhas. "Ha-safeq be-halakhah u-ve-mishpat." *Jewish Law Annual* 1 (1974): 328–52.
Schmitt, Carl. *Der Begriff des Politischen: Text von 1932 mit einem Vorwort und drei Corollarien*. Berlin: Duncker & Humblot, 2015.

———. *Der Nomos der Erde im Völkerrecht des Jus Publicum Europaeum*. Berlin: Duncker & Humblot, 2011.
———. *Politische Theologie: Vier Kapitel zur Lehre von der Souveränität*. Berlin: Duncker & Humblot, 2009.
———. *Politische Theologie II: Die Legende von der Erledigung jeder politischen Theologie*. Berlin: Duncker & Humblot, 2017.
———. *Römischer Katholizismus und politische Form*. Stuttgart, Germany: Klett-Cota, 2016.
Schofer, Jonathan Wyn. *Confronting Vulnerability: The Body and the Divine in Rabbinic Ethics*. Chicago: University of Chicago Press, 2010.
Scholem, Gershom. *Es gibt Geheimnis in der Welt*. Frankfurt: Suhrkamp Taschenbuch, 2002.
———. *On Jews and Judaism in Crisis: Selected Essays*. Edited by Werner Dannhauser. New York: Schocken, 1976.
———. *On the Kabbalah and Its Symbolism*. New York: Schocken, 1965.
———. *The Messianic Idea in Judaism and Other Essays on Jewish Spirituality*. New York: Schocken, 1995.
Schwartz, Baruch. "The Pentateuchal Sources and the Former Prophets: A Neo-Documentarian's Perspective." In *The Formation of the Pentateuch: Bridging the Academic Cultures of Europe, Israel, and North America*, edited by Jan C. Gertz, Bernard M. Levinson, Dalit Rom-Shiloni, and Konrad Schmid, 795–812. Tübingen, Germany: Mohr Siebeck, 2016.
Secunda, Shai. *The Iranian Talmud: Reading the Bavli in Its Sasanian Context*. Philadelphia: University of Pennsylvania Press, 2013.
Segal, Moshe Zvi. *Sefer Ben Sira ha-Shalem*. Jerusalem: Mosad Bialik, 1958.
Segré, Ivan. "Controverse sur la question de l'universel (Alain Badiou et Benny Lévy)." *Lignes* 30, no. 3 (2009): 169–200.
Seneca. *Epistles*. Translated by Richard M. Gummere. 3 vols. Cambridge, MA: Loeb Classical Library, 1917.
Shemesh, Aharon. "The Holiness according to the Temple Scroll." *Revue de Qumran* 19, no. 3 (2000): 374.
Shinan, Avigdor. *Midrash Shemot Rabbah Chapters I–XIV: A Critical Edition Based on a Jerusalem Manuscript with Variants, Commentary and Introduction*. [In Hebrew.] Jerusalem: Dvir, 1984.
Shkop, Shimon. *Ḥiddushei Rebbe Shimon Yehudah Ha-Kohen*. 4 vols. Jerusalem: Printed by the author's family, 2011.
Simon-Shoshan, Moshe. *Stories of the Law: Narrative Discourse and the Construction of Authority in the Mishnah*. New York: Oxford University Press, 2012.
Sion, Avi. *Judaic Logic: A Formal Analysis of Biblical, Talmudic and Rabbinic Logic*. Charleston, SC: CreateSpace, 2014.
Sklar, Deirdre. *Dancing with the Virgin: Body and Faith in the Fiesta of Tortugas, New Mexico*. Berkeley: University of California Press, 2001.
Smyth, Mary M. "Kinesthetic Communication in Dance." *Dance Research Journal* 16, no. 2 (1984): 19–22.
Sokoloff, Michael. *A Dictionary of Jewish Babylonian Aramaic of the Talmudic and Geonic Periods*. Baltimore: Johns Hopkins University Press, 2003.
———. *A Dictionary of Jewish Palestinian Aramaic of the Byzantine Period*. Ramat Gan, Israel: Bar Ilan University Press, 1992.
Solomon, Norman. *The Analytic Movement: Hayyim Soloveitchik and His Circle*. Atlanta: Scholars' Press, 1993.

Soloveitchik, Hayyim. *Ḥiddushei Rebbenu Ḥayyim Ha-Levi: Ḥiddushim u-Be'urim al Ha-Rambam*. Jerusalem: Published by the author's family, 2002.
Soloveitchik, Joseph B. *Halakhic Man*. Translated by Lawrence Kaplan. 1944. Reprint, Philadelphia: Jewish Publication Society of America, 1983.
———. *The Halakhic Mind: An Essay on Jewish Tradition and Modern Thought*. New York: Free Press, 1986.
Sommer, Benjamin. *The Bodies of God and the World of Ancient Israel*. Cambridge: Cambridge University Press, 2009.
Spector, Janet D. *What This Awl Means: Feminist Archaeology at Wahpeton Dakota Village*. St. Paul: Minnesota Historical Society, 1993.
Sperber, Daniel. *A Commentary on Derech Erez Zuṭa Chapters Five to Eight also called Derech Erez Ze'ira*. Ramat Gan, Israel: Bar-Ilan University Press, 1990.
——— ed. *Derekh Erets Zutta (Masechet Derech Eretz Zutta and Perek Ha-Shalom)*. Jerusalem: Tsur-Ot, 1994.
———. "Rabbinic Manuals of Conduct during the Talmudic and Rabbinic Periods." In *Scholars and Scholarship in Jewish History: The Bernard Revel Graduate School Conference Volume*, edited by Leo Landman, 9–26. New York: Yeshiva University Press, 1990.
Spinoza, Benedict. *The "Ethics" and Other Works*. Edited and translated by Edwin Curley. Princeton, NJ: Princeton University Press, 1994.
Stampfer, Shaul. *Lithuanian Yeshivas of the Nineteenth Century*. Oxford: Littman Library of Jewish Civilization, 2012.
Stark, Werner. "Historical Notes and Interpretive Questions about Kant's Lectures on Anthropology." In *Essays on Kant's Anthropology*, edited by Brian Jacobs and Patrick Kain, 15–37. Cambridge: Cambridge University Press, 2003.
Steinsaltz, Adin. *Talmud Bavli*. 44 vols. Jerusalem: HaMakhon HaYisraeli LePirsumim Talmudiyim, 1967–2009.
Stern, Eliyahu. *The Genius: Elijah of Vilna and the Making of Modern Judaism*. New Haven, CT: Yale University Press, 2013.
Stone, Suzanne Last. "Rabbinic Legal Magic: A New Look at Honi's Circle as the Construction of Law's Space." *Yale Journal of Law & the Humanities* 17 (2005): 97–123.
Stuczynski, Claude B. "Converso Paulinism and Residual Jewishness: Conversion from Judaism to Christianity as a Theologico-Political Problem." In *Bastards and Believers: Jewish Converts and Conversion from the Bible to the Present*, edited by Theodor Dunkelgrün and Paweł Maciejko, 111–33. Philadelphia: University of Pennsylvania Press, 2020.
Sturm, Thomas. *Kant und die Wissenschaften vom Menschen*. Paderborn, Germany: Mentis, 2009.
Swenson, Kristin M. "Care and Keeping East of Eden: Gen 4:1–16 in light of Gen 2–3." *Interpretation* 60, no. 4 (2006): 373–84.
Talmud Yerushalmi According to Ms. Or. 4720 (Scal. 3) of the Leiden University Library with Restorations and Corrections. [In Hebrew.] Jerusalem: Academy of the Hebrew Language, 2001.
Theodor, J., and H. Albeck. *Midrash Bereshit Rabba: Critical Edition with Notes and Commentary*. 3 vols. Jerusalem: Wahrmann, 1965.
Tommasi, Francesco Valerio. "Somatology: Notes on a Residual Science in Kant in the Seventeenth and Eighteenth Centuries." In *Knowledge, Morals and Practice in Kant's Anthropology*, edited by Gualtiero Lorini and Robert B. Louden, 133–46. New York: Palgrave, 2018.
Urbach, E. E. *The Sages: Their Concepts and Beliefs*. Translated by Israel Abrahams. Skokie, IL: Varda, 2006.

van Boxel, Piet. *Jewish Books in Christian Hands: Theology, Exegesis and Conversion under Gregory XIII (1572–1585)*. Vatican: Biblioteca Apostolica Vaticana, 2016.
van de Sandt, Huub, and David Flusser. *The Didache: Its Jewish Sources and Its Place in Early Judaism and Christianity*. Minneapolis: Fortress, 2002.
van Loopik, Marcus. *The Ways of the Sages and the Way of the World: The Minor Tractates of the Babylonian Talmud Derekh 'Eretz Rabbah, Derekh 'Eretz Zuṭa, Perek ha-Shalom Translated on the Basis of Manuscripts and Provided with a Commentary*. Tübingen, Germany: Mohr Siebeck, 1991.
Vidas, Moulie. *Tradition and the Formation of the Talmud*. Princeton, NJ: Princeton University Press, 2014.
Vroom, Jonathan. *The Authority of the Law in the Hebrew Bible and Early Judaism: Tracing the Origins of Legal Obligation from Ezra to Qumran*. Leiden: Brill, 2018.
Wagenaar, Jan A. *Origin and Transformation of the Ancient Israelite Festival Calendar*. Wiesbaden, Germany: Harrassowitz, 2005.
Weinrib, Ernest J. "Legal Formalism: On the Immanent Rationality of Law." *Yale Law Journal* 97, no. 6 (1988): 949–1016.
Weisberg, Alexander M. "Before There Was Nature: Affect, Ontology, and Ethics in the Early Rabbinic Sabbatical Year Laws." PhD diss., New York University, 2019.
Weissman, Moshe. *Sefer Yetsi'ot ha-Shabat: le-varer dine r. ha-r. de-oraita ve-isur tikun 'eruv be-Bruklin . . . u-she'ar 'ayarot gedolot: muva'im bo pesakim mi-gedole ha-rabanim be-Amerika lifenei ke-me'ah shanah u-pesakim mi-gedole ha-dor she'avar; u-metsorafim la-zeh Kuntres Pirtsot ha-'ir; ve-Kuntres Delatot ha-'ir*. Brooklyn, NY: Mosheh Yitshak Vaisman, 2002.
Werman, Cana. "Appointed Times of Atonement in the Temple Scroll." [In Hebrew.] *Meghillot: Studies in the Dead Sea Scrolls* 4 (2006): 89–119.
White, Geoffrey. "A Short Political Philology of Visceral Reason (A Red Mouse's Long Tail)." *Parallax* 11, no. 3 (2006): 8–27.
Wiese, Christian. *Challenging Colonial Discourse: Jewish Studies and Protestant Theology in Wilhelmine Germany*. Translated by Barbara Harshav and Christian Wiese. Leiden: Brill, 2005.
Wimpfheimer, Barry Scott. *Narrating the Law: A Poetics of Talmudic Legal Stories*. Philadelphia: University of Pennsylvania Press, 2011.
Wimsatt, W. K., and M. C. Beardsley. "The Intentional Fallacy." *Sewanee Review* 54, no. 3 (1946): 468–88.
Wise, Michael Owen. *A Critical Study of the Temple Scroll from Qumran Cave 11*. Chicago: Oriental Institute of the University of Chicago, 1990.
Wittgenstein, Ludwig. *Philosophical Investigations*. Translated by G. E. M. Anscombe, P. M. S. Hacker, and J. Schulte. Malden, MA: Wiley-Blackwell, 2009.
Wood, Allen W. "Kant and the Problem of Human Nature." In *Essays on Kant's Anthropology*, edited by Brian Jacobs and Patrick Kain, 38–59. Cambridge: Cambridge University Press, 2003.
Wozner, Shai Akivah. *Ḥashiva Mishpatit Be-Yeshivot Lita: 'Iyyunim Be-Mishnato Shel Ha-Rav Shim on Shkop*. Jerusalem: Magnes Press, 2016.
Yadin, Azzan. *Scripture as Logos: Rabbi Ishmael and the Origins of Midrash*. Philadelphia: University of Pennsylvania Press, 2004.
Yisraeli, Yosi. "Constructing and Undermining Converso Jewishness: Profiat Duran and Pablo de Santa María." In *Religious Conversion: Historical Experience and Meanings*, edited by Ira Katznelson and Miri Rubin, 185–216. Farnham: Ashgate, 2014.

Young, Charles M. "Plato's *Crito* On the Obligation to Obey the Law." *Philosophical Inquiry* 27, nos. 1–2 (2006): 79.

Zammito, John H. "What a Young Man Needs for his Venture into the World: The Function and Evolution of the 'Characteristics.'" In *Kant's Lectures on Anthropology: A Critical Guide*, edited by Alix Cohen, 230–48. Cambridge: Cambridge University Press, 2014.

Zellentin, Holger. *Rabbinic Parodies of Jewish and Christian Literature*. Tübingen, Germany: Mohr Siebeck, 2011.

Žižek, Slavoj. "Dialectical Clarity versus the Misty Conceit of Paradox." In *The Monstrosity of Christ: Paradox or Dialectic?*, edited by Creston Davis, 234–306. Cambridge, MA: MIT Press, 2009.

Zohar, Noam. "Idolatry, Idols and Their Annulment." [In Hebrew.] *Sidra* 17 (2001–2002): 64–77.

———. "Partitions around Common Public Space: The Relation to Goyim and Their Idols According to Mishna *Avodah Zarah*." [In Hebrew.] *Reshit* (January 1, 2009). https://heb.hartman.org.il/partitions-around-a-shared-cultural-space/.

Zunz, Leopold. "Remarks on Rabbinic Literature." Translated by James Adam Redfield. In *Classic Essays in Early Rabbinic Culture and History*, edited by Christine Hayes, 27–41. London: Routledge, 2018.

INDEX

Abbasid Caliphate, 211
Abortion, 174
Abraham, prophet, 28
Absolutism, 22, 37, 39, 41
Academics, 3, 8, 53, 60, 98
Adam, 149, 207, 216, 217, 221, 223; Adamic naming language, 229n3; Adam and Eve, 46,
Adler, Rachel, 161
affective economy, 206, 222–228
aggadah, 8, 25
Albeck, Hanoch, 187, 193, 207, 217
Alfonsi, Peter, 255
Amora, 9, 117, 134, 142, 148n77, 151n109, 151n112, 154n132, 178, 179, 187, 190, 201n31, 204, 208, 211, 215, 216
anarchism, 69
animals, 129, 188, 192–195, 201–202n35, 205, 218, 235, 237–239, 245–249
aphorism, 71–74, 148n79, 148n82
Apocrypha, 5
Aramaic Levi Document, 246
Archaeology, 181
Aristotle, 2, 86, 120, 145n28, 232–234, 240, 248; Aristotelianism, 11, 13; *organon*, 7, 12
Asher, Jacob ben, 163–166; *Arba'ah Turim*, 163–164
Ashkenazic rabbis, 182
Assi, Rav, 207, 211
Assmann, Jan, 87, 88, 92, 110n13
atheism, 34, 38, 42, 43, 50n56
Athens, 87

Augustinian, 254, 255
avodah zarah, 77–81; *avodah* as prayer, 208, 211, 215

bar mitzvah, 10
Benjamin, Walter, 18, 204–206, 217–228, 230n26, 230n31, 231n37
Benveniste, Emile, 91 *see* survivor
Berakhiah, Rabbi, 85, 86, 95, 109n4, 109n6
Berkovits, Roger, 160
Bible, 3, 9, 45n7, 55, 79, 154n132, 218, 219, 257
Blanchot, Maurice, 90–92, 94, 100, 106
blood, 129, 132, 236–240, 243–245, 250n9
Bloom, Harold, 23, 30, 45n10
Blumenberg, Hans, 34, 38–42
Boyarin, Daniel, 10, 21, 34–38, 45n10, 46n11, 57–63, 70, 73, 76, 248
Burnyeat, Myles, 232, 233, 242

Caesarea, 85–89, 93, 95, 106
Canpanton, Rabbi Isaac, 10–13, 30–33, 40, 42
Christiani, Pablo, 256
Christianity, 19, 26, 43, 46n13, 94, 253–257; Catholicism, 66–69, 72, 74, 77; censorship, 256–258; Protestant, 256, 258; theologeme, 97, 98, 105
Church Fathers, 3
Cicero, 4, 232
Citation, 85, 86, 90–108, 142
Classics, 4, 18, 248
Cohen, Hermann, 13, 46n13
commandments, 88, 110n13, 129, 132, 135, 137, 140, 163, 165–167, 174

converts, 142, 256–260
correspondence theory, 6
covenant, 24, 27, 28, 41, 227, 228
creation, 25, 41, 132, 162, 204–208, 215, 216, 220–228

dance studies, 180
Derrida, Jacques, 27, 30, 37, 41, 44, 90, 91, 94, 106
Descartes, René, 29, 38–44, 118
Detienne, Marcel, 87, 88, 109n10
Diaspora, 61, 76, 77, 255
Didache, 134
Dogma, 67, 68, 71, 76, 102–107; dogmatism-relativism, 99, 103
Dolgopolski, Sergey, 15, 16, 29, 30, 33, 51–54, 57–66, 70, 73–76, 184, 259
Donin, Nicholas, 256
doubt, 33, 40, 42, 73, 187, 188, 196, 249
dualism, 27, 37, 134, 149n95

Eden, 206, 207, 215, 216, 228
Eiger, Akiva, 163, 165, 166
Elijah, prophet, 23
emotion, 31, 43, 129, 178, 181, 183, 195, 228
Enlightenment, 2, 16, 79, 113
enthymeme, 18, 19, 31, 232, 235, 240
epistemology, 53–63, 71, 72
eruv, 178, 186–190, 194, 195
eschatology, 81
ethics, 13, 18, 116, 118, 132, 140, 257, 259
evil, 24, 64, 67–72, 74, 79, 134, 142
exile, 71, 72, 77, 81, 226, 227, 239
existence, 26, 40–43, 56–59, 67, 76, 224, 228
Exodus, 238
Ezekiel, 240, 243

feminists, 161, 179, 181
finite thinking, 22, 24, 34, 38, 40–44
Flusser, David, 134
forgetting, 15, 16, 54, 87, 88, 110n13
formalism, 60, 157–159, 161
formalistic reductionism, 161, 174
Freedman, Harry, 207, 216
Furstenberg, Ariel, 179

Gemara, 6, 72–75, 80
Genizah, 205–216, 221–224

gentile/*goy*, 78, 80, 116, 257
Gibbs, Robert, 26, 31
Ginzburg, Carlo, 110n16, 258
Greece, 2, 87
Guin, Ursula K. Le, 195, 196

Hahn, Tomie, 180
Halakhah, 8, 16, 17, 22, 23, 32, 49, 112, 113, 138, 155, 161, 168, 172, 174, 247
Halberstam, Chaya, 6, 248, 249
Halbertal, Moshe, 79, 80, 249
Halivni, David Weiss, 249
hamar gamal, 177–197
Hananel, Rabbenu, 188, 194
Hanasi, Rabbi Yehudah, 233, 248, 252n42
Handelman, Susan, 30
Haraway, Donna, 206, 226
Hasmonean age, 244
Hebrew, 3, 5, 36, 179, 182
Hegel, Georg Wilhelm Friedrich, 30, 63, 75
Heidegger, Martin, 2, 15, 30, 33, 54, 56, 57
Hidary, Richard, 185, 233
Hobbes, Thomas, 41, 65, 68
Holy of Holies, 236, 238
humanism, 2, 59, 66

idolatry, 78–80
imperialism, 71–74, 77, 80
intolerance, 254
Iran, 2, 142
Irshai, Ronit, 161, 174
Islam, 3, 8; Muslim 2, 15
Israel/ Yisrael, 15, 27, 42, 55, 77–81, 105, 133, 249
Israelite, 130, 233

Jeremiah, 225, 226
Jesus, 46n15, 95, 134, 257
Jewish Studies, 19, 20, 55, 60, 78, 257
Jewish: thought, 2, 73, 155; law, 26, 112, 155, 156, 159, 161, 168, 170–173; tradition, 3, 23, 28, 173, 255, 258; culture, 55, 63, 183, 211, 257
Jhering, Rudolph von, 160
Job, book of, 24, 45n7, 227, 228
Josephus, Flavius, 142, 185
Judaism, 2, 13, 22, 23, 26, 28, 37, 43, 55, 161, 183, 254–258
Judea, 77, 185, 253
jurisprudence, 2, 160

INDEX

Kabbalah, 10, 55, 73
Kadushin, 132, 133, 136
Kant, Immanuel, 14, 16, 34, 73, 74, 102, 112–129, 135–141
Karaites, 8, 9
Kelsen, Hans, 64, 158
kenosis, 24
kinesthetics, 178, 180, 181, 195, 196
Knohl, Israel, 239
Kosstrin, Hannah, 180, 196
Kripkean rule, 27
Kunin, Seth, 69, 246

LaMothe, Kimmerer, 180
Leibniz, Gottfried Wilhelm, 156, 159, 160
Levi, Rabbi, 85, 86, 93, 95
Levinas, Emmanuel, 2, 13, 18, 21, 28, 42–44, 50n57
Levine, Baruch, 238–240, 243, 245
Levitical priesthood/tradition, 241, 244, 247, 249
Leviticus, 234–249
liability, 158, 168–172
liberalism, 59, 69, 70, 80
Lithuanian Talmudism, 155, 156, 162
Locke, John, 14
logo-politics, 51, 57–81
longue durée, 15, 16, 108n2
Luhmann, Niklas, 156, 157, 159
Luther, Martin, 256
Luzzatto, Moshe Chaim, 13

MacLeish, Archibald, 35
Maimonides, Moses, 7–10, 13, 73, 78, 163, 164n1, 167, 172; *Mishneh Torah*, 7, 8, 163; *The Guide for the Perplexed*, 8
Mannah, Rabbi, 85, 86
martyrdom, 92, 93, 95, 100
Marx, Karl, 2, 70
materialist, 34
mediation, 23, 28, 254, 257, 258
Melamud, Yitzhak, 160
memory, 4, 5, 10, 11, 15, 52, 54, 62, 63, 76, 86–89, 95, 106, 118, 240; memorizing, 5, 10; remembering, 4, 5, 15, 62, 73, 74, 76, 87–89
Meshel, Naphtali, 238, 239
Mesopotamia, 184
metalepsis, 97–99, 105

metaphysics, 37, 64, 66, 70–73, 218, 222, 225, 228
Middle Ages, 2, 3, 7, 9, 15, 17, 86, 254
Milbank, John, 37
mimetics, 12
miracles, 26, 39, 43
Mishnah, 5, 6, 9, 18, 19, 62, 72–81, 86, 93, 95, 101, 129, 168–171, 181, 185–190, 232–235, 244–250
modern state, 64–70, 74
monotheism, 26, 43, 110n13
morality, 16, 43, 112–128, 131–141, 159
Morrison, Toni, 181
Mosaic distinction *see* Assmann
Moscovitz, Leib, 179
Moses, prophet, 9, 27, 30, 48n27, 88, 130, 244
Mount Sinai, 23
muses, 87, 88
myth, 95

Nails, Debra, 248
Nancy, Jean-Luc, 59
natural law, 114, 133, 134, 140, 168, 173, 174
Neusner, Jacob, 207, 216
New Testament, 97–99, 105, 106, 110n17, 255, 256
Nietzsche, Friedrich, 31, 34, 38, 41, 43
Nihan, Christophe, 240
Noahide laws, 133, 173, 174
nomos, 64, 75, 76, 92
nonhuman, 80, 118, 204–206, 218–227
normative closure, 155–165, 174
Novak, David, 133, 136, 173, 174
Numbers, 234–249

oblivion/*Lethe*, 54, 86–89, 92, 106, 108n1, 109n10, 110n13
Ockham, William, 39, 40
Old Testament, 94, 97, 254
ontologies, 18, 31, 60, 81, 204–206, 216–224, 227, 228; deontologies, 80, 131
oral tradition, 3, 114, 141, 142, 208, 215
orthodoxy, 41, 47n16, 161
ownership, 157, 169–172, 175

Palestine, 2, 4, 15, 87, 93, 114, 142, 178, 184, 233
Papa, Rabbi Chananya bar, 215
Particularism, 55, 56, 61, 63, 77

Passover, 163–167
Paul, the Pharisee, 26, 46n11
pedagogy, 120, 121, 138, 160
Peirce, Charles Sanders, 175
performance studies, 178
Persia, 81, 211
persuasion, 18, 232, 234
Peter the venerable, 255
Phaedrus, 232
Pharisees, 93, 95, 110n17
phenomenology, 53, 57, 58, 61, 63, 71
philosophy: Anglo-American, 175; contemporary 54, 57, 259; Continental, 54; Greek, 18; philosophers, 1, 6, 11, 16, 21, 114, 178, 197; of language, 13, 18, 179, 181, 183, 204, 206
physiognomy, 123, 124
Pirqe Avot, 27, 134
Plato, 2, 30, 61, 86, 232; Platonism, 2, 7, 12, 18, 29, 30, 34, 86, 109n10; Platonic dialogue, 248; Platonic distinction, 88, 92; Neoplatonism, 10, 37; *Crito*, 232, 233, 250n1
polis, 55–59, 64–81
political philology, 96–99, 105
political theology, 63–72, 99, 105
positivism, 157–159, 162, 173, 174
praesens historicum, 102, 103
prayer, 182, 204–211, 214–217, 220–228, 231n33, 249
pre-Socratics, 2, 86
priestly source, 241, 242
print shops, 257
Psalms, 226
psychology, 117, 123, 144n10

Quintilian, 232, 233
Qumran, 134, 241, 242

Rabbinic: courts, 5; schools/academies, 2–7, 15, 86–89; interpretation, 2, 35, 45n10, 86; thought, 14, 16, 17, 96, 113, 114, 132, 139, 197, 249
racism, 115, 116
Rashi, 188, 192
Rationalism, 10, 11, 13, 133
Raz, Joseph, 158, 159, 174

Raz-Krakotzkin, Amnon, 257, 258
reading, 89, 90, 108
redemption, 67, 225–227, 231n33, 231n38
Reischer, Rabbi Ya'akov, 182
relativism, 37, 80, 99, 102–107, 118, 259
religion, 2, 13, 16, 26, 37, 43, 73, 116, 180, 254, 257
Renaissance, 2
Responsa, 5, 182
revelation, 22–28, 46n13, 68, 71, 101, 133, 162, 247
rhetoric, 2–19, 33, 58, 86, 184, 198n3, 232, 248, 250
ritual, 129, 174, 238, 244–249
Roman, 9, 35, 74, 77, 80, 92, 113, 129, 185, 233
romanticism, 2
Rosenzweig, Franz, 11, 21, 42, 43, 44n6

Sabbath, 9, 146n61, 178, 182–190, 196
Sacrifice, 226, 233–247, 251n34
Sasanian, 142, 211
Schaefer, Donovan, 206, 222–224
Schiffman, Lawrence, 242–245
Schmitt, Carl, 59, 63–74, 77, 78, 80
Scholem, Gershom, 21–23, 27, 50n56
Science, 34, 42, 55, 64, 70, 117, 128, 138, 159, 160, 257
scribes, 10, 93, 110n17, 142
scripture, 3, 25, 47n19, 86, 129, 130, 135, 140, 254, 255
Second Temple, 142, 233, 235, 237, 240, 242, 247, 249
secularism, 50n56, 64, 66, 69, 156, 159
Seforim, Mendele Mokher, 182
Sephardic, 30, 182
Sepphoris, 86
Sermon on the Mount, 93, 106, 110n17
sexual intercourse, 131, 132, 142
Shema, 85, 100, 101, 130
Shemesh, Aharon, 241
Shkop, Shimon, 156, 162, 163, 168–175
slaves, 142
social norms, 114, 124, 130–135, 140
Soloveitchik, Hayyim, 156, 162–168
Soloveitchik, Joseph, 155, 156
Sophists, 38; sophistry, 7, 184; Second Sophistic, 233, 234, 244

soul, 218–220
sovereign, 37, 65, 66, 69–72, 77, 81, 222
Spector, Janet, 181
Spinoza, Baruch, 26, 33
spirit/spiritual, 19, 35, 40, 205, 206, 227, 240, 255, 258
Stoicism, 9, 232–234, 242
subject/object divide, 205, 206, 225, 229n3
subjectivity, 11, 25, 37, 42, 106, 107, 256–259
supersessionism, 19, 37, 46, 48n44, 59, 105, 106, 255, 258, 260
survivor/*superstes*, 91, 92, 95, 106, 110n16
syllogism, 18, 19, 232, 240, 242
Syria, 2, 87
System: legal, 65, 70, 155–163, 189; halakhic, 155, 156, 161, 162, 168, 172; normative, 158, 159
systems theory, 156, 157

Tarski, Alfred, 33
tautology, 33, 34, 42, 111n22
teleology, 255, 256, 260
telos, 13, 119, 129, 136
Temple Scroll, 235, 240–247
testimony, 91–96, 100–107, 208, 254
tetragrammaton, 88, 89, 108n1
Tiberias, 86
tiqqun ha'olam, 133
Torah, 22–29, 42, 43, 75, 76, 81, 129–137, 140, 141, 161, 170, 171, 183, 256
Tosefta, 5, 181, 235, 245–248
Totalitarianism, 59, 62, 64
tradition of tradition, 1, 2, 13–15, 89, 96

transcendentalism, 99, 102–106
truth, 6, 7, 15, 24–34, 38, 40–43, 56, 61–65, 68–72, 87, 160–162, 183, 196, 232, 234, 237, 242, 249, 254–256

universalism, 55–61, 67–70, 116
universe, 39, 224, 225, 228

visceral reason, 97, 98
visualization, 181, 196

Wagenaar, Jan, 239
Waite, Geoffrey, 97
war, 59, 66–70, 79
Weinrib, Ernest, 157, 158
Werman, Cana, 234, 245, 247
Wise, Michael, 241
Wissenschaft des Judentums, 55, 258
women, 145n31, 161, 174, 181, 199-200n18
Wozner, Shai, 168, 173

Yannai, Rabbi, 137
Yavneh, 86, 93, 95
Yehudah the Prince, Rabbi, 85, 86, 93
yeshiva, 86, 162
Yiddish literature, 182
Yom Kippur (Day of Atonement), 233, 234, 237, 239–244, 248, 249
Yosel, Yosel ben, 43
Young, Charles, 232

Žižek, Slavoj, 25, 26, 37, 38, 48n44
Zunz, Leopold, 258

FOR INDIANA UNIVERSITY PRESS

Anna Garnai, *Editorial Assistant*
Dan Crissman, *Acquisitions Editor and Editorial Director*
Gary Dunham, *Acquisitions Editor and Director*
Anna Francis, *Assistant Acquisitions Editor*
Brenna Hosman, *Production Coordinator*
Katie Huggins, *Production Manager*
Darja Malcolm-Clarke, *Project Manager/Editor*
Dan Pyle, *Online Publishing Manager*
Michael Regoli, *Director of Publishing Operations*
Leyla Salamova, *Artist and Book Designer*
Stephen Williams, *Marketing and Publicity Manager*

www.ingramcontent.com/pod-product-compliance
Lightning Source LLC
Chambersburg PA
CBHW021347300426
44114CB00012B/1120